Helping and
Human Relations

Helping and Human Relations

VOLUME II
Practice and Research

ROBERT R. CARKHUFF

Human
Resource
Development
Press

1969 Library of Congress Catalog Number: 73-82021
1984 Library of Congress Number in Publication Data

ISBN 0-914234-90-0

Manufactured in the United States of America

Printing by BookCrafters, Inc.

To my children

FOREWORD

In every generation there arise, in every field of human endeavor, a few who stand out by making a significant contribution in advancing the field by taking a giant step forward. The author of these volumes is one of them. This is a major contribution to counseling and psychotherapy. I have commented verbally that the earlier work of Carkhuff and Truax and of Carkhuff and Berenson (*Toward Effective Counseling and Psychotherapy* and *Beyond Counseling and Therapy*) was the most significant advance in counseling and psychotherapy since the 1942 book of Rogers. The present volumes are even more significant, since they incorporate and extend the earlier work.

Carkhuff here speaks out on the problem of the ineffectiveness of therapy, placing the responsibility squarely where it belongs—on the therapist (or helper) who is incomplete (incompetent), often using the relationship to satisfy his own needs. The extension of the treatment beyond the formal counseling or psychotherapy relationship makes these volumes very useful to those concerned about all kinds of interpersonal relationships. The introduction of the "helper-helpee" terminology facilitates this application.

Volume I, although concerned with selection and training, is not a routine or usual treatment of this area. Nor is the training a "how-to-do-it" or technique-oriented treatise. It develops a comprehensive model of the helping relationship or process which is necessary as a basis for adequate selection and training.

The model of the helping process which is presented is true to life. It is not an artificial model apart from other human relationships; it brings the helping relationship clearly into line with all good human relationships. The epitome of the relationship is the concept designated by the Greek word, *agape*. This relationship is not one in which the helper remains aloof from the helpee, presenting a mask and providing a sterile, neutral atmosphere. Rather, the helper becomes highly involved, and, because he cares deeply, he cannot be neutral or unconditional in his responses. If I care for you, what you are and what you do make a difference to me, and I must react accordingly, sometimes approving but sometimes disapproving, sometimes with pleasure but sometimes with disappointment—yet always caring. The extension of this aspect of a good, close human relationship, recognized in the concept of good family relationships, to helping relationships in general is again a contribution in bringing together all interpersonal relationships in a comprehensive model.

The development of the concept of the two main phases of the helping relationship, the facilitative and the action phases, is a major contribution. To me, facilitative relationships lead inevitably to action. To be sure, Carkhuff does not make a sharp separation of the phases; he recognizes that they overlap. And he acknowledges that some helpees can act without stimulation by the helper, though he feels these are a minority. I perhaps would hope the helpee could go through this phase more on his own, unless there is some handicap such as lack of knowledge or skill or need for training or retraining or reeducation, in which case perhaps others might be more effective than the therapist. Carkhuff does recognize that referral may be desirable at this stage. He also cautions against the helper moving too quickly into this phase: "It should be understood that many would-be helpers attempt to move to this stage prematurely." That many may need specific assistance must be recognized, and this assistance is provided through what Carkhuff calls preferred modes of treatment. My own definition of counseling or psychotherapy would not include these methods or modes, which to me are beyond therapy, or are teaching rather than therapy. Indeed, Carkhuff refers to "the more cognitive problem-solving kinds of activities." But it must be remembered that Carkhuff is concerned about helping relationships in a broad sense.

Counselor educators have long been asking for guidelines in the preparation of counselors. Now they have them. The comprehensive model presented here provides materials for both teacher and student as they embark upon the process by which the student becomes a helper. The model is a humanistic, not a mechanistic model. It focuses upon the modification of the person of the trainee, not upon the acquisition of techniques. The effective factor in the training is the person of the trainer, not gadgets or gidgets such as those which are the focus of attention of too many counselor educators—videotapes, computers, simulation devices, etc., etc. None of these will substitute for the level of functioning of the trainer, or counteract the harmful effects of a low functioning trainer. Yet the model does break the relationship down into manageable parts; it also puts the parts together again.

A major contribution is the demonstration that the most important element in the preparation of counselors or other helpers is the relationship of the teacher with the student, just as the most important factor in counseling is the relationship between the counselor and the client. It is, of course, pleasing to me that Carkhuff has developed, on the basis of extensive research and experience, a didactic-experiential approach to training very similar to the approach I have been using in practicum, though my method has been less systematic or less structured.

A very significant development is that summarized in Chapter 14 of Volume I and Chapter 10 of Volume II. It appears that direct training of "patients" and helpees in the conditions of good interpersonal relations was more effective than therapy. Perhaps therapy is not necessary! What we may need is direct training or education of everyone in the conditions of good human relations—not only "normal" people and children, but the emotionally disturbed as well. If we can prepare counselors to provide higher levels of the core conditions of interpersonal relationships, why can't we educate others to do so? Carkhuff shows that we can, whether they are mental hospital patients or parents of problem children. We can then make psychotherapy unnecessary or obsolete in a short period of time.

Carkhuff's presentation is hard hitting. Hopefully, it will jar us out of the rut of our predominantly gloomy outlook regarding the effectiveness of counseling and of counselor education. I have found these volumes to be packed with practical, useful help for teaching. They will be useful to the student learning to be a helper, but I think they will be most useful to the teacher. The student will need the help of an experienced helper to get the most from them and to avoid misunderstanding or the misplacing of emphases at the different stages of the learning process.

Chapters 8 and 10 in Volume II convey by illustration the humanness, the genuineness of the relationship which Carkhuff writes about in other chapters. Here is the evidence of the credentials of the writer. They can be summarized in the statement: "Here is a therapist, a man, a human being."

C. H. Patterson, Ph.D.
Professor of Education and Psychology
University of Illinois

PREFACE

The three R's of helping—the *right* of an individual to intervene in another person's life, the *responsibility* he must assume when he does intervene, and the *role* he plays in the process of helping—are most critical to those who give least thought to these questions. Those who are committed to being less than they can be, both within helping and outside it, can only doubt the possibility of constructive change in human beings. They never ask the critical questions because the answers might expose them, not only to others but to themselves as well.

Those who are not being less than they can be do not doubt themselves or others. But they constantly raise important questions about themselves, about others, about the helping process.

Ultimately the helper must face the fourth *R* of helping—the *realization* of his own resources. At the heart of successful helping is the helper's commitment to himself. *The effective helper, indeed, the effective person, is personally committed to his own emergence, at whatever level, and this alone frees him to make personal commitments to others.*

In attempting to realize his own resources, then, the effective helper is committed to his own well-being and fulfillment and in so doing lives independent of many of society's norms and goals. He is actively committed to his own personal experience in a lifelong learning process and is fully aware of the personal implications *for him* of not being committed to constructive potency in his world.

The effective helper views the helpee as he views himself and will do anything for the helpee that he would do for himself under the same conditions. Such an individual is committed to personal and intimate involvement with the helpee in a fully sharing relationship. He is aware that if the helpee fails as a person, he himself has failed, although he is willing to risk failure in order to achieve success.

There are no limitations to the helper's commitment to himself or the helpee, although he will take neither more nor less than he is entitled to in life. In his commitment to expand his own boundaries his movement extends as much into the life of the helpee as into his own. Finally, he is committed to nourishing constructive forces and fighting destructive ones both within and between individuals, wherever and whenever he finds them.

If the helper cannot actualize his own potentials, he cannot enable another to do so. The focus of training, as the focus of treatment, then, is upon the change or gain of the trainee himself. This is most critical, for without an effective person in the helping role all else is futile.

In a very real sense these volumes are part of my own process of self-realization. Having gotten my hands dirty in practice and research, having tested the limits of theory, and having recorded in broad brush strokes my insights into it, I found that I was not home free. I found that I must go back, as my clients say, to the "nitty gritty." I must attempt to explicate and implement in the most basic form the constructs that underlie the helping process. I have attempted to articulate this often vague and amorphous experiential process which we term "helping" while at the same time leaving its essence inviolate.

In a way these volumes are in reverse order, for we select and train helpers on the basis of what we know about the helping process. Indeed, we have begun with what we have learned about what makes successful helping and worked backwards. On the other hand, for the prospective helper the process begins with his selection, moves through his training, and continues as he himself assumes the role of helper. It concludes only with the satisfactory emergence or re-emergence of the people with whom he is working.

This second volume is based upon a great body of existing literature, only some of which is explicitly summarized here. The purpose of these volumes, however, has been to bring together in as straightforward a form as possible the conclusions of our efforts in theory, research, and, particularly, practice. My conclusions will, to be sure, change as I change. *And I will change!* My objective has been to transmit to a wider audience the kinds of learnings that have been reserved for and, indeed, discovered in conjunction with my training groups and teaching classes.

Part One introduces the literature on the current state of affairs in the treatment processes, including the results of the ongoing search for sources of efficacy in helping.

Part Two elaborates effective modes of treatment, including operationalizations of the goals of the exploratory and emergent directionality phases of treatment as well as of the intermittent crises of therapy and life.

In Part Three emphasis is given to some of the issues and problems involved in making systematic and enlightened inquiries into effective modes of training and treatment.

Part Four, a summary and overview, is devoted to some of the larger issues of life, those that are not easily summarized and operationlized in a primer for human relations.

In compiling this book I am in debt to those who have shared the adventures of my learning experiences, my family as well as my students and colleagues. In particular, I wish to acknowledge Dr. Bernard G. Berenson, Dr. George Banks, Dr. Ralph Bierman, Dr. David Donofrio, who conducted a case which was restated in Chapter 9 of this volume, and Mrs. Miriam Conable, who made specific contributions to another of the chapters of this volume.

R. R. C.

Springfield, Massachusetts
August 1969

CONTENTS

xv

Helping and
Human Relations

PART ONE

Introduction

PART ONE of this text introduces several fundamental propositions and examines the evidence behind them: helping processes are additional instances of interpersonal processes which may have constructive or deteriorative consequences and which in their constructive instances are in large part a function of core, facilitative, and action-oriented dimensions. The implications for treatment and training are profound. The programs that have been built systematically around these core conditions have been most effective while those that have not been so constructed have been the least effective.

1

FACILITATION AND RETARDATION IN HELPING PROCESSES

Traditional training and treatment programs in the helping professions have not established their effectiveness in terms of translation to helpee benefits. Reluctance to investigate has gradually given way to systematic inquiries, yet the research programs that have been conducted have yielded essentially negative results. In the training area the data indicate little change, no change, or negative change on those dimensions related to helpee benefits (Anthony & Carkhuff, 1970; Bergin & Solomon, 1963; Carkhuff, 1966, 1969; Carkhuff, Kratochvil & Friel, 1968). In the treatment area no differences are indicated between treated and untreated children and adults (Eysenck, 1965; Levitt, 1963; Lewis, 1965). That is, on indexes relevant to constructive helpee change or gain, on the average the helpee has as much chance of changing constructively over time without professional help as he has with such help.

There are directional answers to these very basic challenges. First, several meaningful propositions flow directly from a fundamental assumption concerning all interpersonal processes.

Assumption I. Helping processes and their training programs are all instances of interpersonal learning or relearning processes.

The direct implication of this assumption is that the same dimensions that are effective in other instances of human relations are effective in helping processes. Thus, while secondary dimensions may vary in parent-child, teacher-student, counselor-counselee, and therapist-patient relationships, the primary interpersonal dimensions remain the same. In this regard, in training processes in which interpersonal processes incorpo-

3

rating the level of functioning of both the helper trainer and the helpee trainee are calculated to effect significant improvement in the helpee's level of interpersonal processes, we can account for the greatest amount of change in the level of functioning of the helpee trainee (Carkhuff, 1969). These processes are straightforward in the sense that they are devoid of the usual ancillary objectives such as the learning of developmental tasks, a particular subject matter, or a new cosmology. They tell us the most about the core dimensions of human relations because the ingredients are not confounded by secondary objectives.

Thus, two or more persons encounter each other in relation to the accomplishment of definable tasks or goals. One person is considered and designated the "more knowing" person, the other the "less knowing." One is helper and one is helpee. Hopefully, one is committed to enabling the other to achieve a given level of functioning in areas in which the former has expertise. Hopefully, being so committed, the helper will employ all of the means available to him to enable the helpee to achieve an adequate level of functioning in an area of benefit to the helpee.

In the hope that we may more fully comprehend the helping processes, then, we must attend to helper, helpee, and contextual and environmental variables, alone and in their various interactions. We must study the characteristics of the helper that make the helpee open and amenable to the helper's influence. We must study the characteristics of the helpee in order to determine which treatment procedures will be most effective with which helpees. We must study the conditions of the environment in which the helpee evolved and that to which he will return after helping as well as the setting in which the helping process takes place.

PROPOSITIONS

A number of general propositions flow from the general assumption and deserve special attention because of their critical significance.

Proposition I. All interpersonal processes may have constructive or deteriorative consequences.

If we can effect positive change or gain in persons, we can also bring about negative change. The deteriorated schizophrenic may be seen most fruitfully as a product of a succession of retarding relationships just as the psychologically healthy person may be seen as the end result of a number of facilitative relationships. As a result of some helping processes the helpee may go on to flourish as he has never flourished before. As a result of others the helpee may be retarded in his growth or, worse yet, may deteriorate.

Corollary I. Counseling and psychotherapy may be "for better or for worse."

At all levels on the psychological health continuum there are data to indicate that counseling and therapeutic activities may have constructive or deteriorative consequences. There is evidence to indicate a significantly greater variability on the posttreatment change indexes of the treatment groups when compared to the control groups. Thus, a significant increase of both constructive and destructive consequences in treatment groups when compared to controls has been found in programs of intensive treatment with hospitalized schizophrenics (Rogers, Gendlin, Kiesler, & Truax, 1967; Truax & Carkhuff, 1967), outpatient neurotics (Barron & Leary, 1955; Cartwright & Vogel, 1960), and relatively nonpathological guidance populations (Mink & Isaksen, 1959).

In general, then, the relevant findings seem to offer an explanation for the puzzling mass of data already existing concerning the over-all ineffectiveness of the helping relationship. That is, the constructive changes of some clients are balanced out by the deteriorative changes of others. Consequently, when we average the increased number of positive and negative changes in the treatment group we find no *average* differences between treatment and control groups. Together these studies suggest one very consoling and one very distressing message to those of us who have dedicated our lives to helping others. *We have an impact!* The findings, however, force us to examine the nature of this impact. Counseling and psychotherapy may indeed be for better or for worse.

Corollary II. Parent-child, teacher-student, and other significant relationships may be for better or for worse.

A growing body of literature indicates that parent-child and teacher-student relationships may have facilitative or retarding consequences. In regard to the parent-child relationship there is evidence to indicate the negative effects of early retarding parental relationships in terms of the child's social maladjustment (Cass, 1953; Montalto, 1952), the manifestation of hostility (Chorost, 1962), and the emergence of schizophrenia (Bateson, Jackson, Haley,

& Weakland, 1956; Baxter, Becker, & Hooks, 1963; Bowen, 1960; Lidz, Cornelison, Fleck, & Terry, 1957; Lidz & Lidz, 1949; Weakland, 1960; Wynne, Ryckoff, Day, & Hirsch, 1958). In the teaching area there is evidence to indicate the facilitative and retarding effects upon the child's social adjustment (Truax & Tatum, 1966) and learning achievement (Aspy, 1969; Aspy & Hadlock, 1969; Carkhuff & Berenson, 1967; Carkhuff & Truax, 1966; Christensen, 1960; Kratochvil, Carkhuff, & Berenson, 1969). Thus, there is substantial support for the proposition that all interpersonal processes may be for better or for worse. An often overlooked example of interpersonal learning experiences is training in the helping professions. This area deserves special attention because it is often forgotten and because it further illustrates the phenomena involved.

Corollary III.   Training in the helping professions may be for better or for worse.

In the few studies that have been conducted of the traditional graduate programs the results have been negative. There is a pronounced tendency for professional trainees to deteriorate over the course of training on those dimensions related to constructive helpee change. Thus, when cast in the helping role trainees function at slightly higher levels at the beginning than at advanced stages of training (Carkhuff, 1968, 1969; Carkhuff, Kratochvil, & Friel, 1968), and these levels are low (Anthony & Carkhuff, 1970; Bergin & Solomon, 1963). There is, in addition, a tendency for the programs to eliminate those trainees functioning initially at the highest levels (Carkhuff, Kratochvil, & Friel, 1968) and demonstrating the greatest action orientation (Holder, 1969).

We know, on the other hand, from some intermediate-level (guidance counselors, rehabilitation counselors, teacher counselors), subprofessional (nurses, dormitory counselors, community volunteers, hospital attendants), and helpee (racial relations workers, outpatients, inpatients) training programs that training may have constructive consequences in terms of facilitating the positive outcomes of schizophrenics, inpatients as well as outpatients; outpatient neurotics; individuals with marital difficulties; student clients; and situationally distressed normals (Berenson & Carkhuff, 1967; Carkhuff, 1966, 1968, 1969; Carkhuff & Berenson, 1967). These lower-level training programs have been the only programs that have consistently demonstrated their effectiveness in terms of translation to client benefits. At a minimum the results suggest that lay persons systematically selected, trained, and supervised can learn to do whatever a professional can do—perhaps more.

Thus, at different developmental stages we find that helping relationships can be facilitative or retarding in terms of their intrapersonal and interpersonal results. The problem then becomes one of looking at outcome and then tracing back through the helping process (and this makes a strong case for recording the process) in an attempt to determine the variables that facilitate positive movement and those that inhibit this goal or even contribute to individual deterioration. In spite of the bewildering array of theories and practices, there have been many recurring themes.

Proposition II. All effective interpersonal processes share a common core of conditions conducive to facilitative human experiences.

Again we can assume that those interpersonal conditions that are facilitative in one instance of human relations are facilitative in others. For example, the conditions that are facilitative in the parent-child relationship are facilitative in the teacher-student and counselor-counselee relationships, and vice versa. In addition, we can assume that the helpee will move in the direction of the helper in his level of functioning on these interpersonal dimensions. That is, if the helper functions at a high level, the helpee will demonstrate constructive change; if the helper functions at a low level, particularly at a level significantly lower than the helpee, the helpee will demonstrate deteriorative change.

Corollary I. Clients of counselors who offer high levels of core, facilitative, and action-oriented conditions improve while those of counselors who offer low levels of these conditions deteriorate.

Widely divergent orientations to counseling and psychotherapy have emphasized the critical nature of the counselor's empathic understanding and respect for the helpee, his genuineness in the therapeutic encounter, his specificity in emphasizing emotional experiencing, his concreteness in problem-solving, his ability to confront the helpee when appropriate, and his ability to interpret the immediate experiencing of the helpee's relationship with the helper. Other sources of more limited theory and research have variously supported dimensions such as self-disclosure, openness and flexibility, confidence, commitment, and other more dynamic personality characteristics. Many of these dimensions, especially empathy, respect, genuineness, concreteness, confrontation, and immediacy, have

been related to constructive process or outcome or both in hospitalized schizophrenics, including those in both individual (Berenson &
Mitchell, 1974; Rogers *et al.*, 1967; Truax & Carkhuff, 1967) and
group psychotherapy (Truax, 1961; Truax, Carkhuff, & Kodman,
1965), as well as with outpatient psychiatric populations (Pagell,
Carkhuff, & Berenson, 1967) and outpatient neurotics or situationally
distressed populations (Barrett-Lennard, 1962; Berenson & Mitchell,
1969; Carkhuff & Berenson, 1967; Halkides, 1958; Pagell *et al.*, 1967;
Truax & Carkhuff, 1967). The accumulation of studies offers substantial support for the relationship of these core, facilitative, and
action-oriented dimensions to client and patient outcomes.

These findings also constitute a second possible response to the
challenges of Eysenck, Levitt, and Lewis, the first being that the
treated helpee may get both "better" and "worse" than the controls.
The effective ingredients of counseling and psychotherapy may not
be what we have traditionally considered to be the critical dimensions of therapeutic processes. Since a large part of the effectiveness
of a given counselor or therapist may be accounted for by how effective and facilitative a human being he is, these conditions may be
available to the control group clients and patients from other than
the professional helper. That is, *control groups may not be control
groups.* In all probability the likelihood of a given patient in the
treatment group seeking the help of a nonprofessional helper is
minimal because these patients have already been assigned counselors. On the other hand, the probability of a given patient in the
control group seeking the help of a nonprofessional is maximal since
these patients have not been assigned counselors. Thus, the clients
under control conditions may find a facilitative relationship with persons selected from those in the group around them (Bergin, 1963;
Frank, 1961; Gurin, Veroff, & Feld, 1960; Powers and Witmer, 1961).
The relationship of facilitative and action-oriented conditions to
outcomes of helpees also holds in other instances of interpersonal
processes.

*Corollary II. Children and students of parents, teachers, and other
significant persons who offer high levels of core, facilitative, and
action-oriented conditions improve while those of persons who offer
low levels of these conditions are retarded in their development.*

An extensive body of evidence supports the view that the core,
facilitative, and action-oriented dimensions are related to learning
in teaching (Aspy, 1969; Aspy & Hadlock, 1969; Carkhuff & Beren-

son, 1967; Carkhuff & Truax, 1966; Christensen, 1960; Davitz, 1964; Isaacson, McKeachie, & Milholland, 1963; Kratochvil *et al.*, 1969; Pace & Stern, 1958; Thistlewaite, 1959; Truax & Tatum, 1966; Willis, 1961) and child-rearing situations (Bateson, 1956; Baxter *et al.*, 1963; Bowen, 1960; Carkhuff & Berenson, 1967; Carkhuff & Truax, 1966; Cass, 1953; Chorost, 1962; Lidz *et al.*, 1957; Lidz & Lidz, 1949; Montalto, 1952; Weakland, 1960; Wynne *et al.*, 1958). Again there is evidence to indicate that the benefits accrued from relationships involving high-level conditions are not restricted to social adjustment gains but are also evident on more traditional educational indexes.

The effective teacher or parent is not simply a knowledgeable person who imparts his accumulated wisdom to a learner without taking into consideration the experience of the learner. Rather, the effective helper appears to be an individual who offers his learnings in the context of a relationship involving high levels of facilitative and action-oriented dimensions.

Corollary III. Trainees in training programs in the helping profession that offer high levels of the core, facilitative, and action-oriented conditions improve while those in programs that offer low levels of these conditions deteriorate.

The evidence here is clear. In all instances the trainees move in the direction of their trainers in their level of functioning (Carkhuff, 1968). Thus, trainees who are functioning at higher levels than their trainers will deteriorate (Carkhuff, Kratochvil, & Friel, 1968) while those who are functioning at levels similar to their trainers will be retarded over the course of training (Anthony & Carkhuff, 1970; Pierce, 1969; Pierce *et al.*, 1967). On the other hand, trainers who are functioning at levels significantly higher than their trainees will have trainees who demonstrate significant improvement in functioning (Berenson, Carkhuff, & Myrus, 1966; Carkhuff, 1969; Carkhuff & Banks, 1970; Carkhuff & Bierman, 1970; Carkhuff, Friel, & Kratochvil, 1970; Carkhuff & Truax, 1965; Kratochvil, 1969; Martin & Carkhuff, 1968; Pierce *et al.*, 1967; Pierce & Drasgow, 1969; Vitalo, 1968). The evidence is not restricted to process measures. The helpees of these trainees improved in functioning as measured by a variety of outcome criteria.

Again the trainers are not simply imparters of accumulated wisdom but also constitute models for effective living. If they themselves are living effectively, the trainees have an opportunity to learn to live effectively. In this regard the programs that demonstrate negative effects neglect to emphasize the core, facilitative, and action-oriented dimensions or concentrate only upon discrimination learning. Those demonstrating positive effects attempt specifically to provide an experiential base in which the trainees have the firsthand experience of high levels of conditions while at the same time they teach didactically the necessary discrimination and communication of both facilitative and action-oriented conditions.

CONCLUSIONS

These propositions carry a number of implications which we can systematize in order to understand their significance.

Conclusion I.   Those treatment and training programs that are not built systematically around the core, facilitative, and action-oriented dimensions are least effective in translating their efforts to helpee benefits.

In general, traditional programs of both treatment and training do not concentrate effectively upon a core of facilitative and action-oriented dimensions. Often traditional programs emphasize the communication process only from a particular frame of reference. If the orientation employed happens to meet the helpee's needs, it may constitute a preferred mode of treatment and thus be helpful, but it may exclude critical aspects of an effective helping process. Too frequently these programs do not develop courses of action for the helpee, or, if they do, they do not do so out of the learnings from the earlier phases of helping, but, instead, operate from a predetermined frame of reference. There are several related corollaries.

Corollary I.   Traditional treatment and training orientations are the consequence of a particular interaction of helper, helpee, and contextual and environmental variables.

The very evolution of a variety of different approaches to helping is attributable for the most part to a more or less unique interaction of variables (Berenson & Carkhuff, 1967). A particular group of counselors, therapists, or educators who, having many interests and beliefs in common, converge and linger in a given setting and interact with a helpee population which is screened to have many characteristics in common. Certain methods or approaches come to connote more effective practices. A set of beliefs takes hold, and the helpers, shaped by what they believe to be effective methods, promulgate a theory of practice. Unfortunately, all too often the process ends there. The beliefs based upon generalizations from the helpers' own experiences are passed on as doctrine and applied by students in contexts involving a very different interaction of variables. If trainees have not learned to trust their own experience and feedback and have not learned to be shaped by what is effective for them in terms of helpee outcome, then they may themselves indoctrinate their students in their own externally imposed theory and practice and the group will have succeeded in establishing a more or less dominant school or "cult" of helping. The particular orientation, in turn, is not dominated in its approach by a concentration upon the core dimensions of all human relations processes.

Corollary II. Traditional treatment and training programs have been built around secondary factors which are a function of a particular interaction of variables.

Built around the central core of primary, facilitative, and action-oriented dimensions are secondary factors predicated upon a particular interaction of helper, helpee, and contextual and environmental variables (Carkhuff, 1966; Carkhuff & Berenson, 1967). Thus, the psychoanalytic approach, which focuses upon a diagnostic kind of empathy, may serve to elicit helpee self-exploration during the exploratory phase of helping with neurotic-type populations in outpatient psychiatric clinics. The nondirective or client-centered approach, which concentrates upon empathy, warmth, and unconditionality, elicits self-exploration during the exploratory phase of helping with neurotic types and situationally distressed normals in college counseling centers and other clinics. The existential approach, which focuses upon empathy, regard, and genuineness, serves to elicit self-exploration during the initial phases of helping with neurotic and situationally distressed normal populations in a variety of settings. The trait-and-factor approach, in turn, which emphasizes concrete problem-solving in the development of courses of action in the latter phases of helping, offers (1) information and success probability statements during the second phase of helping with neurotic-type and possibly situationally distressed normals in educational centers and (2) assignment for inpatient populations. The behavioristic approaches, which also emphasize concreteness in problem-solving, contribute to the reduction or elimination of symptoms during the second phase of helping with inpatient and out-patient populations with more definable and isolated symptomatology in more experimental settings.

Our training programs in psychiatry, clinical and counseling psychology, social work, and education have concentrated upon secondary factors which may in given instances make significant contributions to the effectiveness of the helping process. These approaches may well constitute possible preferred modes of treatment given that particular interaction of variables, and in the context of high levels of core conditions may contribute a significant and additional amount of effectiveness to the helping process. However, if employed in the absence of the particular interaction of variables involved, these approaches may contribute nothing or may actually retard the helping process at the helpee's expense— the tragedy in inappropriate applications of doctrinaire modes of practice.

Conclusion II. Those treatment and training programs that are built systematically around the core, facilitative, and action-oriented dimensions are most effective in translating their efforts to helpee benefits.

The most effective treatment and training programs are those that (1) focus systematically upon the facilitative and action-oriented dimensions constituting the core of all interpersonal processes and (2) are complemented by the systematic development of courses of action calculated to lead the helpee out of his difficulties. That is, systematic attention to the core conditions does not exclude the employment of all means available to enable the helpee to have the best success probability. Accordingly, all potential preferred modes of treatment are analyzed in order to discern their unique contributions to helpee change or gain over and above those accounted for by the core conditions (Carkhuff, 1966; Carkhuff & Berenson, 1967).

Corollary I. The helper's effectiveness may largely be accounted for independent of his orientation and technique by assessing the level of core conditions he offers.

At this point we can account for a large measure of the effectiveness of a practitioner, whatever his orientation, by assessing the level of facilitative conditions he offers as well as the consequent level of process involvement engaged in by his helpees (Carkhuff & Berenson, 1967; Truax & Carkhuff, 1967). Thus, the helpees of psychoanalytic or client-centered or existential or trait-and-factor or behavioristic helpers who are functioning at high levels improve in functioning on a variety of change indexes with perhaps little regard for the helper's cognitive map of what is taking place and where it is going. A significant exception to the lack of research evidence concerning the effect of a particular orientation is the work of the behavioristic conditioning schools. Given experimentally oriented helpers in experimental settings with anxiety reaction cases involving more or less isolated fears such as phobic reactions, the evidence of a distinct contribution is positive. Even here, however, the learning theory model that determines the mechanisms employed does not necessarily dictate that the helper be an impersonal programed reinforcement machine. Indeed, everything that we know about the reinforcement contingencies and their effect upon social variables dictates a very personal interaction (Carkhuff & Berenson, 1967). In this regard Wolpe (1958) concedes that as much as 60 percent of the effectiveness of the counterconditioning process may be due to "nonspecific relationship factors."

Thus, helpees are helped most when they are offered high levels of core conditions complemented by a searching for and operationalization of constructive courses of action. First, the helper-products of programs built around core dimensions offer at least minimal levels of those facilitative and action-oriented dimensions and involve their helpees in a process leading to constructive helpee change or gain. Second, the helper-products of programs concentrating upon core conditions focus upon the communication process as a source of directionality for the helpee. Only in the deepest understanding of the helpee and in enabling the helpee to understand himself can helper and helpee together effectively consider alternative courses of action and develop a constructive directionality for the helpee.

Corollary II. Both professional and nonprofessional persons can be brought to function at levels of core conditions that effect positive gains in others.

In developing the different levels of programs—intermediate, subprofessional, and helpee as well as professional—we have systematically attempted to develop sensitivity and skill in communication. It is important to note that these different programs concentrate upon practice in discriminating and communicating the central core of facilitative and action-oriented dimensions before focusing on the

development of courses of action and the implementation of preferred modes of treatment. On the other hand, the traditional programs have concentrated upon theory and technique almost to the
exclusion of practice in implementing the core conditions. The outcomes of the nontraditional programs have been exciting, however.
It is clear that persons without professional qualifications can become facilitative agents. Indeed, in a number of areas in order to
fill the need for qualified individuals it is essential that lay persons
be trained and employed. For example, in the area of racial relations the employment of selected and expertly trained members of
minority groups may constitute a preferred mode of treatment rather
than a last resort measure.

In summary, in response to the many challenges to the helping professions, we have offered and examined a substantial body of evidence
for several fundamental propositions: Helping processes are additional
instances of interpersonal processes which may have constructive or
deteriorative consequences and which in their constructive instances are
in large part a function of core, facilitative and action-oriented dimensions. We have explored the implications for treatment and training:
those programs that have been built systematically around these core
conditions have been most effective while those that have not been so
constructed have been least effective. If trained lay persons can achieve
results comparable to those of professionals, then what do those who hold
doctorates have to offer if not some skill in explicating, operationalizing,
and implementing in training, practice, research, and consultation the
dimensions of effective interpersonal learning and relearning processes.
Surely the rights of the people being served are paramount. We must
strive to broaden our treatment and training efforts so that new understanding can be translated into human benefits by trained helpers. The
need for doctoral-status "pure" practitioners would appear to be *superfluous* except insofar as their doctoral training equips the practitioners
to make enlightened and systematic inquiries into what they are attempting to accomplish and provide the appropriate training and consultation
in the hope of improving the effectiveness of the helping process.

The ultimate appeal is not to theory and research; rather, it is to the
experience of the reader. He must, if he is honest and free of distortion,
decide what makes a difference and what does not make a difference in
the lives of others. The further removed that any mode of practice comes
to be from the "truth" concerning the dimensions of effective human
encounters, as each of us who has had constructive relationships knows,
the greater the likelihood that such a practice will be discarded.

REFERENCES

For a more detailed discussion of the issues considered in this chapter see the asterisked readings and the references upon which the readings are based.

Anthony, W., & Carkhuff, R. R. The effects of rehabilitation counselor training upon discrimination, communication and helping attitudes. *Rehabilitation Counseling Bulletin*, 1970, **13**, 333–342.

Aspy, D. The differential effects of high and low functioning teachers upon student achievement. *Florida Journal of Educational Research*, 1969, **11**, 39–48.

Aspy, D., & Hadlock, W. The effects of high and low functioning teachers upon student performance. Unpublished research, University of Florida, Gainesville, 1969.

Barrett-Lennard, G. T. Dimensions of therapist response as causal factors in therapeutic change. *Psychological Monographs*, 1962, **76**, No. 43 (Whole No. 562).

Barron, F., & Leary, T. Changes in psychoneurotic patients with and without psychotherapy. *Journal of Consulting Psychology*, 1955, **19**, 239–245.

Bateson, G., Jackson, D., Haley, J., & Weakland, J. H. Toward a theory of schizophrenia. *Behavioral Science*, 1956, **1**, 251–264.

Baxter, J. C., Becker, J., & Hooks, W. Defensive style in the families of schizophrenics and controls. *Journal of Abnormal Social Psychology*, 1963, **66**, 512–518.

*Berenson, B. G., & Carkhuff, R. R. *Sources of gain in counseling and psychotherapy*. New York: Holt, Rinehart and Winston, Inc., 1967.

Berenson, B. G., Carkhuff, R. R., & Myrus, P. The interpersonal functioning and training of college students. *Journal of Counseling Psychology*, 1966, **13**, 441–446.

Berenson, B. G., & Mitchell, K. *Confrontation*. Amherst, Mass.: Human Resource Development Press, 1974.

Bergin, A. E. The effects of psychotherapy: Negative results revisited. *Journal of Counseling Psychology*, 1963, **10**, 244–250.

Bergin, A. E., and Solomon, S. Personality and performance correlates of empathic understanding in psychotherapy. *American Psychologist*, 1963, **18**, 393.

Bowen, M. A family concept of schizophrenia. In D. Jackson (ed.), *The etiology of schizophrenia*. New York: Basic Books, 1960. Pp. 346–372.

*Carkhuff, R. R. Training in counseling and therapeutic processes: Requiem or revielle? *Journal of Counseling Psychology*, 1966, **13**, 360–367.

Carkhuff, R. R. Differential functioning of lay and professional helpers. *Journal of Counseling Psychology*, 1968, **15**, 417–426.

Carkhuff, R. R. Critical variables in effective counselor training. *Journal of Counseling Psychology*, 1969, **16**, 238–245.

Carkhuff, R. R., & Banks, G. Treatment as a preferred mode of facilitating relations between races and generations. *Journal of Counseling Psychology*, 1970, **17**, 413–418.

*Carkhuff, R. R., & Berenson, B. G. *Beyond counseling and therapy.* New York: Holt, Rinehart and Winston, Inc., 1967.

Carkhuff, R. R., & Bierman, R. Training as a preferred mode of treatment of parents of emotionally disturbed children. *Journal of Counseling Psychology*, 1970, **17**, 157–161.

Carkhuff, R. R., Friel, T., & Kratochvil, D. The differential effects of sequence of training in counselor-responsive and counselor-initiated dimensions. *Counselor Education and Supervision*, 1970, **9** (2), 106–109.

Carkhuff, R. R., Kratochvil, D., & Friel, T. The effects of professional training. The communication and discrimination of facilitative conditions. *Journal of Counseling Psychology*, 1968, **15**, 68–74.

Carkhuff, R. R., & Truax, C. B. Training in counseling and psychotherapy: An evaluation of an integrated didactic and experiential approach. *Journal of Consulting Psychology*, 1965, **29**, 333–336.

Carkhuff, R. R., & Truax, C. B. Toward explaining success and failure in interpersonal learning processes. *Personnel and Guidance Journal*, 1966, **44**, 723–728.

Cartwright, R. D., & Vogel, J. L. A comparison of changes in psychoneurotic patients during matched periods of therapy and no therapy. *Journal of Consulting Psychology*, 1960, **24**, 121–127.

Cass, L. K. Parent-child relationships and delinquency. *Journal of Abnormal Social Psychology*, 1953, **47**, 101–104.

Chorost, S. B. Parent child-rearing attitudes and their correlates in adolescent hostility. *Genetic Psychology Monographs*, 1962, **66** (1), 49–90.

Christensen, C. M. Relationships between pupil achievement, pupil affect-need, teacher warmth, and teacher permissiveness. *Journal of Educational Psychology*, 1960, **51**, 169–174.

Davitz, J. R. *The communication of emotional meaning.* New York: McGraw-Hill Book Company, Inc., 1964.

Eysenck, H. J. The effects of psychotherapy. *International Journal of Psychiatry*, 1965, **1**, 99–178.

Frank, J. D. *Persuasion and healing.* Baltimore, Md.: The Johns Hopkins Press, 1961.

Gurin, G., Veroff, J., & Feld, Sheila. *Americans view their mental health.* New York: Basic Books, 1960.

Halkides, G. An investigation of therapeutic success as a function of four variables. Unpublished doctoral dissertation, University of Chicago, 1958.

Holder, B. T. A follow-up study of the activity-passivity and facilitative-non-facilitative dimensions of continuing and terminated graduate trainees. *Journal of Clinical Psychology*, 1969.

Isaacson, R. L., McKeachie, W. J., & Milholland, J. E. A correlation of teacher personality variables and student ratings. *Journal of Educational Psychology*, 1963, **44**, 110–117.

Kratochvil, D. Changes in values and interpersonal functioning of nurses in counselor training. *Counselor Education and Supervision,* 1969, **8,** 104–107.

Kratochvil, D., Carkhuff, R. R., & Berenson, B. G. The cumulative effects of facilitative conditions upon physical, emotional and intellectual functioning of grammar school students. *Journal of Educational Research,* in press, 1969.

Levitt, E. E. Psychotherapy with children: A further evaluation. *Behavior Research and Therapy,* 1963, **1,** 45–51.

Lewis, W. W. Continuity and intervention in emotional disturbance: A review. *Exceptional Children,* 1965, **31,** 465–475.

Lidz, T., Cornelison, A., Fleck, S., & Terry, D. The infrafamilial environment of schizophrenic patients: II. Marital schism and marital skew. *American Journal of Psychiatry,* 1957, **114,** 214–248.

Lidz, R. W., & Lidz, T. The family environment of schizophrenic patients. *American Journal of Psychiatry,* 1949, **106,** 332–345.

Mink, O. G., & Isaksen, H. L. A comparison of effectiveness of nondirective therapy and clinical counseling in the junior high school. *School Counselor,* 1959, **6,** 12–14.

Montalto, F. D. Maternal behavior and child personality. *Journal of Projective Technique,* 1952, **16,** 151–178.

Pace, C. R., & Stern, G. G. An approach to the measurement of physiological characteristics of college environment. *Journal of Educational Psychology,* 1958, **49,** 269–277.

Pagell, W., Carkhuff, R. R., & Berenson, B. G. The predicted differential effects of the level of counselor functioning upon the level of functioning of outpatients. *Journal of Clinical Psychology,* 1967, **23,** 510–512.

Pierce, R. Graduate training of facilitative counselors: The effects of individual supervision. *Journal of Counseling Psychology,* in press, 1969.

Pierce, R., Carkhuff, R. R., & Berenson, B. G. The differential effects of high and moderate level functioning counselors upon counselors-in-training. *Journal of Clinical Psychology,* 1967, **23,** 212–215.

Pierce, R., & Drasgow, J. The effects of human relations training upon V. A. neuropsychiatric patients. *Journal of Counseling Psychology,* in press, 1969.

Powers, E., & Witmer, H. *An experiment in the prevention of delinquency.* New York: Columbia University Press, 1961.

Rogers, C. R., Gendlin, E., Kiesler, D., & Truax, C. B. *The therapeutic relationship and its impact.* Madison, Wisc.: University of Wisconsin Press, 1967.

Thistlewaite, D. L. College press and student achievement. *Journal of Educational Psychology,* 1959, **50,** 183–191.

Truax, C. B. The process of group psychotherapy: Relationships between hypothesized therapeutic conditions and intrapersonal exploration. *Psychological Monographs,* 1961, **75,** No. 7 (Whole No. 511).

Truax, C. B., & Carkhuff, R. R. *Toward effective counseling and psychotherapy: Training and practice.* Chicago: Aldine Publishing Company, 1967.

Truax, C. B., Carkhuff, R. R., & Kodman, F. The relationships between therapist-offered conditions and patient change in group psychotherapy. *Journal of Clinical Psychology*, 1965, **21**, 327–329.

Truax, C. B., & Tatum, C. An extension from the effective psychotherapeutic model to constructive personality change in preschool children. *Childhood Education*, 1966, **42**, 456–462.

Weakland, J. H. The "double-bind" hypothesis of schizophrenia and three-party interaction. In D. Jackson (ed.). *The etiology of schizophrenia*. New York: Basic Books, 1960.

Willis, M. *The guinea pig after 20 years*. Columbus, O.: Ohio State University Press, 1961.

Wolpe, J. *Psychotherapy by reciprocal inhibition*. London: Oxford University Press, 1958.

Wynne, L. C., Ryckoff, J. M., Day, J., & Hirsch, S. J. Pseudomutuality in the family relations of schizophrenics. *Psychiatry*, 1958, **21**, 205–220.

Vitalo, R. The effects of training in interpersonal skills upon psychiatric in-patients. Unpublished research, V.A. Hospital and Buffalo State Hospital, Buffalo, N.Y., 1968.

Toward Effective Helping

PART TWO INTRODUCES the critical categories of helping variables—the helper, the helpee, and the helping
program (Chapter 2). The goals of helping are then
examined. The entire helping process is based upon
the helper's skill in enabling the helpee to explore
himself in his problem areas (Chapter 3). The direction that helping takes following the exploratory
phase is based for the most part on the helper's experience of the helpee during exploration. In the highly
interactional process of helping it is most effective to
attempt to build or rebuild the communication process
to a point where some level of self-understanding will
provide minimal structure for helpee action (Chapter
4). Helpee action, in turn, will provide the necessary
feedback to modify the gross discriminations upon
which the action was based and thus prepare the
helpee for more constructive action based upon finer
discriminations (Chapter 5). An overview of the core
of helping is then presented, with special attention
given to an operationalization of crises in helping and
life (Chapter 6) and the operationalization of the
stages of the individual dimensions involved in the
helping process (Chapter 7). Applications in effective

helping involve variations of the core conditions (Chapter 8) and employment of a preferred mode of treatment, in this instance behavior modification approaches to helping (Chapter 9). In addition, Part Two moves from consideration of individual processes to consideration of group processes (Chapter 10). In an integration of both training and practice, a case study in training a group of parents of emotionally disturbed children is presented with both written and taped material.

2
THE DEVELOPMENT OF EFFECTIVE
HELPING PROCESSES

Perhaps the major assumption with which we initiate the exploration and development of effective helping processes is that these processes are interpersonal in both origin and nature. The helpee's problems are almost exclusively interpersonal ones. He may have behaved in a way that got him into trouble with other persons, or he may not have developed sufficiently in his interpersonal functioning. Even the term "emotional" is synonymous with "interpersonal" for the most part. When it is employed in an intrapersonal sense to refer to what is going on within the helpee, there are no behavioral referents and, accordingly, few visible difficulties in functioning. It is the interpersonal expression of experiences that leads to the helping process. It is assumed that the ability to handle experiences in a given problem area interpersonally will reflect the ability to handle these problem areas intrapersonally. In a sense, interpersonal communication reflects intrapersonal communication, or communication by the individual with himself. In this context the need for means to assess an individual's level of interpersonal functioning is manifest.

Interpersonal functioning can be assessed inferentially from an individual's behavior or empirically by casting the individual in the helping role or in some related operation. When we do so, while we obtain an over-all level of functioning from our indexes, we also obtain different levels of functioning within the same individual. Thus, we find that some persons function at higher levels in one problem area than in another or in one affect area than in another. Similarly, while programs maintain the potential for making their own unique contributions, they do reflect by and large the disposition and development of their promulgators and in this sense may concentrate on specific areas by emphasizing one orientation or the other. It is important to note that there is a significantly greater over-all consistency both within and between different problem areas and affects with an individual who is functioning at a high level than with one functioning at a low level. The high-level–functioning person is effective in almost all areas. It appears that the low-level–functioning person frequently does develop a "specialty" area. However, while he may be more proficient in this area than in others, his level of functioning is usually inadequate in terms of minimal levels as well as inferior to that of the high-level–functioning person in the same area. It can readily be seen, then, that it is imperative that the helper be functioning at higher levels than the helpee in the area of treatment. As we will see, the relative differences demonstrated by individuals in level of functioning from area to area establish the basis for effective helping processes between areas and between individuals.

Level of functioning, then, can be assessed both empirically as well as experientially, since the constructive or destructive consequences of the helping process may be accounted for by the differences that occur within and between the critical helping variables. This may be further broken down in propositional form.

Proposition I. Constructive or destructive consequences of the helping process may be accounted for in part by the level of functioning of the helper.

The level of facilitative and action-oriented dimensions offered by the helper will account in large part for the effects upon the helpee's level of functioning. In general, there is evidence to indicate that traditional practitioners neither concentrate effectively upon the core dimensions nor offer high levels of these dimensions in their helping. The data indicate that many of these helpers are less than minimally facilitative, and some have a retarding effect upon their helpees. On the other hand, helper-products of programs, whether lay or professional, built around the primary core conditions and offering minimally facilitative levels do themselves offer at least minimal levels of facilitative and action-oriented dimensions and involve their helpees in a helping process leading to constructive helpee change or gain.

Proposition II. Constructive or destructive consequences of the helping process may be accounted for in part by the level of functioning of the helpee.

The effects of the level of functioning of the helper, in turn, depend in large part upon the level of functioning of the helpee. With the general expectation that persons functioning at higher levels may help lower-level functioning persons to function at higher levels, we need to analyze helper and helpee level of functioning both within and between different areas. Again it is imperative that the helper be functioning more effectively than the helpee over-all as well as in the helpee's problem areas. As with training, the effects of the helping process are contingent in large part upon the degree of discrepancy between the levels of functioning of the helper and helpee, with those helpees functioning initially at the highest absolute levels tending to function finally at the highest absolute levels and those helpees deviating the most from a high-level–functioning helper demonstrating the greatest change.

Proposition III. Constructive or destructive consequences of the helping process may be accounted for in part by the type of helping program implemented.

Again helping programs reflect the helping persons. In general, helpees are helped most when they are offered high levels of facilitative and action-oriented dimensions. However, they appear to be helped most when the high levels of core conditions emanate from a systematic, albeit open-ended, frame of reference. The helper has to know what he is doing and his helping program has to be going somewhere. While structurally directionful, the helping program is constantly shaped by the feedback from the helpee concerning what is effective for him. Thus, in a highly interactional process the facilitative and action-oriented dimensions are complemented by a searching for and operationalization of constructive courses of action or preferred modes of treatment. In contrast, traditional helping processes usually emphasize the communication process only from a particular frame of reference. If the orientation happens to meet the helpee's needs, it may indeed constitute a preferred mode of treatment and thus be very helpful, but all too often it excludes critical aspects of an effective helping process. Only in understanding the helpee as well as in enabling him to understand himself can helper and helpee together effectively consider alternative courses of action and develop a constructive directionality for the helpee.

THE EFFECTS OF HELPER LEVEL OF FUNCTIONING: A CLOSER LOOK

Obviously differences in effectiveness are not to be accounted for solely in terms of whether a treatment process is traditional or not. There are traditional, professional practitioners who function at high levels and there is an abundance of low-level–functioning nonprofessional persons ready and willing to offer help at any time. However, the literature with regard to both process and outcome in helping indicates the critical nature of the helper's level of functioning. The accumulated evidence from a number of naturalistic studies is extensive and consistent: helpees of high-level–functioning helpers demonstrate constructive change on a variety of indexes while those of low-level–functioning helpers do not change or even deteriorate (Berenson & Carkhuff, 1967; Carkhuff & Berenson, 1967; Rogers, Gendlin, Kiesler, & Truax, 1967; Truax & Carkhuff, 1967).

More specifically, while the outcome criteria are not directly comparable, as are the training indexes (see Volume I, Chapter 10), the predictive evidence is similar for counseling and psychotherapy (Pagell, Carkhuff, & Berenson, 1967), education (Aspy, 1969; Aspy & Hadlock, 1969; Kratochvil, Carkhuff, & Berenson, 1969), supervision (Pierce, 1969), and parent-child treatment (Carkhuff & Bierman, 1970). In developing data directly comparable to the training data, one study (Pagell *et al.*, 1967) searched a variety of indexes of possible client gains in interpersonal functioning over therapy, including expert, therapist, helpee, and self-ratings as well as objective ratings prior to and following the helping process. Those therapists who were functioning both (1) above minimally facilitative levels and (2) at least a level above their clients had clients who demonstrated the greatest growth in interpersonal functioning. (These results are very similar to those obtained with the training groups in Table 10-1, Volume I.) In addition, it is noteworthy that a client of one of the high-level–functioning therapists was functioning at minimally facilitative levels following the helping process, something that most of the therapists had not been able to achieve over a lifetime. While a few of the clients of some of the low-level–functioning therapists demonstrated some minimal change, the most significant changes occurred in the clients of the high-level–functioning therapists. This study of treatment is, however, not without qualification. Thus far we have concentrated primarily upon the absolute level of helper functioning. The results of one study (Kratochvil, Aspy, & Carkhuff, 1967) have taught us that the directionality of movement, when such changes are significant, may in some cases be more critical than the absolute level of functioning: counselors and therapists who demonstrate significant growth movement from the beginning to the end of helping will have clients who demonstrate constructive change; those helpers who decline in functioning over the course of helping will have helpees who decline.

Another source of learning concerning the effects of helper level of functioning has been the process studies in which helper level of functioning was manipulated and the effects upon helpee functioning studied. In studies of both inpatient schizophrenics (Cannon & Pierce, 1968; Truax

& Carkhuff, 1965) and low-level–functioning college students (Holder, Carkhuff, & Berenson, 1967) it was found that relatively high-level–functioning helpers influenced the low-level–functioning helpee's level of functioning by the level of facilitative conditions they offered (Figure 2-1). When the helper offered high levels of conditions the helpee explored himself at high levels; when the helper offered low levels of conditions the helpee explored himself at low levels. Similarly, when we introduce low-level–functioning helpers (Piaget, Berenson, & Carkhuff, 1967) we find different effects upon low-level–functioning helpees, with the low-level helper tending to pull low-level helpees down toward his modal level of functioning over time (Figure 2-2). These studies have implications for the progress of helping. *The high-level–functioning helper engages all of the helpee's resources in a process that culminates in the helpee's constructive growth. The low-level–functioning helper involves the helpee in a subtractive process that results in deterioration over time.*

HELPEE LEVEL OF FUNCTIONING: A CLOSER LOOK

Few studies have systematically assessed the effects of the helpee's level of functioning. Nevertheless, this remains a critical dimension which in interaction with the helper's level of functioning dictates the

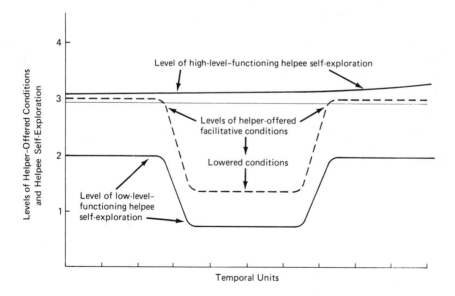

Figure 2-1. Effects of the experimental manipulation of a high-level–functioning helper's facilitative conditions upon helpee self-exploration.

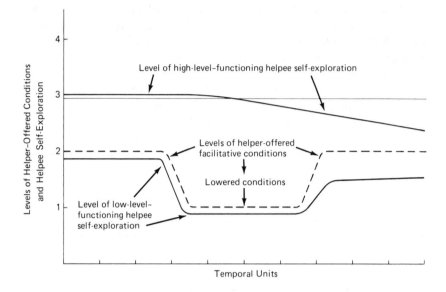

Figure 2-2.   Effects of the experimental manipulation of a low-level–functioning helper's facilitative conditions upon helpee self-exploration.

outcome of the helping process. Again the main source of evidence comes from the process manipulation studies. Whereas, for example, the depth to which low-level–functioning helpees explore themselves is a function of the level of facilitative conditions offered by high-level–functioning helpers (Cannon & Pierce, 1968; Holder *et al.*, 1967; Truax & Carkhuff, 1965), the findings are quite different when we introduce relatively high-level–functioning helpees (Piaget *et al.*, 1967). In general, we find that the higher the level of functioning in the helping role, the higher the disposition to explore and experience oneself. In particular, in interaction with a high-level helper the high-level helpee continues to explore himself independently of the helper's lowering of the conditions he offers. When the helper restores high levels of conditions the helpee proceeds to even higher levels of self-exploration than those at which he began (see Figure 2-1). On the other hand, where the low-level–functioning helpee drops to a level from which he does not recover in conjunction with the low-level helper, the high-level helpee continues for a while to explore himself at his modal level of functioning. Gradually, however, the low levels of conditions take their toll and the otherwise high-level helpee explores himself at less and less effective levels (see Figure 2-2).

Perhaps the significance of this work is this: if a helpee is cast in a relationship with a low-level helper *and cedes him the power in the relationship,* he will deteriorate over time, with those helpees functioning at the lowest levels deteriorating most rapidly, although the others will deteriorate just as surely. If, in turn, a helpee cedes a high-level helper the necessary recognition, the helper will influence the helpee toward the helper's level of functioning, with the high-level helpee moving most rapidly and the low-level helpee most slowly. A temporal factor based on previous experiences, then, may modify these generalizations. While the high-level–functioning helpee stands to gain the most in interaction with a high-level helper and lose the most with a low-level helper, he may also be more likely to move more rapidly in the positive direction and more slowly in the negative. The general rule is, the more successful experiences an individual has had, the higher his level of functioning and the more amenable he is to treatment by high-level–functioning persons and the less accessible he is to low-level–functioning persons. Similarly, the low-level helpee may move more slowly in a positive direction, and while he may lose very little, he may lose what he is going to lose rather rapidly. The general rule is, the more failure experiences an individual has had, the less reachable he is by high-level–functioning persons and the more accessible he is to low-level–functioning persons.

These inferences are further buttressed by the results of studies that manipulated the client's level of functioning and studied the effects upon the therapist (Alexik & Carkhuff, 1967; Carkhuff & Alexik, 1967; Friel, Kratochvil, & Carkhuff, 1968). When a client who has been exploring himself at reasonably effective process levels suddenly ceases to explore himself we might say that he had in effect presented the therapist with a therapeutic crisis. The results indicate that the higher the level at which the therapist is functioning, the greater the likelihood that he will increase the level of conditions he is offering. Conversely, the lower the therapist's level, the greater the likelihood that he will offer even lower conditions, and following the independent reinstitution of high levels of self-exploration by the client the low-level–functioning therapist does not recover to function again at the level at which he was functioning initially (Figure 2-3). The implication is that the level of helpee functioning and the crises that he presents will have a different effect upon high- and low-level–functioning helpers. The high-level–functioning helpers will be responsive and will, in turn, have a constructive effect upon the helpee over the course of helping. The low-level–functioning helpers will be overwhelmed and thus will have a destructive effect upon the helpee over the course of helping.

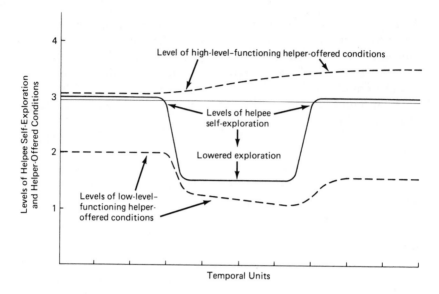

Figure 2-3. Effects of experimental manipulation of helpee self-exploration upon helper-offered conditions.

THE HELPING PROCESS: A CLOSER LOOK

The helping process may be divided into two principal phases: (1) the downward or inward phase and (2) the upward or outward phase or the phase of emergent directionality. During the initial phase the goal of helping is to learn not only the nature of the individual's problems but also how the helpee views himself and his world. During the latter phase the goal is to establish and operationalize a constructive direction or problem resolution for the helpee.

The Phases of Helping

During the initial phase the helper offers high levels of conditions, his goal being the helpee's self-exploration and self-experiencing. Initially the helper concentrates more on the facilitative dimensions of empathic understanding, warmth, respect, and concreteness in order to create an atmosphere in which the helpee can come to trust him and the experience he offers. The helper will usually find that he is most effective when he offers minimally facilitative levels of the facilitative conditions. This is in large part simply a function of the depth or perhaps the lack of depth of the relationship at this stage of development. That is, in actuality there is little basis for a depth of empathic understanding or for a high degree of positive regard. The helper usually does not know the helpee and there is little basis for a constructive relationship other than the fact that one person is disposed toward helping while the other has a set for being helped.

The period of getting to know each other may be very brief in some helping processes where there is a basis in past experience for high levels of understanding early in helping. For example, shared cultural or sub-cultural backgrounds may give the helper a depth of understanding that he might not have with another helpee who might require a great deal more time. However, even in this event cultural stereotypes should not be allowed to cloud the uniqueness of the particular helpee's life experience. In summary, whether the period is brief or long, the goal of the initial phase—the helpee's self-exploration of relevant areas of concern —must be effectively attained. In order to accomplish this the initial phase of the helping process must take place in a context of at least minimal levels of helper-communicated genuineness.

Gradually, as the helper establishes a basis for experiencing and understanding the world as the helpee does, there is increasing reason for the helper to institute higher levels of facilitative conditions. Concomitantly, the helpee's increasingly higher levels of self-exploration in interaction with interchangeable levels of understanding on the part of the helper enable the helpee to clarify and sharpen his experiences. This increased level of self-understanding, in turn, signals a readiness for the institution of higher levels of conditions. Whereas helpee self-exploration constitutes the goal of the first phase of helping, and, indeed, the very basis for helping, higher levels of understanding on the part of both the helper and the helpee constitute the transition into the action-oriented phase of helping—that is, doing something about the problems that were explored and that have come to be understood.

Still within the first phase of helping, then, yet providing a transition into the second phase, are the more action-oriented dimensions. Gradually as the helpee comes to trust his own experience in the relationship and to make this experience known to the helper, at least at minimal levels, there will be an increasing basis and need for the helper to communicate increasingly higher levels of genuineness and, often concurrently, self-disclosure. This direction will be in part a function of the helpee's need to come to be able to know the helper at even deeper levels. It will also pave the way for the helpee's being able to make himself known at deeper levels. Again the helper is both model and agent.

As the helper and helpee come to know each other at these deeper levels there will be increasing opportunity for and meaning to the helper's confrontations of discrepancies in the helpee's behavior and interpretations of immediacy in the relationship. Whereas initially there was no strong relationship to incorporate these thrusts without a breakdown in communication, increasingly these modalities provide the levers into deeper and deeper levels of experiencing and understanding for the helpee as well as the helper. In addition, and most significantly, the helpee learns in direct experience both how to interpret and act upon his immediate experience of himself and another.

Thus, within the initial phase the helper concentrates early upon minimal levels of facilitative conditions in a minimally genuine context and moves toward higher levels of facilitative conditions as he introduces the more highly action-oriented dimensions at minimally effective levels. There is evidence to indicate that effective helpers do just that. Bierman (1968) studied therapeutic process movement along two dimensions, the active-passive and the affectional-rejecting. He found that while most therapists attempt to function initially in a more passively affectional manner, those who function most effectively in this manner move toward functioning in the more active-affectional realm while those who function least effectively in a passive-affectional manner move over time and with, we might add, crises (Carkhuff & Berenson, 1967) toward one or both of two dominant modalities, passive rejection or active rejection. Finally, those who moved from passive- to active-affectional functioning had the most constructive effects upon client functioning.

This is not to say that there are not many qualifications and modifications upon this model. There are many. For one thing, the level of functioning at which a helpee enters helping and the levels to which he moves within the helping process may make a great difference. For example, with a very high-level–functioning helpee the initial phase of self-exploration leading to self-understanding may be very brief indeed. Such a helpee need only experience the briefest communications to make discriminations concerning the level at which the helper is functioning. If he is fortunate enough to be involved with a high-level helper who has made similar discriminations, most of the time may be spent on the more cognitive pursuits of the second, problem-solving phase. On the other hand, a very low-level–functioning patient may, in effect, require phase 2 treatment prior to phase 1. The helper may, for example, choose to manipulate both the patient and his environment in order to bring the patient to a level of functioning at which he can interact with another human being.

The action-oriented dimensions, at minimal levels, provide a bridge into the second phase of helping. These dimensions take on increasing significance and, accordingly, movement toward higher levels as the emphasis shifts from responding to initiating. It is in those moments when the helper, and consequently the helpee, acts upon his experience that the significant learnings of helping and life take place. The second phase of helping merely brings the helpee back to the problems that led him to seek help in the first place.

During the second phase of helping the helpee comes not only to learn to act in terms of experiential dimensions (he learns to do all that the helper does) but also to become involved in more cognitive, problem-solving–type activities. Having effectively explored himself and having come to some highly functional understanding of himself, the helpee comes once again to address himself to the difficulties that brought him to counseling. The issue is, "Now what are we going to do about what we understand?" The answer is threefold: (1) "We are going to consider the various alternative courses of action available to you"; (2) "We are going to consider the advantages and disadvantages, long term as well as immediate, of each"; (3) "We are going to take steps to operationalize the best mode of action available."

During the phase of emergent directionality, then, the helper, often in conjunction with the helpee, considers the implications of the interaction of all of the relevant variables involved. Frequently the conclusion may involve the implementation of one or another preferred mode of treatment—for example, systematic counterconditioning or vocational testing and counseling or environmental manipulation or a combination of all of these and more—as the means that will best enable the helpee to overcome obstacles to his actualization of his growth potential. The second phase brings the helpee back to the realities of his environment and, indeed, his life. In a very real sense the direction of the second phase flows directly from the explorations and understanding of the first phase. Thus, while the helper has some structure in mind for the helping process, he begins essentially atheoretically and allows himself to be guided by the feedback he gets from the significant dimensions of client behavior. A bias toward one or the other mode of treatment may negate the effectiveness of the two-phase sequence, excluding the mode that might offer the helpee the prospect of the most constructive change.

The two-phase sequence, then, is essential. It requires the courage of a strong helper who can face the unknown, without the safety of the known. It requires the maturity and patience of a responsible helper who does not have to have solutions before he fully understands problems. It requires the openness of a flexible helper who can move in any one of innumerable directions, some that he has not experienced before but that are, nevertheless, dictated by the conditions of this particular case. It requires the skill of a competent helper to implement the courses of action dictated. In short, it requires a whole person and a whole helper, one who is not fractionated in his existence and thus unable to offer the helpee anything more than he himself has.

In this context one of the most interesting studies involves a series of factor analytic studies of a correlational matrix involving all of the facilitative and action-oriented dimensions as well as several other dimensions of both high- and low-level—functioning helpers (Friel 1971). Following helpee crises precipitated by helper confrontations, three factors emerged for the high-level—functioning helpers. The first we might call a more feminine factor incorporating those more passive dimensions of respect and understanding. The second factor is a more masculine factor involving dimensions such as genuineness, immediacy, and confrontation. Finally, the third factor involves the explorations and more reality-oriented, problem-solving kinds of activities of the helpee. In effect, this is to say that the effective helper is both male and female, both father and mother, and he knows when to employ each or both dimensions appropriately in a manner integrated with his effective style of life. In addition, the effective helper is an expert in the assessment and implementation of many possible directionalities. He is an expert on how and when to employ a given course of action and, in particular, a variety of potential preferred modes of treatment; if he cannot himself implement any one of these treatment modes, he knows how and where to make the appropriate referral.

For the low-level–functioning helpers essentially only one factor was found. We could find no other name than the "stupid question" factor, since the dominant mode of functioning of the low-level–functioning helper was to ask numerous questions. The very best that can be said for these questions is that they lead the nondiscriminating helpee to the expectation that his answers will lead to even more significant answers from the helper. Unfortunately, this is not the case. There is no delivery. Most frequently the helper apparently has no intention of providing the helpee with directionality—a directionality that, we might add, the helper has been unable to find in his own life. Less frequently the helper provides a directionality that may be overwhelming for the helpee, a directionality with which he appears to have begun the helping process and one that he imposed independently of the helpee. Perhaps the greatest significance of this work lies in the contrast of the functioning of high- and low-level helpers, with the built-in flexibility of the former serving to offer the helper the highest-level human experience and the built-in rigidity of the latter providing only debilitating experiences.

REFERENCES

For a more detailed discussion of the issues considered in this chapter see the asterisked readings and the references upon which the readings are based.

Alexik, M., & Carkhuff, R. R. The effects of the manipulation of client depth of self-exploration upon high- and low-functioning counselors. *Journal of Clinical Psychology,* 1967, **23,** 210–212.

Aspy, D. The effect of teacher-offered conditions of empathy, positive regard and congruence upon student achievement. *Florida Journal of Research,* 1969, **11,** 39–48.

Aspy, D., & Hadlock, W. The effects of high and low functioning teachers upon student academic achievement and truancy. Unpublished research, University of Florida, Gainesville, 1969.

Bierman, R. Therapist activity-passivity and affection-rejection in therapeutic *psychotherapy.* New York: Holt, Rinehart and Winston, Inc., 1967.

Bierman, R. Therapist activity- passivity and affection-rejection in therapeutic processes. Unpublished research, University of Waterloo, Waterloo, Canada, 1968.

Cannon, J. R., & Pierce, R. M. Order effects in the experimental manipulation of therapeutic conditions. *Journal of Clinical Psychology,* 1968, **24,** 242–244.

*Carkhuff, R. R., & Alexik, M. The differential effects of the manipulation of client self-exploration upon high- and low-functioning counselors. *Journal of Counseling Psychology,* 1967, **14,** 350–355.

Carkhuff, R. R., & Bierman, R. Training as a preferred mode of treatment of parents of emotionally disturbed children. *Journal of Counseling Psychology,* 1970, **17,** 157–161.

Donofrio, D. The effects of level of therapist-offered conditions upon parents in group therapy and their children. Doctoral dissertation, State University of New York at Buffalo, 1968.

Friel, T. Factor analysis of levels of therapist functioning and confrontation. *Journal of Counseling Psychology,* 1971, **27,** No. 2.

Friel, T., Kratochvil, D., & Carkhuff, R. R. The effects of training upon the manipulation of client conditions. *Journal of Clinical Psychology,* 1968, **24,** 247–249.

Holder, B. T., Carkhuff, R. R., & Berenson, B. G. The differential effects of the manipulation of therapeutic conditions upon high and low functioning clients. *Journal of Counseling Psychology,* 1967, **14,** 63–66.

Kratochvil, D., Aspy, D., & Carkhuff, R. R. The differential effects of absolute level and direction of growth in counselor functioning upon client functioning. *Journal of Clinical Psychology,* 1967, **23,** 216–218.

Kratochvil, D., Carkhuff, R. R., & Berenson, B. G. Cumulative effects of parent and teacher offered levels of facilitative conditions upon indices of student physical, emotional and intellectual functioning. *Journal of Educational Research,* 1969, **63,** 161–164.

Pagell, W., Carkhuff, R. R., & Berenson, B. G. The predicted differential effects of the level of counselor functioning upon the level of functioning of outpatients. *Journal of Clinical Psychology,* 1967, **23,** 510–512.

Piaget, G., Berenson, B. G., & Carkhuff, R. R. The differential effects of the manipulation of therapeutic conditions by high and low functioning counselors upon high and low functioning clients. *Journal of Consulting Psychology,* 1967, **31,** 481–486.

Pierce, R. Graduate training of facilitative counselors: The effects of individual supervision. *Journal of Counseling Psychology,* 1969.

Rogers, C. R., Gendlin, E., Kiesler, D., & Truax, C. B. *The therapeutic relationship and its impact.* Madison, Wisc.: University of Wisconsin Press, 1967.

Truax, C. B., & Carkhuff, R. R. The experimental manipulation of therapeutic conditions. *Journal of Consulting Psychology,* 1965, **29,** 119–124.

*Truax, C. B., & Carkhuff, R. R. *Toward effective counseling and psychotherapy: Training and practice.* Chicago: Aldine Publishing Company, 1967.

3

THE EXPLORATORY
PHASE OF HELPING

The person with a problem seeks help. He has some difficulty or area in which he does not function effectively and he wants to change. Or perhaps he is functioning at a fairly adequate level but desires to gain or grow in some way. The changes and gains he seeks may be emotional, intellectual, or physical or a combination of these.

A critical aspect of an individual's dysfunctioning is his inability to understand himself in depth and/or to act constructively in his problem areas. In cases in which such a person's level of understanding is adequate it may be assumed that he is unable to act upon this understanding. Perhaps because of past learning experiences or experiences in other problem areas in which his understanding was not adequate, he has found that at a minimum when he acts he is not rewarded, or, worse yet, he may live in fear of being punished for acting. He seeks help because in certain areas he is unable to attain an effective level of functioning either by himself or with the help of his acquaintances. He seeks help to enable him to make finer discriminations and to be able to act upon these discriminations.

The goals of the helping processes, then, are facilitative communication and constructive action both as an individual relates to himself and to others. Consistently constructive action is not possible without the fine discriminations of sensitive understanding; consistently sensitive understanding is not possible without the learning that comes from the feedback of action. In healthy people understanding is simultaneous with action, and the achievement of this balance is the ultimate goal of the helping process.

Under ordinary circumstances in order to accomplish these ends two

35

phases of helping must take place: (1) the downward or inward phase involving movement inward toward a depth of exploration of the problem areas and (2) the upward or outward phase in which there is movement toward resolving the problems. In this regard self-exploration is not to be confused with self-understanding. Although some degree of self-understanding may be involved in self-exploration, there is no necessary relation between the processes. To be sure, the higher the person's over-all level of functioning, the greater the relation between exploration and understanding. Among low-level–functioning persons, which means the majority of helpees, however, there should be no expectation that exploration leads automatically to understanding. For such individuals the two processes are for all intents and purposes separate and distinct. Often the self-exploration process operates more for the helper's benefit, to provide him with the directionality necessary for the ensuing stages of helping, than for the helpee's, whose very dysfunctioning usually implies the he neither understands nor knows what to do with his explorations.

It is true that a high-level–functioning helper will employ his own understanding of the helpee's dysfunctioning to enable the helpee to understand himself. However, depending upon the helpee's level of functioning as well as upon a variety of other variables, the helping program leading to this understanding may be implemented in either the first or second phase of helping. For example, with the knowledge that understanding may lead to action among high-level–functioning helpees, the process of simultaneous understanding with exploration that typifies the activities of these helpees may be effectively reinforced by the helper. On the other hand, this approach will not be effective with helpees functioning at low levels. The helper will employ his understanding of the helpee's dysfunctioning to develop his own directionality and to implement a program leading to improved understanding of both himself and others as well as constructive action in regard to himself and others. Even here, however, the helper may have to decide upon the order of learning.

Following the stage of self-exploration, then, the helping process proceeds in two principal ways: (1) helpee self-understanding precedes helpee constructive action and (2) helpee constructive action precedes helpee self-understanding. Again these two modalities are not mutually exclusive—indeed, they usually play complimentary roles in a highly interactional process. An improved level of understanding involves a process of perceptual reorganization on the part of the helpee. An improved capacity to act involves a process of practice with all of the behavioral shaping it implies. Whether the emphasis in helping is upon understanding before action or upon action before understanding, the helper aids in accomplishing both of the objectives by involving the helpee in a process of self-exploration and self-experiencing. The helping process cannot be initiated until a self-exploration process has taken place. *There is no basis in the experience of either the helper or the helpee for helping until the helpee has thoroughly explored his past, present, or future difficulties.* Helpee self-exploration, then, may lead to improved self-understanding and/or the improved capacity for constructive action, initially one before the other, ultimately both simultaneously.

Helpee self-exploration, as the helper-offered core conditions, cuts across a variety of orientations to helping and is a common ingredient of all effective helping processes (Carkhuff & Berenson, 1967). Self-exploration makes possible not only a relearning process but also a learning process by the necessary assumption of the learner's frame of reference by the teacher that makes possible the communication process of teaching. The goal of the first phase of helping, and indeed the criterion by which we can assess the effectiveness of the first phase, is the depth to which the helpee is able to explore himself in his problem areas. Finally, there is extensive evidence to relate the degree to which a helpee explores himself, *particularly early in the helping process*—for that is when exploration is appropriate—to a variety of final outcome criteria (Carkhuff & Berenson, 1967; Truax & Carkhuff, 1967).

THE EXPLORATORY PHASE OF HELPING: A VIEW IN DEPTH

As we noted earlier, while the helpee may be functioning at a given level over-all, his level of functioning usually varies from area to area. Thus, we may assume that the helpee is functioning at high or low levels depending upon a variety of related variables. For example, having developed a rigid competitive cosmology in response to early childhood threats to his well-being, the helpee may find that while this approach serves him well in his educational-vocational areas of endeavor it serves him poorly in his social-interpersonal, sexual-marital, and child-rearing areas. Another individual may find an other-directed orientation effective in social-interpersonal relations but ineffective in other areas. Such individuals do not have the understanding or the flexible cosmologies available to them to allow them to be shaped by what is effective. In addition, they do not have the responses in their repertoire that enable them to act effectively.

We may arrive at assessments of differential functioning experientially or experimentally. We can make inferences from behavior or we can obtain objective indexes of levels of functioning. We may, for example, cast the persons involved in the helping role with persons with problems in the areas of concern, or we may assess their respective levels of functioning by their responses to standard stimuli, as in the selection procedures developed in Volume I. Thus, we may obtain indexes that can be tested empirically as well as experientially.

In a similar manner we may assess the helper in the same areas of functioning. We will find that while a healthy and integrated helper also functions differentially in different areas, he demonstrates a much greater over-all consistency. In addition, and this is imperative, he must be functioning above minimally facilitative levels in all relevant areas. These are the minimal conditions that enable him to elicit process involvement and movement on the part of the helpee to higher levels of functioning.

The goal of the exploratory phase of helping may be operationalized as in Scale 1. At the lowest level, level 1, the helpee does not discuss

SCALE 1
SELF-EXPLORATION IN INTERPERSONAL PROCESSES
A SCALE FOR MEASUREMENT [1]

Level 1

The helpee does not discuss personally relevant material, either because he has had no opportunity to do so or because he is actively evading the discussion even when it is introduced by the helper.

EXAMPLE: The helpee avoids any self-descriptions, self-exploration, or direct expression of feelings that would lead him to reveal himself to the helper.

In summary, for a variety of possible reasons the helpee does not give any evidence of self-exploration.

Level 2

The helpee responds with discussion to the introduction of personally relevant material by the helper but does so in a mechanical manner and without demonstrating feeling.

EXAMPLE: The helpee simply discusses the material without exploring its significance or attempting further exploration of his feelings in an effort to uncover related feelings or material.

In summary, the helpee responds mechanically and remotely to the introduction of personally relevant material by the helper.

[1] This scale is a revision of earlier versions of self-exploration scales (Carkhuff, 1968; Truax & Carkhuff, 1967).

Level 3

The helpee voluntarily introduces discussions of personally relevant material but does so in a mechanical manner and without demonstrating emotional feeling.

EXAMPLE: The emotional remoteness and mechanical manner of the discussion give it a quality of being rehearsed.

In summary, the helpee introduces personally relevant material but does so without spontaneity or emotional proximity and without an inward probing to newly discovered feelings and experiences.

Level 4

The helpee voluntarily introduces discussions of personally relevant material with both spontaneity and emotional proximity.

EXAMPLE: The voice quality and other characteristics of the helpee are very much "with" the feelings and other personal material being verbalized.

In summary, the helpee introduces personally relevant discussions with spontaneity and emotional proximity but without a distinct tendency toward inward probing to newly discovered feelings and experiences.

Level 5

The helpee actively and spontaneously engages in an inward probing to newly discovered feelings or experiences about himself and his world.

EXAMPLE: The helpee is searching to discover new feelings concerning himself and his world even though at the moment he may be doing so perhaps fearfully and tentatively.

In summary, the helpee is fully and actively focusing upon himself and exploring himself and his world.

personally relevant material while at the next level he responds to the introduction of such material but does so in a mechanical manner and without demonstrating his feelings. At the minimally effective level, level 3, the helpee may voluntarily introduce discussions of personally relevant material, but he does so in a mechanical manner and again without demonstrating feeling. Finally, at the higher levels, levels 4 and 5, the helpee voluntarily introduces content areas with both spontaneity and emotional proximity.

The self-exploration process, in turn, is a complex process that involves at least three key aspects: (1) the over-all level of helpee functioning in a given area and its relation to self-exploration; (2) the initial disposition of the helpee to respond to the crisis areas, which more often than not are areas in which he is functioning at the lowest levels; (3) the generalization of learning from past exploration experiences to new exploration experiences. Just as the helpee functions at different levels in different problem areas, so will he also explore himself differentially. When the data from high- and low-functioning persons are combined there is a pronounced relation between levels of interpersonal functioning and levels of intrapersonal exploration in a given area (Holder, Carkhuff, & Berenson, 1967; Pagell, Carkhuff, & Berenson, 1967; Piaget, Berenson, & Carkhuff, 1967). Thus, the helpee tends to explore himself at the highest levels relatively in the areas in which he is functioning at the highest levels. Accordingly, in some areas the helpee may be functioning and capable of exploration at minimally facilitative, self-sustaining levels.

On the other hand, the crisis area that most frequently precipitates the search for help involves an area in which the helpee is functioning at the lowest levels. Whether the intention is to deal with the resolution of the immediate crisis, as in short-term crisis therapy, or to deal with all relevant areas of functioning, as in long-term treatment, the helper will most effectively initiate the exploration process by assuming a stance responsive to the helpee's initial disposition, although in the instance of the latter alternative other revelant areas will be explored.

Finally, the explorations in one area will have some generalization to explorations in another area. Thus, an initial disposition to exploration in a second area at a given level may be modified by the exploration experience in the first area. This characteristic becomes most apparent in longer-term treatment in which several successive areas relevant to the helpee's over-all functioning are dealt with. The helper must stay constantly attuned to these changes by checking the feedback he gets from the helpee.

The goal of phase 1, then, is to enable the helpee to explore himself at the deepest possible levels in the areas of concern. The ultimate goal of helping to which the first phase contributes emphasizes the helpee's ability to function at minimally facilitative levels himself, that is, not only at minimal levels of understanding of himself and others but also at levels that enable him to act upon this understanding.

Helpee Self-Exploration: Guidelines for the Helper

A number of guidelines are available to assist the helper in achieving the goal of the exploratory phase of helping.

1. *The helper will find that he is most effective when he establishes helpee self-exploration as his immediate goal.*

The goal of the first phase of helping is the exploration by the helpee of his feelings and experiences in relation to the problem area at hand. Without this starting point no amelioration of the condition of the helpee is possible. As we have seen, helpee self-exploration incorporates both immediacy of experiencing and extensiveness of problem expression. Thus, at minimally effective levels the helpee introduces personally relevant material while at higher levels he does so with emotional proximity and at the lowest level he avoids doing so or is unable to do so.

2. *The helper will find that he is most effective in eliciting helpee self-exploration when he initially attempts to understand the helpee at the level at which the helpee presents himself.*

Usually the helpee brings his own problems for exploration. Nevertheless, these areas will be complimented by areas of inquiry encouraged by the helper. However, even when the helper may direct the explorations of the helpee to a given problem area, he will find that exploration of personally relevant material is most effectively reinforced by essentially interchangeable levels of understanding and a suspension of potentially deleterious attitudes and judgments. Thus, the helpee may move increasingly to initiate his own explorations and increase his emotional proximity to these explorations in a free yet responsive atmosphere.

3. *The helper will find that he is most effective when he initially offers minimally facilitative levels of facilitative conditions.*

When the helper offers minimally facilitative levels of empathy, respect, warmth, concreteness, and genuineness he establishes a relationship within which the helpee can explore, experience, and experiment with himself. Again the emphasis is upon interchangeable understanding (level 3 of empathy) and a kind of functional unconditionality (level 3 of respect), the implicit assumption being that at this stage of helping the helpee cannot utilize more than these levels of these conditions. Not only do higher levels of these conditions not have functional utility for the helpee but they also may have harmful effects at this stage of helping. The minimally facilitative conditions enable the helpee to know that someone can understand him on his terms in addition to providing him with the feedback necessary for later reformulations. The minimally facilitative conditions are sufficient in and of themselves to elicit a depth of self-exploration in all relevant problem areas.

4. *The helper will find that he is most effective when he employs the helpee's self-sustaining level of self-exploration as his guide for movement to the next stage of helping.*

The goal of the first stage of helping is the exploration of relevant personal material in the helpee's problem areas. Within a given area the criterion for movement to the next stage of helping will be the helpee's ability to develop his own explorations with emotional proximity. When the helpee is able to do so the helper proceeds systematically to focus his effort upon either helpee self-understanding or action, depending on his understanding of the helpee's explorations. While the self-exploration process may lead to some self-understanding and/or action, the learning is usually fragmented and operates from a distorted base.

5. *The helper will find that he is most effective when he is open to a repetition of the cycle of self-exploration both within and between different content areas.*

Within each content area the helpee may repeat the following cycle: (1) responding to material introduced by the helper (level 2 of self-exploration); (2) introducing personally relevant material mechanically (level 3); and (3) introducing personally relevant material with emotional proximity (level 4 or higher). Thus, within an area the emphasis will be upon more personally meaningful material while between areas the cycle will be repeated with more personally difficult material. It must be emphasized that *at all times the helper must direct the focus of the helping process toward the highest problem area in which the helpee is not functioning at minimally facilitative levels,* that is, the highest of the problem areas in which the helpee is functioning at less than minimally facilitative levels.

HELPEE SELF-EXPLORATION: ILLUSTRATIONS

Thus, we may assume that both helpees and helpers function at different levels in different problem areas. In fact, we can objectify the differential levels of functioning (Table 3-1). Accordingly, helpee 1 may not be functioning at minimally facilitative levels in any of the relevant content areas while helpee 2 may function effectively in one area, the social-interpersonal area. The helper, in turn, is functioning at minimally facilitative levels significantly above the helpee in all relevant areas.

As indicated earlier, under ordinary circumstances the initial explorations will be in the crisis area, or the area that precipitated the helpee to seek help in the first place. The helping process, however, is by no means restricted to that problem area. Except under circumstances in-

Table 3-1. Helper and Helpee Levels of Functioning

	Social-Interpersonal	Educational-Vocational	Child-Rearing	Sexual-Marital
Helper	4.1	4.0	3.9	3.7
Helpee 1	2.1	2.3	1.9	1.7
Helpee 2	3.0	2.2	1.8	1.9

volving the very briefest duration of helping the helper will seek an index of the helpee's level of functioning in other areas. If the helpee does not explore himself spontaneously in these other areas the helper will find that he must direct the helpee to do so. The helper may obtain an estimate of the helpee's level of functioning inferentially from the helpee's behavior or he may do so experimentally, as we suggested earlier, by casting him in the helping role with helpees with representative problems or by related means.

In a crisis situation, then, the helpee may seek help in the area in which he is functioning at the lowest or near lowest levels. Thus, helpees 1 and 2 might appear for help in the child-rearing area as a result of crises in the lives of one or more of his children. Whereas the treatment process may be initiated in a different area with longer-term treatment, *all exploratory phases of helping begin with the helpee's presentation of his problem area. Except under extreme crisis conditions the helper is at first exclusively a responsive participant in the helping process.* As more time is available the helper will direct the helpee to explore himself in relevant areas. Thus, in the example we may assume that the difficulty associated with child-rearing is not an isolated problem, and the helpee will be directed to explore himself in the other areas, in particular the sexual-marital, the social-interpersonal, the educational-vocational, and other areas not mentioned here.

As Table 3-2 and Figure 3-1 show, during the stage of problem pres-

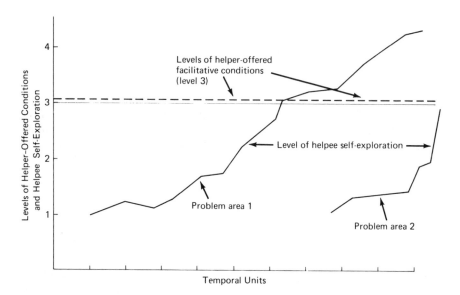

Figure 3-1. Helper and helpee activities in exploratory phase of helping.

Table 3-2. Helper and Helpee Activities in Exploratory Phase of Helping

Long-Term Treatment *(Helpee Development)*		*Short-Term Treatment* *(Crisis Resolution)*	
Helper	*Helpee*	*Helper*	*Helpee*
(1) Level 3 of facilitative conditions in response to area 1	→ Level 2 self-exploration in crisis area ↓ Level 3 and	(1) Level 3 of facilitative conditions in response to crisis area	→ Level 2 self-exploration in crisis area ↓ Level 3 and
(2) Level 3 of facilitative conditions in response to area 2	← more exploration in crisis area Level 2 exploration in area 2 ↓ Level 3 and	Introduction of treatment leading to crisis resolution	← more exploration in crisis area
(3) Level 3 of facilitative conditions in response to area X	← more exploration in area 2 → Level 2 exploration in area X ↓ Level 3 and more exploration in area X		

entation the helper will concentrate upon offering minimal levels of facilitative conditions. Whether the treatment program is to deal solely with crisis resolution or with over-all helpee functioning, the process begins here. In short-term treatment, however, the helper will employ the helpee's self-sustaining exploration as his cue for introducing treatment procedures. (These procedures will be examined in later chapters.) In a sense the short-term treatment constitutes an analogue of long-term treatment with one major exception: the long-term treatment process involves a survey of all relevant areas of functioning prior to the initiation of treatment, and the sequence of and the treatment procedures themselves are contingent upon the helpee's relative levels of functioning in these different areas. In order to establish the basis for long-term treatment, then, the helper must continue to offer minimal levels of facilitative conditions in all problem areas, moving from one to the other as the helpee is able to sustain exploration with emotional proximity. Thus, as the helpee is able to explore himself effectively in the child-rearing area the helper will direct his attention to another, related area and repeat the cycle.

In longer-term treatment before introducing a specific program the helper encourages the helpee to explore himself in all potentially relevant problem areas. He does so in order to establish the basis for a meaningful and effective treatment procedure. In effect he suspends any inclination that he might have to effect immediate gains by attempting to establish a sound basis for expecting significant long-term benefits for the helpee.

In summary, *a key objective of the exploratory phase of helping is to enable the helper to gauge the helpee's level of functioning in his problem areas. Much of later treatment is based upon a thorough knowledge of such functioning.* If the helpee explores and simultaneously understands himself at relatively high levels, the helper may be a *facilitative agent* in aiding the helpee to sharpen his discriminations, encourage his action, and embellish his learnings based upon this action. If the helpee cannot understand himself at relatively high levels, the helper must become a *directive agent*, basing the further movement of the helping process in *his* experience of the helpee's dysfunctioning.

REFERENCES

For a more detailed discussion of the issues considered in this chapter see the asterisked readings and the references upon which the readings are based.

Berenson, B. G., & Carkhuff, R. R. *Sources of gain in counseling and psychotherapy.* New York: Holt, Rinehart and Winston, Inc., 1967.
*Carkhuff, R. R., & Berenson, B. G. *Beyond counseling and therapy.* New York: Holt, Rinehart and Winston, Inc., 1967.
Carkhuff, R. R. (ed.) *The counselor's contribution to facilitative processes.* Buffalo: State University of New York, 1968.
Holder, B. T., Carkhuff, R. R., & Berenson, B. G. The differential effects of the manipulation of therapeutic conditions upon high and low functioning clients. *Journal of Counseling Psychology,* 1967, 14, 63–66.
Pagell, W., Carkhuff, R. R., & Berenson, B. G. The predicted differential effects of the level of counselor functioning upon the level of functioning of outpatients. *Journal of Clinical Psychology,* 1967, 23, 510–512.
Piaget, G., Berenson, B. G., & Carkhuff, R. R. The differential effects of the manipulation of therapeutic conditions by high and low functioning coun-

selors upon high and low functioning clients. *Journal of Consulting Psychology*, 1967, **31**, 481–486.

°Rogers, C. R. (ed.), Gendlin, E., Kiesler, D., & Truax, C. B. *The therapeutic relationship and its impact.* Madison, Wisc.: University of Wisconsin Press, 1967.

°Truax, C. B., & Carkhuff, R. R. *Toward effective counseling and psychotherapy.* Chicago: Aldine Publishing Company, 1967.

4
SELF-UNDERSTANDING IN HELPING

Following the stage during which the helpee explores his problem areas the helping process may take one of two directions, the first concentrating upon sensitive understanding as a precondition of constructive action and the second emphasizing action as a precondition of understanding. These next phases are not, to be sure, mutually exclusive. Indeed, both understanding and action are integral and complementary components of the very highly interactional process of helping. Understanding serves to facilitate action and action, in turn, aids understanding.

Although it is the traditional view that Western man's emphasis is upon insight as a precondition of action, there is enough evidence to the contrary to make the choice to focus initially upon understanding an arbitrary one. In practice, however, we have found that an introduction to the self-understanding process before concentration on action-oriented efforts is a meaningful stage in helping. Accordingly, the following stages appear to be operative in the most effective helping processes: (1) a minimal translation of the helpee's explorations into self-understanding; (2) the development of some direction, however tentative, based upon this minimal understanding; (3) acting upon this directionality; (4) incorporating the feedback from the action; (5) reflecting back upon prior understanding and sharpening earlier discriminations; and (6) acting more constructively based upon finer and more sensitive understanding.

The major assumption that gives significance to the process of self-understanding is that psychopathology or dysfunctioning largely derives from problems in interpersonal functioning. The problems may also be of an intrapersonal character—that is, the individual cannot communicate with himself in any meaningful way in given areas. However, it is the verbal and behavioral expressions in the problem areas that lead the individual into difficulty. Given this assumption, the goal of the helping process becomes the helpee's reconstruction of the communication process both with himself and with others. The key ingredient in the reconstruction of the communication process is helpee self-understanding. When the helpee understands himself effectively he will be able to understand others and then communicate his understanding.

HELPEE SELF-UNDERSTANDING: A VIEW IN DEPTH

Again we assume that individuals function at different levels in different problem areas. Having established these differential levels, the alternatives are clear. In short-term treatment the inferences from explorations or the experimental indexes of functioning lead to treatment programs that emphasize either understanding leading to action or action leading to understanding. Where possible the former emphasis is to be preferred, since it provides at least minimal structuring for the action experience, one that can be modified by feedback. In longer-term treatment the process is quite different. Attention is not focused exclusively on the crisis area. Instead the indexes of differential functioning may be composed in a hierarchical fashion from the highest to the lowest levels of functioning. Since the success probabilities are greatest in the highest areas of functioning, the helper will attend initially to those areas that meet the following conditions: (1) the ones in which the helpee is functioning below minimally facilitative, self-sustaining levels and (2) the ones in which the helpee is functioning at the highest relative levels below minimal levels. Again this focus is in sharp contrast to that of short-term crisis therapy, which concentrates on the area that precipitated the search for help and, in particular, which gives attention to the fact that this is the area in which the helpee is functioning at the lowest level.

In defining understanding we are not so concerned with dynamic definitions of "feeling knowledge" as we are with more functional and operational definitions. Accordingly, we may employ modifications of the scales that we employ to assess the helper's level of functioning to assess the helpee's level of functioning (see Chapter 8, Volume I; Carkhuff, 1968; Carkhuff & Berenson, 1967; Truax & Carkhuff, 1967).[1] Indeed,

---

[1] The relevant scales and their implications are presented and fully developed in Volume 1 on selection and training. Employing the cues elaborated in this section, these scales may be modified to meet the needs of assessing the helpees on these dimensions.

both helper and helpee can be assessed on all dimensions by essentially the same scales. Thus, in response to his own explorations, or later in the helping role in response to the helper and others, the helpee's responses may not add or subtract noticeably from the expressed feeling and content at the lowest levels or add noticeably to his own expressions or to those of others in such a way as to enable him to express deeper feelings at the highest levels. At minimally facilitative levels, the minimal goal of helping, the helpee is to respond in such a way as to reflect in terms of feeling and meaning what he or others might have said. In relation to the helper the cues for the higher levels of understanding are: (1) when the helpee has responded to himself as an effective helper might have responded to him—and the response is essentially interchangeable in affect and meaning—the response can be said to be level 3; and (2) when the helpee has responded to himself as an effective helper might have responded to him—and the response enables the helpee to go on to explore and understand himself at deeper levels, then the helpee's response can be said to be higher than level 3.

The translation of self-understanding to the understanding of others becomes apparent when the helpee responds in a similar manner to others, in particular the helper, at least during the initial stages of helping. Thus, when the helpee responds to the helper's expressions in such a way as to reflect essentially interchangeable affect and meaning, then the response can be rated level 3. When the helpee responds to the helper's expressions in such a way as to add significantly, enabling the helper to explore himself at deeper levels, then the response can be rated at level 3 or more. The latter cue establishes the fact that the helpee is functioning at high levels in that particular problem area. Indeed, if he were to function in this manner in all problem areas we could hardly label him a helpee.

We can readily understand the functional relations between exploration and understanding. Helper understanding facilitates helpee exploration. *When the helpee's understanding reaches the level at which he is able to express to himself what the helper might have expressed to him in order to facilitate his own further exploration then we say that the helpee has not only attained minimally facilitative but also self-sustaining levels of functioning in that particular problem area.* The helpee can sustain for himself what he has been dependent upon others to do for him in his search for direction. Similarly, just as the helper has facilitated the helpee's self-exploration, so also can the helpee facilitate self-exploration on the part of the helper. This is the highest level of functioning within the helping process. Again when the helpee is able to generalize this level of functioning to all content areas as well as to all significant others outside of the helping process then we may say that the communication process has been effectively constructed or reconstructed.

In a similar manner other key interpersonal dimensions, both facilitative and action-oriented, may be applied specifically to the helpee. The scales that were presented in Volume I on selection and training may be systematically modified to apply to the helpee in a manner similar to empathic understanding. *In effective helping the helpee will ultimately be able to do everything that the helper does and at levels very close to those at which the helper is functioning.*

Helpee Self-Understanding: Guidelines for the Helper

A number of guidelines have been designed to enable the helper to achieve the goal of helpee self-understanding.

1. *The helper will find that he is most effective when he focuses upon the construction or reconstruction of the helpee's communication process as a goal of helping.*

With constructive action, the construction or reconstruction of a communication process is a primary goal of helping. Indeed, these two goals are interrelated. On the one hand, effective communication may be seen as the first stage of effective action, since in a very real sense it involves acting upon discriminations. On the other hand, the very notion of the constructiveness of action implies the ability to make fine discriminations.

2. *The helper will find that he is most effective when he invests his energies initially in the highest spheres or areas of the helpee's functioning.*

Obviously in order to accomplish this objective the helper must be functioning at levels higher than the helpee in the area of the helpee's difficulties. Simply stated, the probability of the low-level–functioning person's understanding and acting upon his world is greatest in those areas in which he is functioning at the highest levels. Those areas in which he is already functioning effectively need not be considered. However, from among the areas below minimal levels the success probability is greatest among those that are relatively highest. The success experiences, in turn, will increase the probability of understanding and action in other areas and, thus, the probability for success in the helping process.

3. *The helper will find that he is most effective when he initially offers minimal levels of facilitative conditions in reconstructing the communication process.*

When the helper offers minimal levels (level 3) of the facilitative conditions of empathy, respect, concreteness, and genuineness he establishes a facilitative relationship within which the helpee cannot only explore, experience, and experiment with himself but also come to understand, respect, and be genuine with himself. Thus, the helper will emphasize an empathy that is interchangeable with the helpee's—and complimented by specificity of experiencing—a regard that is operationally unconditional and a genuineness that, while it does not emphasize helper-initiated responses, is nevertheless responsive to the helpee's needs and is not negative or destructive in any way. Level 3 responses will enable the helpee to know that someone can understand him on his terms in addition to providing him with the feedback necessary to establish a basis for reformulation.

4. *The helper will find that he is most effective when he employs the helpee's minimal level of self-understanding as his cue for increasing his level of facilitative conditions.*

The sign for the helper to increase the level of facilitative conditions he offers, or to make additive responses within a given content area, is the indication that the helpee can make effective responses for himself. One key index for effective responses will be those that are interchangeable in nature with those of the helper. *When the helpee makes responses that the helper could have made in a given content area the helper must respond to the helpee's readiness to move toward deeper levels of both exploration and understanding.*

5. *The helper will find that he is most effective when he employs the helpee's minimal level of self-understanding as his cue for introducing action-oriented dimensions at minimal levels.*

When the helpee can respond to himself with minimal understanding the helper not only increases the level of facilitative conditions but also introduces action-oriented dimensions. The action-oriented dimensions are introduced in an open-ended manner at minimally effective levels. They are introduced to provide a transition from understanding to action. They represent the helper's assumption of greater initiative in the helping relationship and define his potential to act upon his experience of the helpee.

6. *The helper will find that he is most effective when he employs the helpee's self-sustaining level of effective understanding as his cue for movement to the next stage of helping.*

When the helpee is able consistently to offer minimally facilitative or higher-level responses to himself with a given problem area the helper must respond to the helpee's readiness to move to the next stage of helping within that problem area, that of acting upon his understanding. In a very real sense self-understanding leads to action of one kind or another. The helping process within a given problem area has not been brought to culmination until the helpee has implemented a course of action.

7. *The helper will find that he is most effective when he employs his own self-exploration in response to high helpee-initiated levels of conditions as his cue for movement to the next stage of helping.*

The highest levels of helpee functioning in the communication process of helping involve the helpee's eliciting of self-exploration from the helper. This movement again signals a readiness for assumption of the full adult responsibilities of action. The helpee indicates that under some specifiable circumstances he could be the helper. The helpee indicates a readiness for a growing, equal relationship in which each participant is free to initiate or respond to the other.

8. *The helper will find that he is most effective when he is open to a repetition of the cycle of self-understanding both within and between different content areas.*

The cycle of movement from exploration to understanding to action will be repeated over and over both within and between the relevant problem areas. In addition, the cycle will not always move in an orderly way. The early structure of minimal understanding will focus the action in a gross sense. The action will provide feedback which modifies the original discrimination, sometimes eliciting further exploration, and it will always involve a deeper level of understanding. *The helping process has not been brought to culmination until the helpee has acted upon the directionality dictated by understanding,* and has reflected upon and modified the understanding accordingly and acted again—only this time even more constructively and with a greater degree of simultaneous understanding.

HELPEE SELF-UNDERSTANDING: ILLUSTRATIONS

Again we assume that both helpee and helper are functioning at different levels in different problem areas. In the attempted construction or reconstruction of the helping process Tables 4-1 and 4-2 represent helpee and helper level of functioning. The tables give estimated potential gains over a long-term relationship as well as probable minimal gains as a function of the helping goal of minimally facilitative, self-sustaining functioning, which assumes that the helpee may or may not go on to function at higher levels. As can be seen, with the same helper the gains will be different in different problem areas for different helpees. These gains represent those possible under conditions where the necessary duration of treatment is available. They will be modified by the conditions of short-term treatment or crisis therapy where the helper will attempt to ameliorate the disabling conditions in the crisis area, often with only as much change or gain on the part of the helpee as is necessary for accomplishing this goal. Frequently this change or gain

Table 4-1. Illustration of Helper and Helpee Level of Functioning and Potential Helpee Gain

	Social- Interpersonal	Educational- Vocational	Child- Rearing	Sexual- Marital
Helper	4.1	4.0	3.9	3.7
Helpee 1	2.1	2.3	1.9	1.7
Potential gain	+2.0	+1.7	+2.0	+2.0
Helping goal (minimal)	3.0	3.0	3.0	3.0
Probable gain	+0.9	+0.7	+1.1	+1.3

Table 4-2. Illustration of Helper and Helpee Level of Functioning and Potential Helpee Gain

	Social- Interpersonal	Educational- Vocational	Child- Rearing	Sexual- Marital
Helper	4.1	4.0	3.9	3.7
Helpee 2	3.0	2.2	1.8	1.9
Potential gain	+0.9	+1.8	+2.1	+1.8
Helping goal (minimal)	3.0	3.0	3.0	3.0
Probable gain	None (approximately same level)	+0.8	+1.2	+1.1

is significantly less than the usually desired goals of minimally effective functioning.

To continue the example, in short-term treatment the helpees might seek help for a problem focused in the child-rearing area. Whereas in long-term treatment the helper would not initiate helping in that area, he must do so under crisis conditions dictating short-term treatment. Following helpee self-exploration, then, the helper continues to offer increasingly higher levels of facilitative conditions (level 3 and above) in the crisis area in order to develop some necessary, albeit gross, discriminations concerning courses of action. With helpees functioning at relatively low levels, as in the example, the courses of action will come more from the helper and his experience of the helpee than from the helpee. Some degree of understanding is essential simply to insure that the helpee is not overwhelmed any further by the prescribed action. Accordingly, both helpees 1 and 2 might gain only small portions of the potential or probable gains. Obviously, even with resolution or amelioration of the crisis condition further treatment, if possible, would be both desirable and necessary.

Longer-term treatment involves a somewhat different process and effects very different results. As has been seen, helpee 1 has the potential for gaining approximately two or more levels of growth in all problem areas in a long-term helping relationship with this helper. With the exception of the social-interpersonal area, helpee 2 is in much the same position. However, the probable gains, calculated in terms of a helping goal of minimally facilitative and self-sustaining levels (3.0), are less than the potential gains, which average around one level. The processes by which the helpees might achieve these changes are much different from those in short-term treatment.

Similar to his approach in short-term treatment the helper offers moderately or minimally facilitative conditions (level 3). However, he does so in the area below level 3 in which the helpee is functioning at the highest level. In the case of helpee 1 this involves all content areas beginning with the educational-vocational area. With helpee 2 the social-interpersonal area in which the helpee is already functioning at minimally facilitative levels may be disregarded temporarily and attention directed to the sexual-marital area. The highest level of functioning below level 3 established that area in which the helpee is strongest, that is, the one in which his assets and resources are greatest. Accordingly, the prospects for the success of this aspect of the helping process are greatest. In fact, if constructive consequences cannot be achieved here, then there is no basis for further helping efforts.

As the helpee approaches minimal levels of self-understanding the helper will increase the level of facilitative conditions he offers to levels above 3. As the helpee achieves level 3 or more within one aspect of the relevant problem area the helper will direct the helpee's attention to other aspects. As the helper increases the levels of facilitative conditions and as the helpee approaches level 3 himself, the helper will introduce the action-oriented or helper-initiated dimensions. Decisions concerning the helpee's gains can be made according to the effectiveness of his own response-making, in particular the possibility of his making responses that are interchangeable with those of the helper. The relevant question is, *"Did the helpee offer himself what the helper might have offered him?"* The answer to this question will be the explicit guide to the helper's decision to move on or not. At the very highest levels the relevant question might involve whether or not the helper finds himself making self-explorations in response to the level of conditions the helpee offers the helper.

If the relevant aspects of a given problem area have been exhausted, understood in depth, and acted upon, the helping process moves on to the next highest area of helpee functioning. For helpee 1 this was the social-interpersonal area initially, while for helpee 2 it was the sexual-marital area initially. However, additional observations and inferences may be necessary at this point, since some generalization from the first learning experience may have taken place. Thus, for example, in the case of helpee 2 some of the effects of significant progress in the sexual-marital area may have generalized to the child-rearing area, an area that potentially has many elements in common with the sexual-marital area. The helpee may find that as a result of success in the sexual-marital area he is now functioning more effectively in the child-rearing area than in the educational-vocational, and the helping process may be directed accordingly to the child-rearing area.

The cycle is repeated until the helpee is functioning above minimally facilitative levels in all areas of relevant concern. The helping process, it can be seen, moves from those aspects of areas, and from those areas, in which the helpee is strongest and the probability of success is greatest toward more personally difficult aspects and areas. While the difficult aspects and areas offer initially low probabilities of successful treatment, the probabilities are increased with the reinforcement of successful surmounting of obstacles and attainment of effective levels of functioning in other areas.

Table 4-3 and Figure 4-1 provide an overview of helper and helpee

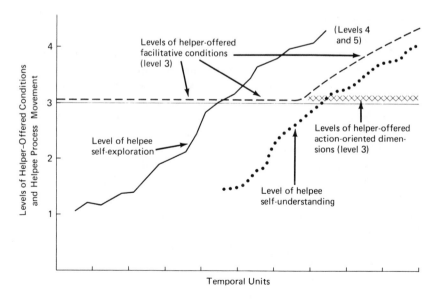

Figure 4-1. Helper and helpee activities to and during reconstruction of the communication process in helping.

Table 4-3. Helper and Helpee Activities in Self-Understanding Stage of Helping

Long-Term Helping		Dealing with Short-Term Crises	
Helper	*Helpee*	*Helper*	*Helpee*
Level 3 facilita- → tive conditions	Level 3 self-exploration in all problem areas ↙ ↓	Level 3 facilita- → tive conditions	Level 3 self-exploration in crisis area ↙ ↓
Level 3 facilita- → tive conditions	Level 3 self-understanding in first highest area below level 3 (area 1) ↙ ↓	Level 3 and above facilita- tive conditions plus	→ Some degree of structured ← understanding in crisis area preparatory for action
Level 4 and above facilita- tive conditions	→ Level 3 or above self-understanding preparatory for action	Level 3 and above action-oriented dimensions	
Level 3 action- ← oriented dimensions	action		

activities in this stage of helping. As can be seen, the long-term helpee development and the short-term crisis helping processes are, with one exception, analagous during the initial phase. In long-term treatment the process ordinarily focuses upon areas in which the helpee is functioning at higher levels while in short-term treatment the process focuses upon areas in which the helpee is usually functioning at lower levels. However, while the helpee's structural understanding may be considered "shored up" in short-term treatment, the helpee does not reach the level of development of the successful helpee in long-term treatment. In each instance, though, a high-level helper is essential to the accomplishment and solidification of helpee gains in understanding. When the helper offers minimal levels of facilitative conditions he focuses the helpee's efforts intrapersonally, and the helpee explores and comes to understand himself at increasingly high levels. The signal for movement to higher levels of facilitative conditions and the introduction of action-oriented dimensions is the helpee's demonstration of responses that the helper might have made. The signal for movement to the next stage of constructive action is the fact that the helpee is functioning at self-sustaining levels of all dimensions in the problem area involved.

REFERENCES

For a more detailed discussion of the issues considered in this chapter see the following readings and the references upon which the readings are based.

Carkhuff, R. R. *The counselor's contribution to facilitative processes.* Mimeographed book, State University of New York at Buffalo, 1968.
Carkhuff, R. R., & Berenson, B. G. *Beyond counseling and therapy.* New York: Holt, Rinehart and Winston, Inc., 1967.
Truax, C. B., & Carkhuff, R. R. *Toward effective counseling and psychotherapy.* Chicago: Aldine Publishing Company, 1967.

5
EMERGENT DIRECTIONALITY
IN HELPING

The explicit search for directionality and its implementation in action constitutes the second or final phase of helping. The initiation of this phase assumes an intensive exploration of the relevant problem areas. It involves an extension of exploration to self-understanding in these areas to the point where a directionality emerges from this understanding. It emphasizes an acceleration of the action-oriented dimensions in an attempt to answer the questions, "Now that we know what we do about the difficulty area, what do we do, where do we go?"

Phase 2 involves an intensive consideration of the directionality dictated by a depth of understanding of the helpee. With each party to the relationship now sharing more fully his experience of the problems involved and the directions or goals indicated, the relevant and available alternative courses of action are explicitly considered and the advantages and disadvantages of each course weighed. In an effective helping process the alternatives are usually limited. Based in a depth of understanding, there will be relatively few possibilities that will be congruent with a given individual's make-up. Indeed, the deeper the understanding, the more alternatives will be available, but fewer alternatives will be appropriate. In the very highest-level helping process as often as not it becomes increasingly obvious to both helper and helpee that only one course of action is meaningful and functional at a given point in time. Accordingly, programs and gradations of these programs are developed in order to successfully achieve the appropriate courses of action.

Along with his reinforcement of helpee self-understanding and helpee action initiated on the basis of the helpee's experience, then, the helper will consider a variety of approaches or techniques that will best enable the helpee to achieve his goals. On the basis of the goals that are most functional for the helpee the most effective mode of treatment is introduced and implemented in the helping process.

EMERGENT DIRECTIONALITY: A VIEW IN DEPTH

The upward or outward phase, or the phase of emergent directionality, involves three principal considerations: (1) a more intense emphasis upon a depth of helpee understanding; (2) an increasing emphasis upon helpee initiation of action-oriented dimensions; and (3) a consideration of a variety of courses of action calculated to get the helpee where he wants to go. The first two considerations indicate the helpee's readiness to act constructively for himself and upon his world. The third provides a path for overcoming the obstacles and achieving higher levels of functioning. As we indicated in Chapter 15, Volume I, each of these considerations must be firmly based in, and reflective of, the helpee's very personal experience of his world.

In regard to the more intense emphasis upon a depth of helpee understanding, this may be accomplished with increasingly additive empathic responses. That is, the helper formulates the emerging picture or pattern of the helpee's problems based upon earlier explorations and understanding. The helper indicates to the helpee what it all adds up to for the helper: "What I hear you saying is that. . . ." In a sense the helper puts together a pattern based in large part upon the music behind the words. He expresses the problem in the most complete way and at the deepest level possible in terms of the way the helpee experiences himself. The emphasis upon more intense self-understanding may lead quite readily to the introduction of more action-oriented dimensions such as confrontation and interpretations of immediacy. For example, the helpee might reject or qualify the helper's attempt at additive empathy in such a way as to ultimately, following reflected understanding of the helpee's position, lead the helper to confront the helpee with his experience of the helpee or his experience of the helpee's experience of the helper in the moment.

Concerning the initiation and increasing acceleration of the action-oriented dimensions on the part of the helpee, we must begin again with the differential levels of helpee functioning in the different problem areas discerned by the self-exploration process. With the helpee's approach to achieving minimal levels of self-understanding in a given problem area the helper not only increases his level of facilitative conditions but also introduces the more action-oriented dimensions in an open-ended manner. As the helpee achieves minimal levels or above of self-understanding, the need to learn to act upon this understanding becomes increasingly obvious to both the helper and the helpee. An accurate reflection at this point might be: "Now that you know what you do, you're increasingly aware of your need to act upon it." An effective confrontation, in turn, might be: "Now that you know what to do, what are you going to do about it?" Indeed, at the highest levels of functioning high levels of helpee understanding in relation to himself and others are related to action-oriented dimensions. The highest levels of responsiveness lead directly to initiated action.

Again the same action-oriented dimensions with which we assessed the helper in Volume I (Berenson & Mitchell, 1974; Bierman, 1968; Carkhuff, 1968; Carkhuff & Berenson, 1967) may be employed with the incorporation of appropriate helpee cues to assess the helpee. Accordingly, we may look for increasing movement from the simple absence of discrepancies in the helper's behavior or congruence only in response to the helpee to helper-initiated communications of genuineness. Similarly, we may look for movement from an openness to discrepancies in the helpee's behavior to explicit confrontation of these discrepancies and from an openness to interpretations of immediacy to a direct relating of the helpee's expressions to the helper by the helper. Finally, there is increasing movement toward a consideration of the specifics of program implementation for the helpee.

Continuing his role as both model and agent, the helper increasingly elevates his level of action-oriented dimensions as the helpee moves toward higher levels of understanding and approaches the stage at which he initiates action out of his own experience in his relationship with the helper. Obviously the goal of helping is not simply a matter of the helpee acting upon his experience in his relationship with the helper. However, his ability to do so will cue the helper of his readiness to act upon his experience in his everyday world, and the helper will make relevant homework assignments accordingly. Finally, in a fully sharing relationship in which each person acts upon his experience and responds to the experience of the other, the helper and the helpee explore and implement a course of action geared to the helpee's welfare.

Both at the point of establishing such a program as well as during the stages leading up to it a number of more formalized courses of action may be considered. Indeed, these are a direct outgrowth of an increasing action orientation. For want of a better term we may call these courses of action preferred modes of treatment. Again, however formalized, these modalities must reflect the very personal phenomenology of the helpee. Primarily they are step-by-step procedures leading to the elimination or neutralization of nonfunctional vestiges of past functioning or existing difficulties in the helpee's present world that impede the helpee's progress toward higher levels of functioning. However, these programs need not deal solely with difficulties. They can also extend into the future in very positive approaches to achieving the goals of higher levels of functioning. Thus, for example, we might employ one preferred mode of treatment to eliminate existing neurotic symptomatology and another to systematically train an individual to function more effectively interpersonally.

The existing traditional potential preferred modes of treatment are numerous. However, upon closer examination we find that the unique contributions of a number of these approaches are limited (Carkhuff & Berenson, 1967). For example, while the nondirective or client-centered approach might be most effective during the initial interactions of the exploratory phase of helping, its value during the phase of emergent directionality is severely restrictive. It focuses upon empathy and respect in the form of moderate reflections and unconditionality and thus involves minimal risk while accomplishing much exploration and some understanding from which some limited directionality might emanate. However, the client-centered approach can *conceivably* be considered appropriate only during phase 2 for a person functioning himself at minimally effective levels who needs only a continuation of a kind of support by another person functioning at minimally effective levels in order to insure full integration, but where neither helper nor helpee wishes to risk movement to higher levels.

In general, the existential approach has the most to offer during phase 1 because it focuses upon the greatest number of facilitative dimensions, genuineness along with empathy and respect, and its techniques do not, at least theoretically, put a limit on the level of functioning to which both helper and helpee can rise, as does the client-centered approach, for example. During phase 2 the existential approach might have some limited application with a higher-level–functioning helpee who wishes to function at still higher levels. However, even here we often find that in practice its elaborate systems are restrictive rather than freeing. Its unnecessary bias against the incorporation of more behavioristic approaches as preferred modes of treatment in the helping process is only one example of this tendency.

From among the more traditional approaches the psychoanalytic probably has the least to offer—and to the fewest number of people. For most purposes it is inappropriate simply because it focuses upon a kind of diagnostic understanding which the helpee is often not able to employ meaningfully in his life. Its psychodynamic interpretations might better be replaced by a communication of an understanding of the helpee's phenomenology. The psychoanalytic communication process, then, is inherently subtractive since it does not offer usable communications; when psychoanalysts offer usable communications they need not maintain their psychoanalytic orientation. Although it is calculated to clear up the distortions of a neurotic population, people who distort cannot employ the kind of insights dictated by the analytic model without distorting them. The appropriate employment of the psychoanalytic approach as a preferred mode of treatment would require a unique interaction of variables not yet clearly articulated by its proponents. During the phase of emergent directionality the psychoanalytic approach could *conceivably* be considered appropriate only with well-integrated persons with an interest in a broad, inclusive, well-established frame of reference as a source of intellectual stimulation rather than the morbid and masturbatory curiosity that dominates many of its adherents.

From among the more formalized and traditional approaches only the trait-and-factor vocational counseling approach and the behavioristic approaches may be considered legitimate potential preferred modes of treatment. These approaches are largely inappropriate for the first phase of helping, however, since they focus only upon a periodic emphasis on concreteness. The behavioristic approaches do have some application with very low-level–functioning patients in what might be considered pre-phase I treatment, which involves shaping patients who do not interrelate at all to do so. However, each such approach flows from an effective implementation of the exploratory and understanding phases.

Briefly, during phase 2 the trait-and-factor approach involving vocational and educational counseling, including testing and interpretation, must be considered a preferred mode of treatment for otherwise well-functioning helpees with vocational and educational conflicts or problems. Vocational and educational assignment must be considered a preferred mode of treatment for similarly troubled persons functioning at lower levels. The instrumental behavioristic approaches must be considered most appropriate in "shaping" behavior, particularly among the lowest-functioning helpees. The classical conditioning approaches are most effective with persons who often are otherwise functioning with relatively specifiable symptomatology.

Perhaps the main contribution of the trait-and-factor and behavioristic approaches, however, is in the structure they provide for operationalizing the construct of preferred modes of treatment. This is best illustrated when the two approaches are employed in a complimentary fashion: the trait-and-factor approach serves most effectively to describe the critical dimensions of the directions or goals of treatment, while the behavioristic approach may be most effectively employed in providing the means for attaining these ends.

To be sure, *a systematic approach of almost any kind may provide benefits for the individuals employing it*. Independent of the seeming relevance of the program, a systematic approach might provide the structure within which effective helping can take place. A system has the additional bonus of helper confidence. Again, however, the systems employed as preferred modes of treatment need not be formalized. We are really talking about the development of very individualized treatment goals and some effective step-by-step procedures for attaining them. While some of the traditional systems are helpful in enabling us to think in these terms, *the most effective helpers need no system; they draw upon all systems and create their own to meet the very unique and individualized programs that will enable helpees to function effectively*.

Helpee Action: Guidelines for the Helper

A number of guidelines are available to assist the helper in achieving the goal of constructive helpee action.

1. *The helper will find that he is most effective when he employs constructive helpee action as the goal of helping.*

The ultimate goal of helping is constructive action both in terms of oneself and others. Again there is an interrelationship between understanding and action, with each serving to sharpen up the basis of the other. Thus, constructive action implies the accuracy of the discriminations upon which the action is based as well as the increasing accuracy of the discriminations.

2. *The helper will find that he is most effective when he emphasizes action orientation in the area in which the helpee best understands himself.*

The area in which the helpee understands himself at the highest levels offers the highest probability of successful translation into constructive action. The helper, accordingly, concentrates upon this area both to increase the helpee's level of understanding as well as to make the translation to action. Initially he will concentrate upon minimal levels of facilitative dimensions.

3. *The helper will find that he is most effective when he increases the level of action-oriented dimensions as the helpee moves to higher levels of understanding and approaches minimal levels of action.*

As the helpee approaches level 3 of action-oriented dimensions 'and moves to higher levels of understanding the helper will increase his emphasis upon action orientation. What this means operationally is that the helper begins to initiate more activities based upon his experience of the situation, thus serving as both model and agent for the helpee to do likewise. Again and again the increase in action is employed to sharpen up new and higher levels of understanding and thus more constructive action in the problem area. In addition, while the emphasis is upon acting on one's experience in helping, a systematic attempt will be made to insure generalization of learning and acting to extrahelping relationships and situations.

4. *The helper will find that he is most effective when he is able to describe the directions and/or goals emerging from helping in functional and operational terms.*

When a full description of the goals of helping can be achieved the means of obtaining these goals can be implemented. Accordingly, the full description must include dimensions that can be operationalized. Vague and amorphous goals such as those delineated by many of the traditional approaches are of no use in developing step-by-step procedures for their attainment.

5. *The helper will find that he is most effective when he is able to operationalize step-by-step means for attaining the goals of helping.*

When functional and operational goals have been described step-by-step procedures for their attainment can be developed. Each step will represent a systematic progression toward the functional goals. The more fully the goals have been described, the more fully the steps to their achievement can be implemented. Descriptions of functional goals are discussed more fully in Part Three on research applications.

6. *The helper will find that he is most effective when he employs constructive action in one area as his cue for movement to repeating the cycle in another area.*

Within each problem area constructive action will signify satisfactory achievement of minimal levels of effective functioning and thus a readiness on the part of the helpee to move to the next area. Again the helper must be open to a repetition of the understanding-action-understanding-action cycle in each area until the helpee has achieved a minimal level of effective functioning in both action and understanding.

7. *The helper will find that he is most effective when he employs constructive action in all relevant areas as the basis for termination of helping.*

When the helpee demonstrates his increasing ability to act constructively on increasingly finer discriminations in all relevant problem areas he is indicating a readiness for termination of the helping process. Just as the helper responds initially to the helpee's need for minimal understanding and intermediately to his need to be able to act upon this understanding, so must he now respond to the helpee's need to function independently of the helper's efforts on his behalf. The helpee learns to understand himself through helper understanding on his behalf and he learns to act through helper action on his behalf. The helpee learns to act independently through the highest level of responsiveness and independent action on the part of the helper. Constructive action initiated by the helpee for himself independent of the helper represents the highest level of functioning that the helping process can achieve.

HELPEE ACTION: ILLUSTRATIONS

We have established the differential functioning of the helpees (Chapter 3) and the potential and probable gains through helping (Chapter 4) in the different problem areas. The helpee has not successfully concluded the helping process in a given area until he can act constructively in that area. He has not successfully concluded helping until he can act constructively in all areas.

Thus, as Table 5-1 and Figure 5-1 indicate, the self-exploration process

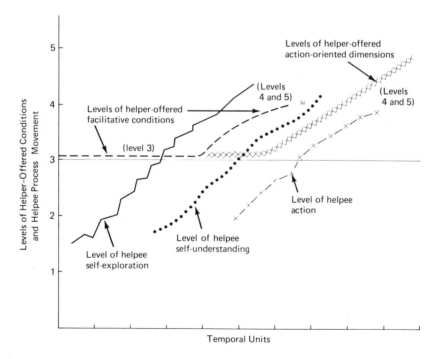

Figure 5-1. Helper and helpee activities to and during the phase of emergent directionality.

Table 5-1. Helper and Helpee Activities in Phase of Emergent Directionality

Long-Term Treatment (Helpee Development)		Short-Term Treatment (Crisis Resolution)	
Helper	*Helpee*	*Helper*	*Helpee*
Area 1		*Crisis Area*	
Level 3 facilitative conditions →	Level 3 self-exploration in first highest area below level 3 (area 1) ↓	Level 3 facilitative conditions →	Level 3 self-exploration in crisis area ↓
Level 3 and above facilitative conditions plus	← Level 3 self-understanding in area 1	Level 3 and above facilitative conditions plus Level 3 action-oriented dimensions →	← Improved self-understanding
Level 3 action-oriented dimensions →	Level 3 and above self-understanding ↙		Constructive action
Level 3 and above facilitative conditions plus Level 3 and above action-oriented dimensions	→ Level 3 and above self-understanding plus Level 3 and above action-oriented dimensions ↓ Constructive action in area 1		
Area 2 . . .			
Area 3 . . .			
Area X .			
. . → Functioning at level 3 or above in all relevant areas			
Termination			

is initiated in order to establish a base for the understanding-action interaction. Some attempt is made to attain at least minimal understanding prior to the initiation of action-oriented dimensions. As there is movement to higher levels of helpee self-understanding in a given area there is a convergence with the need to act upon this understanding. This is best exemplified in the helpee's initiated responsiveness to some condition of the helper, so that the helper finds himself exploring himself in an apparent role reversal. In a very real sense the very highest level of responsiveness is initiated action. At this point the action-oriented dimensions are introduced at minimal and open-ended levels. With the feedback of each to the other the helpee moves simultaneously forward on both understanding and action-oriented dimensions. As the helpee increases his readiness to act, as indicated by movement toward level 3 of the dimensions, the helper increases his initiated behavior, offering higher levels of action-oriented dimensions.

To follow the example, then, the area in which the helpee is functioning at the highest level initially will be brought to the culmination of constructive action. In the instances described the initial focus of helping will be upon the educational-vocational area for both helpees 1 and 2. Short-term crisis helping will be brought to culmination when the helpee is able to act constructively in the problem area. In long-term treatment, upon successful action and the integration of the learning from the feedback of action, the helper will ascertain if any significant changes have taken place in the helpee's functioning in different areas and proceed to repeat the learning or relearning cycle in the next highest area.

Thus, the helpee is guided through several phases of action. Initially, and most often in response to the helper, he explores himself. Then he is brought to communicate with himself and others. This very communication, however responsive rather than initiated it is, is a kind of action. In turn, the initiated action within the helping relationship is represented in the increasing demonstration of action-oriented dimensions. Finally, the helpee is able to act independently in his problem area both within and without helping. As we indicated earlier, at each step along the way preferred modes of treatment may be employed to achieve the next goal or subgoal.

In culmination, then, the problem area or areas are defined and described as a consequence of the efforts of the exploratory and understanding phases of helping. The directions and/or goals dictated are fully explored and their critical dimensions analyzed. Alternative courses of action that enable the helpee to achieve these dimensions of the goals are considered in terms of the inherent long-term as well as short-term advantages of each. Physical, emotional-interpersonal, and intellectual programs that offer the highest probability of successfully implementing the most promising course of action are initiated in step-by-step progressions that insure success. In reverse order a 10,000-mile trip does indeed begin with the first step. The helpee must concentrate all of his efforts on his first assignment, since success in implementing that assignment increases the probability of successfully implementing the program leading to the achievement of the most rewarding course of action in terms of the goals or directions defined for ameliorating or resolving his problem areas.

The model presented represents a pattern of helping put together from extensive research and experience. The helping process does not always unfold so nicely or so neatly. The model as well as the helping process is to be modified according to the needs of the helpee. The guiding phenomena in helping is the feedback we get on what is and what is not effective for the helpee. We must check each step of the way with the ongoing experience of the helpee.

There may, however, be instances in which the helpee does not go along with the courses of action formulated. At least four different stages are involved here. The first may be thought of as the helpee taking the bit in his teeth and formulating his own courses of action and programs independent of the helper. This stage is possible only if the helpee is at, or has been brought to, very high levels of functioning. The second, and most frequent, stage involves the helper and the helpee jointly sharing in the consideration of courses of action and the creation of programs. The third, and more difficult, stage involves the helpee who will not assume the responsibility for implementing a course of action. Here the helper has the additional burden of responsibility to bring the helpee to a point at which he can assume such responsibility. That is, the responsibility for putting a course of action into operation becomes a goal of helping, and the helper sets up step-by-step gradations to enable the helpee to achieve that goal. Finally, and most disappointing, the helpee may choose not to implement a course of action that even he knows is both desirable and necessary, for in the end he is free to choose. The helper has discharged his responsibility when he has offered the helpee alternative ways of living his life, but the helpee is free to decide how he wishes to live his life. Such a decision does not imply abandonment by the helper of the helpee, but it does imply temporary abandonment of the course of action involved in favor of the development of new treatment areas.

The model for helping is testable both empirically and experientially. The essential ingredient is a helper who is functioning above minimally facilitative levels in the content areas in which the helpee is not functioning effectively. The helper calls upon all of his resources in involving the helpee in a process leading to the utilization of all of his resources. At the termination of successful long-term helping the helpee may be functioning in some or perhaps even many areas at levels as high or higher than the helper. In the end it is the helper's ability to integrate the sources of learning in both the means and the ends of helping that enable one person who was not functioning effectively to function effectively both in relation to himself and his world.

REFERENCES

For a more detailed discussion of the issues considered in this chapter see the asterisked readings and the references upon which the readings are based.

*Berenson, B. G., & Mitchell, K. *Confrontation*. Amherst, Mass.: Human Resource Development Press, 1974.

*Bierman, R. *Counseling and child-rearing*. Mimeographed manuscript, University of Waterloo, Canada, 1968.

Carkhuff, R. R. *The counselor's contribution to facilitative processes*. Mimeographed manuscript, State University of New York at Buffalo, 1968.

*Carkhuff, R. R., & Berenson, B. G. *Beyond counseling and therapy*. New York: Holt, Rinehart and Winston, Inc., 1967.

6
CRISES IN HELPING AND LIFE

When the distressed person seeks help he is usually in a crisis or precrisis condition. Some major or minor functions, essential in some way to his existence as he experiences it, have broken down. Or sensing a growing uneasiness and the fragmentation of a once-tight world, he anticipates a breakdown in major or minor functions. His rigid cosmologies, perhaps once functional in a restrictive range, no longer serve him in some critical area. His assumptive world, perhaps once validated in limited ways, has been exposed by new and broadening experiences for its error-laden base. His feeling responses, once adequate to handle a restrictive range of behavior, are no longer appropriate or readily available. His energy reservoir, once capable of supplying the necessary resources, no longer delivers. He comes to the realization that he is deteriorating. He needs help and he seeks help. The commonality in crises, then, is the experience of "falling apart," of being overwhelmed, of deteriorating—and the fact that it matters to one person or another. ". . . we can see most clearly the essential character of the crisis: whether physical or psychological, it is of life and death urgency" (Carkhuff & Berenson, 1967).

While crises or the anticipation of crises lead the individual to seek help, they also provide the potential vehicle within the helping process that will enable him to go on to function at higher, self-sustaining levels where he can deal appropriately and resourcefully with future crises. Thus, while the initial crises are most often external to helping, these crises are reflected directly in the more relevant or basic crises that are internal to the helping process. Crises are an integral part of the helping process, and how they are handled determines the effectiveness of the helping process.

The crisis is the essence of helping. Crises yield rich opportunities to reach new heights and higher levels of functioning if they are encountered fully and if all available resources are drawn upon to resolve them. On the other hand, if crises are avoided or handled inappropriately, they may lead to depths of depression never before experienced. Crises in helping, as in life, may be for better or for worse.

The crises for the helpee may be both external and internal to the helping process. In addition, the helper may be affected in a similar manner. Extrahelping crises in the helper's life may translate their effects directly to the helping process just as they do with the helpee. Whereas most therapeutic efforts are concentrated upon the resolution of the helpee's external crises, the external influences also manifest themselves directly within the helping processes. Indeed, external crises have very little meaning if they do not handicap an individual's effective functioning in some interpersonal area. We can deal with the external crises by recognizing, understanding, and treating the crises internal to the helping session. This will be our starting point.

CRISES IN HELPING: A VIEW IN DEPTH

While there may be obvious external crises for both helpee and helper, those that we can readily discern and remedy are the crises within the helping process. We begin with the crises of the helpee.

Within the helping process a number of helpee crises manifest themselves. Depending on whether the helper is equipped to deal effectively with these crises, they may or may not become crises for the helper. The evidence indicates that helpers functioning above minimally facilitative levels not only acknowledge the crises in the helpee's behavior but deal swiftly and effectively with these experiences (Alexik & Carkhuff, 1967; Carkhuff & Alexik, 1967; Friel, Kratochvil, & Carkhuff, 1968). On the other hand, those helpers who are not functioning at minimally facilitative levels themselves are unable not only to recognize the existence of a crisis in the helpee's behavior but also to deal with the crisis. Indeed, whereas high-level–functioning helpers actually elevate the level of helping conditions they offer during the crisis, low-level–functioning helpers deteriorate in functioning during the helpee's crisis, offering significantly lower levels of conditions at that time. At another level we might infer from his behavior within the helping process how the helper relates to crises in his own life: the helper who is functioning at a high level confronts the crises in his own life directly and forthrightly; the helper who is functioning at a low level does not confront the crises in anyone's life, least of all his own.

Helpee crises may be manifested in a number of ways. The most common crises involve the discrimination of a significant decrement or the prospect for such a decrement in functioning from an established level of helpee functioning. Thus, when enough helpee behavior is available to the helper the helper may make certain discriminations concerning the helpee's modal level of functioning. The helper is alerted to the possibility of crisis in the helpee's life when there is a significant decrement from this established level of functioning. For example, in a given content area within the helping process the helpee may have established a given level of self-exploration. A long delay in movement toward higher levels will allow the helper to infer that some obstacles or barriers are precluding further development in the area. The crisis will become explicit when the helpee deteriorates or regresses to an earlier and lower-level mode of exploration.

Each new barrier brings back old feelings and behavior. When we experience ourselves as unable to cope with a crisis, we are thrown back upon our old and ineffective means of functioning. Whether we can make the necessary fine discriminations and develop the new behaviors to cope effectively with the crises will determine whether we move on to higher or lower levels of functioning.

Having discriminated the crisis, the helper knows that he must give the process directionality. He knows that the helpee is aimless, that he is experiencing a feeling of being overwhelmed, that his behavior is fragmented, and that his energy level is low. The helper knows that he must act to put things together for the helpee, to reintegrate the helpee and the helpee's world. He knows that he can not rely solely upon the experience of the helpee. He knows that he must have his own directionality to depend upon. Accordingly, he elevates the levels of action-oriented dimensions while continuing to emphasize the facilitative dimensions (Berenson & Friel, 1969; Friel, Berenson, & Mitchell, 1969). The experience for both helpee and helper is one of heightened intensity of both the facilitative and the action-oriented dimensions.

The helper's directionful efforts provide the helpee with the structure that will ultimately enable the helpee to understand the conflicts he is unable to see and which are contributing to his regression. To be sure, at the crisis point the helpee is most receptive to the directionality of the action-oriented dimensions. These dimensions provide him with a firm foundation based momentarily in the helper's experience but only as a take-off point for the reintegration of the helpee's experience at higher levels. The helpee is most amenable to the helper's directionality, and indeed he gives his assent for such directionality by virtue of the fact that his deteriorated state is immediately available to his experience.

The helper may also precipitate crises within the helping process either intentionally or inadvertently. He may do so unintentionally as a result of external crises in his own life. For example, he may not be able to proceed further within a given content area. He can no longer offer minimal levels of relevant conditions or he cannot increase these conditions sufficiently in a given content area to effect a constructive helping process. Obviously this difficulty is lessened by a consistently high-level–functioning helper. Nevertheless, it is possible for the helper to regress to a lower level of functioning and, depending upon the helpee's level of functioning and his present predicament, this possibility may or may not have consequences for the helpee. The evidence indicates that high-level–functioning helpees will under ordinary circumstances continue to explore themselves constructively independently of such a crisis with a high-level–functioning helper (Holder, Carkhuff, & Berenson, 1967). On the other hand, low-level–functioning helpees will be severely affected by any regression or lowering of conditions on the part of the helper (Cannon & Pierce, 1968; Truax & Carkhuff, 1965). With helpers functioning at low or moderate levels a drop in the level of functioning will lead to the deterioration in functioning of both high- and low-level–functioning helpees (Piaget, Berenson, & Carkhuff, 1967).

In general, a helper will seek his modal level of functioning. Thus, a high-level–functioning helper will become aware of his self-initiated crisis and will intensify his efforts to confront and understand himself in this regard. He may, depending upon the helpee's level of functioning, share with the helpee the difficulty he is encountering. If he cannot do so, or even if he can, he should seek guidance from a high-level–functioning colleague. The low-level–functioning helper, since he likely denies the possibility of the existence of a crisis, will not take the constructive action necessary to deal with the difficulty.

In the absence of crises the helper may intentionally precipitate a crisis for the helpee. He may, for example, confront the helpee with discrepancies in the helpee's behavior which the helpee has not encountered before. The helpee may then choose to defend or explore his behavior. With a high-level–functioning helper the tendency of the helpee is to explore himself, since he feels more secure and understood and since chances are that the helper's confrontation reflects insightful and is helpful. With a low-level–functioning helper the confrontations are most likely less than accurate and thus are subtractive; consequently, the helpee is less likely to explore himself meaningfully (Carkhuff & Berenson, 1967; Friel, 1971).

Similarly, the helpee may precipitate a crisis for the helper whether inadvertently or purposefully. He may, for example, confront the helper with discrepancies in the helper's behavior, and future therapeutic movement may be dependent upon whether the helper can handle the confrontation or not. Again the high-level–functioning helper is more likely to be able to respond with immediacy and make open-ended inquiries into the source of the helpee's discrimination (Collingwood, Renz, & Carkhuff, 1969).

Crises in Helping: Guidelines for the Helper

A number of guidelines are available to assist the helper in handling crises in the helping process.

1. *The helper will find that he is most effective when he views the crisis as the necessary means to constructive growth.*

The effective helper views crises within the helping process as an integral part of the process. Rather than avoiding these crises he recognizes that there is no possibility for constructive growth without them. He also feels a great responsibility for responding to or initiating such crises because he knows that the outcomes may be deteriorative as well as constructive.

2. *The helper will find that he is most effective when he is attuned to significant decrements in the functioning of the helpee as well as himself.*

The helper may discriminate the precrisis condition by a slow-down in helpee movement and a crisis condition by a decrement in helpee movement in a given area. To be sure, there may be contradictory signs emanating from the helpee's behavior, depending upon whether or not the helpee is resistant to the helper's efforts. However, the guiding index is the helpee's performance in the behavior criterion. That is, whatever other activities the helpee engages in, either he is or he is not progressing in the behavior criterion. During the initial phase of helping the behavior criterion may involve helpee self-exploration, whereas during the latter phase it may involve the helpee's constructive action in resolving given difficulties.

3. *In the absence of crises the helper will find that he is most effective when he precipitates crises in the helping process.*

The helper will not only respond to crises that the helpee brings with him to helping but he may also initiate or precipitate crises. Upon discerning a leveling off or slowing down process he precipitates crises in order to provide the opportunity for movement toward higher levels of functioning in the behavior criterion. He may precipitate these crises by confronting the helpee with discrepancies in the helpee's behavior, usually pointing up the discrepancy between where the helpee says he is going or what he is doing and the helper's experience of the helpee's movement.

4. *The helper will find that he is most effective when he makes open-ended inquiries into the sources of the crises.*

Rather than becoming bogged down within the crisis and, accordingly, being unable to recognize it in its life perspective the helper will find that he is most effective when he, however momentarily, rises above the condition of the crisis. In doing so he raises open-ended questions about his own role as well as that of the helpee. In effect, he questions his own movement as well as the helpee's. His readiness and ability to confront life's crises not only contribute to the resolution of the crisis but also provide a model for a person who effectively copes with the periodic difficulties of life. The helpee will be able to commit himself only as the helper is able to commit himself to growth at the crisis point.

5. *The helper will find that he is most effective when he is directionful and elevates the level of action-oriented dimension he offers.*

Having discerned or precipitated the crisis, the helper has no alternative than to provide the helping relationship and the helpee with the directionality of the helper's experience. In effect, a momentarily blind helpee employs the helper's eyes to find his way, avoiding pitfalls through the darkness of the crises to the light of effective functioning. In order to achieve this goal the helper must himself be functioning at levels high enough to trust his experience so as to be able to screen and decipher the often contradictory feedback he gets from a helpee in distress. If the helpee can make it through the initial crisis, he has the direct experience of knowing just that, that people can effectively encounter and resolve the difficult moments of life in such a manner as to enable them to go on to even higher and more rewarding levels of functioning. Given this positive reinforcement, the probabilities of making it through succeeding crises are increased significantly.

6. *The helper will find that he is most effective when he views the helpee's movement to the next highest level as the criterion for effective crisis resolution.*

If the crisis is effectively resolved, the helpee will demonstrate movement to higher levels of functioning within the problem area. Thus, within phase 1 of helping the helpee will explore himself at higher levels, while within phase 2 he will demonstrate an increased ability to act constructively upon his discriminations. His functioning in both phases will, in turn, increase the probability of his doing similarly upon termination of the helping process.

CRISES IN HELPING: ILLUSTRATIONS

The crises may be implemented in a variety of ways. In particular in relation to the helpee the helpee may progress to the point where he cannot sustain his movement. For example, due to early developmental experiences he may be confronted with obstacles he sees as insurmountable and overwhelming. Consequently, he regresses to an earlier and lower level of functioning. Of course, the helper may also precipitate the crisis. He may confront the helpee with the fact that he expresses himself at one level and acts at another. For example, the helpee may be expressing himself at level 3 and acting at level 2 or perhaps not at all. Along these lines the helper may attempt to confront the helpee with more additive material that the helpee has not before encountered, and thus the helpee experiences a crisis.

Of course, some crises may be unnecessary. For example, the helper may inadvertently attempt to make additive responses that, if he misses the meaning for the helpee, may become subtractive responses. In effect, he may aim for level 4 or 5 and hit level 1 or 2, thus precipitating crises. In this context the probability for unnecessary crises is diminished with high-level–functioning helpers, since low-level helpers are unable to make additive responses even when they are called for while high-level helpers can. These constructs lead directly to a consideration of helper behavior, because it is how the crisis is handled that is critical. The existence of a crisis, whether originally necessary or not, creates an opportunity for growth, depending upon how the helper handles the crisis.

Whereas the helper has been offering minimally facilitative conditions (level 3) and, as the helpee approached higher levels of functioning, increasingly higher levels of facilitative conditions (level 4 and higher) in an attempt to enable the helpee to discover his own directionality, the helpee can no longer do so and the helping process breaks down. The high-level–functioning helper is immediately aware of a precrisis or crisis condition and intensifies his efforts to give the helping process directionality. Having introduced the action-oriented dimensions at minimal levels (level 3), he does not, however, discontinue his emphasis on the facilitative dimensions. He simply offers higher levels of the action-oriented dimensions (level 4 and above) in addition to the already high levels of facilitative dimensions.

The process must be differentiated from the short-term treatment of external crises. There the external crises are dealt with directly and related crises internal to the helping process may never take place. Thus, the short-term treatment may or may not involve a helping process in which internal crises take place. On the one hand, the helpee may progressively move toward dealing with the external crisis and he may do so with or without breaking through to new levels of functioning. Often his and his helper's goal is simply restoration of former levels of functioning, however low they might be. On the other hand, internal crises may reflect the helpee's difficulty in dealing with many aspects of the problem area.

The crisis may occur within phase 1, as reflected in the helpee's inability to explore himself, or it may occur in phase 2, as reflected in the helpee's inability to implement a constructive course of action. The crises within phase 1 may be portrayed as in Table 6-1 and Figures 6-1 and 6-2.

Table 6-1. Helper and Helpee Activities During Crisis in Helping (Internal Crisis Helping)

Helper		*Helpee*
		Area 1
Level 3 facilitative conditions	→	Level 2 self-exploration in crisis area
		↓
	↘	Level 3 self-exploration in crisis
Level 4 and above facilitative conditions	←	area
plus		
Level 3 action-oriented dimensions		*Breakdown in process* (CRISIS)
Level 3 facilitative conditions	←	Regression to level 2 self-exploration in crisis area
plus		
Level 4 and above action-oriented dimensions	→	Level 3 and above self-exploration *Constructive Action in crisis area*
		Area 2
		.
		.
		.
		Area 3
		.
		.
		.
		Area X
		.
		. Functioning at Level 3 or
		. above over-all
		Termination

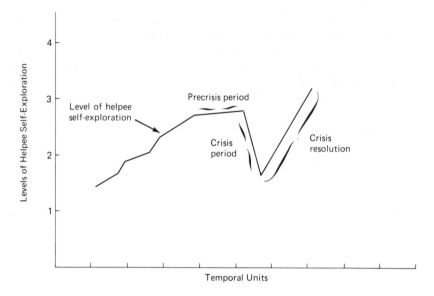

Figure 6-1.   Helpee movement and crisis in self-exploration in a given content area.

Crises within phase 2 may be similarly portrayed, although for the present we have no readily available means of describing the implementation of an action orientation. However, we have already seen how these constructs converge, as in the example of the confrontation of a helpee expressing himself at one level (for example, level 3) and acting at another (for example, level 2).

As can be seen, the helpee may progress in self-exploration from below level 2 to almost self-sustaining levels (level 3) and then, in the face of some seemingly insurmountable difficulty, demonstrate changes in functioning. He may slow down or level off inappropriately, as portrayed in the precrisis condition, or he may demonstrate a regression to lower levels of functioning, as portrayed in the crisis condition. The helper, in turn, while he continues to emphasize the facilitative conditions, increases the level of action-oriented dimensions. With the directionality based in the helper's experience the helpee is once again able to get back on the track. He goes on once again to explore himself at levels sufficient to culminate in constructive action in the crisis area. Of course, the cycle repeats itself within different problem areas, some of which incorporate crises and some of which do not.

All of this is not to say that the crises within helping are dealt with to the exclusion of the crises outside of helping. Quite the contrary. The

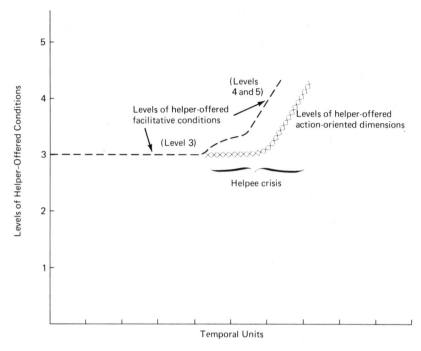

Figure 6-2. Helper-offered levels of facilitative and action-oriented dimensions during helpee crisis.

internal and external crises are interrelated. The helper, however, must learn to deal with the internal crises before he can deal effectively with the external crises. With external crises, as we noted earlier, the crisis area is fully defined, the related directions and goals are explored in terms of their critical ingredients, the courses of action are considered and chosen on the basis of the greatest probability of success, and a program is implemented. While the crisis is most often experienced as emotional in nature, it is interrelated with physical, interpersonal, and intellectual phenomena. Accordingly, the program implemented will have physical, emotional-interpersonal, and intellectual components. For example, there is a physical component for all crises: the individual must have enough physical energy to deal with the crises. A physical program would dictate appropriate rest, diet, and exercise. The crisis may have an interpersonal component. The interpersonal program might dictate training in responsive and assertive behavior. The crisis may have an intellectual component. The intellectual program would involve the development of an effectively working assumptive world.

In summary, crises reflect not so much insurmountable difficulties as they do opportunities to break through to new and higher levels of functioning. Often the helper assumes a more responsive stance during the early phases of helping. Increasingly, and particularly with the incidence of crises, the helper will initiate activities based in his own experience and calculated to give directionality to what would otherwise be a directionless process. It is as if the mother prepares the child for the father. But it is always the father, representing a directionful thrust in life, who dominates the crisis with his directionality.

REFERENCES

For a more detailed discussion of the issues considered in this chapter see the asterisked readings and the references upon which the readings are based.

Alexik, M., & Carkhuff, R. R. The effects of the manipulation of client depth of self-exploration upon high and low functioning counselors. *Journal of Clinical Psychology*, 1967, **23**, 210–212.

Cannon, J. R., & Pierce, R. M. Order effects in the experimental manipulation of therapeutic conditions. *Journal of Clinical Psychology*, 1968, **24**, 242–244.

*Carkhuff, R. R., and Alexik, M. The differential effects of the manipulation of client self-exploration upon high and low functioning counselors. *Journal of Counseling Psychology*, 1967, **14**, 350–355.

*Carkhuff, R. R., & Berenson, B. G. *Beyond counseling and therapy*. New York: Holt, Rinehart and Winston, Inc., 1967.

Collingwood, T., Renz, L., & Carkhuff, R. R. The effects of client confrontations upon levels of immediacy offered by high and low functioning counselors. *Journal of Clinical Psychology*, 1969, **25** (2), 224–226.

Friel, T. Factor analysis of levels of therapist functioning and confrontation. *Journal of Counseling Psychology*, 1971, **27**, No. 2.

Friel, T., Kratochvil, D., & Carkhuff, R. R. The effects of training upon the manipulation of client conditions. *Journal of Clinical Psychology*, 1968, **24**, 247–249.

Holder, B. T., Carkhuff, R. R., & Berenson, B. G. The differential effects of the manipulation of therapeutic conditions upon high and low functioning clients. *Journal of Counseling Psychology*, 1967, **14**, 63–66.

*Piaget, G., Berenson, B. G., & Carkhuff, R. R. The differential effects of the manipulation of therapeutic conditions by high and low functioning counselors upon high and low functioning clients. *Journal of Consulting Psychology*, 1967, **31**, 481–486.

Truax, C. B., & Carkhuff, R. R. The experimental manipulation of therapeutic conditions. *Journal of Consulting Psychology*, 1965, **29**, 119–124.

7

THE STAGES OF INDIVIDUAL
DIMENSIONS

Throughout the helping process the effective helper is making accurate discriminations and acting upon these discriminations. Communication is one kind of action in this regard. Depending upon his discriminations, the helper may assume a responsive posture or he may take the initiative in relation to the helpee. In the highly interactional process of helping the boundaries of responsiveness and initiative may fade. To be sure, we may view the helper as taking the initiative in response to the helpee's urgent pleas, or we may view the helper as initiating a responsive disposition in order to elicit certain movement from the helpee. Thus, the phenomena are not only interactional but they are continually repetitive, as we will see in later chapters. In all cases, however, there is no way to avoid the helper's assuming the responsibility for the individual discriminations upon which the various modalities are based.

Thus, we may say that in the context of this high discriminating-high communicating relationship, one that is both responsive and initiative, the helpee learns to discriminate first his own experiences and then the expressions of the experiences of others. Whereas he learns through the helper's responsiveness to him to respond to himself with accuracy, he concurrently learns the ingredients of responding effectively to others. The response to others involves not only discrimination but also communication as a first action based upon discrimination. Similar to the helper in relationship to him, his communications and other actions may be initiated by him or may be respondent to the needs of others.

The helpee is guided through stages in preparation for acting upon his accurate discriminations. Following exploration the helpee learns to

81

discriminate, then to communicate, and finally to act in other ways. The communications and other actions yield him a harvest of learning in the feedback he gets from his environment to sharpen up his earlier understanding. The finer discriminations, in turn, lead to more constructive action. Again all of this is not to say that the process is predetermined or irreversible. Often the helpee must be led to act before he can make the necessary discriminations. Indeed, frequently the helper must act before he can discriminate. *Ultimately, however, the goal of effective helping as well as of effective living is to act as constructively as possible upon the finest discriminations available.*

THE FUNCTIONAL STAGES OF INDIVIDUAL DIMENSIONS

In the following exploration of dimensions a number of assumptions are made. The first and foremost is that the helper is capable of functioning at high levels of all of the dimensions involved and is flexible in his employment of these dimensions. Again the dimensions do not follow any necessary sequence. However, independent of any one orientation, the very assumption of which discloses only such data as we invest and thus resultingly discern, a picture emerges of practices that can be and have been verified in research. To describe this picture we employ a breakdown by stages to characterize the functions of the facilitative and action-oriented dimensions. While these stages of the dimensions cut across the two phases of helping, the downward or inward phase of self-exploration and the upward or outward phase of emergent directionality (Carkhuff & Berenson, 1967), they are not solely a function of the phases. Between the phases, for example, there are transitional stages within some of the dimensions. In general, the facilitative dimensions, because they are instituted earlier in helping, generally move through more stages over the course of helping than the action-oriented dimensions, which are instituted during latter phases of helping and/or with helpees functioning at higher levels. Accordingly, then, there are a number of guidelines to understanding the stages of the individual dimensions that will enable the helper to function most effectively throughout the helping process.[1]

1. *The helper will find that he is most effective when he views and implements the empathy dimension in stages.*

Empathy is perhaps the most critical of all helping dimensions (Berenson & Carkhuff, 1967; Carkhuff & Berenson, 1967; Rogers, 1967; Truax

---

[1] The dimensions involved and the relevant considerations are fully developed in Volume I.

& Carkhuff, 1967). *Without empathy there is no basis for helping.* From it flows the appropriate and meaningful employment of all other dimensions and ultimately the resolution of the helpee's problems. Without a depth of understanding on the part of the helper there is little hope for the helpee to come to understand himself at deeper levels. It can readily be seen that the helper's own self-understanding is the critical resource for the effects of this dimension, the didactic and modeling as well as the experiential. Our definition of empathy, then, is a functional one in which the activities of helper and helpee cannot be separated. The emphasis is upon the helpee's ability to employ constructively the communications of the helper. If the helpee cannot employ *for his own purposes* the communications of the helper, then we cannot say that the helper is accurately empathic. It does not matter what level of understanding the helper is alleged to have. If, on the other hand, the helper's communications enable the helpee to continue to understand himself at meaningful levels or to understand himself at even deeper levels, then we can discriminate effective levels of empathic understanding. Perhaps we must emphasize not only the accuracy of empathy but the appropriateness of its communication, that is, whether or not the communication has functional utility in terms of how the helpee employs it rather than whether or not its accuracy is agreed upon.

To be sure, empathic understanding is often not directly communicated nor are its effects immediately observable. A depth of understanding may dictate the introduction of some other dimension (for example, confrontation is response to an implicit plea for someone to "pull me up short") or action (for example, problem-solving activities in response to the need for the resolution of immediate conflicts). In addition, the effects are not always immediately evident. However, often the helpee needs no more than time to chew, digest, and translate the helper's formulations to effective utilization. *If there are no long-term manifestations of the helpee's assumption of responsibility for the effective employment of his own resources in his own service, than there is no basis for concluding that the helper's empathic understanding and, indeed, his helping activities have been effective.*

A functional definition of empathy, then, depends upon the level at which the helpee is functioning, a consideration that leads directly to the functional stages of this dimension.

Stage 1 of Empathy

During the initial stages of empathy as well as during the initial phases of helping the focus is upon interchangeable formulations in both discrimination and communication. Reflections and other such interchangeable communications are most effective here. The establishment of such a base of communication enables the helper to identify and identify with the ways in which the helpee is expressing himself. So to speak, an interchangeable basis for communication allows the helper to try the helpee's expression of himself "on for size." Generally, it enables the helper to gauge the level at which the helpee is functioning and thus his readiness for entering further phases of empathic understanding and helping. Specifically, it enables the helper to estimate the helpee's depth of understanding in relevant areas. Similarly, it allows the helpee to determine how well the helper can comprehend his world as he has expressed his experience of it. Thus, while stage 1 of empathy establishes the helper's readiness to proceed to higher or deeper levels of functioning, it also helps to establish a secure base for the helpee's readiness to proceed to the next level of attempted self-understanding. It is as if the helpee were saying, "If the helper can stay with me and be with me as I present myself, then there is basis for my attempting to explore and understand myself at levels that I have not yet successfully reached."

Stage 2 of Empathy

During the second stage of helping the helper attempts to extend the limits of his own understanding of the helpee and thus the helpee's self-understanding, particularly in the areas of functioning in which the helpee does not demonstrate a depth of understanding. Here it is as if the helper, having successfully formulated the helpee's world, stands up in it and stretches out his arms and legs to reach its corners and crevices. The effective mode of communicating during this stage approximates the depth reflection of the client-centered approach or the moderate interpretation of the psychoanalytic orientation (Carkhuff & Berenson, 1967), again the utilitarian criterion being whether or not the helpee can effectively utilize the helper's formulations in his own life. Whereas the helper must usually initiate entrance into this stage—since the helpee is reluctant to go where he has not been before, at least in a constructive way—in its more successful instances this stage becomes a highly interactional process during which both helper and helpee enable the other to move to deeper and deeper levels of understanding. Again whether or not the helpee achieves the deepest possible levels of self-understanding is contingent upon the depth to which the helper understands himself; indeed, over the course of helping the helper often comes to expand his self-understanding. With high-level–functioning helpees it is possible for the empathic process to move directly to stage 2 after only the briefest of interchangeable communication. However, the second stage of empathy is an essential stage within the helping process, one that makes possible the depth of understanding necessary for conflict resolution.

Stage 3 of Empathy

The third stage of empathy like the second phase of helping concentrates upon the problem-solving activities that emanate from a depth of understanding of the problem areas. It is as if the helper, having extended himself to the limits of the helpee's experience, now discovers that, given this helpee at his developmental level, there really are few alternatives available to him. There is a directionality that emerges from understanding. In the ideal the helpee will have made similar—hopefully, often shared—discoveries. Often the helper in his eagerness to help attempts to proceed prematurely to stage 3 of empathy. He dissipates much energy in considering multiple alternative courses of action without having any basis for them. Where a shallowness of understanding once precluded constructive resolution, however, now the alternatives flow directly from the second stage of empathy. Rather than concentration upon the communication of empathic understanding to the helpee, the changing emphasis is upon the helper's own expression of his experience of the helpee's situation. In the third stage, then, the emphasis is upon action, both within and without the helping process, based upon a depth of understanding. Often the empathy upon which the action is based remains implicit. That is, having established a viable communication process, there is no need for continual articulation of this most critical of all dimensions. *The highest and ultimate form of empathic understanding is action.*

2. *The helper will find that he is most effective when he views and implements the respect dimension in stages.*

Just as the helper's self-understanding and consequent understanding of others is the source of the helpee's self-understanding and ultimate understanding of others, so also is the helper's respect for himself and, when appropriate, for others a critical source of the helpee's self-respect and ultimately respect for others (Carkhuff & Berenson, 1967). Thus, the communication of respect by a healthy and integrated person is the critical source of experiential, didactic, and modeling effects. As with empathy, the effective communication of respect also involves making discriminations about the levels at which the helpee is functioning. While respect is seldom communicated directly, the modalities that are employed to convey this critical dimension are contingent upon the level of the helpee's development. In a sense we might conceive of this differentiation in terms of the feminine or facilitative and the masculine or action-oriented dimensions. It is as if the mother nourishes the child so that he is strong enough to experience and identify with the directional thrusts of a potent father. The dimension of respect, then, moves through different developmental stages, leading ultimately to the helpee's functioning at his highest possible level.

Stage 1 of Respect

Similar to the operation of empathy, in early stages the emphasis upon unconditionality or unconditional positive regard enables both the helper and the helpee to experience the helpee as fully as possible. The essential communication, and often it is implicit, is, "With me you are free to be who you are." This is not to say, however, that there are no limits set. There are but they primarily involve those behaviors that are harmful or potentially harmful to the helpee or others. In this sense the terms, unconditionality or unconditional positive regard, are misnomers, for no one is totally unconditional in relation to another. While the communication of warmth may be a modality for communicating respect, translated functionally *unconditionality merely involves the suspension of all potentially psychonoxious feelings, attitudes, and judgments on the part of the helper—that is, those that might have a restrictive or destructive effect upon the expressions and behaviors of the helpee.* Such a communication establishes the basis for a secure relationship within which the helpee can experience and experiment with himself. Further, it provides the basis for the helper as well as for the helpee to come to know the helpee well enough to discern those aspects of the helpee that are deserving of positive regard, the second stage of respect.

Stage 2 of Respect

As the helper comes to know the helpee, then, he comes to experience aspects of the helpee to which he can respond positively. If he cannot do so, there is no basis for continuing further, since there is no hope that the helpee will come to have respect for his own capacities for making appropriate discriminations and acting with responsibility in relevant areas. The principal modalities for communicating positive regard involve the communication of accurate or attempted empathic understanding and, to a lesser degree, the genuinely positive responses of the helper to the helpee. In particular, the degree to which the helper is committed to and can with intensity understand the helpee will reflect the degree to which he communicates respect in its second stage. At a minimum the communication, "You are worthy of my effort to understand" establishes a basis for the helpee's experience of his own self-worth. At a maximum a depth of understanding on the part of the helper communicates his readiness and desire to be able to know the helpee more fully. In a sense we might view the respect dimension in more traditional behavioristic terms. We need first to know who this person is before we can respond positively to some or all of his assets. However, since not all of his characteristics are functional and thus deserving of positive reinforcement, we must also deal with those that are nonfunctional and even self-destructive. This consideration leads readily to the third stage of respect.

Stage 3 of Respect

As we come to know the helpee fully we determine that there are many aspects of his behavior that we want to reinforce positively and many that at a minimum we want to extinguish and at a maximum to reinforce negatively or punish. In a very real sense stage 2 has already initiated an extinction process by the selective reinforcement of some behaviors and the absence of reinforcement for others. In this context stage 3 is more critical in rehabilitation treatment processes than it is in socioeducational processes. The last stage of respect, then, emphasizes a conditionality of respect. That is, "Given your developmental stage, I will respect you *only if* you function at your highest level." *The central message of this stage involves not accepting an individual at less than he can be.* The main modality for its communication is the genuineness of the helper, a level of spontaneity that allows the helper to disclose fully in his attitudes and behaviors both his positive and negative feelings about the helpee's behaviors. To be sure, many helping processes may never reach this stage. In the ideal, however, successful completion of the helping process will dictate a helpee who has incorporated a standard of not accepting himself at being less than he can be. At the highest levels, this has implications for full and creative productivity, and, indeed, self-actualization. The helper's conditionality is not predicated upon "doing things as I do them" but rather upon "finding your own way, employing me as a model for someone who strives to be fully himself not only in the moment but in life."

3. *The helper will find that he is most effective when he views and implements the concreteness dimension in stages.*

Concreteness or specificity of expression serves to increase the level of understanding of both the helper and the helpee of specific feelings and experiences, not only those of the helpee in extrahelping situations but also the feelings and experiences of the immediate interaction between the helper and the helpee (Carkhuff & Berenson, 1967; Truax & Carkhuff, 1967). The only critical qualification for this dimension is that the material be personally relevant to the helpee. The nature of the contribution of this dimension revolves around (1) the necessity for a complete comprehension of the specifics of phenomena potentially relevant to the helpee's problem area and (2) the implementation of specific courses of action to ameliorate the helpee's condition. Accordingly, concreteness is emphasized during early and late phases of helping. Thus, initially this dimension is largely complementary or supplementary to attempts to achieve not only a depth but also a breadth of understanding of the helpee's problem area. Finally, after intermediary phases of helping during which concreteness is deemphasized, the helper returns with new perspectives on the helpee's problems to emphasize specificity in dealing constructively with the problem areas.

Stage 1 of Concreteness

During the initial stage, then, the helper employs his resources to influence the helpee to discuss fluently, directly, and completely specific feelings and experiences regardless of their emotional content. Again the helper influences the helpee through the critical sources of learning. He may employ specificity in his own communications, whether basically reflective or interrogative, so that he enables the helpee not only to have the facilitative experience of having the specifics of his problems understood but also the experience of being encouraged to make his own relevant discriminations and communications. In addition, the helper provides the helpee a role model for a person who can deal concretely with problem areas, his own as well as those of others. Finally, the helper may didactically teach the helpee to communicate concretely in both his questions and his directions. In summary, then, during stage 1, the helper's concreteness serves several critical functions: (1) it ensures that the helper's response does not become too far removed emotionally from the helpee's current feelings and experiences; (2) it encourages the helper to be more accurate in his understanding of the helpee, and thus misunderstanding can be clarified and corrections made when the feelings and experiences are stated in specific terms; (3) it encourages the helpee to attend specifically to all problem areas and emotional conflicts.

Stage 2 of Concreteness

Stage 2 of concreteness is something quite different, for, having enabled the helpee to deal with the specifics of his problem areas, it now becomes imperative for the helper to decrease his emphasis on this dimension in an attempt to achieve a fuller, freer exploration on the part of the helpee. Thus, in the intermediary phase the helper may not only allow but also actively encourage the helpee to explore himself in more abstract, less specific ways. In particular, in dealing with material that is not readily available to the helpee's awareness it would seem most effective to facilitate a more vague and general course of exploration. Suffice it to say that this is the form that less conscious or unconscious processes take and it is simply not effective to attempt to impose concreteness on what is not concrete. The modalities of the second stage involve nonspecific probing and free associations on the part of both the helper and the helpee. Although not always apparently immediate in relevance, the second stage enables the helpee to break the binds of rigid cosmologies, restricted thinking, and blunted emotionality. Such a course enables both the helpee and the helper to return once again to the relevant areas with a new and fresh perspective necessary to discern and design a constructive course of action during the last stage.

Stage 3 of Concreteness

During the final stage the dimension of concreteness once again takes on a critical function of the helping process. Whereas it initially served responsively as a necessary supplement to understanding all specific and relevant aspects of the helpee's problem area, now it functions actively to consider all specific and relevant aspects of educative or remedial action. Concreteness is, at this point, the key to a consideration of potential preferred modes of treatment. It involves a consideration of alternative courses of action, including in particular the details of the advantages and disadvantages of each. At this point its modalities include both questions and answers on the part of both the helper and the helpee. It may also include, among many other possibilities, representational balance sheets, topological portrayals, and specific homework assignments. The second stage, having provided new and fresh perspectives, lays the base for breakthroughs in the development of modes of problem resolution. On the one hand, it becomes apparent to the helpee that he has many more degrees of freedom available to him than he once thought he had. On the other hand, in conjunction with a depth of self-understanding, the helpee's improved discriminations allow him to discern the subtle cues that determine the course of action most suitable for him. It should be underscored that many would-be helpers attempt to move to this stage prematurely.

4. *The helper will find that he is most effective when he views and implements the genuineness dimensions in stages.*

The goal of effective helping processes is the constructive change of the helpee in the direction of becoming a more genuine or authentic person, that is, more fully, spontaneously, and, consequently, more creatively himself in the moment. Thus, authenticity is the end of helping. Authenticity is also the means of helping. The base for the helping relationship is the establishment of a genuine relationship between the helper and the helpee (Carkhuff & Berenson, 1967; Rogers et al., 1967; Truax & Carkhuff, 1967). The degree to which the helper can be honest with himself and thus functionally integrated in his relationship with the helpee establishes this base. Thus, the entire helping relationship is based upon the proposition that the degree to which there is a congruence between the experience, the awareness of this experience, and the communication of this awareness in the helping person will be related to the congruence between the experience, the awareness, and, ultimately, the communication in the person being helped. One important qualification upon this construct is the concept of facilitative genuineness; that is, the helper must inhibit potentially destructive responses (Carkhuff & Berenson, 1967). In this context, while the movement throughout helping is toward deeper and deeper levels of genuineness, it is to be reiterated that the helping process does not function for the benefit of the helper, although he may benefit personally over the course of helping. Genuineness beyond certain levels may not be helpful and, indeed, may even have deleterious effects. At a minimum the dominance of spontaneity may detract from the substantive problems at hand. At all times, then, the helper serves the helpee, being guided by what is effective for the helpee.

Stage 1 of Genuineness

There are really only two stages of genuineness, the initial stage involving only minimally facilitative levels of that dimension. Not unlike empathy and respect, the initial emphasis is upon minimal congruence of the helper or, perhaps more important, the absence of incongruence. One step toward accomplishing this end involves a minimization of maintaining a façade and playing the role, except insofar as it is necessary to meet certain critical role expectations of the helpee. However, the helper has no need to demonstrate his level of authenticity. Indeed, the experience of such a need is a cue to inauthenticity to which the helpee is attuned. Rather, the key to the helper's congruence is his intense concentration upon his own accurate awareness of his own ongoing experiences in the helping relationship. If he is guided by what is effective for the helpee, his behaviors do not have to be predetermined and can instead flow from his awareness of ongoing experience, particularly of the helpee in relation to him. In this regard there is initially no necessity for full or spontaneous communication of genuineness to the helpee. Instead, the helper will find that he is most effective when he concentrates upon understanding the helpee in relation to himself rather than making himself and his own direction known to the helpee. The question concerning how the helper can be genuine while he is employing the technique of reflection to communicate interchangeable understanding can best be answered as follows: it is quite natural to employ tentatively some techniques or stereotyped modes of responding during early phases of all significant human interactions—indeed, it would be quite unnatural to be fully oneself with someone one does not yet know or respect; conversely, to attempt to remain completely unknown while attempting to come to understand and know someone is also quite unnatural.

Stage 2 of Genuineness

Whereas genuineness in stage 1 is seen in a responsive context, in stage 2 genuineness is seen in an initiative context. The movement throughout helping is from technique to person. That is, the helper moves toward becoming more fully and freely himself in the helping relationship and, accordingly, enables the helpee to become more fully and freely himself. In this regard somewhere in the intermediary stages of helping the dimension of self-disclosure, particularly insofar as it establishes a model for self-disclosure on the part of the helpee, takes on significance and then fades again in later stages. In effective helping, then, there is continual movement toward a highly genuine, highly interactional, and hopefully—however conditional the helper and ultimately even the helpee might be—a highly equalitarian and fully-sharing relationship. Again, high levels of genuineness must not be confused with license. When the only genuine responses in regard to the helpee are negative, the effective helper makes an effort to employ his responses as a basis for further inquiry into the helping relationship. However, in relation to his genuine reaction to self-destructive behavior on the part of the helpee the helper may actively indicate his negative regard in an attempt to extinguish such behavior. Finally, the emphasis upon the functional integration of the helper is not restricted to his helping relationships alone. He must be functionally integrated in all areas of his life. If he is functionally integrated in his own life he can be so in the helping process. Indeed, genuineness flows as easily and readily in helping as it does in other aspects of life. *In regard to the helpee, if there*

*is no authenticity in helping there can be none in life. In regard to the
helper too, if there is no authenticity in life there can be none in helping.*
5. *The helper will find that he is most effective when he views and
implements the confrontation dimension in stages.*

The highest level of understanding within the helping process involves
a translation to action within the helping process. Confrontation is one
of the assertive communications available to the helper (Berenson &
Mitchell, 1969; Carkhuff & Berenson, 1967). The helper is most effective
when he employs confrontation in response to the helpee's plea, whether
implicit or explicit, for an undistorted, external observation and evaluation of his behavior. Whether asked for or not by the helpee, the confrontation of helpee discrepancies in self versus ideal, insight versus
behavior, self versus other experiences, loving versus harming, or resources versus deficits precipitates a crisis in the helpee's life. The crisis
poses the helpee with the choice between continuing in his present mode
of functioning or making a commitment to attempt to achieve a higher-
level, more fulfilling way of life. If the helper is effective in following
through on his confrontation, he will make it impossible for the helpee
to avoid full responsibility for this choice. In this context the effects of
confrontation are not necessarily immediately observable, since the act
of confrontation elicits helpee defenses multifold. Similarly, in following
through the helper may not be responsive to the helpee's communications. Thus, the helper may appear to be functioning at low levels of
facilitative conditions. Having found his direction in his experience of
the helpee, he is tenacious in deterring the helpee's attempts to neutralize the effects of confrontation. Thus, the helper will persevere in
the face of attacks, both subtle and frontal. However, the proof of the
dimension is in its effects, and over time, following effective confrontations by high-level–functioning helpers, the helpee will explore himself
at deeper and deeper levels, finally demonstrating positive movement
toward higher levels of functioning himself.

Stage 1 of Confrontation

Except for the necessity for a transition into direct confrontations there
is really only one stage of the confrontation dimension. Some kind of
preparatory phase may be necessary, however, both in order to prepare
the helpee and in order to gauge his readiness for confrontation. During
this first stage of confrontation the helper concentrates upon tentative
formulations concerning discrepant communications from the helpee.
The modality usually employed involves probing inquiries rather than
directionful confrontations. Tentative comparisons of diverging commu-

nications are both natural and appropriate for both helper and helpee at this point. The helper will most likely not have full and clear directionality, and the helpee's responses will aid in sharpening the development of these dimensions in the helper's experience. By contrast, prematurely direct confrontations may have a demoralizing and demobilizing effect upon an inadequately prepared helpee. The helpee's response, then, provides a means of assessing the helpee's readiness for directionful confrontations, or stage 2 of confrontation.

Stage 2 of Confrontation

Directionful confrontations create crises that offer the helpee the possibility of movement to higher levels of functioning. Thus, when the helper discerns critical discrepancies in the helpee's behavior, whether the discrepancies are between the helpee's insights and actions, between his self and ideal concepts, or between the helpee's experience of himself and the helper's experience of the helpee, the helper confronts the helpee with these discrepancies. The critical nature of the discrepancies with which the helpee is confronted will, of course, be dependent in large part upon the helpee's level of functioning, the discrimination of which is dependent upon the preliminary stages of all of the dimensions involved, including in particular confrontation. At the point of confrontation the helpee is pressed to consider the possibility of changing and, in order to do so, utilizing resources that he has not yet employed. Whether or not he resists the implications of the confrontation, he cannot avoid the responsibility for his choice, whether self-constructive or self-destructive. He cannot avoid the responsibility for these choices that he has so far denied that he has because the helper in his follow-through will not allow him to do so. The high-level–functioning helper is free to employ both the didactic and the experiential modality for confrontation, although he tends to prefer the latter. Similarly, he feels free to confront the helpee with both deficits and assets that the helpee has denied, again tending to prefer the latter. Finally, the ultimate positive effect of confrontation is to enable the helpee to confront himself and, when appropriate, others. *Confrontation of self and others is prerequisite to the healthy individual's encounter with life.*

6. *The helper will find that he is most effective when he views and implements the immediacy dimension in stages.*

The highest level of action within the helping process is incorporated in interpretations of immediacy. Again immediacy involves the question, "What is the helpee really trying to tell *me* that he cannot tell me directly" (Berenson & Mitchell, 1974; Carkhuff & Berenson, 1967; Kell,

1966). Thus, interpretations of immediacy translate the helper's immediate experience of the helpee in relation to the helper directly into action, in this case a direct communication to the helpee of messages he is trying to communicate to the helper. Immediacy differs from the psychoanalytic concept of transference in two significant ways: (1) it takes the helper's stimulus value into consideration in interpreting the helpee's communications and (2) it is not tied to any single personality theory and thus is open to more broad expressions of the helpee's experience of the helpee's phenomenology in terms that both persons can come to understand. Many helpees distort all experience by continually making comparisons of their level of functioning with that of others. It is as if they are saying, "I know me only in relation to others." The healthy individual, in turn, commits himself to knowing himself first and others only secondarily in relation to himself. It is as if the correctional action that the effective helper takes is saying, "I know you by how you respond to me." Thus, the modality by which an essentially directionless helpee who knows himself only in relation to others comes to discern his own direction is interaction with a directionful helper who, knowing himself, knows others in relation to himself.

Stage 1 of Immediacy

As with confrontation, there is a preliminary or transition stage into direct interpretations of immediacy. This is also dependent upon the level at which the helpee is functioning. With most helpees the helper will tentatively approach the immediacy dimension. He may do so with formulations that do not define precisely the helper's experience of the immediate moment, either because he is not in full contact with it or because the helpee lacks readiness for it, or both. The formulations may take the form, "You're trying to tell me something more, something about yourself in relation to me." The helpee's response will not only provide the helper with feedback that will sharpen his discrimination and communication but also will prepare the helpee for directionful communications of immediacy.

Stage 2 of Immediacy

Healthy persons communicate what they are communicating. They say what they are saying. They are about what they are about. Unhealthy individuals communicate their distorted comparisons indirectly. They are never talking or living about what they are talking or living about. The healthy person, the only effective helper, lives fully in the moment.

The unhealthy person, the helpee, does not and is never fully in anything. The medium by which the unhealthy person becomes healthy is the immediacy of the healthy person. The helper who is fully and intensely himself in the moment knows the helpee by how the helpee responds to him. Not only does the helper have a far better grasp of himself than the helpee with his distortions could ever hope to have but also a far better grasp of who the helpee really is. *Only the person who is living and working fully and intensely in the present, with minimal infringement from the past and future, can live a productive and creative life and thus enable others to live a productive and creative life.*

THE INTERACTION OF INDIVIDUAL DIMENSIONS IN HELPING: AN OVERVIEW

Perhaps the simplest way to understand the dimensions involved in the helping relationship is to understand these dimensions as essential characteristics of the fully functioning person, characteristics that the helper has and the helpee does not have to a sufficient degree. Thus, through the didactic, experiential, and modeling sources of learning high levels of empathic understanding in the helper serve to develop in the helpee high levels of understanding of himself and others. In a similar manner the helpee's respect for himself and others, his ability to be concrete in distressing problem areas for himself and others, his genuineness with himself and others, his ability to confront himself and others, and his facility to understand with immediacy the interrelationship between himself and others are developed to degrees that enable the helpee to function effectively in his world. We are really talking about a reconstruction of certain critical, functional personality characteristics with certain developmental stages similar to those a child encounters in his development. The point at which we initiate the helping process, then, is contingent upon the helpee's prior development. Let us consider again all of the dimensions in interaction with each other.

Early Stages of Helping Dimensions

In the usual case helping is initiated through the dimensions of genuineness and empathy in a complementary relationship. The helper's authenticity, or perhaps more precisely the absence of inauthenticity or incongruence, for the helper has no need to demonstrate his authenticity during the initial stages of helping, contrasts vividly with the inauthenticity of the helpee in both the helper's and the helpee's eyes. Most important, who the helper is in the helpee's eyes—that is, the fact that he is not a "phony," and so on, however distorted this may be initially —establishes that the helper has something that the helpee feels he wants or needs. Thus, the genuineness dimension even at the prevailing minimally facilitative (level 3) levels of early phases of helping establishes the necessary power base for helping, that is, the recognition by the helpee of the helper as an agent of the helpee's change. In addition, minimally facilitative levels of genuineness provide the context within which all other helping communications may take place. Empathy, respect, and all other dimensions are only as effective as they are genuine.

Empathic understanding, in turn, is the key ingredient in the establishment of a viable communication process. At minimally facilitative levels (level 3) the interchangeability of the helper's communications with those of the helpee indicates to the helpee that the helper will initially accept the helpee's experience at the level at which the helpee is expressing himself. The helper will neither press too hard nor offer a depth of more diagnostic understanding prematurely. In all, the interchangeable communications of the early phase of helping institute a hope for the helpee to one day see and communicate himself clearly and without distortion.

The interchangeable empathic communications of early helping are not unrelated to the institution of unconditionality as a first stage in the development of the respect dimension. Here, although the emphasis is upon at least minimally facilitative levels of respect (level 3) throughout the early stage, the concentration upon a qualitatively unconditional respect during the early stages indicates to the helpee that at least initially he will not be hurt, punished, or destroyed for expressing himself increasingly as he experiences himself. The helper's readiness to understand and his suspension of potentially negative reactions communicates to the helpee the possibility that the helper can find aspects of the helpee that he can respect and institutes the hope that the helpee may some day come to respect himself in critical areas of functioning.

In turn, the concreteness dimension is also related to empathic understanding, initially serving a complementary role in sharpening up the understanding of both the helper and the helpee of the helpee's problems at hand. Without the more dynamic meaning of empathy, respect, and genuineness, concreteness of at least minimally facilitative levels (level 3) is critical to providing specific affective and intellective feedback for areas of helpee functioning that the helper can do something about. In addition, this dimension provides perhaps a first experience in concretizing areas of dysfunctioning for the helpee and institutes the hope that he will one day be able to do likewise for himself.

The emphasis during the earliest stage of helping, then, is upon minimally facilitative levels of at least four key dimensions. In particular, the absence of inauthentic responses, even without the presence of definitively genuine responses, in conjunction with the interchangeable emphasis upon empathy, provides the necessary context for the entire helping process as well as the basis for deepening levels of both dimensions. That all of the dimensions converge in their functioning during this stage of helping will become immediately obvious. In a very real sense, for example, *the suspension of very genuine responses in conjunction with interchangeable empathic communications defines unconditionality at this stage of helping.* That is, all of the dimensions converge and function simultaneously in allowing the helpee complete freedom to explore, experience, and experiment with himself in the context of minimally facilitative levels of genuineness, empathy, respect, and concreteness. The key perhaps is that *the helper does not commit too much of himself in the interest of offering the helpee as much opportunity as possible to develop himself as fully as possible.* The helper's position serves at least two critical functions: (1) the helper does not impede the helpee's development of himself and his problem in any respect; and (2) the helper has an opportunity to assess the helpee's level of development. Conclusions concerning the helpee's level of development will determine the length of time spent in this initial stage of helping. With very low-level–functioning helpees the stage may be very long, perhaps lasting even years; with very high-level–functioning helpees the stage may be very brief, often amounting only to minutes.

Intermediary Stages of Helping Dimensions

Again the stages of the helping process are not the equivalent of the phases of the process. When we view the individual dimensions we see that it is necessary to describe a more intermediate stage before we are fully in the second phase of helping, the period of emerging directionality. During this stage the dimensions of genuineness, empathy, and respect move toward higher levels of facilitation (approximately level 4 and sometimes level 5 where possible) in effective helping processes. Thus, the helper moves simultaneously on several dimensions toward increasing his level of functioning in his relationship with the helpee. He moves toward becoming increasingly genuine, particularly at this stage in regard to his positive feelings about the helpee. In relation to his negative feelings he is less likely to communicate them than he is his positive feelings. He introduces, perhaps for the first time, the dimension of self-disclosure, providing a model for increasingly deep levels of self-disclosure on the part of the helpee. Concomitantly, his empathic communications are increasingly probing and dynamic as he attempts to assist helpee in understanding himself at deeper and deeper levels, particularly in those areas of dysfunctioning in which the helpee evidences a lack of understanding. It can readily be seen how higher levels of genuineness and empathy converge, with helper disclosures implicitly and depth reflections and interpretations explicitly calling for deeper levels of exploration and awareness on the part of the helpee. Concreteness has less of a role here, since the probings often yield abstract explorations as a function of dealing with material that is often less than readily available to the helpee's conscious processes. Similarly, the same dimensions again converge with regard to the respect dimension. Through deep levels of empathic understanding the helpee now makes himself known in ways that enable the helper to respond positively to him. There are aspects of the helpee that elicit positive regard from the helper, and he freely and genuinely communicates this respect to the helpee. Where the helper's genuine responses are negative he will most likely not respond, or at least initially, simply in effect placing the helpee on an extinction schedule (that is, the absence of any reinforcements) with regard to the helpee's more self-destructive characteristics. Again we find that the dimensions operate concurrently both with regard to function and time. An interactional process ensues. *As the helper becomes more fully himself so does the helpee. As the helpee becomes more fully himself the helper is increasingly free to respond fully to the helpee, and the helpee, in turn, to himself.*

In this context the intermediary stages introduce for the first time the more directional thrusts of helping, confrontation, and interpretations of immediacy. These dimensions flow freely and naturally as a function of the increasing genuineness on the part of both the helper and the helpee. As crisis-precipitating dimensions for the helpee they are most effectively introduced at minimally facilitative levels (level 3). Thus, these dimensions are presented more in tentative formulations, pointing up questions rather than directions concerning behavioral discrepancies and interrelationships. Nevertheless, the introduction of these dimensions serves to prepare the helpee immediately for these direct and immediate helper dimensions and offers him the promise for ultimately living himself in a direct and immediate manner.

Thus, whereas the early stages of helping function to enable the helpee to make himself known in his own way, the intermediary stages take on the characteristic of tentative helper initiative and directionality. The development of the helper's directionality does not function to the exclusion of the helpee's development of his own directionality. Rather, it is internally directed within the helping process, its probes and reinforcements serving to give directionality to the helpee's own efforts to come to understand himself at deeper levels in areas in which he is not now functioning effectively. Indeed, at one level it is very empathically responsive to the helpee's urgent plea for directionality. Again the duration of time will be contingent in large part upon the helpee's level of functioning, specifically his level of functioning in the relevant problem areas. In the usual case, however, the helpee will experience either or both of the initial and intermediary stages of the individual helping dimensions before entering the final phase of helping.

Later Stages of Helping Dimensions

With the transition into the period of emergent directionality accomplished we turn to a consideration of the individual dimensions within the later stages of helping. The dimensions of confrontation and immediacy, insofar as they flow from very high levels of genuineness, take on a very critical character in the problem-solving activities of the second phase of helping. The helper is now freely and fully himself (levels 4 and 5). However, with the qualification that he still serves the helpee's interests, he continues to concentrate upon the helpee, with dimensions such as self-disclosure now assuming a more subordinate function. Thus, in the consideration of alternative solutions the helper directly confronts the helpee with discrepancies in the helpee's behavior that preclude constructive resolution (levels 4 and 5 of confrontation). He actively interprets with immediacy his experience of the helpee's motives and attitudes toward the helper that present obstacles to progress, both in terms of internal understanding and external action (levels 4 and 5 of immediacy). In this manner he offers the helpee at the highest level the translation of his own experience (of others and others in relation to him) to action within the helping process. All of this is not to say, of course, that the helper does not act outside of the helping process. When appropriate he does so as actively as is necessary. However, with the helping goal in mind of the helpee's own authentic and autonomous action based upon his own discriminations the helper continues to concentrate upon the helpee's translation to action of his own experience within helping. With the hope in mind that the helpee will generalize from his experience in helping to critical experiences in other areas of his life the helper continues to concentrate upon the helpee's translation of his own experience to action outside of the helping process.

In the later stages of the helping dimensions the dimension of respect moves even further toward being incorporated within genuineness. Thus,

along with positive regard directed toward self-constructive helpee behaviors the helper also generates negative regard toward self-destructive
helpee activities. He introduces a conditional attitude based upon his
clear and genuine perceptions of the helpee. *He will not accept the
helpee at less than he can be. He will employ all of his resources in
differentially reinforcing the helpee in order to enable him, in turn, to
employ all of his resources in searching for the highest levels of productivity and creativity within himself.*

As can readily be seen, the dimensions in the second phase of helping
are not as easily described in terms of levels or any other more traditional characteristics. They are qualitatively different. Whereas empathy
appears to have a more subordinate function—although in reality it continues to constitute the basis for the entire helping process—serving now
only to provide periodic feedback as a check on level of understanding,
concreteness, which was once complementary to empathy, becomes
prominent. The concreteness now, however, deals more with the specifics
of problem resolution and implementation, operationalizing both a consideration of advantages and disadvantages of alternative courses of
action as well as the ultimate directionality taken. It is clear that such
a dimension is essential to effective achievement of the ultimate goal of
helping, constructive helpee action in relation to himself and his world.

Table 7-1 provides an overview of the stages of the individual dimensions within phases of helping. As can be seen, the emphasis during the
initial stages of phase I is upon level 3 of empathy, respect, concreteness, and genuineness. The emphasis in empathy is upon interchangeability; in respect upon unconditionality; in concreteness upon specificity
of feelings and experiences in explorations; in genuineness upon the
absence of inauthenticity.

With the exception of concreteness, which is deemphasized in favor
of more abstract explorations, the focus during the intermediary or transition stages is upon higher levels of the facilitative dimensions. For
empathy the emphasis is upon additive responses, depth reflections,
moderate interpretations, and the like; for respect the emphasis is upon
positive regard. More action-oriented dimensions are also introduced.
Genuineness at higher levels incorporates self-disclosure and spontaneity.
At the same time confrontation and immediacy are developed in an
open-ended manner.

Upon completion of the transition into the final phase of helping, the
period of emergent directionality, the dimensions as they were introduced during the initial phases are deemphasized. Except for periodic
feedback the communication of empathy does not receive explicit attention. The nature of respect changes qualitatively as the helper differen-

Table 7-1. The Stages of the Individual Dimensions Within the Phases of Helping

Dimensions	Initial Stage of Individual Dimensions	Phase I (Downward or Inward Phase of Self-Exploration) Intermediary Stages of Individual Dimensions	Phase II (Upward or Outward Phase of Emergent Directionality and Action) Final Stage of Individual Dimensions
Empathy	Level 3 (interchangeability)	Levels 4 and 5 (additive responses)	Levels 4 and 5 (emphasizing periodic feedback only)
Respect	Level 3 (unconditionality)	Level 4 (positive regard)	Levels 4 and 5 (regard and conditionality)
Concreteness	Levels 3 and above (specificity of exploration)	Deemphasized (abstract exploration)	Levels 4 and 5 (specificity of direction)
Genuineness	Level 3 (absence of ingenuineness)	Levels 4 and 5 (self-disclosure and spontaneity)	Levels 4 and 5 (spontaneity)
Confrontation		Level 3 (general and open)	Levels 4 and 5 (directionful)
Immediacy		Level 3 (general and open)	Levels 4 and 5 (directionful)

tially reinforces the helpee and in so doing introduces the dimension of conditionality. Once again concreteness is stressed, only now the emphasis is upon the specificity involved in exploring and operationalizing courses of action. The more action-oriented dimensions, in turn, operate at the highest levels. The helper functions from a base of authenticity and is fully spontaneous. In addition, he is directionful in the confrontations and interpretations of immediacy that he shares with the helpee.

In summary, the early stages of the helping dimensions enable the helpee to make himself known, the intermediary stages to allow the helper to give the helping process internal direction. The later stages of helping emphasize a shared, highly interactional process in which both the helper and the helpee concentrate upon the interrelationship of the internal and external worlds of the helpee and the resolution of his areas of dysfunctioning within and between these worlds. These descriptions are in some ways artificially specific. Indeed, as didactic means of learning they must be so. They are, however, verbal articulations of many effective helping experiences of the writer and others. As such they have all of the limitations of words and constructs. *In helping and in life these highly interactional processes flow naturally, with each movement shaped by the feedback from the last and each process shaped by what is, in the end, most effective for the helpee.*

REFERENCES

For a more detailed discussion of the issues considered in this chapter see the asterisked readings and the references upon which the readings are based.

Berenson, B. G., & Carkhuff, R. R. *Sources of gain in counseling and psychotherapy.* New York: Holt, Rinehart and Winston, Inc., 1967.
*Berenson, B. G., & Mitchell, K. *Confrontation.* Amherst, Mass: Human Resource Development Press, 1974.
*Carkhuff, R. R., & Berenson, B. G. *Beyond counseling and therapy.* New York: Holt, Rinehart and Winston, Inc., 1967.
Kell, W. *Impact and change: A study of counseling relationships.* New York: Appleton-Century-Crofts, 1966.
Rogers, C. R., Gendlin, E., Kiesler, D., & Truax, C. B. *The therapeutic relationship and its impact.* Madison, Wisc.: University of Wisconsin Press, 1967.
*Truax, C. B., & Carkhuff, R. R. *Toward effective counseling and psychotherapy.* Chicago: Aldine Publishing Company, 1967.

8

APPLICATIONS OF CORE
CONDITIONS IN EFFECTIVE
INDIVIDUAL HELPING PROCESSES

The helping process is not always as neat as it appears when we formulate it in the abstract. Although it contains many of the dimensions attended to in these volumes, it does not always follow the patterns we have learned so well. The translation from theory to practice is not an easy one. It should not be otherwise. If the helping process does not contain the spark of nuance and change, then it does not contain the spark of life. As helpers we must be ever open and flexible in the discharge of our commitment to translate our efforts to tangible helpee benefits. We must be guided by our learnings concerning what works for the helpee and not simply what works for us. When the two merge, as they often do in the most experienced, high-level–functioning helpers, then the prospects for the constructive gain of the helpee are greatest. When they do not merge the effective helper must choose what works for the helpee even if, or perhaps because, it means new learning for him.

Our experiences in individual and group helping processes range so wide as to preclude the possibility of reviewing all of them. In our work we have found ourselves at different times with different or even the same helpees conducting helping processes in a manner that is compatible with just about every orientation possible. Always, however, the processes are built, however briefly, around variations of the approach described in these volumes. Since the following chapters deal with individual behavior modification, group processes, and group training experiences as preferred modes of treatment, we will concentrate here upon some of more recent experiences in individual counseling, with particular emphasis upon the independent experience, albeit at the helper's request, of the helpee as well as the helper.

"THE LONG WINTER": THE HELPER'S EXPERIENCE

A depressed, highly anxious middle-aged woman unable to mobilize her resources alone or in conjunction with any of her acquaintances to counter self-destructive tendencies was referred to this helper for help. Avoided by professionals who felt inadequate to handle such a threatening person, the helpee was lost and alone. This helper offered very early in the first contact that he could understand the threat the woman might pose to others and added candidly that of those therapists who were known to him and available to her he alone could help. However, having no motivation other than to establish himself as having something that the helpee wanted, that is, to achieve the "power" role in the relationship, the helper referred the woman to several professionals so that she could make the decision for herself. When she returned, convinced that she "could handle the others easily," the helper had established a relative power base much different from the initial random selection procedure. Formal sessions began.

Counteracting the helpee's set to "take" him, the helper quickly established that the helping process would be on his terms. For example, whereas the helpee dictated long-term treatment, the helper offered only the structure of time-limited counseling. Whereas the helpee dictated nondirective counseling, the helper made it clear that he did not believe that she could benefit from such an approach exclusively nor could he hear her really asking for it. Rather, he interpreted these demands as tests by the helpee to ascertain the constructive directionality of the helper. In addition, early in helping the helper found the helpee employing misleading maneuvers, such as providing cues that appeared only for a moment to be leading to personally relevant and revealing experiences but that, in fact, always came around in circular fashion to some superficial starting point. As he took these defenses away from the woman one by one with often gentle and sometimes not so gentle firmness he found her moving quickly through her lines of resistance.

A helping process more compatible with our formulations began only after these initial forays concerning whose terms would prevail. Had the helpee won, she would have had no hope, since her terms were not only destructive of others but also of herself. It was almost as if she were saying, "If I win I lose." If I win in my battle with the helper, I lose in my struggle for myself. Indeed, at the deepest level of understanding the helper hears the helpee's pleas to lose the battle: "If only someone will take me. If I lose I win." But the battle will not be won if the helper is not for real, for the helpee will come back time and again to search out the helper's vulnerabilities. Even if it is real for the helper, the helpee will do so periodically, perhaps not so much to discover the helper's adequacies as to renew her confidence in her earlier judgments. She wishes to know that the helper has constructive directionality in his own life. The helpee discovers that, having established the superiority of his position, the helper is now willingly responsive to her. Having lost the battle with the helper, the helpee is now surprised to find that the depth of her openness and vulnerability is matched only by the depth of her helper's sensitivity and concern. A constructive helping process ensues.

Alone with a terrible guilt that she had earned, the helpee found someone who was able not only to understand it, at least at the level at which she presented it, but also to make her face her guilt at deeper and deeper levels. Along with her explorations in response to the now helpee-centered process she started putting pieces of her picture together. For example, having hidden the voids in her own make-up in a somewhat complementary marriage, she had panicked at the prospect of her husband's imminent death and did things she could not at first admit to herself and then could not forgive. As the helpee achieved higher levels of self-understanding the helper communicated his understanding at deeper and deeper levels. As the helpee hit the "bottom" of her depression the helper put her on a "demand schedule," seeing her frequently at crisis points. As she was in the depths of her depression he reached out his hands to hold hers, as she shivered in fear and panic. Always, however, the helper focused his efforts upon either translating deeper and deeper understanding to action or shaping action and discovering the understanding later, according to the helpee's level of development in a given area. In response to her own sense of urgency the helpee came to know that the helper would if necessary force her to do something about her problems.

Again, in spite of her stated preference, some areas in which the helpee was functioning well were skipped in favor of those in which she was not. The helper simply acknowledged those areas in which the helpee was functioning at minimally facilitative levels. For example, in relation to her child-rearing efforts, given the time-limited nature of the process, the helper simply acknowledged, "Whatever mistakes you made, whatever your limitations, I think it would have been rewarding and at times exciting to have been a child with a mother like you." Instead, the helping effort was concentrated in those areas where the focus was more urgently needed.

As the helpee came to be able to make responses that the helper might have made the helper introduced the action-oriented dimensions in a natural way. As the helpee was able to initiate offering high levels of facilitative conditions to both herself and the helper the helper elevated the level of action orientation. In terms of weekly homework assignments the helper became more and more conditional, increasingly not allowing the helpee to be less than she could be until he found that she could take over a particular function for herself and, indeed, until finally she could periodically call the helper up short when he was being less than he could be. When the helper and the helpee could interchange roles the process was approaching termination. Needless to say, the helpee was ultimately equipped to surmount her own obstacles and search out her own fulfillment in life, something she has done well.

While this description covers only some of the highlights of the case and does not fill in all of the relevant material, it does serve to point up some new learnings. If the helper is truly shaped by what is effective for the helpee, he may find himself doing things that he might not otherwise tend to do. Thus, he finds it necessary first to establish his superiority before there is any basis for the helping process. The superiority must be legitimate, however. The helper in this case established that he is "for real" and as such would not be pulled into the helpee's sick little games. He established that he had something that the helpee wanted, and thus set the first of the conditions necessary for the helpee's commitment to living. *In the process the helper was not misled by the helpee's smokescreens nor did he flee in terror from the helpee's threats, since he knew that his fears were the helpee's fears and only if he did not run would the helpee not run.* The helper learned that not only is he most effective when he is most sensitively responsive but also that the highest level of understanding is not to respond to what is there but to respond to what is missing and to act upon this. There are many other learnings. The helping process in this case moved ultimately to a fully sharing, equalitarian relationship. Both persons were better able to act more constructively and upon more sensitive discriminations; or, in the absence of accurate insights, to act as is necessary to do what has to be done, trusting their ability to integrate the experiences, initially at a point following action and ultimately simultaneously with the action.

Even in our modifications we often lose the essence of helping as it is experienced by the helpee. To be sure, helping does not proceed effectively except on the helper's terms, at least initially. However, this is not to say that the helper's formulations invariably capture the necessary ingredients of the helping process. Indeed, while the helpee's terms may not be trusted initially, following effective helping the successful helpee, in this case a person who went on to become a successful professional helper, has perhaps the most claim to an understanding of what went on over the course of helping that made a difference in her life.

"WELCOME TO SPRING": THE HELPEE'S EXPERIENCE

Full attention: that's uppermost as I remember our hours of therapy together. I'd never before known, even from my husband when he was alive, such total awareness of what I was saying and not saying, and how. Once you said:

> "When something happens, you have a strong impulse to handle it intellectually, that means communication. Sometimes at the deepest level you don't need to communicate. . . . I think you can get glimpses of the need not to communicate, the lack of the need to communicate, when you look in my eyes sometimes. That's enough."

You listened with such empathy, so much *with me*, that you heard the core of my messages, even when I myself didn't recognize what that core was. I remember vividly that early on you'd listen for long periods and then you'd say, "What I hear you saying is . . ." and give me, with uncanny accuracy, the essence of what I had meant. The first time we really talked you said,

> "*You* want to tell *me* these things, and I want to hear them. You want me to know that you're a full woman and have had beauty in your life such as few people ever know. I could infer it from hunches, but I'd rather hear it from you."

I remember, physically and spiritually, the wonderful feeling when I left our first real session: "good, warm, and relaxed," I wrote later in my journal. As I passed you in the doorway I got a sense of being caressed, without your touching me. I felt my spine unshrivel. I hadn't even known it *was* shriveled. I mattered to you; you cared in a quite unself-seeking way. I had been blessed.

But the very next week, though you'd put me on a "demand schedule," came the first crisis. I couldn't get to you when I desperately needed to. I'd started a story there wasn't time to finish—an ugly one—and after the session I wrote and sent you a long, self-revealing letter telling the end of it. For nearly a week thereafter I needed a response. I was stuck on a turntable, round and round and round, wild with frustration at being able to get no feedback. When I called you turned me down—deliberately, I thought, but it had been circumstance. Finally, angry and humiliated and tense, I tried to sublimate and rationalize my feelings—in vain. I wrote in my journal:

> "I have been crying wildly about my husband—and really resenting R.C. He makes me feel refused, thwarted. My husband would never have let me suffer for a whole week from doubting me and my motives.
>
> "I want to hurt R.C. But I can't. I'd only hurt myself. I'll have to learn humility from this and go back to him supplicant again.
>
> "This is the sort of neurotic misery I was warned about by my reading. Once the lid is off there's no defense against it.
>
> "I feel hurt by this week. I want to go to sleep—I just want to escape.

"I needed help and he refused me. I needed help and he turned me away, repeatedly. It makes me know that I am alone and that I may live 30 years alone and I can't do a damned thing about it."

The next morning you telephoned me:

RC: I was not here late yesterday.
M: I know.
RC: You sound tired.
M: I'm beaten.
RC: It was a rough night?
M: It's been a rough week. . . . I thank you for calling me.
RC: Are you alone at home? . . . Is that partly the trouble—that there's nobody to talk to?
M: I need to talk to *you* . . . I feel so goddamned exposed.
RC: You're not going to be hurt because of it.
M: I *am* hurt.
RC: You mean you're hurting?
M: Yes.
RC: Can you make it through till tomorrow, M?
M: Somehow. (*Long silence*)
RC: Why don't you come in later this morning?

I hung up and burst into tears—relief, grief, goodness knows what, saying, "He does have some sense of mercy."

When we met a few hours later:

RC: Is it something about your husband and me?
M: I hadn't thought of it that way. Between my husband and you, you've insured that I'll be a widow the rest of my life.
RC: Your husband is dead and you can't have me?
M: Between the two of you, you've set me a standard.
RC: And that scares you.
M: Yes, I might live 30 years. . . . I love you.
RC: O.K.
M: Can you understand how complex and simple that is?
RC: Yes. . . .

. . . .

RC: Go ahead.
M: I can't . . . I'm afraid. I don't want to be slapped again.
RC: You know that the slaps weren't intended to hurt you.
M: Of course, but they did.

. . . .

M: I want you to read the letter.
RC: Tomorrow.
M: Now.
RC: But you're here now and I won't sit here and read it.
M: I'll read it to you; I have enough nerve for that.

RC: I'll read it by tomorrow, and we can discuss it then.

M: You're stubborn, aren't you?

RC: I don't think the letter is as important as how you've been feeling these two days.

M: I'm frozen.

RC: What does that mean? Do you feel cold? cold toward me?

M: Not that so much, just dead . . . I've said all there is to say.

The next day, after you had read the letter, we talked:

RC: What was in the letter except for details that mostly I already knew. It had three messages: you and L., you and yourself, and you and me. There isn't going to be another L. I'm mostly interested in you and yourself. You haven't let it all the way in—about your husband since he died.

M: I hear you saying to me, "Suffer."

RC: I don't want you to suffer.

M: The children need to have me carry on.

RC: Is that what you want to teach them about facing a thing like this— not to look at it, to shut it out? You've shut it out for almost a year now.

M: I can't force it. Sometimes I know it. Once recently K. was exercising a sore muscle in my arm the way I'd exercised my husband's paralyzed arm last year. And I cried, suddenly overwhelmed by memory.

RC: Let it out.

M: You don't want me to howl.

RC: It's all right.

M: I howled after you called me yesterday. . . . I can't really let go unless you hold me, and you're not going to hold me.

RC: You need someone strong to let go to. . . . You're afraid to let in the beauty of your relationship with your husband.

M: I did at the first interview and you approved.

RC: And you felt good.

M: I'm afraid to lie down and consent to let it wash over me for fear I couldn't get back up again.

RC: There's a lot of you left, in spite of the loss of your husband from your life. You don't know how much. He gave you strength, but there was a lot there to begin with. . . . I'm not just being supportive.

M: I don't know how deep I actually am—maybe a lot shallower than you think.

RC: You know you wouldn't get so far down you couldn't get back up.

M: Suppose I had decided to give in today, not to get up, not to keep this appointment, not to go to the quiz this afternoon. You wouldn't have come to my house to see what was wrong with me.

RC: I'd have expected you to come, no matter what.

All that session you were struggling to know what to say, how to put what you wanted to say. It was work for both of us—the hardest we'd been through yet.

In the early days of the therapy I often planned what I'd begin talking about, before a session. I'd been a long-time list-maker. But when I was with you I never really knew what I'd say next. I often heard myself express things I hadn't known were in me. I needed less and less to plan.

As we went on together there were fewer long monologues from me and much more natural interaction, in which we talked on a basis of equality. You made it quite plain that I would be in no way your equal until I earned it. But in *my* definition of equality—nothing to do with experience or skill or knowing or strength, but springing from a basic acceptance of each other—in that to me crucial sense we did communicate as equals, from the beginning.

Prime among your qualities the most characteristic and the most essential to my respect for you is your utter *realness*. Just that—without qualification.

Next: your *honesty*. I never heard you speak a single word that was even the slightest shade off completely honest, nor fail to speak when silence would have been dishonest. Once I asked, "Is that policy or truth?" and you answered, "There's no policy here." Another time you said, "The two cardinal virtues are honesty and work. You understand work. I can't teach you a thing about that. But I can teach you a lot about honesty." And so you did. First, by your un-flinching integrity. Next, by refusing to accept from me anything in word or act that smacked of inaccuracy, even of "harmless pretense," particularly of kidding myself, let alone you. The seed you planted in me (or replanted after my husband's initial planting) is still growing. You know that, as you know most of what there is to know about me.

Concrete self-disclosure, to the extent that it would be helpful to me, always came from you most naturally. For example:

RC: Last hour you wondered why I'd make myself available for counseling you. Now I know. Now I can say it. I think I can learn from you.
M: I honor you for saying that to me. It makes you more vulnerable.
RC: You don't *know* how vulnerable.
M: I know. (I tried to start an intellectual discussion about it.)
RC: Let's just leave it at what I said.
M: O.K., we'll do it your way.

I spoke of the "best moment of the day" with my husband, when we'd lie, like spoons, together in bed and *breathe*.

M: I hope you know how that feels.
RC: I couldn't help you if I didn't, could I?

RC: I didn't think there was anybody else around here strong enough to handle you. . . . You didn't want the woman counselor because you were afraid she couldn't handle you, that you could manage her. And you didn't want that. . . . Sometimes you make me fight for my direction.
M: I don't want to threaten you.
RC: I'm not afraid of you. But you make me fight for my direction. You hope that my health is stronger than your pathology. . . . I can find my way

through the jungle better. . . . Where you are misusing your strengths, you'll have to find better ways.

M: That's why I'm here.

RC: I can stay with you.

I had no need to manage you, plan for you, be your mother. You set me free to find out who else I was. You were self-moving, competent to know what to do for me and how to do it. In fact, you *would not* let me run the show. What a blessed relief! I could *wholly trust you.*

I never had a sense that you were using me in any way to satisfy any neurotic need of your own. You never talked too much or ill consideredly, nor refrained from speaking when I needed you to talk. You never manipulated me, even ever so subtly, though I thought you did the second time we met. You called me by my first name, as I'd suspected you would when you asked me what it was the first time we talked. I felt your using it was "technique-y," insincere, and I protested that since I wasn't ready yet to call you by your first name you mustn't call me by mine. The next time you did it, several sessions later, it felt O.K. And finally, weeks later, outside the therapy room I was able to call you by yours, easily. You never gave me a sense that you required anything from me for yourself. Nothing I did or said, or failed to do or say, could hurt you. You obviously did not need me to love you, but when I did you accepted it in a way that added to my growing health. You were happy when I made progress. You could accept gratitude when it felt genuine to you, without in any way indicating that you needed it. You paid me the important compliment of using me for a sounding board at our last sessions when you had things to say about yourself.

During therapy I knew you were evaluating constantly, but I never felt you to be judgmental, in the constrictive sense. I felt completely free to tell you all that lay upon my heart, even things that showed me in an unfavorable light —hell, I could not avoid it. That didn't seem to matter. I knew I could neither shock you nor drive you away, nor need I fear preachment nor rebuke. I could condemn myself, and did, as you know. But I couldn't shake your faith in my worth, beneath all the garbage. I remember that you said to me early, "I respect your strengths. Sometimes you misuse them, but I highly respect them."

Yet when I needed to express my weakness—as in tears—you were *there* just as I needed you to be there—receiving, not speaking until the time was ripe, letting the emotion run itself out, and then responding just exactly as I'd have wanted if I'd been in any condition to know what I wanted. I never felt diminished by such a scene but somehow strengthened and enhanced.

One came during the greatest crisis of the Spring's therapy. You had pointed out that I'd made another relationship too soon after my husband died; in fact, it began to be foreshadowed even before his death. The next time I came I had a justification of myself all prepared. Characteristically, you wouldn't take it as I prepared it but insisted on looking at my present feelings about it—not the historical ones I tried to bring you. I weathered the session pretty well and held off reaction for about three hours. Then I wrote, "It *was* premature. How can I ever forgive myself?" I was deluged with uncontrollable tears. I couldn't see to drive home and knew it was foolish to drive *away* from help. I went to your office, to wait until your class was over and try to see you. During a break you happened to find me there in obvious pain and dismissed the class to join me.

I cried desperately before you for about 20 minutes while you said nothing. Then we talked a little.

M: If I hurt my husband a year ago before he died, I can't make it have been any different. It's too late. I hope he didn't know I was divided in my mind.

RC: He loved you.

M: Will this knowledge stay in me as an open wound?

RC: You won't necessarily have either an open wound nor one skinned over. How you live from here on is what counts.

M: I don't want to look at you. I don't want to be comforted.

RC: I'm not going to comfort you.

M: I know it.

RC: I'm not without conflict about it, but this is *yours*. . . . You've been trying to vomit this up for nearly a year. It's been a nightmare.

M: It's been hard.

You didn't want to talk much; you said just to let the experience *be*.

M: I have no plan.

RC: Good.

M: · You think I plan too much . . . I don't want it to go under and be lost. . . . Will I grow a skin over it? (*Silence from you.*) I might as well be alone.

RC: There's the skin.

M: The Catholics are more merciful.

RC: Yes, you've been looking for punishment and absolution.

M: I don't want to be punished. But if this is mine, I have to figure out how to deal with it—forgive myself.

But the sessions ended before I had done that—nor did I really need to. I knew I could survive and live with the knowledge of myself as, in part, ignoble. And I knew how essentially simple it is to accept help.

I thanked you for letting me come to you.

RC: Today had meaning for me. Your thanks have no meaning.

M: You have a wound on your head. What's that from?

RC: I live a violent life. I'll tell you about it sometime.

M: Don't die before Wednesday.

RC: I'll try to take care of myself.

As I left you touched my shoulder. I had been having a strong impulse to touch you, which I think you'd picked up. I turned and touched your cheek with my open hand. You said, ". . . for today." And I left, smiling, somehow eased in my spirit. Later I felt exhausted but good, and I wrote in my journal, "I want to be more myself now."

When I saw you five days later I wasn't feeling much of anything, after having turned myself inside out the last time. You too were having some trouble finding your footing.

M: Today I'm just wearing a grey dress.

RC: You're in limbo . . . I'm not getting any message.

M: I'm not sending anything.

RC: You waited a long time for Friday—and a long time for the tiredness. . . . Today we both needed to see that each other was still here. We both need to get our feet under us.

M: I think about you all the time. I think: "It's only two days, only a day and a half . . ."

RC: Something real happened Friday. . . . I thought about it a lot Friday night and Saturday—and then I thought about other things. I don't want to talk it to death. When you talk about something sometimes something happens to it. You nail it down and it gets changed.

RC: I get pieces of it but not the whole thing.

M: (*Covering my face*) That scares me.

RC: Why?

M: You told me before to let it all in and when I did it was pretty shaking. Now I'm afraid to let any more of this in.

RC: That isn't what I meant. I meant *I* only get pieces of it. You're not nineteen, and you're not the grieving guilty widow—but something in between—we don't know what yet. There's a lot in between—to mold. You don't know what it's going to be.

M: I don't know, but I'm not worried about it.

RC: That's honest. . . . You're in a refractory stage. You have a right to respite. You can't say what you are, but you can say what you're not. That gives me some handles. . . . If you'd wanted to see me Monday or Tuesday you would have disciplined yourself.

M: I didn't need to.

RC: As in basketball you don't try to force the ball.

M: You dribble.

RC: Too much effort. Not even that, you do nothing. You flow with the game and when the opportunity comes you do something with it. . . . Most times *you* work quite hard. Now you have a right to do nothing and just see what happens. What do you want to do?

M: (*Suppressing an impulsive answer, smiling*)

RC: Now you're smiling.

M: Uh huh, but I'm not going to say why. There's a lot going on in my mind, but it's extraneous.

RC: About me?

M: Yes.
RC: You'll have to tell me sooner or later.
M: No.
RC: You'd better share it.
M: You're a hard man.
RC: No, I'm an easy man.
M: I wonder what you mean by that.
RC: I'm easy.
M: Are you? You're gentle even though you do lead a violent life—whatever that means.
RC: You'll have to decide.
M: It's all been decided. There *is* nothing in it. . . . I have no plan at all. I'm learning, I think, not to panic when I have no plan. Just be spontaneous.
RC: But you consciously decided that. It's *not* spontaneous.
M: I can't help that. I can't decide and be spontaneous at the same time.
RC: It's good though.

I remember my happiness the day you said, "You'll have more crises. I wouldn't take pain away from you even if I could, which I can't because it's part of life. But you'll be able to cart away your own crud now." The confidence you expressed about me has buoyed me through some damned trying times this academic year of my first counseling experience. No matter how low I got—full of self-contempt, frustration, discouragement, and rejection of those about me—I knew I'd come back up again, would take myself and my life in hand and rebuild in a way I could be proud of and you'd approve. Then one day you said I was no longer bringing you problems but solutions I had worked out, for your comments. In a session near the end I said, "I don't know what I'm going to do or say." You answered, "Find beauty in yourself. I think you can do it. You don't need a flowering spring. . . . This is *now*." Very near the end, when you were forcing me to contemplate leaving you, I finally was able to say:

M: I know I can make it without you.
RC: Well, welcome to Spring. You've had a long winter—over a year. Now, welcome to Spring.

The last crisis came in late May when I was in a tremendous flap of what I now know was preseparation neurosis. I phoned you saying that I was trying to think through my life with the kids, year by year, and *could not* hold my mind from glancing off to all sorts of other subjects.

RC: I think you're making this difficult for *yourself*. You don't have to go through your life systematically. Try letting go; relax and let it come. Let in the full appreciation of what you've been through and what's happening today. Let the important things suggest themselves. Don't work so hard. You don't need to.

M: You mean, don't be so compulsive, just let it happen.

RC: Yes, and we'll talk tomorrow. I have some ideas about why you're operating in the old mode on the new problems.

An immense burden immediately lifted off my shoulders. I was free to sit under the tree in the May sun-dapple, to knit you a sweater, enjoy desultory talk with K., and let come what would. What came was happy stuff: recollections of the good times we had had as a family and of how well my husband and I had done with the children, not how badly. I knew we'd made a bad botch of some of it, but nothing irreparable. We gave them something—or permitted something to grow in them—that enabled them to remake themselves, as all of them are in the process of doing. I think they're all going to grow up more whole than not, within their own limitations, as I am, within mine.

The next day on the way to an extra session with you I had an insight that the only way I could ensure losing contact with you was to clutch. If I simply opened my hand I'd never lose you. This has been a symbol of great significance to me ever since: the symbol of the open, upturned palm, fingers relaxed, ready to respond, support, or let go, but never to clench. They would never crush any butterfly that landed lightly on the palm. I can't always live it, but I can try to fulfill it. When I told you, you reinforced it at once by inviting me to visit you and your family in the summer—not as a client but as a friend—a powerful incentive toward independence and maturity!

About a month before the end of therapy I had a dream: There was a blind woman, and she was telling, in my presence, that she went to someone to whom she would say what it was like to see. She'd tell a little more, and then a little more, and a little more. And she said, "That's why I come, so I can know for a while, at least, what it's like to see." I seem to know how important that was. I was part of the process somehow—and I was glad. When I woke up I thought of you right away.

I was the blind woman, coming to *you* so that I'd know what it is like to see. And many-levelled as dreams are, *I* was the one to whom she came—as I went deep into myself for understanding. Lastly, I am the one to whom others would come so that they could know what it is like to see, and God willing, to begin to see, as I am doing, and as I am beginning to help others to see.

9
INTEGRATED APPROACHES
TO BEHAVIOR CHANGE

Good human relations are not enough! Even when the core, facilitative, and action-oriented dimensions are present in a helping relationship, the helpee may be unable to surmount certain difficult problems or to achieve certain goals. Other means are necessary to enable him to resolve his problems or achieve his goals. To be sure, in some few instances in the context of an effective helping relationship the helpee may go on to develop and implement courses of action on his own. But these instances are rare, occurring only with helpees functioning at the highest level. Most frequently the helper and the helpee together develop some meaningful goals for the helpee. Less frequently the helper may develop goals for the helpee if the helpee is unable to contribute to such development.

The possible approaches to helping are as varied as the goals of helping. While traditional educational and traditional therapeutic orientations enter the picture, good common sense is essential. Almost any approach may be considered a potential preferred mode of treatment in an individual case. The critical questions for any potential preferred mode of treatment are twofold (Carkhuff, 1966; Carkhuff & Berenson, 1967a): (1) what are the unique contributions of a given orientation over and above those contributions accounted for by the core, facilitative, and action-oriented dimensions of an effective helping relationship? and (2) where and under what conditions is this orientation applicable?

Let us review some propositions that enable us to understand the critical nature of the development of effective courses of action.

116

Proposition I. The ultimate understanding in helping is a recognition of the helpee's need to develop a course of action to deal with his difficulty or to achieve his goal.

The realization that understanding is not enough leads readily to the recognition of the necessity for the development of effective courses of action. The courses of action may be rehabilitative or achievement or growth oriented. They may involve remedies for the amelioration or elimination of problems or they may involve steps to be taken to achieve some valued goal.

Proposition II. A consideration of effective courses of action is based upon an operational definition of the critical dimensions of the goals of helping.

The first step in the development of an effective course of action is to describe the goals of helping and to define in operational terms the critical dimensions of these goals. The courses of action that are considered must be operationally related to the critical dimensions of the goals set for the helping process.

Proposition III. The development of effective courses of action is dependent upon an eclectic orientation to helping.

Different orientations produce different changes. Different helpers have different effects under different conditions, and different helpees respond differently to different treatment procedures. The helper must find the treatment that offers the highest probability of achieving the helpee's goals. In this regard the effective helper is limited only by his and his helpee's knowledge and creativity in the consideration of alternative modes of treatment. In developing courses of action the helper must feel free to draw from all existing systems and yet not be bound by any of them (Carkhuff, 1967). He must create his own course of action when there is none that serves the purposes of his treatment.

Proposition IV. Implementation of effective courses of action is accomplished by systematic programs offering the highest success probabilities for achieving the goals of helping.

Alternative courses of action must be considered in terms of their immediate and long-term advantages and disadvantages. The course of action that offers the highest probability of goal achievement over the longest term is the preferred mode of treatment. Physical, emotional, interpersonal, and intellectual programs are developed in progressive gradations of success experiences to effectively implement the course of action prescribed.

Proposition V.   Integrated approaches to behavior change constitute the most effective courses of action.

The systematic programs yielding the highest success probabilities for goal attainment must be integrated into all interpersonal learning or relearning processes. The interpersonal processes that focus upon the core, facilitative, and action-oriented dimensions prepare the helpee for responding with sensitivity to himself and his world and for acting with direction based upon this understanding. The systematic ancillary modes of treatment enable the helpee to resolve problems or to achieve goals that are critical to his effective functioning.

The emphasis upon the systematic development and implementation of courses of action reflects the critical contributions of behavioristic modes of treatment to the total helping process. The technique of particular behavioristic treatment procedures need not be emphasized to the exclusion of step-by-step procedures leading to desired changes or to the exclusion of the helpee's phenomenological experience, which is, of course, the source of the goals of helping. What is critical is progressive practice in the behavior we wish to affect or modify. The traditional approaches do have something to contribute here. Knowledge in the trait-and-factor descriptive approaches will facilitate operational definitions of critical dimensions of desired goals. Experience and practice in behavioristic methodologies will facilitate the attainment of desired goals. Accordingly, the systematic training in responsiveness or assertiveness described in these volumes may be complemented by one or all of a variety of modalities of behavior modification: desensitization; reinforcement; modeling; extinction; behavior rehearsal; role induction; and cognitive reorientation. The helper, however, must not become lost in the modality he employs any more than the helpee. Again the helper must keep the treatment in good perspective.

In the following two cases integrated approaches to behavior change are employed. The first case incorporates an operant or instrumental conditioning procedure (Bandura, 1961; Frank, 1961; Krasner & Ullmann, 1965; Salzinger, 1959; Shaw, 1961; Ullmann & Krasner, 1965) while the second case incorporates classical conditioning procedures (Eysenck, 1960; Salter, 1961; Wolpe, 1958; Wolpe, Salter, & Reyna, 1965).

"TO GET A BIKE": INTEGRATING AN OPERANT CONDITIONING APPROACH

The helpee, a physically strong, intellectually alert 10-year-old boy did no talking with anyone but his mother since his father died when he was three years old. His father's death caused difficulty in many situations, particularly school, where, while his written work was adequate, the authorities felt compelled to fail him because of his inability to verbalize. The helpee and his mother had been seen in conventional, play-oriented therapy for nearly five years by two different psychoanalytically oriented child therapists with no tangible results.

The new helper was able to involve the helpee in a very intense, albeit silent, play-therapy interaction. Thus the helper established a good experiential base for the helpee for the process that followed. At the same time he constructed his role as a potent reinforcer or influencer of behavior in the child's life. The first task of helping was to find out what might be reinforcing in the boy's life. It was determined through interviews with the mother that what the helpee wanted most in his life was a dog, something to which the mother was in no way opposed.

The task was then to figure out how to employ the dog as a reinforcer or reward in a program of therapy designed to produce the helpee's communication with the helper. A problem was how to stretch an all or none item like a dog into rewards that could be allocated over an extended period of time. It was decided that 100 tokens would be made and that the helpee would get one token each time he talked to the helper. The exact criteria of verbalization varied according to the stage of development of the process, and the award of tokens was left to the helper. While the helpee would receive the dog when he accumulated 100 tokens, the process was made more interesting by adding intermediary rewards associated with the dog. Thus, the following schedule was devised: (1) at 10 tokens the helpee received a dog's collar; (2) at 25 tokens, a dog's leash; (3) at 50 tokens, a dog's dish; (4) at 75 tokens, a dog's bed; (5) at 100 tokens, the dog. This schedule served to build the incentive to complete the process because the items obtained were essentially useless without the dog.

The helper presented the schedule to the helpee and they struck a bargain. The helpee demonstrated a nonverbal enthusiasm and together helper and helpee proceeded to create 100 tokens out of cardboard and crayons.

In the sessions that followed the helper emphasized a high level of verbalization in intense play encounters. The helper was as expressive as he could be in all interactions in order to exploit the effects of modeling. The helper also reflected the helpee's fears of talking, which were acknowledged nonverbally by the helpee.

Initially, when the helpee uttered a noise the helper rewarded him with a token. Progress was slow. The first nine tokens were obtained during the first twenty sessions by the helpee for animal sounds, but the helper was highly conditional with the tenth token, demanding a word. The helpee was highly motivated to obtain the collar, and after great difficulty and physical involvement he produced his first word with the helper—the word was "dog."

The following session the helpee brought the dog collar with him and after much of the same physical involvement as the session before produced his second word as time was running out, and quickly added a half-dozen more. It was never easy for the helpee to produce words, and the helper was always attuned to this difficulty. However, as the helpee began to articulate the helper encouraged formal and meaningful sentence development. The helper offered sentences for the helpee to repeat, followed by active elicitation of spontaneous expressions. As the helper wrote the notes for the rewards the helpee was saying, "This summer I'm going to take my dog with us to the country."

As the treatment process ensued the helpee engaged in spontaneous exchanges with the helper, although not without some initial difficulty each session. The helpee got all of the 100 tokens and talked to the helper at length about the difficulties involved in finding his very, very special kind of dog. In the following sessions he spoke freely. Finally, he brought his dog to his helper and both shared in the great excitement.

Throughout treatment the helpee never uttered a sound to anyone else in the treatment setting. He refused the prospect of earning 25 tokens for one interaction with the receptionist in favor of earning them one at a time with the helper. He held firm to his original bargain, not even talking to the helper when others were present. However, he acknowledged that he wanted very much to be able to talk to the others but was held back by the same great fear that precluded him from conversing with the helper initially. At this point it became apparent that the same operant treatment approach that worked with the helper would be employed in helping the helpee to talk with someone else. Only now he wanted a bike!

Questions of who is on who's schedule may be asked. Dynamic interpretations of relationships may be made. What works works! Learning theory interpretations are only explanations of what works—and usually they come after the stability of effects has been established. In this instance it is clear that very concrete operant procedures were effectively integrated into a highly complex, relationship-oriented helping process. The helper was able to respond to the helpee's need to do something about his disability and he did so with great expertise. The helper was able to operationalize the critical dimensions of the goals of helping. The helper was able to draw upon all available resources to develop an effective course of action. The helper was able to develop a systematic program offering the highest success probabilities for achieving the goals of helping. The helper was able to effectively integrate the different approaches in a manner that assured the helpee of the greatest treatment benefits.

The helpee got his dog! And he will get his bike! And he will talk again. And he will live again—more fully and more effectively.

"GET THE BASTARD": INTEGRATING A CLASSICAL CONDITIONING APPROACH

The helpee, a young male college student in his early twenties, had been a severe stutterer since early childhood. He had been seen in relationship-oriented treatment for a semester prior to the development of an intense situational crisis that had great implications for his future life. The helpee wanted to make a career out of the military. He felt that a regular R.O.T.C. commission was contingent upon an effective presentation of his senior military thesis. In his junior year, although his paper was more than adequate, he had failed miserably in his presentation. He stuttered profusely. He knew that the military would be reluctant to commission a leader who fell apart in front of his men and he knew that he would fall apart again.

The helpee, although a person of superior talents and resources, was shaped from early childhood to seek the approval of others. He had learned that to do his best alienated others because his superior performance was a threat. Approval from critical others was always held back, and in his desperate search for acceptance he geared his efforts to a mean or modal level of output. He settled for the "nice guy" role, never threatening, never challenging, always walking a tightrope between failure and a minimally acceptable performance.

The helpee continued treatment with the helper, with the author sitting in as consultant. The helpee was introduced to the treatment procedure of desensitization as a means for diminishing or eliminating his stuttering. Based upon his helper's understanding of the helpee, and in conjunction with the helpee, a hierarchy of experiences involving the helpee's father as well as his instructor were formulated. The hierarchy began with those school and home items likely to elicit a minimal anxiety reaction from the helpee and moved in progressive gradations to those most likely to elicit an intense anxiety reaction. In addition, the process moved from working the individual stress situation through in imagery while the helpee was deeply relaxed to role-playing to acting out weekly assignments and finally to acting in real life. In each instance the helpee would let the helpers know when he experienced anxiety and the program would not move to the next item in the hierarchy until helpee's anxiety response to the particular item had been extinguished.

The helpee moved through the following hierarchy of experiences: (1) walking toward the critical class (home situation) where he must later in the year make an important presentation (explanation); (2) entering the empty classroom (home); (3) entering the classroom (home) in the absence of his instructor (father); (4) entering the classroom (home) in the presence of his instructor (father); (5) greeting his instructor (father); (6) responding to the instructor (father); (7) asserting himself with the instructor (father); (8) presenting his proposal in the presence of his instructor (father). Each of these phases, in turn, was broken down further. For example, after working through the last phase, presenting his thesis in imagery, the helpee actually enacted the following situations in a classroom of students set up specifically for the helpee's learning: (1) the helpee sat silently in class as another presented; (2) the helpee made a comment as one of the students; (3) the helpee made several comments; (4) the helpee's comments were responded to; (5) the helpee's comments were questioned; (6) the helpee's comments were criticized; (7) the helpee made his presentation by reading without comments from the class; (8) the class made comments on the helpee's presentation; (9) the helpee asserted himself in response to the comments; (10) the helpee recited a memorized presentation and responded to the comments; (11) the helpee made his final presentation in a fully spontaneous classroom atmosphere. At each of these substages the experience was repeated until the helpee felt no anxiety. Finally, the helpee made his presentation in military science and was graded for a superior performance by his instructor, who was unaware of the desensitization training.

The desensitization process did not always go smoothly. For example, after ten sessions of relaxation and desensitization training a seemingly impassable plateau was reached. The helpers returned to begin each new session with the last item in the hierarchy on which the helpee had extinguished in his anxiety response. After extinguishing on one item in one session the helpee was unable to demonstrate extinction on that same item in the next two sessions. The helpee recalled those difficult moments in a final and flawless presentation to a staff of professional helpers (Carkhuff & Berenson, 1967a).

HELPER 1: What set of things contributed most to where you are now?

HELPEE: Getting bawled out—a couple of times.

HELPER 2: I remember the day we said, "Let's junk the desensitization today and get the bastard."

HELPEE: Two weeks ago we just walked around the campus. It was a warm day, like today. You asked me about the talk I had to give to the R.O.T.C. class and I began to say things that—I was sure the talk would go lousy, and you jumped on me. Little things help, like "to hell what others think." I could tell that both of you were angry with me. You had a perfect reason to be ticked off at me. I was so foolish. We had some real good talks. I think that's the whole thing. As for (I don't know what it is called) desensitization, it's hard to say if it helps or not. It's been about a month. I think it helped a little bit. It's not the real thing. I used to picture scenes in my mind. I'd be asked if I was anxious, and raise my finger if I was nervous. I got to dislike it after a while. It might have helped a little. I don't know if it worked. It isn't like being here talking to the class.

HELPER 2: Somehow you have to translate the whole thing into action.

HELPEE: Somewhat. I did notice that after picturing the R.O.T.C. going there didn't seem to bother me as much. It helps to a certain extent, not completely, though, because it is not the real thing. . . . Ya, it gets you going. I used to picture classroom scenes; entering the class was a big thing.

HELPER 1: Are you aware of the resources you brought to bear? What did you contribute here?

HELPEE: When I first started, not much of anything really. Later on, my first presentation to this group, I was very embarrassed, everybody sitting around, knowing. It was very hard, very hard, believe me. First, just because it was a class, a group of people, and second, they did not know the whole story. I think the hardest part is going through these different things with other people, *live*. I think I really had to push myself. Had to push myself to come here for the practice sessions. The thing that really did it was sheer drive on my part to go through with it. Now, today, when I first came here it was completely different. I was relaxed.

HELPER 1: What did you tap in on in yourself?

HELPEE: Basically, I learned that what I feared I *could* do. Everything I feared I could not do, like speaking before a class, I found I could do.

HELPER 1: The systematic part gets the client started toward considering problem areas. After handling them in imagery you have to tap in on your own strengths. Maybe that's part of the unique contribution of behavior therapy.

HELPEE: Between sessions I used to try to put into action what we talked about, like, like I'm doing right now, here talking with you.

HELPER 1:   Who are we to you now? (*referring to the therapists collectively or separately*)

HELPEE: Well, I don't look on you as being doctors. I see you as, as friends. I almost think of you as being one of the guys, just a friend. The professional role stuff is gone. You've become people.

HELPER 1:   (*To the group*) I think some of you have to doubt.

HELPEE: (*Looking at the group*) If you want to ask me anything, ask me.

Frustrated by the limitations of relationship therapy yet benefiting from its contributions, the helpers were able to creatively integrate a systematic desensitization process based upon a dual hierarchy of instructor (school) and father (home) into a process offering high levels of core conditions. Again the helpers were able to respond to the helpee's need to do something about his disability, to operationalize the critical goals and the programs available, and to integrate the different approaches in a manner yielding the greatest treatment benefits to the helpee.

SUMMARY AND CONCLUSIONS

Experientially, the helpee reaches a point where he is keenly aware of his need to change distressing behavior patterns but unaware of how to do so. The helper who has been expert in eliciting the helpee's awareness of his need to change must also be expert in determining the courses of action that will enable the helpee to change. The helper must be aware of all treatment modalities available. He is not a helper until he is aware, for he will limit the degrees of freedom of the helpee, a freedom based not only upon accurate discriminations but also upon the availability of a repertoire of responses that are appropriate to the discriminations. The effective helper will know all that is knowable—and more—more because he is able to create in the moment a course of action that was not available before the moment. The effective helper should know how to implement the available preferred modes of treatment or, at a minimum, he should be aware of the treatments so that he can make the referral when it is appropriate or, as in the second case, incorporate an expert in the relevant modality into the helping process.

Again the principles of learning are the same as for any helping process. In regard to the helper's contribution, he establishes an experiential base for the helpee and serves as a model and teacher of appropriate behaviors. The helpee, in turn, explores himself in the relevant areas so that he can come to understand himself and, ultimately, to act upon this understanding.

The unique contributions of the systematic treatment approaches to the helpee are as follows (Carkhuff & Berenson, 1967b): (1) systematic approaches provide the helpee with an understanding of the treatment process and his role in it; (2) systematic approaches provide the helpee with a concrete awareness of his level of progress in the helping process; (3) systematic approaches provide the helpee with a useful knowledge of the history of the reinforcements that have created and sustained his symptoms; (4) systematic approaches provide the helpee with the knowledge that the helpee is guided by helpee feedback insofar as it fits the helper's system; (5) systematic approaches provide the helpee with an opportunity to actively accelerate the treatment process; (6) systematic approaches provide the helpee with an opportunity to deal with maladaptive autonomic functions; (7) systematic approaches provide the helpee with the assurance that the treatment is "curing" what it sets out to cure.

In regard to the contributions to the helper, systematic approaches do the following: (1) they provide the helper with a system of well-defined procedures; (2) they provide the helper with a well-defined role; (3) they provide the helper with a high and extremely useful level of confidence in what he is doing and where he is going; (4) they provide the helper with a means to become meaningfully involved beyond the treatment hour; (5) they provide the helper with an opportunity to make translations from helping to life; (6) they encourage the helper to attend fully to nonverbal cues; and (7) they provide the helper with a specific behavioral base for understanding helpee behavior.

The limitations of systematic approaches for both helpee and helper are primarily a function of rigid employment of the approach. That is, integrated in a helping process offering high levels of the core, facilitative, and action-oriented conditions, the helper will continue to be shaped by the feedback that he gets from the helpee concerning what is most effective for the helpee. Accordingly, the helper will modify the treatment procedures. Thus, the helpee's feedback cannot go beyond the scope of the helper's system. The helping experience will not be geared exclusively to public cues, to a minimal coping with the world, or to helpee complacency or an externalization or depersonalization of his difficulties. The helping experience can be one of creativity, self-fulfillment, and self-actualization for the helpee. Similarly for the helper, the assumption that the helper can become a potent reinforcer for the helpee rests safely in a creatively integrated approach. The dangers of aversive conditioning for both helper as well as helpee and the dangers of developing faulty models or schedules are all minimized by a high-level–functioning helper who is sensitive to the feedback he gets.

In addition to the many potential benefits for both helper and helpee, there are several conclusions that we can summarize concerning the development of effective courses of action.

Conclusion I. The development of effective courses of action provides clear direction leading to well-defined criteria of outcome.

Perhaps the most unique contribution of the development of courses of action is that they do something and they go somewhere. In this regard we can tell whether we arrived at where we intended to go. Accordingly, we can modify both the outcomes and the processes of achieving what can be achieved.

Conclusion II. The development of effective courses of action emphasizes practice of those behaviors we wish to affect.

Effective courses of action deal with what the helping process wishes to deal with. They are not vague and amorphous or only indirectly related to what they are attempting to accomplish. They provide practice in the behaviors we wish to modify or change.

Conclusion III. The development of effective courses of action provides the highest probabilities of achieving the desired outcome.

By developing progressive gradations of experience in which the helpee learns to walk before he learns to run, the approaches offer the highest success probabilities for the over-all treatment procedures. Successive success experiences reinforce the helpee to go all the way to achieve the desired changes.

Conclusion IV. The development of effective courses of action yields all of the benefits of any systematic approach.

Systematic programs may have benefits in and of themselves. Systematic approaches of any kind are preferable to unsystematic ones because they offer the prospect of new learning. In addition to the confidence that they give both helper and helpee, systematic approaches reduce the ambiguity and attendant anxiety in treatment, and this in itself may account for much of their success.

Conclusion V. The development of effective courses of action is accomplished most effectively in the context of a helping process built around high levels of core, facilitative, and action-oriented dimensions.

It is almost as if the formula for effective helping incorporates high levels of core conditions complemented by any systematic program that works. The essence of the eclectic approach is to focus upon the core, interpersonal dimensions that make a difference in human relations and to analyze the unique contributions over and above those of the core dimensions of all potential preferred modes of treatment.

In summary, the development of effective courses of action is in no way exclusive of a relationship-oriented helping process focusing upon high levels of core dimensions. Indeed, the focus upon the latter leads quite readily from exploration to understanding to action in a highly interactional process. Effective courses of action flow directly from and are most creatively integrated in a helping process that incorporates high levels of core, facilitative, and action-oriented dimensions. It is the helper's task to create the conditions that make the helpee amenable to the helper's influence. It is the helper's task to introduce those treatment procedures that offer the best prospects of achieving the goals of helping. It is in this context that the helpee can gain most. It is in this context that the helper can learn the most.

REFERENCES

For a more detailed discussion of the issues considered in this chapter see the asterisked readings and the references upon which the readings are based.

Bandura, A. Psychotherapy as a learning process. *Psychological Bulletin*, 1961, **58**, 143–157.

Carkhuff, R. R. Training in counseling and therapeutic processes: Requiem or reveille? *Journal of Counseling Psychology*, 1966, **13**, 360–367.

Carkhuff, R. R. The contributions of a phenomenological approach to deterministic approaches to counseling. *Journal of Counseling Psychology*, 1967, **14**, 570–572.

Carkhuff, R. R., & Berenson, B. G. *Beyond counseling and therapy*. New York: Holt, Rinehart and Winston, Inc., 1967. (a)

*Carkhuff, R. R., & Berenson, B. G. To act or not to act: The unique contributions of behavior modification approaches. In *Beyond counseling and therapy*. New York: Holt, Rinehart and Winston, Inc., 1967. (b)

Eysenck, H. J. (ed.) *Behavior therapy and the neuroses*. New York: Pergamon Press, 1960.

Frank, J. D. *Persuasion and healing*. Baltimore, Md.: The Johns Hopkins Press, 1961.

*Krasner, L., & Ullmann, L. *Research in behavior modification*. New York: Holt, Rinehart and Winston, Inc., 1965.

Salter, A. *Conditioned reflex therapy*. New York: Capricorn, 1961.

Salzinger, K. Experimental manipulation of verbal behavior: A review. *Journal of General Psychology*, 1959, **61**, 65–95.

Shaw, F. J. (ed.) *Behavioristic approaches to counseling and psychotherapy.* University of Alabama Studies, 1961, No. 13.

*Ullmann, L., & Krasner, L. *Case studies in behavior modification.* New York: Holt, Rinehart and Winston, Inc., 1965.

Wolpe, J. *Psychotherapy by reciprocal inhibition.* Stanford, Calif.: Stanford University Press, 1958.

Wolpe, J., Salter, A., & Rayna, L. *The conditioning therapies.* New York: Holt, Rinehart and Winston, Inc., 1964.

10
GROUP TRAINING AS A PREFERRED MODE OF TREATMENT

Five years ago Matarazzo (1965), in his review of counseling and psycho-therapeutic processes, concluded that group helping processes, particularly group therapy, are primarily a "self taught art with few, if any, established principles to guide (them)." The traditional controversies among Locke, Slavson, Schwartz, and Wolf, who focus upon the individual helpee within the group, and Berne and Leary, who focus upon interpersonal relationships within the group, and Bion, Ezriel, Foulkes, Frank, and Redl who focus upon the interaction between the group and the individual, does nothing to clear this picture. Indeed, the issues of long-term naturalistic group psychotherapeutic processes versus short-term "experimental" group dynamics programs and individually oriented group psychotherapy versus the group as a unit school seem calculated more to cloud the lack of substantive findings and direction than to free us of it. The recent advent of a bewildering array of so-called growth groups (Gazda, 1969; Lubin, 1967)—the encounter and marathon groups (Bach, 1966; Moustakas, 1966; Murphy, 1969; Stoller, 1967), the self-directed groups (Berzon, 1966; Rogers, 1967), and the sensitivity and "T" groups (Benne, 1969; Bradford, Gibb, & Benne, 1964; Schein and Bennis, 1961)—has done nothing to advance an extremely distressing state of affairs (Carkhuff, 1969a). There is little to recommend reviewing any of these positions, for in comparative studies they are not even competitive with more direct, simple, and forthright approaches to effecting change in groups.

In the interest of finding some direction in an essentially directionless body of gimmicks and techniques, let us review and extend some essential propositions giving rise to group helping processes. The first two

129

propositions deal with helping in general and lead directly to the latter propositions, which deal with group processes specifically.

Proposition I. The core of functioning or dysfunctioning (health or psychopathology) is interpersonal.

The assumption here is that interpersonal processes reflect intrapersonal dynamics, or, conversely, that what is going on within the individual is manifested in what goes on between individuals. In any event people are institutionalized in one way or another for what goes on between rather than within individuals.

Proposition II. The core of the helping process (learning or relearning) is interpersonal.

Constructive interpersonal learning experiences constitute the corrective antidote for destructive interpersonal learning experiences. Again the conditions of constructive interpersonal experiences are the inverse of those that led to the development of difficulties in living in the first place. In individual counseling the helper is the helpee's most significant source of new learning in this regard, for he alone offers the prospect of integrating the modeling, the experiential, and the didactic sources of learning.

Proposition III. Group processes are the preferred mode of working with difficulties in interpersonal functioning.

We can do anything in group treatment that we can do in individual treatment—and more. Since groups are inherently interpersonal, they offer the helpee the means not only to relate to the helper and himself with the helper's guidance but also to relate to other members of the group and to the group as a whole. Group processes offer the prospect for the greatest amount of learning for the greatest number of people at one time.

Proposition IV. Systematic group training in interpersonal functioning is the preferred mode of work with difficulties in interpersonal functioning.

We can do anything in training that we can do in treatment—and more. Training in interpersonal skills strikes at the heart of most difficulties in living. Systematic training in interpersonal skills affords a means of implementing the necessary learning in progressive gradations of experience which insure the success of the learning. In making explicit use of all sources of learning—the experiential, the didactic, and the modeling—systematic group training in interpersonal skills provides the most effective, economical, and efficient means of achieving the individual growth of the largest number of persons.

Again the key throughout all group helping processes is the level of functioning of the leader (Carkhuff, 1969b, 1969c, 1969d). If helpees work intensively and extensively with a high-level–functioning helper, the helpees will improve in a variety of significant ways. If the helper provides an atmosphere in which the helpees can move toward higher levels of functioning, then each individual group member has multiple potential helpers. Let us explore one group interaction, one in which the helpees or trainees were parents of so-called emotionally disturbed children.

This training experience was implemented according to the following paradigm: (1) each parent was assessed on his level of interpersonal functioning with each other and with his child; (2) parents from one family were cast in helping interactions with parents from other families about adult concerns; (3) each parent role-played his troubled child in working with a parent from a different family unit; (4) parents from the same family unit worked with each other in helping interactions; (5) each parent role-played his troubled child in working with the other parent (spouse) from the same family unit; (6) both parents from a family unit worked with the troubled child who was brought into the clinic for this purpose.

SYSTEMATIC TRAINING FOR PARENTS OF EMOTIONALLY DISTURBED CHILDREN

The following taped material will provide brief illustrations of systematic training for parents of children designated as emotionally disturbed on the basis of their destructive behavioral patterns. With the assumption that the child's disturbance is at least in part a function of (1) the level of interpersonal functioning between parents and (2) the level of interpersonal functioning between the individual parents and the child, a training program in interpersonal skills was provided for parents on a clinic waiting list. These parents might not otherwise have been seen or in any event would not have been seen for at least a year. In this instance five couples met twice weekly over a two-month period. Both the parents and the children were pre- and posttested on a variety of different testing indexes, including the real-life indexes assessing the parents' interpersonal functioning with each other and with their children.

During the first two-hour session the therapist-trainer introduced himself and some of his relevant background and the parent-trainees did likewise. The trainees were then given a set to write down the most helpful responses they could develop to a number of helpee stimulus expressions. Following this the trainers were instructed to rate alternative helper responses to the helpee stimulus expressions. This pretesting served not only to provide an index of communication and discrimination for each trainee but also to introduce the trainees to a program in communication training. The trainer then introduced very briefly some of the research and theoretical background for the training group and then introduced, also very briefly and in operational terms, the dimension of empathic understanding or empathy specifically.

In the first illustration we hear the trainer, very early in training, introducing himself as a model for a helper in a role-playing experience:

"SOME KIND OF A MODEL"

TRAINER: In a sense, I think I'm—for better or for worse—initially—I'm providing some kind of a model of what I want you to do—and there are two thoughts that I have. One is initially to listen—and that's a hard one—but I'm going to listen for a while. Oh, I might say a little thing or two but I'm going to listen—to try to understand—and just forget about you people as much as I can. And, second, to try and, you know, give you back at least what I do understand.

KAREN: Uh huh.

TRAINER: So. . . .

KAREN: Well, what do you want me—what am I supposed to talk about? . . .

TRAINER: Well, you can just pick up where you left off last week if you want—or things that have gone on between Tuesday and now, or maybe things you have on your mind that you haven't talked about or concerns that you have about this—or just about anything.

KAREN: (*Pause*) Trying to think what I could. . . .

TRAINER: It is hard to get started—but—it is an artificial situation in some ways but an opportunity that you can use. . . .

TONY: Can I give her one word that'll kick her off (*Laugh*), something I know of that came up?

KAREN: Do! Do!

TONY: Lunches.

KAREN: Well, we have a bit of a problem at home. We have five children in school that require lunches, and the girls, there are three older girls—13, 12, and 10—the 12-year-old and the 10-year-old are supposed to do the lunches—and we do it in a manner of every week or every two weeks they make a batch of sandwiches and freeze them, but they don't get it done and as long as it is their job I—I don't know how to get them to do it. You tell them to do it and they stall around and stall around. I get so frustrated that—I don't want to spank them—or, actually, it's just a case of maybe putting a little iron into my soul and actually getting them to do it—and how to do it. I suppose we really haven't—I haven't gotten mad enough or frustrated enough at them to really sit down and solve the problem—to actually get them to do this particular job and other jobs that they're told to do without punishing them physically—well, actually just punishing them.

TRAINER: Well, it's really their will against yours and right now you're losing.

KAREN: Yes, because I don't think I have actually settled—or I guess I just haven't settled it in my own mind—that this is just what is going to be and they. . . .

TRAINER: You're just not sure of yourself. Right?

KAREN: Probably.

TRAINER: Yea.

KAREN: That's right—that's right.

TRAINER: But meantime, it hurts to be taken advantage of.

KAREN: And I want somebody to tell me what to do so I can go turn around and do it and tell them what to do and then if they don't do it and I don't quite know enough to do it, I want somebody else (*laugh*) to tell me what to do in order to get them to do it.

TRAINER: But—kind of crazy but like—"Everything depends on me but I want to depend on somebody."

KAREN: Right. (*Pause*) I. . . .

TRAINER: . . . "I'm not the big strong. . . ."

KAREN: No. That's right because—well. . . .

TRAINER: ". . . person that everyone takes me to be—and take advantage of. . . ."

KAREN: I don't—there are a lot of cases I just don't know what to do with. I don't know how to handle them and as I look back, they often say, "The way you were brought up in your home is the way it's going to be in this home," but while our home wasn't that bad—but there was certainly a lack of leadership on my father's part and I can't remember as I try to think—I just can't remember how things were and so I don't know how to handle these things now.

TRAINER:	Well, it's kind of like—you're—well, you're looking around for something to hang your hat on but that doesn't really feel like the answer, do you think? You don't get the answer—even though people say it—that's not the answer.
KAREN:	No. I want something more or less concrete, something I can . . .
TRAINER:	You also want something more from your husband.
KAREN:	Yea. Right. Right.
TRAINER:	You know, the main thing that's come across, though, is that, "God, everybody thinks that I'm a fountain that never runs out, and I do run out and it does get too much for me sometimes."
KAREN:	Oh, I don't know if I can go along with that.
TRAINER:	O.K. Now, I'm pushing a little bit there. I'm going to stop it here just for a minute. (*To group*): You go ahead and rate it. I did do something there that—that's my problem, though, but go ahead. You go ahead and rate it.
KAREN:	I'm going to get a piece of paper.
TRAINER:	O.K. Come on up here, though. (*Trainee laughs*) This is going to be the first time we're going to go around the class on a rating but—by the way, you're not bound to rate the instructor high—but we're going to do this a lot. You'll become familiar with it. What I ask you to do—by the way, if you can, take out a separate sheet for this kind of stuff because what I'll be asking you to do is write your ratings down first so that you're not influenced by anybody. You know, if everybody's saying 5 and you have 1, you might change it to 3 or 4 by the time it gets around to you and we want to avoid that. O.K.!
TRAINEE 1:	I had rated it 3.
TRAINEE 2:	4.
TRAINEE 3:	3.
TRAINEE 4:	3.5.
TRAINEE 5:	3.
TRAINEE 6:	2.
TRAINEE 7:	3.5.
TRAINER:	All right, then, I think now we come to the critical person. (*To trainee*): What were the experiences going through your mind? I'll share mine with you.
KAREN:	I. . . .
TRAINER:	Well, how did you feel? You know, it was difficult getting started.
KAREN:	Well, after I got started it was easy.
TRAINER:	You know, did you lose the group? Did you forget about them?
KAREN:	Yea.
TRAINER:	Did you feel that—you know—I had some kind of a minimal level of understanding of what you were talking about?
KAREN:	Yes, except for that last point because I never really did look at it quite that way.

TRAINER: Yea. Right. I was going to say that's my problem. And my problem is that it's almost like I want to move on to what I see— to what I see behind and I really started to up it—or depending upon how you look at it—if I was missing her then you would rate me below 3 at the end; if I were hitting it at deeper and deeper levels then you would rate it up toward 4 or 5. Do you follow me now? Just a basic illustration.

TRAINER: *(To member of group):* I think you felt I was missing her at the end.

MEMBER OF
GROUP: Uh huh.

TRAINER: Right. And a couple of the others felt that I was staying with her a little bit beyond where she was presenting herself and they had it at 3.5 or 4. But, in other words, I wasn't doing just what I said I was going to do. I—it just hit me and I shared it. . . .

KAREN: Uh huh.

TRAINER: Your look now tells me that, you know, you're going to have to digest it—you're going to have to think about it.

KAREN: Uh huh.

TRAINER: And you're going to have to work on it.

KAREN: Uh huh. I have to think about a lot of things twice.

The trainer presents himself not only as a model for functioning effectively interpersonally—for listening and, more important, hearing and communicating what he is hearing—but also as a model for someone who is putting himself "on the line," who is making his skills known to the trainees. In this instance the trainer did go beyond his stated original purpose, but he did so because his immediate experience dictated that he make the experience "full," that he communicate the product of all of his senses, what he could see as well as what he could hear from the other person. In a very real sense the trainer was, very early in training, assuming the reins as parent of a parents' group and in so doing implicitly demanding that each trainee do likewise both in training and in his respective family situation.

In the next illustration the trainees begin to take their own turns as helper and helpee in the role-playing experience:

"A MATTER OF HEARING"

TRAINER: Everybody has an idea about what we're going to shoot for at level 3. We're going to try—we're going to do this with each other and I think I'll break up families a little bit. I think we'll do it with each other later but to get started now it might be helpful. I'm even going to structure it more. I'm going to insist that you listen—I won't keep a stopwatch on you, but let's say you have to listen—after you help the person get started if he has any difficulty—you have to listen for a minute and following that minute I want you to begin your response to him or her by saying, "You feel . . ." or "You feel that. . . ." I just want you to start there. I don't use it that much but it gives you some kind of structure and it pins you down a little bit. You know you'll have to make some sort of delivery. You'll have to let us know one way or the other whether you heard this person. O.K.! Those will be the ground rules. Take a deep breath (*laugh*)—"I don't want to be first." (*Group laughs*) O.K.! But the more we practice it the easier it will be—the more courage we'll have to do the kinds of things that we're going to ask our kids to do. Now the other thing is—one of the homework assignments was that you each play with your kid for an hour and you try to get a feel for, you know, what's really going on in this relationship. "Who am I?" and "Who is he?" "How am I helpful?" "How am I harmful?" "How do I make things go well?" "What's he doing to help or hurt the relationship?" O.K. When you assume the role of the helpee, that is a person like Karen, who was the first with me last week, that is, somebody talking about her problems, I want you to talk about that. (*Pause*) O.K.! In other words, you don't have to have that structured— I want you to feel your way around it—and find your own words for it now. As much as you can, you know, lose your self-consciousness of being with a group and don't worry about grammar and so on; I don't too much. O.K.? O.K.! So, these things: the helper listens for a minute and he begins at least his first expression, and he can begin all his expressions with this— and let's just find out, you know, how helpful this can be if you are, in fact, tuned in and the helpee is talking about the experience he had with the kid. O.K.! (*Pause*) Well, Ann, do you want to be helper or helpee first?

ANN: I don't know. I'll be a bad one. (*Laugh*)

TRAINER: I'll tell you what—why don't you be helper, and Tom, why don't you be helpee? In other words, just try to describe as well as you can what the situation was like with your kid. Let's put you together a little bit—or you could just move around. That'll be good. You can come over here.

ANN: Do we have to rate?

TRAINER: Yea. And I want you to rate—and later on I'll give you a way to rate the helpee. We'll call him helpee—I don't know, does anybody know a better word? Tony?

TONY: No, that's very expressive, I think.

TRAINER: O.K. Yea. I—I'm working on a . . .

TONY: I don't like "client."

TRAINER: I'm working on a book now and I have about 16 chapters and I don't think I've mentioned "therapist" or "client" in it.

TONY: That's good!

TRAINER: It's "helper" and "helpee." I just . . .

MARY: How about "rater" and "ratee"? (*Laugh*)

TRAINER: Well, that's appropriate, too.

TOM: Well, I don't think that—we went roller skating—I took him roller skating, which he likes—he's very good at it—but I had a hard time of even driving over to the rink, to really take up, you know, what the start of the conversation would be and I think that in a way he kind of, you know, realized, this attention—to get more attention than the other children—and it was kind of hard for me, you know, to even start a conversation with him, but when we got to the rink we were, you know, all happy and I felt happy, too, but I really don't think that I really got the feeling, you know, like a father and a son should have. When he was happy, you know, when he was learning "shooting the duck," when you bend down and skate on one leg and hold the other one like so and he caught on real well—he done real good—you know, I felt kind of proud of him, you know, being able to do as good as he was when all the other kids were falling down. And I said, "Gee, you do that real good," but I felt that maybe I could even, really, have said more, and praised him more to let him know. There still seemed to be sort of a—little tension there or some kind of a . . .

ANN: . . . barrier.

TOM: . . . some type of barrier. In other words, the feeling wasn't quite—I wasn't getting quite the feeling he was, even though I was really sitting there trying to—this didn't work out the way I thought it was going to, but he, like, he was enjoying it and I was enjoying watching him, you know, performing. But then, on the way home, he wanted cotton candy so we bought that. He didn't want to eat it right away and all I could think of was, you know, "How am I going to explain it to the other kids when we get home?" You know, in other words, I really didn't know how to tell him not to have it and yet it was all right to buy it. I had a hard time explaining and talking to him. I don't think we accomplished a great deal—as much as I would like to have accomplished, but I think we accomplished something, anyway.

ANN: You feel, then, that it was less rewarding than you had thought—it left you with a feeling of frustration that the whole thing didn't quite measure up.

TOM: I don't think that was it. Actually, I don't think I was happy with myself, you know. I was trying to make him feel more—

happier and more—but he accomplished something more—he really accomplished something. I didn't give him that much encouragement. I could have given him a lot more but he still . . .

ANN: Well, you felt really dissatisfied yourself.

TOM: Myself, right.

ANN: Uh huh.

TOM: With myself, but . . .

ANN: But don't you think that might come with maybe more practice, and the more you do it, the more easier it becomes?

TOM: I hope so. I mean, you know . . .

ANN: You also said that you didn't have a feeling of father and son out together. Would you say that you had a sort of unnatural, unreal feeling about it?

TOM: Not really unreal—just felt that—I felt that maybe we could have, well, maybe if I had participated in skating we could have have had a really good time—you know, a ball—if you really want to call it.

ANN: But did you feel that he had a good time?

TOM: I felt he had a good time.

ANN: Did he say so?

TOM: Yes, he said he had a good time. But, you know, it made me feel good, too, but . . .

ANN: He probably did.

TOM: In other words, the most difficult time that comes to mind was getting the conversation started on the way over and on the way back. On the way back I was—not really, you know—I was kind of worried about him buying the cotton candy and coming home and the other five kids, you know, saying "Where's my candy?"

ANN: Uh huh.

TOM: I don't think—you know—I really put myself in his place at that particular time—as much as I should have. Now . . .

ANN: Well, on the way over—on the way over to the skating rink— he knew where he was going. Did he say anything about how happy he was to be going?

TOM: Well, he just wanted to know if he could ask the man about, you know, buying a pair of shoe skates.

ANN: Uh huh.

TOM: And I told him, "If you save up half of the money, you know, then I'll give you the other half."

ANN: Uh huh.

TOM: And he was kind of happy about that, but right way he wanted to know how much it was going to cost and how much they sell for, you know . . .

ANN: (*Laugh*) Uh huh. He's realistic about that, isn't he?

TOM: That he is! But, other than—because I didn't participate, actually, in the roller skating, which I would like to have done but I had to leave to get a haircut and then come back, but— because I was planning on . . . he would be interesting without— making it look . . .

ANN: Real obvious or set up.

TRAINER: O.K. Let's stop it for now. I'm going to ask—immediately I'll just set this as a pattern—I'll ask for ratings and then we'll open up for discussion. Well, Tony? Be as honest as you can on these ratings because we're not going to—O.K.—let me share this with you. In my experience, when we hear somebody responding as we just heard Ann, you say, "Gee, I don't know if I can do as well as she can do," and yet—I'm not trying to rate it for you—and yet you say, "And yet she wasn't, you know, it wasn't really as good as it could be but I don't know if I could do that well so I'll give it a good rating"—and I leave room for me! What I'm really doing is leaving room for me in my rating and I don't think we do learn from it then. I'm not saying this to tell you to be hard and cruel, just to rate it as honestly as you can, and that's what we'll learn from.

KAREN: Well, I felt that—other than—I felt that first she was off at the beginning but then she improved with him. I would say a 3.

STAN: 2.

TONY: Almost 3.

IRENE: I'm inclined to agree with you. I felt it was almost 3.

MARY: I rated it 2. I kind of felt that she missed the point.

TRAINER: O.K. Go ahead, did you want to express further?

MARY: Yes, I was going to say that I felt what he was saying was that he had wanted to communicate with his son but he felt that perhaps he wasn't going about it in the right way or he just didn't really know how to open it up, and at the same time when he went into the bit about the cotton candy, I felt that he had wanted to act out his own role in the way that—he wanted to tell him he couldn't have it because of what he felt would go on at home with the other children but at the same time he didn't know how to do it without making himself look bad in the child's eyes.

TRAINER: Any other comments from the other people? How about having —let's look at one of the central things that's always going to be with you in relation to the child, but let's first just start with Tom and we'll get to this other thing. (*Addressing helpee*): What was your experience, as honestly as you can say?

TOM: About—some things she understood what I was trying to say— and in other things I think that I missed her in that I didn't express myself, you know, the way that I should have, but . . .

ANN: I think it was more listening—just to . . .

TRAINER: You're saying, "I didn't help her as much as I should."

TOM: Probably not—in explaining the situation—of course—my wife, she knew more about it, though . . .

TRAINER: Sure! Sure!

TOM: But . . .

TRAINER: Well, some wives do and some wives don't.
(*Group laughs*)

TOM: But she hit—I think she hit the nail on the head when she said that, you know . . .

TRAINER: O.K. So then, you're really talking about—this is just in relation to your role—you really thought almost about reversing roles. You're saying, "I didn't help her enough to make her a good helper." You're almost saying that.

TOM: Yes.

TRAINER: O.K. Ann?

ANN: Well, I thought I understood what he was saying. I could feel fully his—I would have thought he was frustrated and discouraged as, you know, starting out—he wanted to make this a real father and son communication deal and he felt that he couldn't think of a thing to say to this child that would make the child talk or make him want to talk—in making conversation—and he was angry with himself or frustrated with himself for not being able to do this.

TRAINER: Now, I know you felt similar kinds of things in relation to your own.

ANN: Uh huh.

TRAINER: Could you really feel that now or you could feel that in relation . . .

ANN: Oh, yes! Oh, yes!

TRAINER: You could experience just where he is?

ANN: Um hum.

TRAINER: O.K. One of the thoughts I had was to play that record back if that tape's good enough. I haven't listened to any of these yet. Would you like to hear it back?

ANN: Uh huh.

TRAINER: O.K. (*Plays tape back*)

TRAINER: Here are a few things that I wrote down—just—I don't think I really had to write them down but I did it. I just said, "He tried to get through hard but he couldn't," and, "I had tried real hard." He wanted something more from this thing, and yet he didn't quite get it.

ANN: Uh huh.

TRAINER: I have a need to go beyond that, you know, that he really in a way hoped for so much more and then he raised the question that Mary raised—you know, "If I love this kid and really want to enjoy him, can I set limits too?" And not put the other kids

	in a position of, you know, "How's he getting all this special treatment?"
ANN:	Uh huh.
TRAINER:	And, you know, that in general, I think in the present situation you want to do so much for him. The personal things that I got if you cut it a little deeper—what I have written down here is that "I have so much love in me for this kid that if I only knew how to do it and if this kid will only let me give it to him." But that's cutting a little deeper. That's not the 3 that I'm asking for now, but it wasn't far off if you had let it happen. I'm not far off there. It wasn't bad. Let me say that, in summary, it wasn't bad at all. But I think the thing that we're going to tune in on more and more here is not even a matter of just listening; it's a matter of hearing, and hearing's different from listening. First, we have to learn how to listen, then we have to learn how to hear.

The trainer structures the role-playing experience, particularly for the helper. While the helpee must relate personally relevant material, in this instance based upon a homework assignment in which he had to work with his troubled child, the helper's directions are quite explicit. The helper must listen for a defined period of time—in the hope that he can hear. The helper must formulate responses that are interchangeable in terms of the feeling and personal meaning that the helpee was expressing—in the hope of establishing a base of communication that lets the helpee know that the helper at least understands what the helpee has expressed. The helper must formulate his initial responses in a reflective paradigm beginning with, "You feel . . ."—in the hope of establishing a responsive set on the part of the helper and in the hope of getting the helper to put his understanding "on the line." As we hear, rules are made to be broken. But the basic rule of all effective training is that the rules are made to be broken—at the risk of the learner. The training program does not develop to the exclusion of the very individualistic concerns of the group members. Within the training structure a great deal of a therapeutic nature takes place. In the next excerpt one of the trainees brings up problems involving his own unique phenomenology:

"YOUR CHILD CAN DREAM. CAN MINE?"

BILL:	You take two men that are trying to think what a child thinks—like take ten people from a different race and try to figure what they think—how they feel—if you're not of the same race—you try to figure what their thoughts are but you can't think

what their thoughts are because you're not one of them and it's the same way with a child—we could stay all night, and with all our background and all, the raising of our children and all that—maybe one may have ten, another five—you're trying to put it all together, you're trying to think what is the best for the child and all of us would be thinking—maybe what the thoughts of one individual child would be—but there's no way in—excuse the expression—no way in hell that you could figure what was in your child's mind, because if you did know what was in your child's mind, then you wouldn't have to be coming to these sessions. That's the way I figure, because you would know how to cope with the situation right away if you knew what was in his mind. You'd know what to do about it.

TRAINER: I can hear you at three different levels. At one level, to some degree, you know in terms of the content of what you're saying—to some degree there's a lot to what you're saying, although I think it can be argued . . .

BILL: Well, I guess there are always pros and cons . . .

TRAINER: Ah, at the other level—and it's more basic to me—you're saying, "I'm just not that optimistic any more."

BILL: Well, you could call it optimistic or whatever you want to call it, but it's just bare facts . . .

TRAINER: "I just don't have as much hope now as I had along the way."

BILL: No, it's not that you don't have hope. You always have hope, but it—it's not the idea that you don't have hope—it's just—you just wonder some time, "Is this it?"

TRAINER: Well, that's O.K. Can I—could I really understand how low you can get?

BILL: I can get pretty low some time. I can get as low as, well, let's face it—if you want to go that route—but that's the bottom of the ocean and nobody knows how deep the ocean is.

TRAINER: Or, let me push it even further—could I ever really understand how low a black man can get?

BILL: Yea, That's it. Yea. You can say that. Sometimes you can say that. I mean, you talk about your, I mean you can tell your child one thing but can I tell my child the same thing—you see that's what would be going through my mind—understand—you can make excuses to your child; you have everything to work with, but can I say the same thing to mine? Your child can dream. Can mine dream?

One member of the parents' group brings up a problem to the parent of the parents' group. He poses the question in terms of whether any parent could ever understand a child. In terms of immediacy the trainer answers the question by understanding the trainee. The trainer helps the trainee to know that the trainee as a parent may come to understand his child by helping the trainee to know that the trainer can understand the trainee. The trainer would be unable to do this if he did not assume the reins as parent of the parents' group and thus provide a model for the trainees to assume the reins as parents of their family group. The trainer would also be unable to understand the trainee if he did not accept, at the deepest level, that he could never be black and see the world as a black man. In turn, the parent can understand the child only if he accepts, at the deepest level, that he cannot be a child and see the world as a child.

Along the same lines, in the next excerpt a husband plays his child in interaction with his wife as helper. The interaction leads directly to confrontations between members of the group and its leader:

"YOU SURE IN HELL DIDN'T WANT IT TO BE A WASHOUT"

JOE: So, I wasn't going to fire them off. I was just trying to sell them.

ANN: So you feel that it was perfectly all right to have these fire-crackers.

JOE: Well, why not? Everybody else had them. I'm not the only one, and I wasn't going to shoot them off. I just wanted to make a little money.

ANN: And you feel that the principal had treated you as though you had broken the law.

JOE: Well, yea! I mean, they all jumped on me, and after all I didn't shoot anything off, so dopey over there shot one off and tipped the whole thing. If he hadn't done it nobody would have found out.

ANN: And then it wouldn't have been wrong for you to have taken them there in the first place.

JOE: Why, no. Of course not.

ANN: You think, then, that it was the fault of the boy who shot off one of these firecrackers.

JOE: Well, they were just little bitty ones—I mean—even if he did shoot one off—what's the damage with that? Nothing got broken, nothing got burned up.

ANN: And nobody got hurt.

JOE: No.

ANN: But they could have. Huh?

JOE: Well, I don't know. But nothing went wrong except that I got blamed for it.

ANN: None of the other boys got blamed?

JOE: Oh, yea—they caught the other guys with it but I got the worst of it. They jumped on me—she goes calling you up on the tele-phone.

ANN: Would you have told me about it if she hadn't called me?

JOE: Well, no.

ANN: Well, if you thought it was all right to do this, what would have been the harm, then, in telling me?

JOE: You know as well as I do that you would have taken them away from me.

ANN: And you don't think that you ever would have shot one of these things off—the ones that you didn't sell? Would you really have done this?

JOE: Well, I was going to sell them. I wouldn't have any to shoot off.

ANN: Well, what if you didn't sell them all? What would you have done with the rest of them?

JOE: Well, I don't know. I would have shot them.

ANN: Oh? But you know that's against the law.

JOE: Oh, so what?

ANN: And you feel that getting caught was the real crime?

JOE: Well, yea!

ANN: But no harm was done unless you got caught?

JOE: Sure—well—that's—(I'm losing the phraseology and I should remember it)—but—Yea, as long as you don't get caught. What the heck.

ANN: So you feel that the principal and the teachers and the kids around you—they're the ones at fault, right?

JOE: Well, listen, there are always those finks—this one in particular. He's always, always getting me in trouble and the other guys in trouble, too. I'm not the only one. They blame it on me but there's Jack and Jim . . .

ANN: Why do you suppose they do that? Why do you suppose they single you out to put the blame on?

JOE: Oh, I don't know.

ANN: Do you suppose it could be because of other things that you've done?

JOE: Well, the other guys have been doing other stuff, too, all the time.

ANN: But they don't get caught?

JOE: No. They don't get the kind of stuff I do.

ANN: All right.

JOE: That's just about where it ended up anyway . . .

ANN: Uh huh. It did.

JOE: This being a packet of firecrackers he had picked up from another kid in the neighborhood and he took them down to school with him yesterday to peddle them off to the boys—to get a few cents.

TRAINER: All right. I'm going to follow a routine, but let's go quick around on the ratings. I want you to comment. I want you to dig in a little bit.

JOE: I'm trying to play it back—about as I remember it's a 3.

KAREN: I'm just trying to think. She was—she was understanding in what he was saying and yet . . .

TRAINER: Somehow it didn't go anywhere.

KAREN: She was definitely the mother.

TRAINER: O.K. Give it a rating. Good. That's good.

KAREN: Oh, I would say she was—as far as understanding I would say she was about a 3.

TRAINER: Tony?

TONY: I say a solid 3.

TRAINER: All right. Let's go around once and then pick up . . .

STAN: Pushing 4—hard on a 4.

MARY: I agree that it was a 4.

IRENE: 3 to 4.

TOM: 3.

BILL: I said 3.5.

JANE: It's a 5.

TRAINER: All right. Let's pick up where you left off.

KAREN: Well, I was rating it in a way we rated it before. She was—she didn't seem to give him any . . .

TRAINER: . . . direction. Now we come pretty fully around It was helpful along the way—now we're coming pretty fully around to realizing the limitations of the kind of rating we've been doing.

KAREN: Yea.

TRAINER: And yet we want to know that whatever she's going to do is going to be based in a good level of understanding. All right. Tony?

TONY: Yea, I felt that it was a good 3. I thought she was hearing what he was saying but I—(*laugh*)—I couldn't help but share the same feeling. I didn't know where to go with it. I wouldn't have . . .

TRAINER: That's where you were, Tony—you know—"O.K. So even if I dig in, 'What the hell do I do with this?' "

TONY: I had the same thing happen. I didn't know where to go with it. I got this far and I couldn't . . .

JOE: You see, that's the point. You're not fooling anything. The agreement is there. You're reading . . .

TRAINER: Right. Right.

JOE: O.K. Yea. That's it. That's the way it is. "And I don't give a damn." That was the only thing that I c uld read over and above what he said because he didn't say that, but it was the one thing I was reading all the way through this and I was not in this situation. I was out in the other room tuned in while she was . . .

TRAINER: But you did tune in. As Ann tuned in on you. You felt that you were tuned in at that level.

JOE: Oh, yea, yea. I was reading it about the same that she was—
                as she was making the remarks I gave her a 3—yesterday. But
                that was the "I don't give a damn" and that's all I read be-
                yond it.
ANN: That's in every incident that comes up with him.
STAN: I felt Ann was tuned in. She had to be to direct it to draw out
                more comments. If you weren't tuned in, you couldn't possibly
                be asking the questions to draw out more of what was the in-
                volvement.
TRAINER: But did you have the sense of frustration that—you know—at
                the same time "I wanted to go some place and I don't—I haven't
                brought this thing to any kind of fruition . . ."?
STAN: Well, looking at it from the understanding part, this is where
                I felt that she led it and brought greater understanding but
                then it was a hot potato.
TRAINER: All right. Understanding has to lead someplace.
STAN: Right. The understanding was there.
TRAINER: O.K.
STAN: But all of a sudden, "Who gets it?" (*All laugh*)
TRAINER: Irene?
IRENE: Well, I felt that she was tuned into him, and from the conver-
                sation I took it that the child figured, "Well, I get blamed for
                everything anyway. I might just as well be the big shot and go
                all the way because I'm going to get it whether I do it or not"—
                and . . .
TRAINER: (*To Ann*) Do you hear that? Do you hear what Irene is saying?
ANN: He has said this on some occasions—that he might as well have
                as much fun because no matter what happens he's going to get
                blamed for it.
TRAINER: Well, Irene's saying a little more than that, I think.
IRENE: Well, he might just as well be the big shot.
TRAINER: "Having been caught at it I might just as well be a big shot
                about it—and make you live with this. Let me see what you
                can do."
JOE: Now you're coming back to the indestructible.
TRAINER: For you it'll have to come back there—not necessarily for Ann.
                But for any one of you who's facing this situation—"I'm going
                to see what you can do with this." You know, "I'm caught al-
                ready anyway. Now I'm going to find out . . ."
JOE: "O.K., wise guy, ad lib . . ."
ANN: ". . . how good you are."
TRAINER: And wait a minute, "Let's find out what you can do with it.
                What you got."
IRENE: Yet, I can't help but to sit here and wonder. Is it wise to let the
                children know that we are coming to the clinic for this particu-
                lar—for them—or because of them. Now, I myself have not

told the children that we are going to the clinic because of
Michael. They know we're going to a workshop, and I haven't
really delved into anything. I have had no questions or any
rebuttal and I feel perfectly at ease with talking to them.

TRAINER: But I think that's—are you going to relate it to this situation?
You mean that the effect that it has on the kids . . .

IRENE: Yes, that they might think, "Well, you're going for all the answers, now you . . ."

ANN: Come up with some.

TRAINER: Oh, I see.

IRENE: Come up with the answers.

JOE: Drag it out.

TRAINER: You've had this reaction long before you came to the clinic.

STAN: "I'm going to test you."

TRAINER: This isn't the first time you've lived with this. The only thing
is—this is maybe the first time where you've experienced it as
deeply as you have the frustration in not being able to do something. You could live with not being able to do something before.
Now it's harder to live with.

GROUP: Um hum. True.

TRAINER: But . . .

JOE: The little knowledge that we have is now hurting.

ANN: Yes it is.

KAREN: It's like stirring up a hornet's nest.

TRAINER: Yea. The (*laugh*)—I can't help it—the same thing comes back
to me in some forms, and in a way I set you up for it tonight
by talking about doing this on a national scale and everything.
Here I'm the big shot and you can lean heavy on *me* tonight.
Like they lean on you. You can say to me, "I got problems.
O.K. big shot, now do something about it." Do you hear that?
You can act out with me what they've acted out with you. You
come home like—you know—I'm moving to new levels and
what do you get from the kid. Well, the first incident that comes
along like this, he uses it to test your new levels. "You really
got this? You really own this?" You come to me and you hear
me talking about new levels I'm moving to and you say, "Well,
I'm stuck with this just like my kid's stuck with it. He got
caught, I got caught, and I'm laying it to you. Now what are
you going to do with it?" Do you hear that? Do you hear that
fully?

JOE: No, not fully. Some of it, though.

TRAINER: You got caught with the new Joe Carr just like he got caught
by the teachers with firecrackers.

JOE: Yes, yes, that I . . .

TRAINER: You got caught and, just like he says, "All right, what are you
going to do with it Popsy?" Well, you can say that to me. You

got caught. It's a good moment for you to test now—"I'm stuck with it, anyway. Now I'm going to find out what he's got." Joe?

JOE: Well, of course, you opened it right up and left it to us. O.K., maybe I came around in circles . . .

TRAINER: "I jumped."

JOE: Well, I—all right, I jumped. Could be you set a trap for me—and I don't know.

TRAINER: No.

STAN: Boy, have you become suspicious. (*Group laughs*)

TRAINER: No, I just have to live with it as it develops, that's all.

JOE: I admit quite frankly that I am in the situation of being lost enough to . . .

TRAINER: To stick me with this.

JOE: To stick somebody, anybody.

STAN: A little knowledge is a dangerous thing. (*Group laughs*)

TRAINER: No, it has nothing to do with knowledge, doggone it! It has nothing to do with knowledge.

JOE: It's the, I presume, natural reaction when you're caught with your inadequacies down—look around for a patsy—or a helper.

TRAINER: Where do you want me to look? (*Group laughs*)

JOE: Is there a psychiatrist in the house? (*Someone laughs*)

TRAINER: You don't even believe that.

JOE: No, I don't, but there's . . .

TRAINER: No, it's gotta . . . you know, even if I'm tired, and I get tired, it's just got to end here. I've gotta handle it. I've gotta see it.

JOE: Of course, that's what you're trying to help us to do. Right? So we can look into ourselves and . . .

TRAINER: You—you . . . Go ahead, Ann.

ANN: I have the feeling—I don't know whether any of the other parents have this same feeling—but I get the feeling that these kids don't really want us to understand them too much because if we do that means they have to change. And they don't want to change, really. They're very happy in their present situation. At least they think they are. They think they are and they give this impression that . . .

TRAINER: You're saying that the deepest level of understanding is to know where to leave understanding off.

ANN: Uh huh.

TRAINER: And where to set down the rules of—whatever it means to be an adult. What does it mean to be an adult, Joe?

JOE: Hum?

TRAINER: Well—I mean it's related here. Go ahead.

JOE: It means accepting the burden of responsibility, at least in my mind that's being an adult. It's one of the hardest things being an adult consists of.

TRAINER: But you didn't accept it fully.

JOE:	I probably never have. I've always disliked the idea of . . .
TRAINER:	You brought part of it here and laid it at my feet.
JOE:	Yea.
TRAINER:	And it's yours . . .
JOE:	You're right.
TRAINER:	Not mine, not an ounce of it.
JOE:	If it's worth anything to understanding, I usually find myself by circumstances or perhaps a move I was not consciously making, caught in the situation of responsibility.
TRAINER:	Uh, huh.
JOE:	Because I am basically lazy. Once I'm in a situation, I go to work on it. I do not seek it, and this may be part of a great deal of trouble.
TRAINER:	Yea, and this is one that you've been avoiding for a long time. You've gotten caught by some of the others, but this one you've managed to avoid, but it's yours.
JOE:	O.K.
TRAINER:	O.K. Given that understanding, and if you can really accept that, then we still have questions about what I do even with the kind of thing Ann is saying. You know, even understanding that they don't want to be understood past a certain point, "What do I do?"
ANN:	Exactly.
TRAINER:	What did I just do?
JOE:	What did you just do?
TRAINER:	Yes.
JOE:	You tossed the ball back to me where I will admit it belongs.
TRAINER:	I made you responsible for what's yours. I took responsibility for what's mine by seeing what was going on and then I made you responsible for what's yours. What do you do with him?
JOE:	Now, this is not to say, if we may, at least, belabor this one a little bit more—I did something. I did something last night . . .
TRAINER:	I know you're capable of acting. That's not a question.
JOE:	I don't know whether what I did was right or effective, however.
TRAINER:	O.K. But what do you do with him?
JOE:	All right, so what I did was this. Let me recount it anyway, for what it's worth.
TRAINER:	O.K.
JOE:	Immediately after this scene I had to drive him over to Little League practice, which gave us ten minutes or so together in the car alone and I laid down precepts. I asked him if he would please seriously think on the fact that right is right and wrong is wrong and no matter who does what or anything else that the ancient pagan Spartan idea that it's no crime unless you're caught is as wrong as the wrong itself, and I more or less lec-

tured him on it—kindly—but lectured him in this vein all the
way over to the school . . .

TRAINER: And what kind of a response did you get?

JOE: . . . and dropped him off.

TRAINER: Now . . .

JOE: Yes—I mean, he agreed and . . .

TRAINER: You really let him off the hook.

JOE: . . . how he would think about it.

TRAINER: You really let him off the hook as I would let you off the hook
now if I—if I . . .

JOE: If you sat down and gave me precepts?

TRAINER: Well, if I said, "You did right," or everything else here.

JOE: In other words, I blew the bit.

TRAINER: No, I just think it's the easy way out. I think you have better
impulses than that—even given—I mean given your understanding, in particular, here. Did you stick him with the responsibility? It was his. You stuck him with the words about
responsibility. Did you stick him with the responsibility?

JOE: Did I?

TRAINER: If he won't accept it, you can do things. You are an adult. You
can withhold things or . . .

JOE: Well, that aspect of it did not come into the situation. I mean,
I see what you're getting at. I mean, the point is that "I can
do this and you can't because I'm an adult." Well, this situation didn't, to me, lend itself in such a line of adult conversation.
I mean it was simply trying to emphasize, or reemphasize, a
fact—that wrong is wrong. Without splitting hairs or anything
like that, Ann had spent some time reexplaining the law to him,
which is very much on the books that it is illegal to own, it's
illegal to buy, and it's illegal to sell . . .

TRAINER: Yea. That's up here, though. Did you make him responsible for
what he did?

ANN: How?

TRAINER: Did you hold accountable him for what he did?

ANN: How?

JOE: Well, he is held accountable for what he did in that sense.
Ann . . .

TRAINER: How did it change his day or his life? He did something—you
took him to the Little League game and gave him a little talk
on the way. It was just as good as silence to have that little talk.

JOE: Now I'm with you—a direct application of discipline. Well,
perhaps the application of this particular discipline may not
mean that much to him. I don't know, because he's not going
to be allowed to go back to that school in September.

TRAINER: You're going to have to make the discriminations, but you give
him freedom as he's willing to accept responsibility for it. As he
doesn't accept responsibility for it, you take that freedom away.

ANN:	He's had about everything except Little League taken away from him. He's had everything . . .
TRAINER:	Is that where he is now?
ANN:	Not tonight.
TRAINER:	No, I mean is that . . .
ANN:	That's where he is now.
TRAINER:	In other words, he's off everything but Little League right now?
ANN:	Right.
JOE:	Uh, huh.
ANN:	Right—and it doesn't seem to change a . . .
TRAINER:	And you've—you've hesitated on Little League, though, because it's so basic to him?
ANN:	Yes, because it's sports and it's something I felt to run off this excess energy that let's him get into all this mischief and even seems to prod him into getting into all this mischief. He doesn't always—he has so much energy he doesn't know what to do with it. I thought about Little League, I thought, also, about applying a good fat strap where it would do the most good, and I thought, "Well, what would that accomplish?" After the spanking is over and the pain subsides he will go right back. And I tried to point out to him—he's ridden with me many times, we've come to a stop sign and we stop—maybe there are no cars there, maybe no one is around, maybe the whole four corners are deserted, and I said to him, "Remember when you go riding with me in a car, I come to a stop sign and there isn't anyone there to make me stop, there's no one probably to see it but if I don't stop, I'm breaking the law and this is wrong. And so I might not get caught—in all probability I wouldn't get caught, but it's no less wrong for me to do this," and—"Oh, Mother!"— and he walked out of the room, as if he's retarded.
TRAINER:	So you have some impulses to do some more but you didn't, because you just didn't feel that they would lead anyplace— even, maybe, taking the Little League away.
ANN:	That's right. Maybe that was the thing to do. I don't know.
TRAINER:	You hate to have to be pushed that far.
ANN:	Yes. Yes, I do.
TRAINER:	What does it mean to be pushed that far?
ANN:	Well, it means having a kid around the house—sullen, rebellious, thwarting you in every way that you can think of because you are mean to him. You don't let him do this.
TRAINER:	No, it also means that right now that looks like my last line of . . .
ANN:	Yes, if that isn't effective, where do I go?
TRAINER:	Where do I go? If I use this one—that's my ace in the hole— if I use this one, where do I go?
ANN:	Right. Where do I go after this?
TRAINER:	"And I'm not going to risk it?" And he knows.

ANN:	Yea, I think so.
TRAINER:	"So I tell him I stop at stop signs when no one is around, but I'll compromise with him."
ANN:	I hadn't thought of it that way, but I guess that's right.
TRAINER:	"I won't go all the way with him because I'm afraid if I use my ace in the hole I get wiped out."
ANN:	And it fails. Yea.
TRAINER:	And I know you're afraid to fail.
ANN:	Um, hum.
TRAINER:	"I"—the kid—"I know you're afraid to fail."
ANN:	Uh, hum.
TRAINER:	"You've given me a lot of verbal stuff"—and I think the group has said that to me tonight—"You give me a lot of talk here, but we know you're afraid to fail, too." And, "We hold the keys to whether *you* succeed or not." Me (*aside*)—I don't want to hear from you. Yea, I know, fine, make your individual discriminations on it—it holds for those who've been sending the message to me tonight. (*Pause*) You hear?
JOE:	Yea, I hear. Also, I hear that it's up to us to devise a solution.
TRAINER:	Do you also hear that—you know—if I get pushed far enough I'll risk losing you? (*Pause*) And, in fact, that we can't go any place unless I do—am willing to take that risk?
JOE:	Well, you said way at the beginning of the sessions that the thing had to be made at home—we could be stars in here but if we don't cut it at home the whole thing is a washout—that you were saying right then that you sure in hell didn't want it to be a washout.
TRAINER:	You're right.
JOE:	You were very much against any failure at . . .
TRAINER:	That doesn't change my other statement, though. I just—I'll make it explicit if you're not reading it into it. That's all.
JOE:	Hmm?
TRAINER:	No, I'm just making it explicit in case—you know—just to bring it out in the open. You think you're going to succeed by not risking failure?
ANN:	I haven't, I haven't succeeded. But I just didn't recognize what I was afraid of—his very attitude about "It doesn't matter if you break the law just as long as you don't get caught" frightens me. It frightens me right out of my mind—that a 12-year-old could have this attitude.
TRAINER:	First of all, from his viewpoint, I think that's a smokescreen. Second, it's calculated to frighten you.
ANN:	Uh, huh.
TRAINER:	He's got a hold on you, and some of the things coming toward me tonight were calculated to frighten me—and understanding only does carry you so far—and with Bill, here, I got the mes-

sage that, you know, there were parts he didn't want understood, either—just something that you stated later. I don't know if we're that—I don't know if in our own way—I'm talking about me, too—if we really are that much different from the kids. Seems to me like we act out a lot of the same things we talk about being mysterious in our kids—and we wonder where it . . .

JOE: Well, I feel that everybody has a time for growing up, but I don't really think that many people live long enough to do it.

TRAINER: That would be handy, wouldn't it, Tom? You shake your head yes. (*Group laughs*) "If I could be sure that I won't live long enough to grow up, then I won't have to." (*Group laughs*)

KAREN: Oh, boy! (*Exchange inaudible*)

TOM: It's a much nicer view.

TRAINER: Yea. And you used to think you had forever, but you don't any more. Joe's just talking about a dream now—that's just a fantasy now—it's not real any more. You don't have forever.

This excerpt illustrates more vividly the therapeutic value of the training structure under the guidance of a high-level–functioning trainer. Again the trainees relate to the trainer as the children relate to their parents. The trainees act out the behavior of their children in "sticking" the trainer with their problems or "dumping" on him. The trainer integrates the experiential, didactic, and, most of all, the modeling sources of learning in his discharge of his responsibilities as parent of the parents' family. If the trainer cannot risk, the trainees cannot risk. If the helper cannot risk "losing," the helpee cannot win. In the next excerpt we find that the parents are gradually making contact with their children in a way that they before could not.

"COMING IN LOUD AND CLEAR"

BILL: He had a feeling for me—I felt he had a feeling for me. As a son he was almost playing a man's part there—he had a feeling for me. It was "Dad's got this to do" and "Dad's got that to do" and "that's why I don't feel I should put any more pressure on him." Understand?

KAREN: You're saying you saw a real streak of responsibility.

BILL: He was really showing a streak of responsibility. I would say that, yes.

JANE: And you felt proud of him.

BILL: I—I felt deeply proud of him. I felt that—my heart went out to him—my heart bled for him. It don't usually do that, but it did then.

TRAINER: Those moments are beautiful.

BILL: Those moments are beautiful is right—hearts and flowers.

TRAINER: Rate it. Tom?

TOM: I give her a 3 this time.

MARY: I would say a 3.

IRENE: I say a 3, too.

STAN: A 3.

TRAINER: You really—you know—there was a difference. Maybe you didn't experience it as much, but you were right in there and . . .

BILL: He was right in there then . . .

TRAINER: I like what you're saying, too, and I think it does represent the side of the kids that we do respond to and that's what spoils it when we see the ugly moments because they are so beautiful and it is beautiful to see a kid trying out a man's role.

BILL: He was trying hard to convey something to me, and it just so happens that I was in the mood that I could grasp what he was saying.

TRAINER: O.K. *You* heard him.

BILL: I heard him, yes. He was coming in loud and clear at that time.

TRAINER: Not always the easiest thing in the world for you . . . (*Group laughs*)

BILL: Not always the easiest thing in the world for *any* of us . . .

TRAINER: . . . for any of us.

BILL: . . . to listen to our child—to hear our child when he's coming in loud and clear. Sometimes, you know, it comes in but it's kind of mumble jumble, but this time he was coming in loud and clear.

The parent-trainees were now equipped to listen and, more important, to hear and to communicate what they heard from their children. The children, in turn, were trying out new behaviors. The parents were seeing a new side of their kids. They were finding a beauty where they had only found ugliness before—a beauty that makes the ugliness they see all the more distressing. In the following excerpt one of the trainees attempts to role-play her child in one of his more ugly moments:

"I WON'T EVEN LISTEN TO YOUR WORDS"

TRAINER: All right. Obviously this is going to be harder than anything you've done. For one thing, you're not as good a child as you are an adult. I don't mean good, you know, good, good—you're not as good at being a child as an adult—and that makes it even harder and yet—I'm thinking out loud now—and yet I think you're going to have to be good. You're really going to have to be children if we're going to make this work. That's not going to be easy but you're going to have to say it like they say it—you know—like you say, "Sometimes she makes me very angry!" You know, "Sometimes I hate her!" or whatever it is. How would it be to crawl inside of him? How much can you feel of it? I guess this is one of the problems. How much can you really feel? How much can you really feel what he feels? Now, I felt you started to feel it. By the way, I'm avoiding the ratings on them because I'm going to ask you to do it again—where I felt you started to feel it or express it—you know—you're saying things like, well, I write my own interpretations on it, "She really loves the others more than me even though she may make special exceptions for me. I can tell she loves the others more than me." You know, "What do I owe her if she loves the others more than me?" "Even though she spends more time with me, she still loves the others more than me. I don't care what you say." I felt you got some of this. Go ahead—any other people want to comment? It's going to be—you know—I think what each of us is saying to ourselves is, "My God, I've got to go through that!" Jane?

JANE: I felt this for sure because when you said, "Pretend to be a child . . ."

TRAINER: What do you mean, *pretend*? I mean *be* a child.

JANE: All right, *be* a child. It's very hard to . . .

TRAINER: Yes!

JANE: . . . to pretend to be a child when you've got one child in your mind. I mean, I could enact something that my child did . . .

TRAINER: I'm not going to ask you to be a child when you leave this room.

JANE: Oh! I mean it's impossible . . .

TRAINER: Yea.

JANE: I could think the way my kid would say it—you know—

TRAINER: Say it like it is . . .

JANE: Yea—I could think the way he would say it but I can't . . .

TRAINER: Tell it like it is. You say it the way your kid would say it— fine. I don't want it to be any other kid.

JANE: You know this is the way—I—you know—

TRAINER: No, I know what you're talking about are all the things that get in the way of hearing children, all the things that make—in part, they make us an adult—fine—and I don't want to take that away, but what about the part that's getting in the way? For our purposes now, we're going to do it here. Look—at a minimum it's opening us up to things that we feel a little bit uncomfortable with—very uncomfortable with. Mary, be a child . . .

MARY: You're being funny. (*Group laughs*)

TRAINER: . . . or I'll give you a spanking. (*Group laughs*) (*Inaudible interaction by group*)

MARY:	Who does my mother sometimes think she is? Always telling me what to do, and I don't want to do what she tells me to do all the time. I want to do just as I darn well please, and boy, sometimes she makes me so mad I could punch her one right in the face!
TONY:	You feel like she's pushing you around.
MARY:	Definitely. She's always pushing—always telling me what to do. She's always taking those other kids' sides. Well, I hate them when she—I hate them! Well, I'm going to smack them when she does that because I can't smack her.
TONY:	You can get back at her by hitting them.
MARY:	Yea. She makes me so darn mad at her. She tells me not to do the things that I want to do and that I feel like doing.
TONY:	You feel like she ought to keep the house clean and not ask you to do it.
MARY:	Oh, I want to do it, too, but I want to be sloppy and I want to go out and play when I want to go out and play and I think she's just unfair all the time, and she loves those other kids and my Daddy more than me.
TONY:	You feel that she wants you to be something that you aren't. She wants you to be somebody else—to be like her.
MARY:	Oh, I can't ever be like her, always telling me what to do. Sometimes I get back at her. Sometimes I lie to her . . .
TRAINER:	O.K. Mary, you told it like it was. It was beautiful. I think you taught us—I guess we all learned something. You called on some courage—and that's what it is—courage. O.K. But Tony is the one who's stuck with the ratings. (*Some of group laugh*) How is that for 5-finger rating? Jane, what do you have?
JANE:	I'd give her a 3 . . .
TRAINER:	Who?
JANE:	Her—
TRAINER:	I give her a 5.
JANE:	Oh, she was excellent!
TRAINER:	What do you give Tony?
JANE:	I'd give him a 3.
KAREN:	A 3.
TOM:	Not over 2.
IRENE:	I'd say about a 2.5.
DON:	3.5.
TRAINER:	All right.
BILL:	I said 3.
TRAINER:	I forgot about you. (*All laugh*)
BILL:	Don't worry about it—you won't be able to—I got a *big* mouth.
TRAINER:	O.K. Mary?
MARY:	Do you want to know what I felt? If he was with me?
TRAINER:	Yea.

MARY: Well, frankly it was a little hard to hear what he was saying, but I was trying so hard to crawl into my son's mind that I . . .

TRAINER: No, I think you climbed in and I think if you were your son and this guy were there he'd almost be irrelevant.

MARY: Right. I really—well, I felt he was relating to me on an adult level.

TRAINER: That's right! Well, what I said to you before, "Now, Mary, say it with feeling," I'm now saying that to Tony. Yea, he had the words. There was nothing wrong with the words, "Sometimes she kind of makes you angry." That's not communication. In terms of what you were communicating to him, that's not communication. "She makes you *furious!*"—for openers. Look, I'm not telling you to go home and give this to your kid—you're not there yet. But it was that loud, Tony! It wasn't a mild, intellectualized, screened, strained adult—you heard it—the words were right and all feelings were subtractive. I know you want to defend that. Go ahead.

TONY: No, I don't want to say anything.

TRAINER: So I think—yea, your ratings are 3—in terms of the words, if we looked at it in writing, I guess we would have to say 3, but we heard it. Tom?

TOM: In response to the child, the feeling, you know, the part he wanted to hear is, you know, in other words, if a child is talking to an adult he wants some advice or . . .

TRAINER: "You know, I almost won't even listen to your words! Give me the feeling. I won't even listen to your words." You know, we talked last week, "Hold them" or make something direct and hold them . . .

TOM: Or take them out to the woodshed or something.

TRAINER: Or take them out to the woodshed. That's direct. There's messages in that and one of them is love—that I care enough—and he said it before—fine—but we're not talking about that right now. We're talking about Mary and Tony, and we all heard and Tony did too. We all heard Mary.

It is difficult for the parent to really crawl inside of her child's skin, to really see the world the way the child does, to really express herself the way the child does. The trainee had failed in her first attempt to portray her child—she intellectualized his problems in an adult way. The trainer is critical and structures the role-playing situation to enable the trainee to cross the barrier. When the parent can overcome the barrier to the world of the child she discovers not only a new understanding of her child but also a new understanding of herself—in this instance in spite of the fact that the helper didn't really stay with her. The trainer not only shapes behavior within the training sessions but also influences the direction of the parents' behavior with their children outside of training. In the next excerpt, following a discussion of the implication of a previous role-playing experience, the parents of the same family unit work with each other on their children's problems:

"WE CAN HEAR THE BIG GUNS GO OFF"

TOM: . . . Could it be that sometimes, generally, you know, they know that this is wrong and they ought to be recognized? And then they're expecting, you know, really to be pampered over or talked about or something and then all of a sudden all you have to do is take them back to the start and everything is . . .

TRAINER: No, I think it runs deeper than that. I think it runs to the kinds of things that we're talking about here in this instance where— you know—"For some reason because of something probably in my parents' attitude I think I'm entitled to do this and I'm entitled to get away with it and if you catch me at it, I think you're the one that's in the wrong because I'm still basically entitled to the same kinds of things." You know, whether you want me to guess at—you know—"Look, you steal some love from me, I steal some money from you," or, "You don't give me some things, I take them," or, "If I steal, the worst that happens is I get some attention," and, "I sure like that, even negative attention." I—you know—here's three. I think we can push it. I'd like to see you and Tony push it together when he comes back Thursday. I think we can push it. I think you can look at those things. Ben, what do you think?

BEN: I always get caught with the same feelings with this kind of thing. You're saying that at some level all our kids take things that don't belong to them. It doesn't matter whether it's in school or some place else—they all do it, and the message I'm sending out is—the message that you're sending is that in the end the child knows that you're going to revolve around her. In the end, "You're going to revolve around me and I'm the center of my world" and you're a part of the world you revolve around, no matter what, and that gives me the cold right to take anything . . .

TRAINER: "If you don't give, I take. If you don't give, you're stealing from me, and I got a right to steal from you." But I think the point before—I like the way you handled it when you finally took a stand—and you used the point that you didn't know what decision to make in the moment—you say, "I'll decide later even if I don't do it now"—you know—"That's my prerogative— I'm the mother." You set up these boundaries and you make the decisions on them. One thing you know for darn sure is that they

	can't function as adults and parents in a world revolving like that, around them.
BEN:	The child is my satellite. I'm not his.
TRAINER:	That doesn't change the understanding that we're talking about. They're not mutually exclusive.
STAN:	In regard about the child—in effect—thinking that the parents are going to revolve around them—backtracking a ways you also commented on the fact that the child would set parents up for their fall—where they could pull the plug . . .
TRAINER:	Right.
STAN:	Do they do this consciously?
TRAINER:	No.
STAN:	Deliberately?
TRAINER:	It doesn't matter, really, Stan.
STAN:	Well . . .
TRAINER:	It doesn't matter—at some point some do, but it really doesn't matter. It's the same thing anyway. They got it in the picture.
BEN:	They're aware of it to the extent they know the payoff shots. When I communicate I revolve around my child; he has every right to come into my room, my workbench, my desk, and take anything he wants, and I've been through this with the children—and I just have to make decisions that in large pieces of life they revolve around *me*—you know—I love them—but they're my satellites, I'm not theirs, and I have to keep reasserting it. If I forget it for too long a period of time . . .
TRAINER:	In other words, what you're saying is they're . . .
BEN:	Janie's in my wife's jewelry and jewelry box—you know—Ted's in taking things . . .
TRAINER:	You're saying they're free within the boundaries of freedom I give them, and I revolve around them in terms of the boundaries that I set, so these are my decisions.
BEN:	They don't—there are certain things they can't violate—they're mine, period. They just don't violate them. They can't invade certain areas of mine—they need not be physical areas. I may give them permission to do so, but they can go just so far; otherwise, I hate to think what they would do.
TRAINER:	You want to go through it, Stan and Irene? Stan, why don't you just begin with the thoughts that are running through your mind related to your kids and Irene—does this come out of my experience or are you all about as tired as I am tonight?
STAN:	I don't know . . .
TRAINER:	I don't know. Why the hell doesn't . . .
BILL:	It just seems to be one of those nights for me.
TRAINER:	All right. Irene you're the helper. (*Pause*)
STAN:	My thoughts weren't on this—I need time—
TRAINER:	O.K. You're just trying to understand what was the exception.

STAN: . . . trying to get a—you know, we go along with it until it gets to the point—we try to do what we can for them—get them what we can, and yet I still figure they need a pretty heavy hand at this point, and I suppose I tie them down pretty hard, don't want to take any back talk from him. And generally speaking, you tell him not to do something and he acts like he never heard you. I keep wondering, "Why?" "Where did I miss him?" I spend some time with him and things go real swell—like we had a good time out in the woods, we really had a ball! And then the same old thing. Ask him to do a simple little thing like, "Leave your sister alone" and he never even hears me, he keeps right on after her, and then I lay down with him and talk with him for a while and the same sweet kid—I just can't see it—those in between times. I miss him entirely and I don't know where—just like dealing with two different people in a couple of hours. He changes three and four times a day.

IRENE: You feel that he doesn't understand you and you definitely don't understand what makes him tick—what he's thinking.

STAN: I can't figure it out—how when he's having a real good time and a couple of hours later or even a couple minutes later he just goes along and does the opposite of what we expect from him, and it kind of burns me that a kid eight years old trying to virtually openly defy a simple little request—and this is what he does. Ask him to hurry up and get out of the bathroom and instead of getting out in half an hour he takes an hour.

IRENE: You think he does this to really—because he knows that he's making you mad?

STAN: I think so.

IRENE: And you get that impression as you stand there and holler at him to get out of the bathroom.

STAN: Yea. I just think that. I think he figures out the way to aggravate and does things to push it—and then he pushes.

IRENE: You feel helpless—you feel as if you're almost drowning—you can't quite reach for that extra help.

STAN: I can't quite reach him . . .

IRENE: He listens but then he doesn't hear—he can tune you out.

STAN: Like a radio. You know he hears you—you can tell by the expression on his face that he's listening, but then you say it the second time and he'll say "What?" as though he never heard the expression before. Boy, that sends me right up a . . . to go back over it.

IRENE: Then you lose patience with him.

STAN: Yes.

IRENE: And then he does it all the more.

STAN: Yes.

IRENE: He seems to enjoy that.

STAN: Well, I don't know whether he really enjoys it. He usually has sort of a chagrin attitude afterwards. It's like he did something wrong—not enjoying it—but he did something wrong. Just putting it in perspective—like we even said tonight—that's negative attention. But I never looked at it that way before. All I know is I can't quite reach him.

IRENE: You're lost.

STAN: With him, yes.

IRENE: Yet when he's having a good time at something he really enjoys he's really tuned in.

STAN: We can have a ball.

IRENE: Well, when you took him out in the woods he said to me what a good time he had and he said, "Daddy didn't even have to scold me or tell me to do anything twice." He was proud of that and he was enjoying it. He knows—and he knows he can get to us by deliberately defying and making us feel helpless—like he's the boss.

STAN: Yea, but what I don't understand is that he seems to enjoy it so much when he's "normal," in other words you might say, "going on an even keel or having a good time." Why he goes the other route and then has that real sad attitude about him—even while he's doing it, even while he's being defiant—this I don't get. But if you never experience going off and having a good time I could see the sadness here—his more or less deliberate agitation—and yet there are times when the only identity he does have are good happy feelings and happy attitudes about . . . I just can't . . .

TRAINER: O.K. Tom?

TOM: I say a 3.

MARY: I say 2.5.

ANN: I'd say 3 plus.

KAREN: 2.

JOE: 3.

BILL: I said 3, too.

JANE: I said 2.5.

TRAINER: Near the end? There were some real good things that you heard communicated, but it got off a little bit—Stan?

STAN: She had part of it.

TRAINER: It's almost like, "If we continue this way we'll never really get to anything." One of the—go ahead.

STAN: That's it. I was just going to say that about wraps it up—start down a path and it looks pretty good then all of a sudden you're on a detour again.

TRAINER: You know that this is just not going to come to conclusion.

STAN: You come along with the encouraging sign and then when its cut out from under you, you're still up in the air.

TRAINER: Yea, but you're not just talking about a kid now, you're talking about in relation to Irene hearing you, too.

STAN: Firstly, yea.

TRAINER: Yea, but there were encouraging signs like, you know, I thought you really were breaking through when you made the point that "The kid doesn't understand *me!*"—you know—because that's part of what Stan was saying—"I'm trying so hard"—you know—"Why doesn't he understand how hard I'm trying?" And then, you know, I think you lost some after that. That's an important piece to really get a hold of and make yours. All right. We said it before you began and then you heard yourself saying it, "I'm on his schedule." The thing—to put the picture together again is—"He's lost and I'm lost" and "If I'm on his schedule, we're both lost." Do you remember the first time you talked about it? You talked about being in the woods and how panicked he was when you couldn't find—when you had that moment when you weren't sure you could find your way out of the woods right away? If you're on a lost kid's schedule, you're lost. This kid lives in fear of being lost in the woods and yet he's strong enough to get you lost, to find out if anybody knows his way out of the woods. Do you? Any other comments? I had another thought, too, and this is just a—this is a directionful thing that my mother taught me—I never did hear her say anything more than once because the second time she was there, she lifted me up and put me wherever she wanted me to be, and if I were in the tub I got lifted out of the tub. The verbal battles are pretty adolescent things. That's coming down to his level. That's getting caught up on his schedule because he's not that bad at it. But physically you could still pick him up, take him out, give him a quick dry, put him to bed, and it's over. And you haven't lost your cool. That's a—(*laugh*) for what we're talking about—it's appropriate. A couple of things—other than being tired myself—I sense there are other things going on in the group. You know, we're a lot slower tonight—a lot more serious. I wouldn't say depressed, I'd just say starting to realize that, "Hey, we're halfway through and we're starting to get the real tests—we've lived through the early periods of enthusiasm and excitement and hope." You know, "We know we're going to get this thing licked now. We've got a real program going there, and now we're coming down to the point where we're starting to test out and see whether we're really going to have a delivery or not." And I'm not saying depressed but serious. "I've pinned a lot on this thing, on this group, and now I'm having some moments and sometimes I deliver and sometimes I don't. I don't know if I'm up to it. I don't know if I've got it."

BILL: I think we've got to the point—we've reached the point where we can hear the big guns going off. Now if you have a soldier there—any kind of serviceman would know—but you know how you start off, real jovial and everything, but the closer you get to that no man's land and you hear the big guns going off you notice that each fellow will settle down and get quieter and quieter—you got your own thoughts. Now we've passed over that stage we were in where it was kind of fun and each one had his little—told a joke—but it's no joke. It's actually reality and we have to realize it is reality. In order to do something about it you got to get down to the nitty gritty. That's where we are now, and that's why each one's got their own thoughts and they're thinking about just what path am I going to take and what would be the best solution for me. I know we're all working in a group, but at the same time—but I think even with us working in a group and each taking a little part of others' hardship and all we still, within ourselves, we feel that our own little problem should get settled and which is the best way to settle it.

STAN: Sort of like, "It's nice to be able to help somebody else, but, buddy, I have to help myself."

BILL: . . . too, at the same time.

STAN: This is the foremost thought.

KAREN: I think at least as far as I'm concerned—I don't know about Tony really—I know the trouble with our kids is the trouble with us and I think this whole group—I know Tony is very excited about it—I think we have come to understand what our problems are and just listening and trying to relate what we learn from others helps us.

BEN: Could I say two things? First, what Bill said, "Less talk before the battle—then men are quiet."

BILL: Very quiet.

BEN: You don't talk before you fight. Number two, I experience parents struggling immensely to understand the children and there's something wrong—there's something beautiful about this, but there's something wrong about it, too. The child has to struggle to get to know you! I'm responding to your *rage* and some of it's maybe because you struggled so hard and talked to the kid, and it doesn't reach him. The other part of—there's another part of the rage, too—that it is appropriate—you don't feel them reaching back and that can break your heart.

TRAINER: Except on his terms when things are going well for him.

BEN: That can break your heart.

Understanding the children does not operate to the exclusion of the parents' understanding themselves and having their own direction based upon this understanding any more than understanding the individual group members operates to the exclusion of the trainer's essential direction. Too often the children's problems are the function of rigid behavior patterns on the part of the parents, whether these patterns are authoritarian or permissive. When the parents search desperately to understand the source of their children's difficulties they often abdicate many of their responsibilities as adults with meaningful direction in their lives. Under the trainer's guidance they return again to find themselves and their own direction and in so doing find their relationships with their children. In the following excerpt the parents from a different family unit act out their difficulties in relating with their children's problems:

"NITTY GRITTY"

TRAINER:	You're gonna have to face the task.
JOE:	Well, what am I, helpee or helper?
TRAINER:	You know what you are.
JOE:	Well, I think I mentioned to you the other day, I don't think I do know.
TRAINER:	Helpee.
JOE:	Very well, helpee. (*Long pause*) In the realm of what's bugging me or . . .
TRAINER:	Joe, if you're really searching—or do you have an idea?
JOE:	Well, I was just about to . . .
TRAINER:	Oh, O.K.
JOE:	In the realm of physical—you and I have long had a basic theoretical agreement in the manner of the disciplining of the children—the setting and enforcing of rules—
TRAINER:	Ann, I'm going to give you—you keep him in there—you don't let him off easy. You cut it deep.
ANN:	What was the theoretical agreement?
JOE:	That we agree between each other as to what we shall do in given situations; that we will not be at cross purposes in that we will countermand each other. Now, when I am not there and you set a discipline, you set a rule, you make an arrangement whereby one of the children must do this or one of the children will have to undergo this or that punishment for an infraction, you inform me of it so this is now a set thing and so it must cover perhaps a space of time. So I think, "No, I don't go along with this," or it must be deprivation, confinement, only to discover within perhaps a short space of time that I'm the only one who is enforcing this rule and you are not because you have forgotten all about it.
ANN:	You feel then that I set up rules and they aren't so important after all because even I don't follow through on them.

JOE: Well, sometimes this has resulted. I feel that when they are set up and if I'm not in agreement and I'd think you'd recall that I let you know that I'm not in agreement with it at the time—my feeling is that I am left hanging in a situation of perhaps being the complete ogre who all by himself goes right ahead and enforces . . .

ANN: . . . enforces a rule that you didn't even make?

JOE: True, although I agreed to it, but I find that I'm the only one enforcing it and you are not, which leads to—well, it leads to confusion on the part of the individual child—a lack of respect for the whole program, whatever it might be.

ANN: You feel, then, that this is the reason you take it upon yourself to be stricter than I then in the way you handle them all by yourself.

JOE: Yes, very frankly, having set them and agreed to them, I feel something must be done, and if there is a relaxation on one side, well probably I have to lay it on harder on my side.

ANN: You don't feel that there are ever circumstances that would cause me to modify something that I have set up? You don't believe then that any of the rules should be modified, right?

JOE: Yes, I'll go along with that. I show an inflexibility, whether justified or not, but I do—possibly a conditioning over a period of time— perhaps a fear that it might end up with both of us relaxing the whole thing and thus becoming permissive parents. I do have an inordinate fear of that situation.

ANN: Don't you think, then, that a rate of communication—maybe foreseeing of circumstances that might cause the rules to be modified. Maybe this would help.

JOE: This might be so, but usually this is not brought out. All of a sudden the relaxation has occurred—perhaps over a period of time it has been relaxed and I don't even know it. I come back after a day of work or perhaps no incident has occurred that perhaps I—which isn't bad and one thing and another over an evening—but a day and a half, two days go by, and I come on the scene and here is a situation in complete variance with whatever the punishment, the rule, or restriction, or whatever it was, and I'm faced with this, perhaps even in your absence, and I proceed to enforce.

TRAINER: Cut it a little deeper. What does it mean to him? See if you can zero in.

ANN: Well, in your mind, then, I must seem like—it must look as though I'm not carrying my end of the bargain.

JOE: Well, that is the result as any given situation demonstrates. The intention is not the consideration as I'm speaking here. It's what happens as a result. Now I feel that in some circumstances there has been an intentional relaxation, but I feel that in more of the cases it's a matter of sheer forgetting the whole scene. It seems to drop right out of your mind.

TRAINER: The *whole* scene.

JOE: Recalling the circumstances under which the kid did something and had to be disciplined. It's not only discipline, you know. I mean it's a matter of—well—assignment of tasks—the doing of this—or the going or coming—the general supervision of the children.

ANN: Does this bug you because you are fearful of the results to the children or because it bothers you so much—it affects you personally—it undermines your feelings—yourself?

JOE: I tell myself that it is the matter of the responsibility to the children . . .

ANN: But really, what is . . .

JOE: Well, it is also a blow to my ego—as I suppose we're both involved in—and it brings me, shall we say, frustration and disappointment in my wife whom I love dearly and would rather not have this situation because it makes me plumb angry. It might also be a case of that very feeling being taken out on the children rather than on you.

ANN: Did you ever ask yourself why, if they're not at fault and certainly they aren't in that case, why not take it out on me?

JOE: Why not take it out on you. Well, I suppose I could put it bluntly that I don't want to hurt you.

TRAINER: Can I—you're—I'm going to stop it now and not because you didn't have some pieces of it but that—he's a hard man to handle, isn't he? He throws a lot at you to keep you off. Mary, let's rate Ann for the time being anyway.

MARY: Well . . . he keeps putting her off. She's just touching on the surface. I feel it goes much deeper.

TRAINER: You know there's more.

MARY: Yea. It's between a 2 and a 3. He's not helping her too much, but I feel it is much deeper than she went.

TRAINER: Irene?

IRENE: 2.5

STAN: 2.5 with one reservation. One remark sounded 4 or better.

TONY: Well, I thought she started out coming up close to 3 and dropped back to 2—particularly in one instance that I thought her question was—seemed to be constructed more in a kind of justification of her activity rather than trying to draw Joe out.

TRAINER: Well . . . Karen?

KAREN: More on the minus side.

JANE: 2.5.

BILL: Well, I say a 3 minus—up to the point where she got too close to the personal. What do you call that?

TRAINER: I like nitty gritty. (*Group laughs*)

BILL: Well, nitty gritty is what it is, but I was—I was trying to use some of these technical words that you've been dropping in there once in a while.

TRAINER: I've thought about that, and I don't think my working vocabulary is that large. Joe, what was your experience?

JOE: Well, I . . .

TRAINER: I handled her.

JOE: I felt that there was a definite feeling of self-defense in many of her responses.

TRAINER: Jane?

JANE: He made a remark about "the whole scheme of things." That was— had I been in Ann's place, I would have asked him what he means about that . . .

TRAINER: I think Ann knows about that . . .

JANE: She didn't grab at it . . .

TRAINER: She only pointed at it.

JANE: . . . make him come out with it when he said "whole scheme of things"—this was the thing to catch.

TRAINER: First of all, you were a tough one to handle other than getting defensive with—you know—in that kind of exchange. You're really, on the surface—you weren't talking much about yourself. You were trying to keep it, you know, keep it off you—keep the focus off you—only in the easy way that you could handle it.

JOE: I could have gone in other directions, I suppose, but I tried to say something which had to do with personal problems between the two of us which I thought . . .

TRAINER: Joe, I wrote down a number of things, but here's where I think it goes—and in part I think probably it comes from my talking the other day where I put some things together—but here's—"I've got to stay on top of the situation or I'll be exposed, and you're working against me and you're going to blow the whole scene, and it's *my* scene I'm talking about—*Me!* I've worked a long time, and I've worked hard on building up my place in the sun and you're helping—you and the kids are helping—to expose me, this image I've built up—and everything else—the strong man. The strong man's not a strong man. He's a responsible person, yes—as strong as he's presented himself, no. Strong, yes—a strong man, no. Joe, if you think I'm pushing too hard you can push back.

JOE: You feel that I am exposing a considerable front . . .

TRAINER: Can I—Yes! Yes.

JOE: All right.

TRAINER: Can I just put a few things together? I can do it now or we can do it later. I'm just going to think out loud a little bit now.

JOE: You made a good start.

From the same session husband and wife reverse roles as helper and helpee after the trainer confronts the husband with discrepancies in the husband's behavior:

JOE:	Does this come in a chance confrontation upon any given situation with a kid?
TRAINER:	Ann, tell him.
ANN:	Well, I think it's just a way of life—it's a way of life. I have always felt that the children thought you were very much superior to me and I didn't even mind this because—well—educationally and most other ways I think you are, but on the other hand, I think they feel I am much more of a human being . . .
TRAINER:	"They're more in contact with me—where you lose you." This is what you're saying, isn't it?
ANN:	Um hum.
JOE:	Do you feel that I make you feel that way?
ANN:	Sometimes. Yes.
TRAINER:	Ann's saying, "I'm more in contact with me and you lose you in all this stuff, and they want you."
ANN:	Um hum.
TRAINER:	And they'll destroy that other stuff one way or another even if it destroys them in the process—even if it destroys them in the process.
JOE:	That's a frightening prospect. (*Heavy sigh*)
TRAINER:	What you're saying is, "I've lived so long with this, I don't know what I'll come up with if I look at this. I might come up empty." You know Ann married you for the "something more" but you don't know if the "something more" is there any more.
JOE:	Isn't that, "What if it ever was?"
TRAINER:	All right. You can almost forget that you ever had it, and even question whether you ever did.
JOE:	Who do I love?
TRAINER:	Well—"Am I capable of love?"
JOE:	. . . loving anybody? It's something to work on.
TRAINER:	You work on it with Ann, and you don't let him off easy. Joe Carr needs somebody to go to, too, whoever he is.
ANN:	I know.
TRAINER:	But you've got to stay in there and not be thrown off by all the stuff Joe Carr built up over a lifetime. If you can't, you can't help him. (*Long pause*)
JOE:	Have you seen an essential selfishness?
TRAINER:	Joe, that won't take us any place.
JOE:	What I'm trying to get at is the front might not hide it.
TRAINER:	O.K. What you're saying is . . .
JOE:	I'm thinking of the children.
TRAINER:	Well, they're funny because they live with you, and there's nobody that good to not give out some cues and some clues—not just on the front but also on the stuff they're after. They may not try so hard for this if they didn't know it was there. Do you know what I mean? If the cues and clues are there that you're not who you represent yourself to be, in part you are, I mean, it's not just

a fiction of somebody's imagination—yea, the clues are there. "I wasn't that damn good at it anyway."

JOE: I had to be flubbing somewhere because things are loused up.

TRAINER: That's right.

JOE: I think . . .

TRAINER: I'm gonna ask you to reverse, right? You must get tired of that sometimes, especially in the deep moments—you couldn't take this and use it. You don't have to do it now—you don't have to do it all now—you can do it later, you know. I want you to reverse and Ann give him what you feel in the moment now.

ANN: Well, I've been thinking that the way I feel now is the way I've felt for years. I think I can only reach you sometimes and the feeling is more of those times are the nonessential times. I think that when we go out on an evening as we do occasionally and we're away from the house and away from the family it's a real close relationship—it's real great, and when we go back to the house, just about the time we step in the door the whole mantel falls over again and there we are. And sometimes when we go out I will bring up the subject of the children and the way to relate to them and sometimes I decide I'm not going to do this because even though it would be nice to talk about these things and it would be an opportunity to talk about these things, they would just cast a cloud on the whole evening.

JOE: You feel generally that when it's a matter of discussion of the family affairs it inevitably ends up in a quarrel.

ANN: Well, you will take the attitude that if I object to something you're saying or some form of discipline or treatment you plan to do then I'm just not with you—that's all—which I suppose is true. It is so often out of proportion and I don't feel this is the way we started out at all. This is not initially the way we started out. I think on my part, anyway, I started out with an awful lot of idealism because I didn't know one thing about raising a family because I was an only child and so I had nothing to gauge by— nothing at all—and I don't see how—even though I had to modify my ideals because they were not always realistic—I don't see how we could have gone so far wrong when we seemed to have been in accord and I used to say to myself, "Well, two people can say things that sound alike and maybe they even mean them alike but actually unless you can see in the other person's mind, you don't know."

JOE: You feel that at one time we were in complete accord, however?

ANN: Oh, yes, before we had any children we were, and I do remember I said one time when you came home so disgruntled—I can't re- member what you were disgruntled about—but I said that I thought we should have the kind of set-up where you saw the children only at their very best and under ideal conditions and sort of had visiting privileges when the house was spic and span and the children looked like dolls and so I guess I was really sending you clues right then.

JOE: You felt also that this was something that could never be accomplished?

ANN: Oh, definitely! Life isn't like that.

JOE: You felt that I was either incapable or unwilling to see this?

ANN: I think not being able to see it often enough—not being privileged to see it often enough.

JOE: No, I mean unable to grasp this.

ANN: I think you could grasp it all right, but you didn't like it. You didn't want it—because very often you'll say, "Tell your son or your daughter to do this or that"—sometime when you were not having anything to do with them because of some rule they had broken or other things. I remember saying to you one time, "Well, they're your children, too. I didn't come to you as a widow with all these nine children, you know. They're yours, too." And I felt that you could be sympathetic and loving and kind to their *friends* who came to the house to visit. You could make quite a big fuss over them, and your own children would be standing around— well, I felt they were jealous at the time—but they were hungering for that same kind of attention which they didn't get.

JOE: Did you ever agree in your mind—not verbally—in your mind with the idea of raising a child and cutting him free as a . . .

ANN: No, never—never. I think that is one of the most damaging treatments of a human being. I don't think any human being deserves this.

TRAINER: All right, I know that's important to you. One of the things you're saying is, "They get more than just clues of what they're hungering for, they've seen it." I don't know if, Joe, you're going to answer that—you know—"I'm really just faking it with the other kids." Are you going to say that?

JOE: The example which she makes specifically—well, I better explain— This was a method of discipline . . .

TRAINER: No, no, no—you introduced coventry. She's talking about visitors. You introduced coventry.

JOE: Well, yes, but what I mean is that these were occasions—probably exclusively—where these kids were under—well—coventry— so friends came right in.

ANN: It didn't matter whether they happen to be at the time.

JOE: Well, this isn't at all so.

TRAINER: All right. Mary, will you rate.

MARY: I think 2.

KAREN: Sounded like a 2.

IRENE: 2 too!

STAN: 2.5.

TONY: I thought about a 3.

TOM: 3.

JANE: 2.5.

BILL: About a 2 for that.

TRAINER: The words sounded like 3 but I think there was other stuff there. Well, what did you think, Ann? Did you think he was with you?

ANN: Not entirely.

TRAINER: Did he really hear you?

ANN: Not entirely.

TRAINER: The words were close but a couple things. One, maybe he's searching for what it means for him but the other thing is, tightening up, Joe. "I can't really hear all this now."

JOE: Could be—I—it's been a brand new experience.

TRAINER: It may not be a bad one for you. First time Bill's rated anyone below 3 since we've been here. It may not be a bad one for you.

JOE: I'm hoping every one is good.

TRAINER: Huh?

JOE: I'm hoping that every one is good—I mean every experience I encounter here. I'm here to look for good.

TRAINER: You've got to pay the price of the purchase like everyone else has to pay, and you can't ask the price of Ann if you can't ask it of yourself.

JOE: I'd be lying if I said this was comfortable.

ANN: I'd like to say something to Joe, though. In the past week or couple of weeks or months I have felt that you were closer to being in sympathy with all of us than you ever have been—much closer—and I marveled at this because you've missed more sessions than anybody here, I think.

TRAINER: Is that real, Joe, or is that role?

JOE: If you are devoting more thought to those around you I imagine that you automatically achieve some empathy.

TRAINER: You're saying it's part real and part role—that you don't really own it yet.

JOE: I have been devoting considerable time to those around me.

TRAINER: You're saying it's part real and part role. "But I really don't own it yet and I haven't paid the price fully yet."

JOE: But probably—simple solutions never seem to be solutions.

Still from the same session another couple discusses their family problems also in the hope of reaching new levels of understanding and direction:

"WALLS TO THE CASTLE"

TRAINER: You know, if you have been hitting that 3, I want you to push it further. You know things and you can start doing things with them.

TONY: I think I feel sometimes with the children that I'm being a policeman or a prosecutor or an administer of punishment. I feel strongly that the best time to teach a child—and I like to try to think of punishment as a teaching situation—is here and now as soon as it occurs, and I quite frankly feel put upon—I feel in an uncomfortable position—when I come home from work and you tell me about something that has happened that day and you feel that I should spank them or that rights should be taken away or whatever it is—that I should do this. And equally also difficult because—I don't know whether it's a sign of weakness or for sure quite what it is—sometimes I may feel that a certain punishment is just but unless I'm the one that feels offended or upset about it I find it difficult to administer the punishment, so that I—any-time that I feel put upon I can also resolve that maybe it's only because I wasn't involved and I'm not upset and I'm not angry and then sometimes I don't agree with the punishment that you want administered. I may either feel it's too harsh or—there I'm also torn because we've tried never to—well, I suppose in a sense we've tried to present a united front to the children. I never like to say to the children, "Well, I don't think Mom was right in doing that. She shouldn't have done that." I'd rather talk to you about it separately and not get into this. I don't want to have all these bad concerns that the kids would try to play both ends against the middle.

KAREN: You feel, then, that I'm ducking my responsibilities when I don't take care of the situation at the moment?

TONY: Yea. Yea. I feel that when a thing happens you have the feeling for what should be done whether I would agree with it or not and you're there and now is the time you should do it. You oftentimes have expressed to me that—well—you felt that I was the one who would know best how to handle it, etc., and sometimes this is kind of flattering and yet, I felt this was mainly a way of kind of duck-ing out and not having to do something.

KAREN: You do feel, though, that we present a united front to the children?

TONY: Well, I think on the whole we do—yea. I don't feel that the dis-agreement over what ought to be done has ever struck me as a major issue. The major issue is who ought to do it, and I think that I usually take care of things when I'm there and when I'm involved in the situation. The thing I have not felt quite fair is to come on the scene afterwards because I, quite frankly, had some feelings about being the big bad guy who was going to administer all the punishment.

KAREN: You didn't like it?

TONY: No, I did not like it. I didn't like it at all.

TRAINER: Karen, you can't quite free yourself up to respond to him.

KAREN: Well, what he's saying is true, and I can't see anything behind it.

TRAINER: All right. Let's rate this. O.K. I do. Let's rate. Bill?
BILL: I say 2 to 2.5.
JANE: I agree.
JOE: 3.
ANN: 3.
STAN: 2.5.
IRENE: 2.
MARY: 2.
TOM: I say 2.5.
TRAINER: It's on the minus side. I'll just say you can't fling words at it. There is something here. You're not free enough to experience it—let it all in. Tony, your experience?
TONY: How I would rate it?
TRAINER: No, just what your experience was.
TONY: I thought she was pretty much with what I was saying.
TRAINER: You want to try this on? And you tell me, but you don't have to tell me—here's what I hear, "And here you've been making a place for me, making me feel like a man, and I think I'd like to try on my own. I think I'd like to try to be a man without you making a place for me all the time any more."
TONY: It doesn't fit . . .
TRAINER: Yea, I know.
TONY: . . . at least it doesn't feel to me like it fits.
TRAINER: It fits for Karen. It doesn't fit for you.
KAREN: No. I don't know—I . . .
TRAINER: No, because your conflict now is—I'm going to push you and you're going to have to show me—your whole set is to defend him now.
KAREN: Well, I would say what he was talking about just now is very true—
TRAINER: And it's so beautiful and so convenient. I'm responding to the way he talked to you—like a boy 16 saying to his mother, "Mom, I think I'm ready to go out and try on my own now." Go ahead— smile. You don't like it.
KAREN: No, I don't feel that way.
TONY: I don't—I tell you, Bob, the way . . .
TRAINER: I'm making a jump. Christ, I know it.
TONY: No, I simply don't feel it's a jump. Let me say what I'm feeling and see where we're leading. I don't feel any difficulty in acting like a man nor have I ever felt that I had any problems with my wife. What I really was trying to say was that I felt like if you're taking care of the kids and they do something wrong and need punishment, go ahead and punish them. Don't wait until I come home.
TRAINER: Look—it's not that I—I don't know how to put it—it may be in Karen more than you, Tony, something that she senses—the

strength that she has—the fact that she can put it out on her schedule—she seems to bring everyone along, right?

KAREN: No. What I was thinking, really, why he happened to pick this topic. I didn't think it was relevant to what our problems are now.

TONY: Maybe I couldn't think of what to talk about.

KAREN: Well, that's what I asked you earlier, "What are you going to talk about tonight," and you said, "I don't know."

TRAINER: I don't like to let you off that easy. I just think you can cut it below that.

KAREN: Well, the last time we were here—no, it was before that—we had the assignment of trying it between ourselves, and I was the helpee, but we never got back to the chance of having him . . .

TONY: It was on the way to the airport.

KAREN: . . . we never got back to hearing how he felt about things so I really don't know . . .

TRAINER: You just don't know anything. That's where we end up every time.

KAREN: That's right! I just don't know.

TRAINER: Well, then, try hearing what I was saying and don't just say, "I don't know," because there is more there, and maybe this doesn't zero in on it but I think there are clues that you give out to Tony. It's not that uncommon, is it Jane? . . .

JANE: No, it's not.

TRAINER: . . . the kind of thing I'm talking about. You know, it's not like you're the first woman who did it or anything like that. And there may even be more reasons in your case—for you, from you. One thing you know is you've lost contact with some kind of basic direction—for you.

KAREN: Right.

TRAINER: And it's something that you're keeping yourself from feeling, from really experiencing fully.

KAREN: Right. Right.

TRAINER: And maybe it's unfair of me, but I'm trying to knock down some of the walls to the castle.

KAREN: That's true, but I really—I've been wondering exactly what happened—where we—where I went off the line—really I didn't know, because . . .

TRAINER: You were once sure of yourself.

KAREN: More so than I had been lately. I would like to be back on the track again.

TRAINER: And not all alone.

KAREN: No. No.

TRAINER: See, this could be more alien to Tony than to you because you're more aware of what you're doing. He's being brought along—you're doing the bringing along. More alien to Bill than to Jane. Karen?

KAREN: Well, I really, when I did tell him to let it wait because I really at the time I just couldn't cope with it any more, I just felt like that was it. I'd had it for the day, you might say, and I was just going to let this one wait until he came home because . . .

TRAINER: O.K. Then more recently—a couple months ago and so on—"What I felt more is just being drained and overwhelmed and just too tired to handle it."

KAREN: Right.

TRAINER: But what I'm suggesting is that in part that comes from losing contact with who you are. If you have your direction you wake up strong and you move strong. And you used to have it and you lost it somewhere. You're talking about the effects. The effects are that, "I'm lost, tired, beat and things get to me quick and I get overwhelmed and then I pass it off to him, but where did I get off along the line?"

KAREN: Right.

TRAINER: Let me come at it from a different viewpoint now. "If I really came on full, really came on strong, as I am a person—basically, underneath there's a strength that I found. It's always been there, if I really came on that strong it might not bring some other people along, like Tony, as much as I would like to. I'd like him to take the dominant role. I'd like him to get out front."

KAREN: Yes, that's right. I've always felt this.

TRAINER: "I'd like him to get out front, like Jane says."

KAREN: No, I've always felt that in the family the father should be the head of the house. He should be the one to . . .

TRAINER: What if the mother is stronger?

KAREN: Well, I don't think I am.

TRAINER: You may not be, but what if she's afraid she's stronger? You may not be stronger. You know, I say that up for questions, but what if she fears she's stronger along the way?

KAREN: I don't know. It would depend on a lot of things.

TRAINER: Sure would. Are you saying, "I'm not even ready for this now; even though I want to I can almost get tired working with this right now"?

KAREN: No, I'm a little confused. I don't quite know what you want.

TRAINER: O.K. Yea. (*Laugh*) You're going to make me be the man, too? (*All laugh*)

KAREN: I don't even know what *that* means.

TRAINER: Well, you do it nicely. You even defer to me and make it my responsibility. I don't buy you at that level—that's all—period, end of report!

KAREN: I don't know what you mean. I really don't. It hasn't sunk in.

TRAINER: Mary?

MARY: He's saying, too, that you're kind of burying yourself and trying to cast the role—you're afraid, perhaps, of the strength inside of you, that it would override Tony as a male and perhaps because of conflicts within yourself this is why you get up and feel drained and that you keep passing the buck back and forth to Bob and Tony—and he's digging and he wants you to dig, but you're not.

Again the trainer interprets the parent-trainees' behavior in terms of the trainees' relationship with the trainer as an analogue of the trainees' relationship with his or her children. If the trainer cannot be real and hold firm with the trainee, the parent will be unable to be real and hold firm with the child. The helpee, whether child or patient, will always turn the image back on the image maker. Life on the child's terms is directionless. Therapy on the patient's terms is directionless. The process of training as a preferred mode of treatment continues with increasingly intensive role-playing and therapeutic experiences. But the training was not restricted to role-playing. The problem children were actually brought in and the play and talking sessions between parents and children viewed by the other parents and children from behind one-way vision screens. The parents acted out their own typical ways of relating to the children before the observant eyes of the trainer and other parents.

What we found is that role-playing in the training group was not the same as meeting the child face to face. To be sure, neither is meeting the child in an experimental training situation in the same way as living with him every day at home. However, the learning from these experiences was vivid. The critiques of the interaction were pointed and sometimes severe in an attempt to directly shape behavior. One of the key learnings was a general one that fit all of the children: there were no "emotionally disturbed" children—only parents with problems—and boys with problems. Finally, the parents were isolated in private rooms for extended interactions with each other in which each served alternately as helper and helpee. The following interaction is an example:

"THE BEGINNING OF ACT I"

TOM: Talking about where I'm going to go—you know—trying something I would like to try such as making a break from _____ Cleaners and really getting my thoughts together and really—you know—setting up a program, getting guidelines to follow and go through with it and really once and for all make up my mind . . .

MARY: . . . make up your mind as a man what direction your life is going to take—yours and ours.

TOM: —the family's, which is, I can see right now, going to be real hard and probably—you know—need your help and understanding, which is always there, which I know, but—you know—let me stand on my own two feet and if I fall, I fall. Let me get up by myself, if I can get up.

MARY: Let you do it alone. In other words, let you see if you can fall even on your own.

TOM: Yea. To make a lot of decisions on my own and if at times you think I'm going way out—that this is another one of my flings—this is where you'll probably maybe have to help me—you know—try to tell me or remind me or what.

MARY: You want to stand on your own, but in a sense you want to know that I'm there to help you when you fall or if you should fall.

TOM: If I'm that blind that I'm going to be making the same mistakes and you think that I'm so blind I can't see I'm making the same mistakes—to maybe—you know, just talk things over, but the main thing is that I want to succeed in something.

MARY: Anything. You don't know what it is yet.

TOM: Well, I'm trying to think of what I actually could do and do fairly well.

MARY: That is your own?

TOM: That is my own, my own ideas. Of course, I've been thinking about this, and when I came home tonight and you told me about Beth calling up and asking if I could help them out in redecorating their house and so forth—this sounds real good and I think that I can do most of it, and I think that I can please her—please myself, I hope, and Ted. It's going to be a lot of work, but this is the type of work that I like, and once I get involved in something like this that's when I—I'm afraid I'll be so involved in my work—or involved in this—that I'll be passing the buck off to you as far as the kids are concerned or something like that. In other words, I'll be gone, come home, be gone. I'll have to try to work something out so that I'll be home sometimes.

MARY: In other words, you want to try it. It is something you do enjoy and you want to try it, but can I take it?

TOM: Yea, because I've been passing the buck on to you as far as almost every other thing goes—see like as far as disciplining the kids now—unless I can work it out until I can be home more often, be a father to them, give them the discipline if they need it, plus go whole-hearted—put my best self forward—in this particular project . . .

MARY: In other words, you do want to try it, but at the same time you're afraid of what it's going to do to us at home because you can foresee what can happen and the time that it will involve, and this scares you because, "Can I take it?" and, "Can the kids take it?" And where do you stand then in the picture?

TOM: In other words, if the same things are going to arise, I don't see where—whether I succeed in this, as something I want to do—the real purpose is succeeding in solving our problems at home, making our own home happier.

MARY: But at the same time you have to resolve this within yourself, and we'll come along. Like you say, "Give you a chance."

TOM: I'm giving myself the chance, but what chance am I giving you?

MARY: Well, give me a chance to see what I can do, and I think we can both work together.

TOM: That's it—if we can both work together and still keep harmony in the home—that any progress we made with Tim or any of them keeps progressing instead of all of a sudden stops because Daddy's being selfish again or self-centered.

In the following interaction the same husband and wife reverse roles as helper and helpee:

MARY: And I told you that I wanted you to take your chance and use it. At the same time, it does scare me. There is some uncertainty in not knowing what the future holds or what will come of it.

TOM: I guess nobody really knows what the future holds. I guess that's what makes us keep going. If we knew, maybe we wouldn't want to go.

MARY: That's true, but what I meant was from a woman's viewpoint. A man kind of looks at it with the uncertainty of his job and where it will lead to, where a woman—I look at it—well, I want you to take it—that it is uncertain for me. I know there will be a lot of times where I'll come across problems, but I feel that I can handle them if I know that you have really found your way in life—that as long as you're happy, I can be happy.

TOM: You feel that this is really what would make you happy even though many times . . .

MARY: . . . even though many times I might, perhaps, in anger or tiredness with the children—perhaps even unthinkingly strike out—this is really what I want. I want what you want. Certainly I'm thinking of the welfare of the children, but I feel that it all rests—not all—but that it will all work out if you find some area where you have found yourself.

TOM: I know that I have your confidence. There might be other problems involved, but do you feel that this is maybe the beginning of Act I? That you and I both going this way, taking these steps, that it will bring us closer together as a family?

MARY: What do you think? What do you think if you went this way? Where would you be?

TOM: I don't know if I can even accomplish this one feat with—maybe not a gold star but a silver star or something—but I think that it'll give me more confidence in myself. I'd be solving some problems of my own that you're not there to help me with as far as—you know—the dimensions of a room or something like that. I'll be on my own.

MARY: It'll be something that would be just yours.

TOM: Yea. And if I really have it or not in this field here—I mean if I have the potential—the basis to go on and learn more, do better. With the understanding that Beth and Ted have I'm sure that if I botched up the whole job I don't even know if they would really say so, but I would know if I did or not—you know—if I did botch it up and didn't say anything to them, I still think they would say it was lovely or beautiful.

MARY: In other words, no matter what you did, they wouldn't really hold you accountable, but you would hold yourself accountable.

TOM: Because I would know.

MARY: And you feel that this is a good starting place because you know that . . .

TOM: . . . maybe it's a crutch or whatever you want to call it—maybe on second thought it wouldn't be too good because I'd be giving myself a false confidence, but I think, though, that I would really know if this was something—you know—when I got finished with if I had really put forth my best efforts and even if they weren't really pleased with it at least I could say I did my best . . .

MARY: . . . you did your best.

TOM: . . . and I know that this is out and from there we can maybe go on to something else. Even so, I think it has a way of letting me be out in front.

MARY: All alone, in a sense.

TOM: Yea.

MARY: And at the same time, like I said, I know there will probably be many times when I feel I could use you at home, and these are perhaps the times when I may be tired, but you know me—you should know me—that I don't always mean what I say—sometimes I strike out in anger, and when I stop to think about it I want what's right and what's good.

TOM: Right. But at the same time, while you're doing this you're trying to tell me something. You know, "Hey, I'm here, too!" Right?

MARY: At the moment, Tom—at the moment, maybe. Yea.

TOM: Even though, even at the moment—even at that moment sometimes I don't even recognize that you're calling for help—not help but recognition.

MARY: But if the moments that you have perhaps to give me—if they're fruitful—I can get through the rest. Do you hear what I'm telling you? If when you are home and with us and you give us what you're capable of—and me—perhaps I'm not putting that . . .

TOM: In other words, when I am there if I do do my duties, so to speak, as a father and as a husband—that I do recognize these symptoms. If I can no matter how short or how long they may be that this would take a—you know—not a burden, but it would help your ego too? Or . . .

MARY: Well, no, not my ego, but help take some of the load off my shoulders, perhaps, because even last night, now, when I had so much to do yesterday and had to take the boys out last night—even just your offering to do up the dishes with Cindy—hey, that was a big thing! It was a small thing maybe to you, and you felt maybe you didn't complete it because you didn't know where all the dishes went, but this was a big thing to me.

TOM: You really appreciated it?

MARY: I really appreciated it. These are the small things that I'm talking about that when you are at home and are rested and the children are there—there's not only one parent in the house, they don't always have to go to Mommy. Hey, I wish that they'd come to you more, and if you took an active part in it, I feel that they would.

TOM: In other words you really don't feel I—lately, anyway—have been taking enough active part in the family?

MARY: Well, sometimes you tend to let me handle it, but maybe there again I start to take it away from you or something when you do. I mean, I've been trying to let you handle some of it, but when they holler or do something, even if they yell, "Mommy," if you went and . . .

TOM: . . . found out what they're yelling, "Mommy" for?

MARY: . . . asserted yourself. Right. I'm not saying all the time, because I know there are many times when you come home and you'll be tired, but a lot of times I guess a woman just hates to say to her husband, "I will never make it in 45 minutes if you don't do the dishes. Will you do the dishes?" And I guess she just kind of expects him to . . .

TOM: . . . to say, "I volunteer, I'll do them."

The husband and wife are no longer role-playing. They are dealing with very real problems, the same problems that have been plaguing them for a long time, only now they are able to communicate effectively with each other. Now they are able to understand themselves and each other with deep sensitivity. Now they are able to share their fullest experiences. Now they are able to take directionful action based upon what they have shared and understood. The parent-trainees have practiced the things that will make a constructive difference in their lives so that they, in turn, can make a constructive difference in the lives of those they love.

SUMMARY AND CONCLUSIONS

Experientially, when the helpee searches for help it is as if his phenomenological world has fallen apart and he is unable to put it back together again. In the instance of the parents, their respective relationships with each other and with their children were deteriorating, so that the parents could neither understand nor act effectively with each other or with their children. It is the helper's task to guide the helpee to put that world back together through the learning of more sensitive understanding and more effective action. Systematic group training yielded positive results for all of its individual members. In particular the interpersonal relationships between the spouses or parents improved significantly (Carkhuff & Bierman, 1970). However, the changes were much greater between parents than between parents and children in part no doubt because the parents received most of the practice experience with each other. Future projects will incorporate more of the direct parent-child experiences. We must practice that which we wish to change.

Again the principles of learning or relearning are the same for group as well as individual modalities. For the helpee, exploration precedes reorganization. Minimal understanding precedes action. Action precedes maximal understanding. Maximal understanding precedes the most effective action.

The advantages of group processes to the helper are multiple (Carkhuff, 1969e), particularly under the guidance of an effective helper: (1) each helpee has an opportunity to act out his characteristic behaviors; (2) each helper has an opportunity to observe the characteristic behaviors of others; (3) each helpee has an opportunity to communicate directly with another person other than the helper; (4) each individual has an opportunity for dispensing with unsuccessful defenses and expressing himself freely in the context of a facilitative group atmosphere; (5) each helpee has an opportunity to share in the helper's clarification and interpretation of the behavior of another; (6) each helpee has an opportunity to try out new behaviors directly with others; (7) each helpee has an opportunity to have the experience of helping as well as being helped; (8) each helpee has an opportunity to be valued by more than one person; (9) each helpee has an opportunity to focus upon the generalities of experience within the group; (10) each helpee has an opportunity to obtain a definition of social reality.

The advantages of group over individual processes for the helper are also numerous: (1) the helper has an opportunity to observe directly the behaviors of the individual helpees; (2) the helper has a direct opportunity to facilitate communication between individual helpees; (3) the helper has an opportunity to create a facilitative group atmosphere within which each group member may come to serve as a helper (4) the helper has an opportunity to focus directly upon the generalities in the group experience; (5) the helper has an opportunity to utilize his resources in such a way as to get a maximum return in human benefits for a minimum of investment of time and energy on the part of the helper.

The limitations of group processes for helper and helpee are relatively few and can be handled by individual treatment that is offered concurrent with group processes. For the helpee, while there may be less intensity and intimacy to his relationship with the helper, this may be countered by the development of a meaningful relationship with another individual in the group. In addition, the group pressures upon the helpee to conform to a socially acceptable mean of the group subculture rather than for the helpee to find his own direction in life really reflects the effect upon the helpee of the helper's inability to influence the conditions of the group. For example, one member's hostility may be blocking the free expression of another. That is, group processes may be more difficult for the helper to control than individual processes, for the helper has more individuals and interactions to attend to. However, under the direction of an effective leader these conditions should be minimized and, when they occur, be dealt with as group crises, just as we would deal with crises in individual treatment.

In addition to the many potential benefits of group processes for both helper and helpee, there are many unique contributions of systematic training processes.

Conclusion I.   Systematic training in interpersonal skills is goal directed and action oriented.

An orientation toward systematic training enables us to discriminate the operational dimensions of the problems we wish to resolve and/or the goals we wish to achieve. Following this, courses of action and programs to implement these courses of action (see Volume I) may be implemented in the most effective way.

Conclusion II.   Systematic training provides a work-oriented structure within which the more traditionally experiential and therapeutic processes can take place.

In the context of a systematic training structure the effective helper can accomplish all the learning and relearning, education, and therapeutic processes that are both necessary and valuable for the helpee. There is always a work-oriented structure to return to following the culmination of some other meaningful learning experience.

Conclusion III.   Systematic training emphasizes practice in the behavior we wish to effect.

The missing link in most treatment processes is the translation to action. With the minimal understanding necessary for action, systematic training emphasizes the most effective means of effecting behavior change—practice in the behavior we wish to effect. Accordingly, systematic training accomplishes constructive changes in understanding and attitude without running into the traditional discrepancies between insight and action.

Conclusion IV. Systematic training leaves the trainee-helpee with tangible and usable skills.

The trainee is left with skills that are valuable in his everyday living —not just memory traces of an experience, whether exciting or debilitating.

Conclusion V. Systematic training promotes longer retention of learned skills.

Systematic training maximally utilizes all sources of learning. Since the skills are in fact learned as a consequence of direct teaching, shaping, and modeling and not simply experienced by the trainee, the probability for retention is multiplied many times over.

Conclusion VI. Systematic training enables us to make systematic selection of group members.

The results of the training programs enable us to generate predictions of trainee change and to choose the trainees accordingly (see Volume I). In general, it is most helpful to have at least one trainee functioning at relatively high levels in order to have an individual group member as a model of a person who makes early movement for the other group members to emulate.

Conclusion VII. Systematic training offers a built-in means for assessing the effectiveness of the program.

Inherent in the nature of systematic training, certain steps lead to certain outcomes. The success in achieving the steps and the outcomes affords a means of evaluating the effectiveness of the program and modifying the next program in order to increase its effectiveness.

Group processes, then, are the preferred mode of treatment for all problems in living which have an interpersonal core, and systematic training is the preferred mode of group treatment. Again these propositions do not operate to the exclusion of other ancillary modes of treatment (see Chapter 9). Quite the contrary! They simply constitute the core of all effective treatment around which all effective ancillary modes of treatment, both group and individual, may be built. In this regard it is clear that individual treatment experiences may have a very real place concomitant to the group experience. In summary, what can be accomplished individually can be accomplished in groups—and more! What can be accomplished in groups can be accomplished in systematic training—and more!

REFERENCES

For a more detailed discussion of the issues considered in this chapter see the asterisked readings and the references upon which the readings are based.

Bach. G. R. The marathon group: I. Intensive practice of intimate interaction. *Psychological Reports*, 1966, **18**, 995–1002.

Benne, K. The self, the group or the task? Differences among growth groups. Paper presented, The growth groups: Encounter, marathon, sensitivity and "T," 9th Annual Conference, Personality Theory and Counseling Practice, University of Florida, January 17, 1969.

Berzon, B., & Soloman, L. N. Research frontiers: The self-directed therapeutic group. *Journal of Counseling Psychology*, 1966, **13**, 491–497.

Bradford, P., Gibb, J. R., & Benne, K. D. (eds.). *T-group theory and laboratory method: An innovation in re-education.* New York: John Wiley & Sons, Inc., 1964.

Carkhuff, R. R. Toward a comprehensive model of facilitative interpersonal processes. *Journal of Counseling Psychology*, 1967, **14**, 67–72.

Carkhuff, R. R. The influence of leader level of functioning on group processes. Address, The growth groups: Encounter, marathon, sensitivity and "T," 9th Annual Conference, Personality Theory and Counseling Practice, University of Florida, January 17, 1969. (a)

Carkhuff, R. R. Critical perspectives on group processes. Address, The growth groups: Encounter, marathon, sensitivity and "T," 9th Annual Conference, Personality Theory and Counseling Practice, University of Florida, January 18, 1969. (b)

Carkhuff, R. R. Critical variables in effective counselor training. *Journal of Counseling Psychology*, 1969, **16**, 238–245. (c)

*Carkhuff, R. R. Critical variables in group therapeutic processes. In *Group Counseling*, J. Hansen and S. Cramer (eds.) New York: Appleton-Century-Crofts, 1969. (d)

*Carkhuff, R. R., & Bierman, R. Training as a preferred mode of treatment of parents of emotionally disturbed children. *Journal of Counseling Psychology*, 1970, **17**, 157–161.

*Gazda, G. *Innovations to group psychotherapy.* Springfield, Ill.: Charles C Thomas, 1969.

Lubin, B., & Lubin, A. W. *Group psychotherapy: A bibliography of the literature from 1956 to 1964.* East Lansing,, Mich.: Michigan State University Press, 1967.

Matarazzo, J. Psychotherapeutic processes. *Annual Review of Psychology,* Palo Alto, Calif.: 1965, **16**, 181–219.

Moustakas, C. E. *The authentic teacher: sensitivity and awareness in the classroom.* Cambridge, Mass.: H. A. Doyle, 1966.

Murphy, M. The growth center phenomenon. Address, The growth groups: Encounter, marathon, sensitivity and "T," 9th Annual Conference, Personality Theory and Counseling Practice, University of Florida, January 16, 1969.

Rogers, C. R. A plan for self-directed change in an educational system. *Educational Leadership,* 1967, **24**, 717–731.

Schein, E. H., & Bennis, W. G. (eds.) *Personal and organization change through group methods: The laboratory approach.* New York: John Wiley & Sons, Inc., 1961.

Stoller, F. H. The long weekend. *Psychology Today,* 1967, **1**, 28–33.

PART THREE

Toward
Effective Implementation
and Inquiry

THE HELPING PROCESS is not complete until we have made inquiries into its effects and have modified it accordingly. Practice is generalized to theory and theory translated to practice in a very highly interactional process (Chapter 11). The problems of process and outcome, in turn, can be placed in perspective only when they are seen in the context of life and the interpersonal processes that dominate life (Chapter 12). The investigation of helping and life, especially insofar as it uses rating scales, employs the criteria of meaning and rigor, with the former serving to make functionally useful translations and the latter to stabilize these translations (Chapter 13). Finally, basic principles in research are made operational, with emphasis upon a basic research model and some innovating applications (Chapter 14).

11
THE TRANSLATION OF THEORY TO
PRACTICE IN HELPING

The helper does not know that he has been a helper until he has made inquiries into the helping process. Similarly, the helping agency has not established that it has provided help until it too has investigated the helping process. These inquiries, then, must be considered an integral part of the helping process. They guide the search for a more effective approach to helping by providing the feedback necessary to shape or modify subsequent practices.

The search for more effective practices leads readily to a consideration of the interaction of theory and practice. Broadly speaking, theoretical formulations are merely means of organizing our experience. We attempt to articulate our experience in some systematic way so that we can comprehend it better. We attempt to understand it so that we can develop more effective formulations and thus more effective practices. This highly interactional process may be termed theory- or model-building or, for that matter, practice-building.

The formulations that we conceive are only as good as the benefits to which they translate. They touch earth, so to speak, in their interpretations of phenomena already experienced and in their structuring of phenomena that are about to be experienced. Thus, for better or for worse these formulations can guide our efforts. In tune with the raw data of human experience they can lead us to more effective and more efficient practices. When they ignore human experience they can lead away from effective functioning.

The pragmatic criteria by which we measure the value of our formulations are tangible human benefits. The effective practitioner cannot get lost in the complexities of his formulations, the intricacies of his methodologies, and the sophistication of his intellect. He does not require a degree in philosophy of science to reflect back upon his past helping experiences, discern the effective elements, interrelate them in a meaningful way, and apply them to his next experience. The more systematic the helper's inquiry, the more systematic will be his formulations and applications and consequently the greater the benefits that will accrue to his helpees. Every effective helper formulates models in one form or another to guide his search for better practices. Let us consider for a moment some fundamental constructs of model-building.

A PARADIGM FOR MODEL-BUILDING IN HELPING

The many views of what is involved in theorizing (Bergman, 1953; Boring, 1953; Feigl, 1945; Harre, 1960; Kaplan, 1964; Koch, 1951; Spence, 1944) converge upon a fundamental purpose of science: explanation. An understanding of the phenomena that science seeks to describe is accomplished by bringing under the fewest possible assumptions, concepts, and principles the greatest number of facts and observations. It has been suggested (Hemple & Oppenheim, 1953) that there exists a continuum that begins with a simple description of immediately observable facts and moves through empirical laws to first-order theories and finally to higher-order constructs of even greater generality.

Much controversy has surrounded the issues involving the inductive and deductive functions of theory (Hull, 1943; Skinner, 1950), and some of the logical problems involved in equating the two processes (Harre, 1960) have been established. However, at the risk of appearing naïve to the sophisticated and perhaps sophisticated to the naïve, we will assume that theory serves both an inductive and a deductive function (Underwood, 1957), and we will present a simplified schema to this effect. To better understand this view of theory we will begin inductively at the point of the raw data (see Figure 11-1).

The stability and reliability of the phenomena and the relationships that obtain between and among independent variables and these phenomena appear to be logical determinants of theoretical readiness (level A in Figure 11-1). Of course, cross-validation of results and all that this process implies is an important consideration at this empirical level. From these raw data certain propositions of a singular nature (facts) or general nature (laws) may be established (level B). In turn, these functional relationships between observed events interact with each other, resulting in first-order theories that relate and "interpret" the relationships (level C). First-order theories may also interact in the

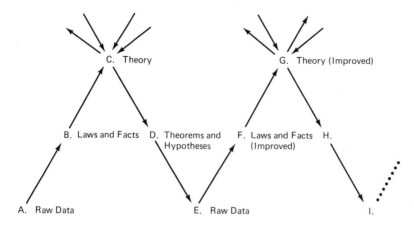

Figure 11-1. A schematic representation of the inductive and deductive functions of model building.

production of higher-order generalizations. Viewed in another way, these theories and higher-order constructs may also produce certain expectations about as-yet unobserved data, that is, serving the deductive function of theory.

The interrelationship of laws and facts accomplished in theory permits the deduction of theorems or abstract generalizations from which hypotheses or inferential statements of a tentative nature may be derived and empirically tested (level D). The statement of relationships in the "if then" form is confirmed, or not, by the significance of the raw data (level E). The results (again cross-validation is important), in turn, serve neither to prove nor disprove theory but rather either to support or not support it.

An investigation may, then, begin at several points, but in all probability it will begin with either the stable body of empirical data (point A), from which it may operate inductivity or with an already existing theory (point C) from which systematic deductions might be made. The usual flow would be inductively from A to C or from C to E. Having arrived at the predetermined objectives, one might find the theory inadequate to the task of explaining some of the data. An obligation to reflect back and qualify, reorganize, or dismiss the theory (the movement from E to G in an attempt to improve the system) now becomes apparent. The interactional process of theory-building continues in perpetuity (H, I, J, K, L, and so on). In this regard Hebb (1959) has stated succinctly the mandate incumbent upon the investigator:

Theory is not an affirmation but a method of analysis and can't produce any belief. Knowledge progresses by stages, so the theory one holds today must be provisional, as much a formulation of one's ignorance as anything else, to be used as long as it is useful and then discarded. Its function is to organize for better evidence. It is really only a working assumption which the user may actively disbelieve.

APPLICATIONS IN MODEL-BUILDING FOR CORE CONDITIONS: ILLUSTRATIONS

Inquiries and formulations that make a difference in the lives of helpees and consequently in the lives of helpers have been a long time coming. In part those elaborate cosmologies that were too far removed from the raw data of human experience were responsible for the delay. Indeed, the relevant statistics on helpee benefits will reflect, no doubt, the degree to which the system relates to human experience. If the relationship is positive, we can expect positive results. If it is negative, we can expect negative results. When empirical methodology finally caught up with psychoanalytic theory, for example, it demonstrated that out of 100 persons treated 67 were likely to improve with no treatment at all over a one- to two-year period while only 44 were likely to improve with psychoanalytic treatment (Eysenck, 1952, 1960, 1965). We lose 23 potential success cases when we employ the psychoanalytic approach. We can make direct inferences concerning the lack of congruence between these systems and the experience of the people who are treated (Carkhuff & Berenson, 1967). Unfortunately, whereas empirical methodology has caught up with these systems, political methodology has not, and the systems continue to survive, if not flourish, in a world that has great need for more effective practices.

Concerned practitioners began to make formulations that were more relevant to the experience of the person with whom they were interacting. Thus, Shafer and Shoben in 1956 wrote of warm concern, nonretaliatory permissiveness, and honesty of communication, while Rogers in 1957 wrote of empathy, unconditional positive regard, and congruence. While these formulations were sketchy and in some cases, as with nonretaliatory permissiveness and unconditional positive regard, needed to be put in perspective, they guided the early investigations of the effects of the helping process. Accordingly, when the Wisconsin Schizophrenic Project, which was, to be sure, attempting to establish the effectiveness of the nondirective mode of treatment with schizophrenic patients, found significantly greater variability in its treatment group than in its control group, the investigators were able to trace back over the recorded cases and establish the differential processes that led to differential effects (Rogers, Gendlin, Kiesler, & Truax, 1967): counselors and therapists who were functioning at high levels of empathy, unconditionality, and congruence had patients who demonstrated positive outcomes on a variety of indexes, while counselors and therapists who were functioning at low levels had patients who demonstrated positive outcomes on a variety of indexes, while counselors and therapists who were functioning at low levels had patients who demonstrated negative outcomes (Truax & Carkhuff, 1967). While the number of patients was very small and the significance of the investigation has been dwarfed by other studies, the results were consistent with those of other research projects (Barron & Leary, 1955; Cartwright & Vogel, 1960; Mink & Isaksen, 1959). Perhaps most important for our purposes, these results led to the development of our own eclectic models.

The movement, then, was from practice to formulations to research of practice (A to C to E in Figure 11-1). The next direction was to reflect back upon the original formulations (E to G). This process led to an attempt to develop a comprehensive model (Carkhuff, 1967) in which both helper and helpee were assessed on the same dimensions and in which all sources of learning, the didactic, the experiential, and modeling, served to influence the helpee to function more and more in ways structurally similiar to the helper. That is, with high-level–functioning helpers helpees who are functioning at low levels gain on the structural dimensions of empathy and the like. The development of such a model necessitated the modification of the dimensions involved. For example, whereas unconditionality might serve a useful function at one stage of helping, the helping process does not seek to enable the helpee to assume an unconditional stance toward his world. If it did, there would be far fewer success cases. The development of an emphasis upon respect rather than unconditional positive regard or nonpossessive warmth was further buttressed by research evidence indicating that assessments of positive regard account for most of the variance of unconditional positive regard (Carkhuff, 1968). Similarly, the congruence which can be intrapersonal was reformulated in terms of the communication of genuineness or authenticity, which is more in keeping with the helpee's experience. Finally, empathy was reconstituted with an emphasis upon its operational translation, the interchangeability of affect and meaning, as a minimally effective base.

Perhaps more important, the model was expanded to incorporate other significant activities of the helper. Thus, a helper who discloses himself will enable the helpee to be able increasingly to disclose himself as it is appropriate. A helper who is concrete and specific in problem-solving activities will enable a helpee to become concrete and specific in his problem-solving activities. A helper who is able to initiate confrontations of the helpee based upon his experience of the helpee will enable the helpee to confront himself and others. A helper who is able to initiate interpretations of the immediacy of the relationship based upon his experience of the helpee's communications to him will enable the helpee to do similarly. In each instance through the various sources of learning the helpee becomes able to do what the helper is effective in doing, although, to be sure, provisions are made in the model for the helpee's going beyond his helper's level of functioning.

Concurrently, the model for interpersonal processes was expanded to include the unique contributions of a variety of potential preferred modes of treatment (Carkhuff, 1966a) in addition to incorporating contextual and environmental variables as well as helper and helpee variables (Carkhuff, 1966b). It was expanded to include extrahelping as well as intrahelping phenomena. Its interpersonal core was extended to incorporate action-oriented as well as facilitative dimensions and it was complemented by the contributions of different treatment modalities over and above those accounted for by the core conditions. In turn, the models had been interrelated in a harmonious manner.

The next step was to generate predictions according to this model. Differential predictions based upon the differential functioning of helpers and helpees on the relevant dimensions were checked out in process and outcome studies. In general, the helpers functioning at the highest levels tended to achieve the most positive results in their helpees while the helpees functioning initially at the highest levels tended to function ultimately at the highest levels. In interaction with each other the helpees who were functioning at the highest levels and whose level of functioning showed the greatest positive differential with their helper's level of functioning (that is, the helpers were functioning at very high levels) made the greatest gains. Other investigations of complementary treatment modalities (Carkhuff & Berenson, 1967) and the effects of the environment (Chapter 5, Volume I) were also conducted.

We must look back to our model and modify it according to the results of this research. We anticipated, for example, that high-level–functioning helpees would gain the most in conjunction with high-level–functioning helpers, and we need now to modify this idea to incorporate the fact that a sizable and positive differential in level of functioning is necessary in order to bring about this gain. We anticipated, for example, the retention of direct and immediate effects, and we must now allow for the indirect and long-term effects of the environment to which the helpee goes. We saw, for example, the potential preferred modes of treatment as complementary in nature, and we have now integrated the interpersonal core with some of these modalities, as the behavioristic, in our approach to training in interpersonal functioning as a preferred mode of treatment.

Again we will return to the soil from which the data evolves in continuing this highly interactional process of model-building. We are continually moving toward greater demonstrable human benefits, which is, after all, our criterion of competence in helping.

APPLICATIONS IN MODEL-BUILDING FOR A PREFERRED MODE OF TREATMENT: ILLUSTRATIONS

A large percentage of teaching, guidance, counseling, and therapeutic activities involve problems of educational and vocational choice. The entire trait-and-factor system is integrally bound with research on the processes of vocational choice. As such, applications of learnings from vocational choice theory and research constitute potential preferred modes of treatment for some helpees. Unfortunately, a logical analysis of the major positions and projects involved in vocational choice processes yields neither theories firmly and inductively rooted in practice nor practice consistently and deductively derived from theory.

The schema of theory elaborated upon will be employed in evaluating the works of Roe, the Michigan group, Tiedeman and O'Hara, Super, and Holland in an attempt to obtain some perspective on these theories, especially in terms of how the various approaches to vocational choice relate to the inductive-deductive process of theory-building.

Roe

Anne Roe and her associates (1956, 1964, 1966) view occupational choice as a process of "self-categorization." Roe looks upon the individual, as does Maslow, as an "integrated, organized whole" whose classification should be based upon his goals or needs, whether conscious or unconscious. Thus, Roe sees an occupation as a primary source of need satisfaction. In an apparent attempt to come to some immediate closure, she seeks to arrange these goals or needs in a hierarchy of prepotency and makes what appears to be a somewhat arbitrary choice of Maslow's somewhat arbitrary hierarchical system. Roe, then, employs her "empirical approach" to select representatives from various vocational fields and to differentiate their personality characteristics and needs. In this regard her choice of perhaps the least empirical of measuring instruments, the Rorschach inkblot test, is an interesting one, again revealing Roe's analytic bias.

Roe's most meaningful contribution remains her very useful level and group classification of occupations. Her later attempts to relate vocational choice to family background (home atmosphere and parental attitudes) have met with little empirical support. Thus, in her schema she finds that persons at level 1 in her classification schema are strongly driven, absorbed in their work, superior in intelligence, and from favorable social climates. She suggests that persons who are freed for creative work through lower need gratification can produce more effectively and with infinitely greater satisfaction than those whose creativity is in spite of, or perhaps partly marshaled by, a hunt for substitute gratifications. Roe's group findings include descriptions of the physical scientist as withdrawn, compulsive, rigid, and anxious; the biologist as restricted and nonsocial; the psychologist as uninterested in intellectual controls and interested in people; and the artist as tending to think abstractly. Further, Roe's studies of the differences between "experimentalists" and "theorists" demonstrate that theorists come from more professional backgrounds, liked school, and developed more adequate social contacts than the experimentalists.

Unfortunately, instead of attempting to generalize her findings into a unique and comprehensive system, Roe apparently seeks to "rationalize" her results by drawing from analytic theory and Maslow's postulates to support her findings. She has neither systematically deduced her hypotheses from these systems nor does she work inductively to these systems. While she feints in the direction of higher-order inductive generalizations (E to F, Figure 11-2), she falls back upon analytic theory and the

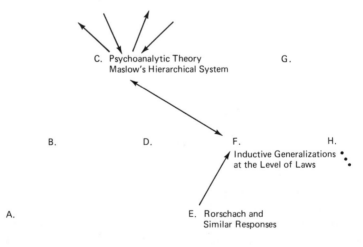

Figure 11-2.   A suggested schematic representation of Roe's (1956) approach.

need hierarchy (F to C), which she apparently had in mind all the while, and from which, to be consistent, she should have operated deductively in the first place. It appears entirely possible that Roe would have made the connections with these systems no matter what her empirical findings were. She does not make systematic derivations from the theories that she proposes, nor is the theory with which she deals a generalization of her findings, thus, serving to organize the available evidence and guide the search for better evidence. Rather, she appears to seek entrance to already existing systems. She does not make a sufficient attempt to qualify the existing theories in terms of her findings, and, thus, she provides no unique theory of her own to encompass her results. In summary, according to the schema Roe makes no justifiable generalizations from her data above the level of what has been defined as laws.

The Michigan Group

The Michigan group (Nachmann, 1960; Segal, 1961; Galinsky, 1962; Bordin, Nachmann & Segal, 1963; Beall & Bordin, 1964; Segal & Szabo, 1964; Galinsky & Fast, 1966; Beall, 1967) has proposed a series of dimensions traceable to infantile physiological functions to account for all of the gratifications that work can offer. Any occupation can be described in terms of the relative strengths of these component dimensions and their relation to a series of modifying characteristics. The theoretical formulations had their original stimuli in studies applying psychoanalytic assumptions regarding personality development to the explanation of occupational activity patterns of accountants and creative writers; lawyers, dentists, and social workers; clinical psychologists and physicists; and engineers. In all of these studies occupational analyses were made to identify what needs might be gratified through what modes of expression. While these studies make passing mention to the effect that this expression occurs within the framework of the environmental pressures and opportunities with which the individual is confronted, Roe (1963) herself is critical of the inability of the Michigan school to incorporate "persons . . . whose occupational motivation is constrained mainly by external forces—economic, cultural, geographical, and other —and persons who have little capacity to get gratification from their work." Because of time and space limitations, we might attend primarily to the first of the studies (Segal, 1961), which initiated a program of research and theory under Bordin's direction.

Segal suggests that analytic concepts such as identification, the development of defense mechanisms, and sublimation in conjunction with the process of role implementation can be used to understand the personality characteristics of individuals who make a specific vocational choice. First, he ascertains the behavioral demands made of practitioners in various fields by an evaluation of occupational information sources. He then selects the vocational fields of creative writing and accounting because they represent widely divergent occupational activities and social stereotypes. He proceeds to determine analytically the personality characteristics expected and employs primarily the Rorschach test in testing his hypotheses.

While Segal presents himself as having proceeded directly from theory, systematically deducing his hypotheses, there are many questions as to whether this is a test of psychoanalytic theory as it has been related by Segal to the vocational process. Segal seems to have engaged in a two-step process here: (1) he moves from the occupational stereotypes to psychoanalytic theory in an *ad hoc* fashion in order to "explain" how the stereotypes may have come about and to determine analytically the implications of the stereotype (D to C, Figure 11-3); and (2) he predicts Rorschach and other responses from the occupational stereotypes (D to E). In general, the main effect of the two steps is to preclude any possibility of testing the theory as related by Segal. The predictions seem to be made according to the stereotypes, not according to the theory, and while an *ad hoc* attempt is made to relate psychoanalytic theory with the stereotypes, there is no direct line deduction. Thus, it appears that Segal is testing essentially either how accurate the stereotyped descriptions and their implications are or how sensitive to these characteristics his instrument is.

In addition, on some of the Rorschach indexes that would be critical to his study Segal does not get expected differences. If as he claims the

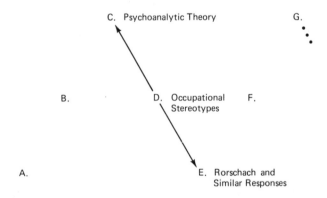

Figure 11-3.   A suggested representation of Segal's (1961) approach.

hypotheses were directly derived from theory, then unless he is severely critical of the sensitivity of the instrument employed he is obliged to reflect back upon the original theory as he interprets it to qualify or reorganize it, since in some way it has been deficient. (Thus, he should have moved from E to G in the schematic representation.) The question must be raised as to whether or not Segal is taking for granted the essential truth of his theory in not looking at the implications of all of his findings.

While Segal's work suggests the possibility that aspects of analytic theory might some day be deductively related to the vocational process, it appears that he has completed only the first step in the process of finding the best system to organize the available evidence and guide the quest for better evidence. His efforts seem quasiempirical. He appears only to have supported Roe's essential finding that on some of the Rorschach indexes that instrument supports the concept of occupational stereotypes.

Tiedeman and O'Hara

Tiedeman and O'Hara (1961, 1962, 1963) view career development as part of a continuing process of differentiating ego identity: just how a person's identity evolves is dependent upon his early childhood experiences with the family unit. the psychosocial crises he encounters at various developmental stages, the congruence between society's meaning system and the individual's meaning system (including his needs, aptitudes, and interests), and the emotional concomitants of each of these factors. Tiedeman and O'Hara have borrowed heavily from the thinking of Freud, Erikson, from Super, Ginzberg, and Roe, and from the social psychologists in developing highly complex, mathematical, and sometimes esoteric formulations of career development: "a concatenation of concepts that seem to be needed as primitive terms in a science of career development relating personality and career through the mechanisms of differentiation and integration as a chooser chooses and experiences the evolution of his life problem."

Their all-inclusive attempt, then, views career development as a sequence of developmental life stages or events. Related to the *aspect of anticipation* or *preoccupation* (of career goals) are the *subaspects* (or steps) of *exploration, crystallization, choice*, and *clarification*. During the *aspect* of *implementation* or *adjustment* the steps of *social induction, reformation*, and *integration* occur. Accompanying each of these developmental stages are certain personality or psychosocial crises, such as the "autonomy versus shame" crisis characteristic of the "anal" period, or the "identity versus role diffusion" crisis of early adolescence. In addition, Tiedeman and O'Hara have concentrated on the developmental crises of later life that occur in school and the world of work, since they feel there is less of a biological and more of an "integrated, or inbalanced, conjunction of the emotional and the rational elements of the personality." Much of their research has characteristically centered on the vocational decision-making processes of children, adolescents, and young adults in school counseling situations, and they have made extensive use of tape-recorded transcripts of counseling or standardized interview sessions, which they analyze and describe in terms of their preconceived paradigm of career development. Each case is presented in terms of the differentiation and integration model, with reference to both career choice and personality development. The vocational choice processes of each case are described, with particular emphasis upon the psychosocial crises relevant to the situation. As an example, in citing the case of Bob, a bright third-grader who identifies with his uncle rather than with his father in his present vocational choice, Tiedeman and O'Hara state that this "transference to another adult in the environment with the same role" may lead to an easy resolution of a potential oedipal crisis. It is apparent that Tiedeman and O'Hara, while contributing little of their own, have attempted an integration of a number of theories and approaches into a coherent and comprehensive theory of career development.

What Tiedeman and O'Hara do have, then, is a massive collection of laws, facts, and theorems, some of which have been derived from systematic research into the career development process and others that have been borrowed from existing theories. They begin with the theoretical systems of the psychoanalytic and the trait-and-factor analysts. From here they proceed deductively toward the establishment of a developmental paradigm at the level of theorem (C to D, Figure 11-4). They have collected a great deal of research evidence, which has also led them to postulate similar developmental paradigms (E to F), that they relate to the deduced theorems (F to D and D to F). However, both their own research and their assumptions based upon other theories have led them to develop similar theorems, apparently independently of each other, the only logical linkage being that they continuously relate their findings back to the preconceived theories with which they began (F to C, Figure 11-4). Their theoretical modifications consist only of extending the specific instances to which their theorems apply (F to H) and never of any real changes in their previous formulations (E to F to G). As a result, their theory cannot emerge beyond the status of a collection of lower-level generalizations. Instead of streamlining and simplify-

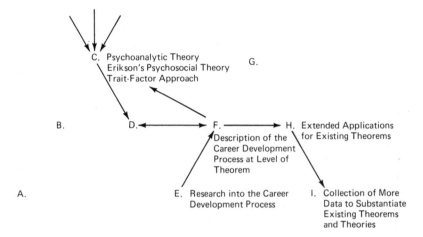

Figure 11-4. A suggested representation of the approach of Tiedeman & O'Hara (1963).

ing their theorems, they seem to be moving in the opposite direction, toward encompassing as diverse data as possible, hoping that in the future out of the midst of chaos order will emerge.

Super

Super and his associates (Super, 1957, 1963; Super & Bachrach, 1957; Super, Crites, Hummel, Moser, Overstreet, & Warnath, 1957; Super & Overstreet, 1960; Super, Starishevsky, Matlin, & Jordaan, 1963) are perhaps most candid in accepting as valid the criticism that much of the work in the occupational area lacks an adequate theoretical framework. In particular, Super derides the trait-and-factor people, who, with their isolated and fragmentary research, forgo the rewards of a systematic, developmental approach that offers the potential for a well-organized theory. Super views each of the major orientations, the trait-and-factor approach, the social systems view, and the personality approach, as partial analytic systems incomplete in and of themselves. His proposal, then, is an integrative one, stressing the interactive nature of the process of vocational development, that is, the interaction of personal and environmental variables. His own unique contribution involves an attempt to synthesize the different orientations with vocational, sociological, industrial, and psychometric learnings. In order to establish the lawful determinism of career patterns, Super borrows heavily from the developmental principles of Ginzberg (1951) and others in order to view vocational development as an ongoing, continuous, and generally irreversible process. While such formulations have been criticized as resting upon a catalog of stages of development for all personalities (Kitson, 1951; O'Hara & Tiedeman, 1959), Super puts them to good use in character- izing the career process as a process of compromise within which his key construct, the development and implementation of the self-concept, operates. The individual chooses occupations whose characteristics will allow him to function in a role that is consistent with his concept of himself, which, in turn, is a function of his own developmental history.

Unfortunately, Super's formulation of the *formation, translation,* and ultimate *implementation* of the self-concept in education and work suffers from his attempt to integrate all possible theoretical and research con- siderations into one system. While this is laudable in the sense that there are many obvious factors that others have neglected, the product is a set of propositions that are too loose, too general, and too inclusive, all of which seem to be fighting for equal weight and none of which allows for any systematic and meaningful theoretical derivations. The reader is overwhelmed by the proliferation of considerations and the difficulties involved in making operational many of these considerations.

Perhaps more interesting than Super's formulations per se is the lack of relationship between the longitudinal and the very valuable, though sometimes fragmentary, studies of career patterns and those formula- tions. While he claims to employ a developmental framework, he gets involved in very low-level, empirical kinds of expectations that bear little relation to his "theoretical" formulations. It must be said that Super has not explicitly stated that his intention is to relate his theory to his investigation. However, he *does* operate at two different levels, and these levels *are not* related. On the one hand, he has taken it upon himself to attempt to integrate all available knowledge or lack of knowledge into one general and loosely connected system in which the weights of the various factors are indiscernible. On the other hand, he is operating at a strictly empirical level with no logically deduced hypotheses, but, rather, with many low-level and probationary expectations limited by the realities of the studies in terms of design, methodology, instruments, and so on. He operates inductively up to the level of laws (A to B, Figure 11-5) but does not establish the connection between his two processes, although he may yet relate B to some future C.

It would seem, then, since very little connection has as yet been estab- lished between the two phenomena, that the longitudinal work offers the most immediate potential because great difficulty is encountered in im- plementing Super's all-inclusive theoretical formulations. His most worth- while contributions are included in his longitudinal work in collecting his data and establishing the presence of stable phenomena.

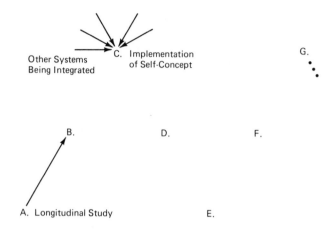

Figure 11-5. A suggested schematic representation of Super's (1957) approach.

Holland

Holland and his associates (Holland 1959, 1962, 1966a, 1966b; Holland & Nichols, 1964; Stockin, 1964; Osipow, Ashby, & Wall, 1966) attempt to delineate a theory of vocational choice "comprehensive enough to integrate existing knowledge and at the same time sufficiently close to observables to stimulate further research." Evident in Holland's formulations are the general influences of need theory, role theory, self theory, social learning theory, psychoanalytic theory, and sociology.

The theory assumes, in accordance with general psychological theory, that at the time a person chooses his vocation he is a product of his heredity and environment. Out of his experiences he develops a hierarchy of habitual or preferred methods for dealing with necessary social and environmental tasks, that is, his life style. This hierarchy or pattern of personal orientations directs the individual toward an occupational environment that will satisfy his particular hierarchy. That is, various classes or occupational groups furnish different kinds of gratifications or satisfactions and require different abilities, identifications, values, and attitudes, and a person's choice of an occupation is an expressive act reflecting his motivations, his knowledge of the occupation in question, his insight and understanding of himself, his personality, and his abilities. In viewing one's occupation as a "way of life, an environment rather than a set of isolated work functions or skills," Holland describes both the working environment and the person in the same terms; out of his own experience he arrived at six major classes of occupational environments and six corresponding personal orientations: the realistic, the intellectual, the social, the conventional, the enterprising, and the artistic. His categorizations bear a heavy trait-factor quality, but his inclination to offer a clinically flavored analysis carries him beyond that approach. One other aspect of Holland's work deserves mention—his attention to extraindividual factors, whose influence is usually recognized, though sidestepped, by most theorists. Thus, he has found that "persons with particular personality patterns achieve in some environments but not in others." Yet, despite his attention to such factors Holland has, in the past, confined his research in large part to persons functioning at higher levels, populations whose members aspire to vocations that require professional training and, in addition, have maximal freedom in their vocational choice.

Thus, we find Holland at level B, implicitly influenced by his own experience, integrating empirical data from previous research and operating with a general "set" indicative of contact with a number of different theories. He has generalized from accumulated raw data and simple facts to the level of laws, which, while they serve to integrate a good deal of existing research and suggest testable hypotheses, do not provide explanations for specified consequences of the interaction of data and laws (B to D, Figure 11-6). For example, Holland hypothesizes that the level within an occupational area that an individual chooses is a function of that individual's self-evaluation and intelligence. Whereas theory would offer some explanatory principle from which this formula might have been derived, Holland merely presents the formula, which, because it is testable, may be verified or modified, but which has yet to be placed within the logical context of theory. Thus, Holland's research efforts do

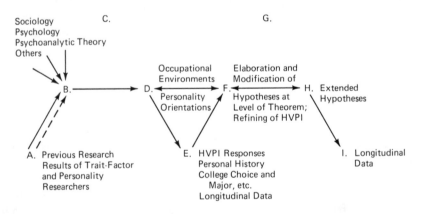

Figure 11-6. A suggested schematic representation of Holland's (1966) approach.

not flow deductively from theory but rather consist of a series of cross-sectional analyses and longitudinal studies that attempt to relate subjects' high-point codes on his preference inventory to a number of other variables: SAT scores, the famous people the individual would like to emulate, self-ratings, teacher ratings, nonacademic activities, choice of college major, background. In addition, Holland has added a great deal of interesting and valuable information to the area of vocational choice and has been open to reformulations of original hypotheses (E to F, Figure 11-6). His predictions, however, are made from descriptive stereotypes, not theory, and his results support, add to, or modify his descriptive categories, not theory. Holland neither logically deduces his hypotheses nor does he make generalizations from his data above the level of laws.

In summary, there does not appear to be any theory of vocational choice that meets the inductive-deductive model of theory-building. The general situation may be represented as one in which we have two sets of constructs: (1) low-level generalizations that offer the potential of being interrelated with one another, and each with rules of correspondence connecting it to observables; and (2) those constructs, also offering the possibility of interrelationship with one another, but of logical or pseudological definition. Notably lacking but indispensable to adequate theory-building are the appropriate inductive-deductive connections between these two sets of constructs.

For the most part preconceived theoretical structures, because they are not modified by empirical results, promote circularity of formulation and inhibit our efforts at theoretical breakthrough. Illustrative here are many of the efforts to transpose psychodynamic theory from the realm of personality to that of vocational choice. Rather than developing lower-level generalizations from the data in the ultimate hope of interrelating these generalizations, or employing the data to modify or qualify the higher-order constructs from which they were derived, these "theorists" all too often restrict their use of new data to those supporting the original theoretical framework. However, while their efforts, and thus their results, are wanting in independent, internally consistent direction, unencumbered and systematic attempts such as those of the Michigan school to discern the potentially unique contributions of the ego-analytic position to vocational development must be applauded.

At the other extreme are efforts such as those of Super that appear to make no attempt to bridge the gap between laws and theory. His theoretical formulations are often difficult, although by no means impossible, to make operational. While beginning with theoretical formulations based upon self-theory, Super has become primarily involved in empirical research that, because it often bears little or no direct relation to his elaborated formulations, avoids entanglement in a closed theoretical network. However, while his system has not emerged beyond the level of low-level generalizations, his efforts to accumulate longitudinal data contribute to the establishment of a basis for theoretical readiness.

Similarly, Holland's large-scale empirical efforts are in large part free from delimiting theoretical bias; the tightly knit quality of his prolific research is supplemented by a continuous process of reformulation and speculation at the level of laws. Because his concepts and measurements are often almost one and the same, he manages to assure the relevance of his research to that supposedly being researched; however, the parsimony of his methodology, while it avoids duplication, must not become a handicap to theoretical aspirations.

A comprehensive attempt that draws both inductively from new bodies of stable data and deductively from already existing formulations is necessary: the dimensions held in common by the various orientations and the potentially unique contributions of each orientation must be discerned and systematically investigated. In this manner we can work toward assigning differential weights to the potentially huge number of forces that influence vocational choice and development (Stefflre, 1966).

It seems, then, that the area of vocational choice, an area of critical concern to the development of potential preferred modes of treatment, does not approximate the highly interactional process of theory-building as, for example, the model-building in core conditions does. Indeed, recent evidence indicating that expressed choice is a better predictor of future choice brings in all of the counseling testing methodologies and the approaches upon which they are based for severe scrutiny. Much of the effort appears academic, almost operating independently of the practice of counseling that led to its emphasis in the first place. In all of our efforts, whether in discerning core dimensions of interpersonal learning or relearning processes or in developing ancillary courses of action, we must ultimately return again to the soil of practice from which our constructs evolved, testing, modifying, and testing again. We must seek continually to move toward greater demonstrable human benefits.

REFERENCES

For a more detailed discussion of the issues considered in this chapter see the asterisked readings and the references upon which the readings are based.

Beall, L. Vocational choice: The impossible fantasy and the improbable choice. *Journal of Counseling Psychology*, 1967, **14**, 86–92.
Beall, L., & Bordin, E. S. The development and personality of engineers. *Personnel and Guidance Journal*, 1964, **43**, 23–32.

Barron, F., & Leary, T. Changes in psychoneurotic patients with and without psychotherapy. *Journal of Consulting Psychology*, 1955, 19, 239–245.

Bergman, G. Theoretical psychology. *Annual Review of Psychology*, 1953, 4, 435–458.

Bordin, E. S., Nachmann, B., & Segal, S. J. An articulated framework for vocational development. *Journal of Counseling Psychology*, 1963, 10, 107–116.

Boring, E. G. The role of theory in experimental psychology. *American Journal of Psychology*, 1953, 66, 169–184.

Carkhuff, R. R. Training in counseling and therapeutic processes: Requiem or reveille? *Journal of Counseling Psychology*, 1966, 13, 360–367. (a)

Carkhuff, R. R. Counseling research, theory and practice. *Journal of Counseling Psychology*, 1966, 13, 467–480. (b)

Carkhuff, R. R. Toward a comprehensive model of facilitative interpersonal processes. *Journal of Counseling Psychology*, 1967, 14, 67–72.

Carkhuff, R. R. *The counselor's contribution to facilitative processes*. Mimeographed manuscript, State University of New York at Buffalo, 1968.

Carkhuff, R. R., Alexik, M., & Anderson, S. Do we have a theory of vocational choice? *Personnel and Guidance Journal*, 1967, 46, 335–345.

Cartwright, R. D., & Vogel, J. L. A comparison of changes in psychoneurotic patients during matched periods of therapy and no therapy. *Journal of Consulting Psychology*, 1960, 24, 121–127.

Erikson, E. Identity and the life cycle. *Psychological Issues*, 1959, 1, 1–171.

Eysenck, H. J. The effects of psychotherapy: An evaluation. *Journal of Consulting Psychology*, 1952, 16, 319–324.

Eysenck, H. J. The effects of psychotherapy. In H. J. Eysenck (ed.), *Handbook of abnormal psychology*. New York: Basic Books, Inc., 1960.

Eysenck, H. J. The effects of psychotherapy. *International Journal of Psychotherapy*. 1965, 1, 99–178.

Feigl, H. Operationism and scientific method. *Psychological Review*, 1945, 52, 250–259.

Galinsky, M. D. Personality development and vocational choice of clinical psychologists and physicists. *Journal of Counseling Psychology*, 1962, 9, 299–305.

Galinsky, M. D., & Fast, I. Vocational choice as a focus of the identity search. *Journal of Counseling Psychology*, 1966, 13, 89–92.

Ginzberg, E. *Occupational choice*. New York: Columbia University Press, 1951.

Harre, R. *The logic of the sciences*. London: The Macmillan Company, 1960.

Hebb, D. O. Intelligence, brain function and the theory of the mind. *Brain*, 1959, 82, 260–275.

Hemple, C. G., & Oppenheim, P. The logic of explanation. In H. Feigl and M. Brodbeck (eds.), *Readings in the philosophy of science*. New York: Appleton-Century-Crofts, Inc., 1953.

Holland, J. L. A theory of vocational choice. *Journal of Counseling Psychology*, 1959, 6, 35–44.

Holland, J. L. Some explorations of theory of vocational choice: I. One- and two-year longitudinal studies. *Psychological Monographs*, 1962, 76, No. 26 (Whole No. 545).

Holland, J. L. *The psychology of vocational choice: a theory of personality types and environmental models.* Boston: Ginn & Company, 1966. (a)

Holland, J. L. A psychological classification scheme for vocations and major fields. *Journal of Counseling Psychology,* 1966, **13**, 278–288. (b)

Holland, J. L., & Nichols, R. C. Explorations of a theory of vocational choice: III. A longitudinal study of change in major field of study. *Personnel and Guidance Journal,* 1964, **43**, 235–242.

Hull, C. L. *Principles of behavior.* New York: Appleton-Century-Crofts, Inc., 1943.

°Kaplan, A. *The conduct of inquiry.* San Francisco: Chandler Publishing Company, 1964.

Kitson, H. D. Review of Ginzberg's *Occupational choice. Occupations,* 1951, **29**, 611–613.

Koch, S. Theoretical psychology, 1950: An overview. *Psychological Review,* 1951, **58**, 295–301.

Mink, O. G., & Isaksen, H. L. A comparison of effectiveness of non-directive therapy and clinical counseling in the junior high school. *School Counselor,* 1959, **6**, 12–14.

Nachmann, B. Childhood experience and vocational choice in law, dentistry, and social work. *Journal of Counseling Psychology,* 1960, **7**, 243–250.

O'Hara, R. P., & Tiedeman, D. V. Vocational self-concept in adolescence. *Journal of Counseling Psychology,* 1959, **6**, 292–301.

Osipow, S. H., Ashby, J. D., & Wall, H. W. Personality types and vocational choice: a test of Holland's theory. *Personnel and Guidance Journal,* 1966, **45**, 37–42.

Roe, A. *The psychology of occupations.* New York: John Wiley & Sons, Inc., 1956.

Roe, A. Comment. *Journal of Counseling Psychology,* 1963, **10**, 117.

Roe, A., Hubbard W. D., Hutchinson, T., & Bateman, T. Studies of occupational history. Part I: Job changes and the classification of occupations. *Journal of Counseling Psychology,* 1966, **13**, 387–393.

Roe, A., & Siegelman, M. *The origin of interests.* Washington, D.C.: American Personnel and Guidance Association, 1964.

Rogers, C. R., Gendlin, E., Kiesler, D., & Truax, C. B. (eds.) *The therapeutic relationship and its impact.* Madison, Wisc.: University of Wisconsin Press, 1967.

Segal, S. J. A psychoanalytic analysis of personality factors in vocational choice. *Journal of Counseling Psychology,* 1961, **8**, 202–210.

Segal, S. J., & Szabo, R. Identification in two vocations: accountants and creative writers. *Personnel and Guidance Journal,* 1964, **43**, 252–255.

Shafer, F., & Shoben, E. J. *Psychotherapy: Learning new adjustments.* Boston: Houghton Mifflin Company, 1956.

Skinner B. F. Are theories of learning necessary? *Psychological Review,* 1950, **57**, 193–216.

Spence, K. W. The nature of theory construction in contemporary psychology. *Psychological Review,* 1944, **51**, 47–68.

Stefflre, B. Vocational development: Ten propositions in search of a theory. *Personnel and Guidance Journal*, 1966, 44, 611–616.

Stockin, B. C. A test of Holland's occupational level formulation. *Personnel and Guidance Journal*, 1964, 42, 599–602.

Super, D. E. *The psychology of careers.* New York: Harper & Row, Publishers, Inc., 1957.

Super, D. E. The definition and measurement of early career behavior: a first formulation. *Personnel and Guidance Journal*, 1963, 41, 775–780.

Super, D. E., & Bachrach, P. B. *Scientific careers and vocational development theory.* New York: Bureau of Publications, Teachers College, Columbia University, 1957.

Super, D. E., Crites, J. O., Hummel, R. C., Moser, H. P., Overstreet, P. L., & Warnath, C. F. *Vocational development: a framework for research.* New York: Bureau of Publications, Teachers College, Columbia University, 1957.

Super, D. E., & Overstreet, P. L. *The vocational maturity of ninth-grade boys.* New York: Bureau of Publications, Teachers College, Columbia University, 1960.

Super, D. E., Starishevsky, R., Matlin, N., & Jordaan, J. P. *Career development: self-concept theory.* Princeton, N.J.: College Entrance Examination Board, 1963.

Tiedeman, D. V. Decision and vocational development: a paradigm and its implications. *Personnel and Guidance Journal*, 1961, 40, 15–21.

Tiedeman, D. V., and O'Hara, R. P. *Differentiation and integration in career development.* Cambridge, Mass.: Harvard Graduate School of Education, 1962.

Tiedeman, D. V., & O'Hara, R. P. *Career development: choice and adjustment.* Princeton, N.J.: College Entrance Examination Board, 1963.

Truax, C. B., & Carkhuff, R. R. *Toward effective counseling and psychotherapy.* Chicago: Aldine Publishing Company, 1967.

*Underwood, B. J. *Psychological research.* New York: Appleton-Century-Crofts, Inc., 1957.

12
PROCESS AND OUTCOME IN HELPING

Persons who have emotional problems search out help from others because they do not feel they can resolve their difficulties alone. The assumption, then, is that they can be helped to resolve their difficulties in conjunction with the activities of a helper. Hopefully, the helper has something to offer, and hopefully, whatever the helper involves the helpee in will in some way be reflected in a significant change in the helpee's behavior.

The ways in which we have attempted to measure the effects of helping have been elusive if not illusive. In the extreme some have mistakenly claimed that helpee changes are so subtle that they defy measurement. We cannot concur. Surely helpees do not invest their time, energy, and often their money in the helping process in the hope of changes too subtle to observe.

In general, the serious investigators in the field divide into two groups, those favoring process research and those advocating the necessity for outcome research. These positions may be summarized in propositional form.

Proposition I. Many researchers favor investigating process variables as a first step in making meaningful explorations of the helping process.

Many researchers have sought significance in process research, determining what process measures—and most often these are determined by one theoretical orientation or the other—relate to what other process measures (Hoch, 1964). This position assumes that all relevant process variables must be discerned and their interrelationships explored before the effects of the helping process can be assessed. They conclude with statements concerning the prematurity of outcome research: "The evaluation of the effects of therapy is not a task we can handle with existing tools" (Hyman & Berger, 1965, p. 322).

Proposition II. Many researchers cite the necessity for incorporating outcome indexes in meaningful studies of the helping process.

It is only through knowing what process variables relate to what outcome indexes that we make the process variables meaningful (Carkhuff, 1966; Greenhouse, 1964). In spite of the many obstacles to outcome research, including sociological dimensions (Parloff & Rubenstein, 1959) as well as the usual methodological difficulties in criterion definition (Zubin, 1964), these investigators suggest that "it is precisely through outcome studies with concurrent measurement or manipulation of variables whose influence is unknown that important variables are likely to be identified" (Paul, 1967, p. 109).

These two dominant positions are not of necessity mutually exclusive and should serve complementary functions. Indeed, a number of conclusions may be drawn from these propositions, the first being that the problems involved in process and outcome research are those associated with exploring and understanding human relations in general.

Conclusion I. A comprehensive understanding of process and outcome research involves a consideration of first person, second person, and contextual and environmental variables.

Both in relation to indexes of process and outcome the effects of first person or helper (parents, teachers, counselors), second person or helpee (children, students, clients), and contextual and environmental variables (including, in particular, the third persons or significant others who are intimately involved in other aspects of the helpee's life) upon each other and upon relevant and meaningful indexes of outcome must be studied (Carkhuff, 1963, 1967; Carkhuff & Berenson, 1967). Although some variables may be more influential than others, both in relation to other process indexes as well as to outcome indexes, these variables cannot be considered independent of their interaction with other related variables. Thus, the helpee variables include descriptions of demographic characteristics, levels of functioning, motivation, and expectations as well as the process variables assessing the helpee on those dimensions in which helpees involve themselves in successful learning and relearning processes. In addition, helpee variables usually constitute the dependent variable outcome measures. Again these variables cannot be considered alone but rather in interaction with the more stable personal-social characteristics of the helper such as demographic and motivational variables as well as level of functioning, including in particular the level of facilitative and action-oriented dimensions the helper offers as well as the effectiveness with which he implements the techniques available to him. Similarly, the immediate social-physical context of helping has a potentially modifying effect in terms of both the physical setting within which the helping takes place and the persons with whom the helpee has contact as well as the variety and duration of treatments available (Carkhuff, 1967; Carkhuff & Berenson, 1967). In addition, the social-physical environment to which the helpee returns following the helping process, including in particular all of the third persons who are influential in the helpee's life as well as a variety of other factors involved in his home and work situation, may qualify the effects of other variables. Finally, Paul (1967) also emphasizes temporal variables because, in addition to task variation, these events also mark points of research focus in time: initial contact; pretreatment phase; initial contact phase; main treatment phase; termination phase; posttreatment phase; follow-up phase.

Conclusion II. A comprehensive understanding of the effects of all interpersonal processes must incorporate meaningful indexes of outcome.

Although science may never account for the totality of experience between two or more parties to a relationship, it maintains the capacity to verify the degree to which the ends of such a relationship are reached or not (Reichenbach, 1938). If helping does not involve visible, measurable, and significant change or gain on the part of the helpee, we simply cannot call the process successful (Carkhuff, 1966). However, outcome indexes of an undifferentiated process are meaningless. The establishment of a relationship between process and outcome variables affords us an opportunity of experimentally manipulating the process variables and studying their differential effects upon outcome.

Conclusion III. A comprehensive understanding of the effects of all interpersonal processes must study meaningful process measures and their effects upon each other.

Although process studies of the effects of process variables upon process variables can be legitimatized only by relating one of the process variables to outcome indexes, it is not enough to know that a variable relates to outcome. Since outcome indexes are almost universally measures of second person variables, the effects of first person and third person variables upon second person variables throughout the process, not solely at termination and follow-up, must be studied in order to understand the process by which the helpee resolves his difficulties. Having established a relationship between one of the process measures and outcome, process studies constitute a potentially rich source of clinical learnings (Cannon & Carkhuff, 1969). Periodic outcome studies must be conducted, however, to avoid possible circularity in construct development.

HELPING PROCESS AND OUTCOME: A VIEW IN DEPTH

A number of unanswered questions dictate a deeper view of the inter-relationship of process and outcome. What is process? What is outcome? Which determines which in the helping process? Who determines which? How do we measure each? How does each relate to real-life functioning?

Part of the confusion in understanding the relation between process and outcome has been a function of the positions from which these phenomena are viewed. To be sure, the more behavioristic positions are outcome oriented. The more traditional therapeutic orientations are process oriented. In effect, for them process becomes outcome—indeed, helpees who are described as being "in process" are considered successful ones.

Depending in large part upon the stance assumed by the viewer, process may determine outcome or outcome may determine process. On the one hand, the process-oriented positions lead directly to discernible outcomes, whether implicitly or explicitly denoted. On the other hand, the outcome-oriented positions determine the step-by-step processes that lead to explicitly defined and operational criteria.

Since both process and outcome studies are based in assessments of second person variables, an open, eclectic stance toward the helpee both in counseling and outside it allows us to view process and outcome as integrally related. Process measures of helpee behavior in counseling may when related to helpee behavior outside counseling become outcome indexes. Thus, for example, the degree to which the helpee explores himself in therapy may, when related to self-exploration in other areas of critical real-life functioning, become an outcome index, particularly in view of the close relation that exists between helpee self-exploration and other external indexes. Similarly, the degree to which the helpee is able to offer high levels of facilitative and action-oriented conditions is related to the helpee's effectiveness in many other areas of his life.

Outcome indexes, however, may be in reality no more than cut-off process measures, or relevant and meaningful indexes of some area of the helpee's functioning. That is, when we take the larger view of the helpee's life outcome assessments of certain aspects of his life become no more than process indexes. *At best, the decision of when to assess the effects of a given process is arbitrary, for the helpee continues to function beyond the first, tenth, or thirtieth session, beyond termination of treatment, and beyond one- or two-year follow-up assessments.* The measures, then, whether process or outcome, must be integral to significant areas of functioning in the helpee's life, both in counseling and, more important, outside it. In this context even the behaviorists must ultimately be concerned that the reduction or elimination of some symptoms makes a difference in the life of the helpee.

The issue of the dependence or independence of the indexes employed to assess the effects of a given process, then, fade to the irrelevant sources in which they originated. If the process is in any way related to its effects, then the measures are not independent. No theory in the world, learning theories in particular, dictates the necessary extension of effects to independent areas of functioning. *The process must be relevant to the effects it attempts to achieve. Outcome indexes cannot be independent of process in effective helping.* The issues are not the dependence-independence of assessment indexes but rather the generalization of effects from functioning within the process to functioning outside the process. For the most part helpees learn what we expect and teach them to learn, all of which leads directly to a consideration of who is to establish the changes expected in the learning and relearning processes.

The problem of who establishes the desired processes and outcomes also takes into consideration first person, second person, and in some cases third person variables. In the absence of a knowledge of cause and effect treatment relationships a number of investigators have called for criteria established by the helpee, indicating that judgments of the success of helping for any given helper must be based upon the requests and/or complaints of the helpee: "Accomplishment of client's goals, not adherence to prescribed procedures, should be the mark of the successful counselor" (Krumboltz, 1965). Although effective helpers obviously serve for the benefit of helpees, they also maintain an expertise in their ability to set meaningful goals and to involve the helpee in a process leading to constructive change or gain. Thus, they do not serve solely to provide the means for attaining the ends desired by the helpee. *The effective helper, functioning at significantly higher levels than the helpee on all relevant dimensions, must be able to make the discriminations necessary to determine what is best for the helpee, whether or not there is agreement or disagreement with the helpee.* In order to accomplish this the helper must not only be able to understand the helpee from the helpee's frame of reference but also to extend this understanding to the point where at the beginning of helping the helper may understand the helpee better than the helpee understands himself in some ways critical to the helpee's growth. In order to accomplish this, in turn, the helper's repertoire of responses must be such that he can provide the means to attain the ends prescribed. Indeed, only helpers with very large repertoires of responses are able to offer differential treatment and, thus, the prospect for the most change on the most change indexes to the greatest number of helpees. Of course, the helper must possess a thorough knowledge of what processes lead to what changes.

In this regard the helper must at a given point in time be willing to make many value judgments concerning which ends are worthwhile and which are not. In this respect the helper is always a living representative of both the means and the ends of the process. He represents effective living in terms of structure and not content—for example, the level of facilitative and action-oriented dimensions at which he functions and not the details of his religious or political beliefs. If he is living effectively, he need only spell out as honestly as possible the dimensions of effective living. If he is living effectively, he has developed a cosmology that, while directionful, is open and flexible. Indeed, it draws upon many systems and is not bound by any single system. If he is living effectively, he is sensitive to his internal and external experiences and possesses the capacity to act forcefully upon the very fine discriminations that he makes. These are some of the goals that the effective helper holds for the helpee. He must be able to summon all of his resources and those of the environment to provide the means for enabling the helpee to attain these ends. In summary, then, the effective helper takes the helpee's phenomenology into consideration in establishing the processes that lead to desired outcomes and, in turn, those outcomes that offer the greatest prospect of involving the helpee in a lifelong learning process.

HELPING PROCESS AND OUTCOME:
A PROBLEM IN INTERPERSONAL FUNCTIONING

In order to understand fully the problems of process and outcome we must return again to the factors that make an individual a candidate for help in the first place. He has been unable to resolve some critical difficulties in living either on his own or with the help of persons immediately available to him. Indeed, it is often precisely an individual's interactions with those immediately available to him that lead to his difficulties, often leading even to hospitalization. While the intrapersonal and the interpersonal processes can be separated, the latter are immediately observable in the behavior of the helpee. Consequently, the interpersonal processes must be accorded greater significance in the processes leading to the search for help. In this context it may be assumed that interpersonal phenomena reflect in large part intrapersonal phenomena—that is, what goes on in the individual's dealings with the world reflect what goes on inside of him or in his dealings with himself. The dynamic process that leads a person to seek help, then, involves difficulties in living. *Difficulties in living are largely interpersonal.* There are profound implications for treatment and its outcome.

If interpersonal phenomena lead to the search for help, then there are implications for both the means and the ends of the helping process. Just as dysfunctioning is a consequence of poor or negative learning experiences, so is effective functioning the result of positive learning experiences. Just as difficulties in interpersonal functioning are a consequence of destructive interpersonal experiences, so is facilitative interpersonal functioning the result of constructive interpersonal experiences. It has been the thesis of these volumes that the means by which low levels of interpersonal functioning are transformed to high levels of interpersonal functioning are experiences involving high levels of interpersonal functioning. Accordingly, *high levels of interpersonal functioning become both the means and the ends of the helping process.* High levels of interpersonal functioning on the part of the helper constitute the means that lead to high levels of interpersonal functioning on the part of the helpee, which, in turn, constitute the ends of the helping process.

It can readily be seen that all sources of learning converge in the interpersonal process of helping. The helper who is himself functioning at high levels of interpersonal dimensions offers the helpee who is functioning at low levels the experience of being understood sensitively and deeply; he offers the helpee the experience of a person who respects certain key qualities of the helpee; he offers the helpee the experience of interacting with a helper who can be specific about certain critical experiences and concrete in his problem-solving activities with the helpee; he offers the helpee the experience of a truly genuine person who is freely and fully himself in his interaction with the helpee; he offers the helpee an experience of being confronted with discrepancies in the helpee's behavior; he offers the helpee the experience of having his indirect communications interpreted directly and with immediacy. Not only does the helper offer the helpee the experience of the facilitative and action-oriented dimensions and their effects but he also actively and didactically teaches the helpee to function effectively on these dimensions. Finally, and perhaps most important, the helper provides the helpee with a role model of a person who functions effectively in terms of these dimensions, for whether the helper's behavior is inadvertent or not, it is the source of the effects of modeling on the helpee's behavior.

Low levels of interpersonal functioning, then, may be raised by a helper who offers adequate levels of facilitative and action-oriented dimensions. *The central occurrence of the effective helping process involves the interpersonal means that lead to interpersonal ends. All other meaningful generalizations in behavior flow from changes in interpersonal functioning.* A large part of the difficulty in resolving the problems of process and outcome has been the inability to define this central occurrence in the effective helping process. Not knowing what we were looking for, we have thrown a battery of traditional tests at the helpees, hoping that something would relate to something else. Usually we have found complex, contradictory, and confusing relationships. However, we have also found that certain helpers elicit changes that are fairly consistent across indexes. The evidence suggests that these are the helpers who give the helpee the highest-level interpersonal experience and who effect the greatest interpersonal changes in the helpee.

If the helpee understands himself at deeper levels and is able to act constructively upon his understanding, then he is also able to understand others and make provisions for their constructive action. Accordingly, the helpee will feel differently about himself, and this will be reflected on the self-reports that are adequate to tapping in on his experienced changes. Similarly, other persons, including the helper and other significant persons in the helpee's environment such as his spouse, his boss, and his neighbor, will feel differently about the helpee. If they do not, this might perhaps reflect some deficiency on their part, deserving of scrutiny in its own right, rather than some inadequacy on the part of the helpee. Finally, if the helpee has indeed made significant changes in his life, they will be reflected on all objective instruments adequate to assessing such changes. With each criterion of outcome it can be seen that there are contingencies involved. If the helpee has manifested overt behavioral changes interpersonally, then the inability of any one of the other sources of outcome criteria to discern these changes reflects upon the inadequacy of the sources rather than upon the inability of the helpee to change. This, of course, presents a strong argument for the establishment of functional and operational criteria of outcome. It also presents a strong argument for the establishment of functional and operational means for achieving this outcome. In our consideration of interpersonal functioning as the central goal of helping, we might again reconsider training in interpersonal functioning as the most efficient and, thus, the preferred mode of helping.

HELPING PROCESS AND OUTCOME:
THE PROBLEMS OF MEASUREMENT

Considering the interpersonal core of helping, then, both helper and helpee can be assessed on their levels of functioning in different problem areas. Thus, differential predictions concerning gains in interpersonal functioning as depicted in the preceding chapters may be generated. The assessments of helpee functioning on these indexes may constitute measures of both process and outcome, depending upon whether the assessments are made during or following the helping process.

In addition, the process and outcome may be individualized according to the needs of the helpee. The problem areas and affects in which the helpee is not functioning at minimally facilitative, self-sustaining levels constitute automatic goals of helping for that particular helpee. For example, an individual may not be functioning effectively in social-interpersonal and educational-vocational areas and these areas will constitute explicit core goals of the helping process. Similarly, the helpee may have great difficulty in handling frustration and anger and these areas will constitute explicit core goals. In each instance the goals may be made operational and specific step-by-step procedures for attaining these goals developed. The effectiveness of the means that are developed depends in large measure on the extent to which the goals of helping are operationalized. Again the measurements of both process and outcome involve the same relevant interpersonal indexes. The means for obtaining indexes of interpersonal functioning, then, should be meaningful. They should be as closely related as possible to real-life goals of functioning. In this context we will briefly review the means for assessing interpersonal functioning, the core means and ends of helping.

Objective Indexes of Interpersonal Functioning

These indexes include casting the helpee in the helping role, with helpees presenting a variety of affects and problem areas. The ratings of the helpee constitute the best means of assessing the maximum level of interpersonal functioning in the areas involved. The tasks can be further individualized to represent conditions or characteristics that are uniquely difficult for the helpee. Standardized means for assessing these changes, such as those illustrated in Volume I on selection and training, may also be employed, with original and alternate forms of these indexes individualized to meet the helpee's personal needs.

While the core of helping is interpersonal, other changes in the helpee may occur concomitantly or concurrently with the interpersonal changes. Helpee change or gain is not necessarily unitary. If a variety of assessment indexes are included, it is entirely possible that the helpee may demonstrate some positive and some negative change (Carkhuff, 1966; Truax & Carkhuff, 1964). In our experience in both practice and research, however, we have found that potent helping or training processes conducted by high-level–functioning helpers reflect rather uniformly positive changes on the indexes they are attempting to affect. For example, in carefully controlled studies of training employing both training control and control groups we found that the gains in the interpersonal functioning of the experimental training group were significantly greater than those in other training or treatment groups as measured by a variety of indexes (Berenson, Carkhuff, & Myrus, 1966; Carkhuff & Bierman, 1970; Martin & Carkhuff, 1968). These changes were reflected not only in objective ratings of functioning in the helping role but also on indexes involving trainee self-reports, helpee reports, and the reports of significant others such as roommates or spouses. The sources for these reports had no basis for knowing whether the trainees were in the training group proper or the training control groups which met during the same time periods for similar purposes. Thus, there is clear generalization from one index of interpersonal functioning to another. Three points are worth reiterating: (1) the interpersonal changes generalized to other spheres of functioning; (2) the interpersonal changes are effected by high-level–functioning helpers; (3) systematic training is the most efficient and the most effective means for obtaining these changes.

In general, then, many of the problems in process and outcome research have been a function of our inability to denote the central occurrences in effective helping processes, the interpersonal core. If we know what effects we are looking for in helping and if we know how to define these goals and how to implement the means for attaining them, then our testing indexes will reflect these changes. The interpersonal changes, in turn, will lead to changes in other relevant areas of human functioning. Indeed, the inability to generalize the effects to traditional testing indexes may reflect more on the questionable nature of the indexes than on the question of the effectiveness of helping.

At this stage of the development of helping, however, in addition to assessments of interpersonal functioning assessment indexes should, if possible, include a variety of different common sense measures of human functioning. The different measures will tell us something of the relation between measures as well as what processes lead to what changes most directly so that we can employ the processes that are most effective in achieving particular goals (Carkhuff, 1966). Depending, then, upon the objectives of helping and the interaction of first person, second person, and contextual and environmental variables, these assessments should include second person indexes both within the helping process and outside it.

Second Person Self-Reports

These indexes include a variety of self-reports, satisfaction inventories, and objective tests as well as quasi-outcome indexes such as assessments of relationship satisfaction and tangential self-report indexes such as projective tests.

First Person Reports of Second Person Functioning

These indexes include both gross and systematic assessments of progress and outcome by the helpers both within and without the process, as for example, inpatient and outpatient therapists in treatment, teachers and superiors, and colleagues in education.

Objective Assessments of Second Person Functioning

These indexes include measures of gross functioning such as institutional discharge and promotion rates due to different helping processes, determinations of whether a treated individual is in or out of the institution, measures of creativity and productivity both in and out of the institution, and criteria assessing educational and vocational productivity.

Third Person Reports of Second Person Functioning

These indexes include outcome indexes that are related to "income"; that is, the opinions of the significant others in the individual's life (spouse, boss, neighbor, friend, and psychiatrist) concerning the factors that led to the individual's institutionalization should be employed in assessing the helpee's readiness for discharge. Also important are the opinions of significant others within the institution—attendants, nurses, doctors—and ward behavior ratings.

Following the establishment of a relation between process and outcome variables we can engage in shorter-term process studies of variables related to constructive change indexes, again always being careful to break free of possible circular research with intermittent outcome studies. The perpetuation of the present state of affairs in process studies in which one process variable may relate to another but neither relates to the constructive change or gain of the helpee is a waste of human energy, talent, time, and money.

We have attempted to put the helping process back into the helpee's life process, calling upon all resources within and without helping to effect the maximum improvement in the helpee's level of functioning in his everyday life. Hopefully, the helping process offers an analogue of life, making possible generalizations to the helpee's real-life functioning. Although for the most part we achieve significant helpee changes in the areas in which we concentrate our efforts and expectations, we do encounter periodically the problem of concomitant or concurrent changes in the helpee. That is, in spite of our emphasis upon one or another helpee achievement, a number of other helpee changes may or may not be taking place simultaneously. Again we must employ multiple measures in order to assess these concurrent effects.

In a very real sense the outcome of the helping process is only part of the ongoing life process of the helpee. In effect the helpee as helper lives through a number of outcome-oriented experiences, and one or another learning or relearning process constitutes only a part of what, in the ideal, may be a lifelong learning experience. In summary, if there is no life in helping, then there is no helping in life.

REFERENCES

For a more detailed discussion of the issues considered in this chapter see the asterisked readings and the references upon which the readings are based.

Berenson, B. G., Carkhuff, R. R., & Myrus, P. The interpersonal functioning and training of college students. *Journal of Counseling Psychology*, 1966, 13, 441–446.

Cannon, J., & Carkhuff, R. R. The experimental manipulation of therapeutic process variables. Unpublished review, American International College, Springfield, Mass., 1969.

Carkhuff, R. R. On the necessary and sufficient conditions of therapeutic personality change. *Discussion papers, Wisconsin Psychiatric Institute*, 1963, No. 47, 1–7.

*Carkhuff, R. R. Counseling research, theory and practice—1965. *Journal of Counseling Psychology*, 1966, 13, 467–480.

Carkhuff, R. R. Toward a comprehensive model of facilitative interpersonal processes. *Journal of Counseling Psychology*, 1967, 14, 67–72.

*Carkhuff, R. R., & Berenson, B. G. *Beyond counseling and therapy*. New York: Holt, Rinehart and Winston, Inc., 1967.

Carkhuff, R. R., & Bierman, R. Training as a preferred mode of treatment of parents of emotionally disturbed children. *Journal of Counseling Psychology*, 1970, 17, 157–161.

Greenhouse, S. W. Principles in the evaluation of therapies for mental disorders. In P. H. Hoch and J. Zubin (eds.), *The evaluation of psychiatric treatment.* New York: Grune & Stratton, 1964. Pp. 94–105.

Hoch, P. H. Methods of evaluating various types of psychiatric treatments: Discussion. In P. H. Hoch and J. Zubin (eds.), *The evaluation of psychiatric treatment.* New York: Grune & Stratton, 1964. Pp. 52–57.

Hoch, P. H., and Zubin, J. (eds.). *The evaluation of psychiatric treatment.* New York: Grune & Stratton, 1964.

Hyman, R., & Berger, L. Discussion of H. J. Eysenck's "The effects of psychotherapy," *International Journal of Psychiatry,* 1965, 1, 317–322.

Krumboltz, J. D. Behavioral counseling: rationale and research. *Personnel and Guidance Journal,* 1965, 44, 383–387.

Martin, J., and Carkhuff, R. R. The effects of training upon changes in trainee personality and behavior. *Journal of Clinical Psychology,* 1968, 24, 109–110.

Parloff, M. B., & Rubinstein, E. A. Research problems in psychotherapy. In E. A. Rubinstein and M. B. Parloff (eds.), *Research in psychotherapy,* Vol. 1. Washington, D.C.: American Psychological Association, 1959. Pp. 276–293.

*Paul, G. L. Outcome research in psychotherapy. *Journal of Consulting Psychology,* 1967, 31, 109–118.

Reichenbach, H. *Experience and prediction.* Chicago: University of Chicago Press, 1938.

Truax, C. B., & Carkhuff, R. R. Significant developments in psychotherapy research. In L. E. Abt and B. F. Reiss (eds.), *Progress in clinical psychology.* New York: Grune & Stratton, 1964. Pp. 124–155.

Truax, C. B., & Carkhuff, R. R. *Toward effective counseling and psychotherapy.* Chicago: Aldine Publishing Company, 1966.

Zubin, J. Technical issues: Discussion. In P. H. Hoch and J. Zubin (eds.), *The evaluation of psychiatric treatment.* New York: Grune & Stratton, 1964. Pp. 122–128.

13
MEANING AND RIGOR
IN ASSESSMENTS OF HELPING

Research in the helping processes has led to the employment of rating scales to assess the process and outcome of these activities. In particular, dimensions that cut across a variety of interview-oriented approaches have been developed and attempts have been made to make them operational. Thus, counselor-offered dimensions such as empathy, regard, warmth, and congruence (Carkhuff & Berenson, 1967; Rogers, Gendlin, Kiesler, & Truax, 1967; Truax & Carkhuff, 1967) have been generalized to all inter-personal processes and have been complemented by additional dimensions such as concreteness or specificity of expression and self-disclosure (Carkhuff, 1968a; Carkhuff & Berenson, 1967; Truax & Carkhuff, 1967) and confrontation and immediacy (Berenson & Mitchell, 1974; Carkhuff & Berenson, 1967). A great deal of evidence has been accumulated to relate these first person process variables to second person or helpee process variables such as helpee self-exploration (Carkhuff & Berenson, 1967; Truax & Carkhuff, 1967), immediacy of experiencing and extensiveness of problem expression (Rogers et. al., 1967), and explorations of relationships with significant others (Berenson & Mitchell, 1974). In turn, both first and second person process variables have been related to a variety of outcome indexes of helpee change or gain (Carkhuff & Berenson, 1967; Rogers et. al., 1967; Truax & Carkhuff, 1967).[1]

The employment of rating scales necessitates a careful consideration of the scales and the dimensions they assess, the rating processes, and

---

[1] These references are by no means exhaustive. There are an extensive number of additional scales and inventories representing a variety of different orientations and assessing not only counseling and therapeutic activities, but also teaching and child-rearing practices.

the methods of selecting and training raters. It is important to view these aspects of rating from the criteria of meaning and rigor.

The criterion of meaning asks esssential questions: "Do the ratings relate to indexes of helpee change or gain and thus enable us to learn better ways of helping people?" For the clinician-researcher the translation of research efforts to human benefits is paramount. In response to his own question he is more concerned with generating working hypotheses (Bakan, 1966) than with replicating and refining his findings. In practice the clinician-researcher, if he must choose, tends to sacrifice the criterion of rigor for the end of immediate and tangible helpee benefits, often, unfortunately, only in the context of his present activities and setting.

The criterion of rigor, in turn, is concerned with further and finer refinements, predictions, and replications. Its proponents develop and diligently follow rules insuring the highest degree of operationalization, concretization, and communication. If the methodologist must choose, he chooses to know the most about what he is most sure of, often to the exclusion of that which he is least sure of—the prospect of increasing human benefits.

We will review the questions that have been raised, the research that has been conducted and the conclusions that we have derived from our research experiences with the criteria of meaning and rigor. Sometimes, to be sure, these criteria may serve not only happy but necessarily complementary functions, as in the case of the first issue raised in proposition form, that of excerpting. As will become apparent, the conclusions that the individual researcher draws may depend in large part upon the purposes and the resources of his research.

RECORDING AND SELECTING

Proposition I. The excerpting of counseling for rating purposes depends in large part upon the constructs and rating scales involved, the media of recording and the source of excerpts, the resources available, and the population to which we wish to generalize.

The Criteria of Meaning and Rigor

The criteria of meaning and rigor converge in their direction on most of the issues of excerpting. In the first place, while issues have been raised by many counselors and clinicians concerning the ethics and effects of recording, the increasing necessity for empirical evidence relating aspects of taped counseling to indexes of helpee change may best be rationalized as follows: (1) since we know very little about helping and its effects, some form of recording that enables us to trace back through the processes leading to positive and/or negative movement is essential (Carkhuff, 1968a); (2) taping, like the introduction of any other technique, will not cause insurmountable difficulties if the helper is competent; put another way, insurmountable difficulties in counseling due to taping are most pronounced when the helper is not competent (Carkhuff & Berenson, 1967). In the second place, although the problem of resources often dictates audio-recording of helping as the only available method, there is work pointing up the necessity for also attending to nonverbal cues such as facial and bodily cues and, thus, the necessity for audiovisual recording of the communication process of helping (Shapiro, 1966). The criterion of rigor, however, dictates the necessary qualification of compatibility between the rating scales and the media employed. That is, a scale that accounts for a limited parameter of behavior should not be employed in rating with a media that goes beyond the stimuli described in the scale. For example, an empathy scale that is described in terms of verbal behavior only would not account for many stimuli in audiovisual recording.

There is further agreement that the excerpt selected should not be independent of helper, helpee, and contextual variables at large. Thus, a pretreatment inequality may be established when individuals are assigned on the basis of convenience and availability. Stratification procedures, involving the random selection of helpers, helpees, and setting on an *a priori* basis will serve to increase the probability of appropriate generalization of findings beyond a particular grouping of relevant variables and also of the representative nature of the excerpts selected. In turn, the excerpts themselves are employed to demonstrate that a construct is a valid index of the effectiveness of helping. Thus, it is imperative that the excerpts to be rated be evaluated to determine if the construct is appropriate to the source of the excerpts under study (that is, the question of external validity). For example, it might be inappropriate to assess the helper's communication of empathy during counter-conditioning or in test interpretation proper while it might be perfectly appropriate to assess helper empathy during the interview employed to establish the problems involved. In addition, the excerpts should be clearly distinguished as either independent or dependent variables. When used as dependent measures procedures should insure that as a measure of outcome they are nonreactive. For example, it might not be appropriate to measure the effects of empathy upon helpee progress by means of a helpee relationship inventory, since while the helpee's experience of the counseling relationship may be related to empathy it may not be related to any other external indexes of helpee change. Finally, in selecting excerpts control and consideration should be given to the effects of dimensions such as content and intensity of affect on the ratings as distinct from helper and helpee "styles" of functioning. Here there is important evidence to suggest that helpers may receive different ratings and, indeed, emit different frequencies of responses depending upon the affective (depression, elation, anger, and so on) and content (social-interpersonal, educational-vocational, sexual-marital, child-rearing, and so on) areas involved (Carkhuff, 1969a).

Depending upon the purposes and resources of the research, the studies and, thus, the taping may be longitudinal or horizontal in nature. All sessions of long-term cases or single, one-shot interviews in cross-sectional studies may be taped for assessment. Again, depending upon purposes and resources, (1) every minute of every session or (2) random or (3) predesignated excerpts (for example, first third, middle third, and last third of an interview) may be selected for rating. While there is precedent for segments ranging from 2 to 12 minutes in length, research indicates that the reliability, range, and discriminatory power of ratings are generally independent of segment length (Kiesler, Mathieu, & Klein, 1964). Therefore, except in certain cases such as experimental manipulation studies where it is important to rate every minute, it is usually most efficient to sample the briefest excerpts. However, segment location may yield different results. For example, there is evidence to indicate greater between-group differentiation for both high- and low-functioning helpers (Carkhuff & Berenson, 1967) and helpees (Kiesler, Klein, & Mathieu, 1965) over time and/or with the introduction of "crises." Thus, both within the helping hour and over the course of helping the discriminations between the levels of conditions offered by high- and low-functioning helpers and the degree of therapeutic process involvement and movement of neurotic and psychotic patients will be sharper in later than in earlier periods. At a minimum, then, the researcher should include excerpts from late within the individual session as well as from later sessions within the total helping program.

The selection of excerpts is ordinarily qualified to include samples of the interaction between helper and helpee. While therapist-patient-therapist interaction unit samples have not been found superior to patient-therapist-patient samples in predicting outcome from level of therapist-offered conditions (Truax, 1966a), the latter approach is preferable in that it allows us to assess both the helper's degree of responsiveness and its effect upon the helpee. In addition, tape-recorded samples obtained from individual patients were not more predictive of therapy outcome than were conditions ratings from ongoing group therapy interactions (Truax, 1966a), another study in the growing body of research indicating that the level of conditions offered is characteristic of the helper. While we may infer from these findings that an excerpter can be confident if he has a minimum of a helpee-helper-helpee interaction, we must raise questions concerning the potential effects of the excerpt sequence upon the "set" of the rater in rating. Finally, the criteria of meaning and rigor are most divergent in regard to the separation of helpee and helper statements for rating purposes. While the finding that the hearing of patients' statements does not influence ratings of therapist empathy and warmth significantly (Truax, 1966b) meets the criterion of rigor, for most clinical purposes it is simply not meaningful to separate helpee and helper responses. One possible inference that we might draw is that the helpers involved in this study were primarily low- to moderate-level–functioning therapists—therapists who, we have found in other research, respond in a manner that is independent of the client: the high-level therapist can be rated only in interaction with someone else. The criterion of meaning does not allow us to separate the high-level helper's empathy from the helpee's self-exploration any more than we can separate the helpee's self-exploration from the high-level helper's empathy (Carkhuff, 1968b). For the present the question of separation of statements remains an empirical question to be explored in research involving a number of high-level–functioning counselors.

In conclusion, the recommendations concerning the excerpting of counseling excerpts for rating purposes may be summarized as follows:

Conclusion I. The excerpting process may be divided into two phases, the preparatory stage and the excerpting proper, and the procedures of each ascertained:

1. In the preparatory phases of excerpting extensive efforts should be made to assess the relationship of the following:
   a. The scale employed and the recording media involved.
   b. The population of relevant variables samples and the population to which we wish to generalize the results of our assessments.
   c. The construct involved and the source of excerpts being studied.
   d. The independent and dependent variables.
   e. The content and intensity of the excerpts and counselor and counselee styles of functioning.
2. Once the relationships of the preparatory excerpting phase have been ascertained, in excerpting proper the following procedures may be followed:

a. It is usually most efficient to employ samples of the briefest duration (approximately 2 minutes), except in certain cases such as experimental studies.
b. Random or predesignated means of sampling or a combination of both (for example, random selections within designated periods) will increase the probability of securing representative excerpts.
c. Excerpts from late within the individual session as well as from later sessions within the total counseling program should be included if at all possible.
d. Excerpts should include at a minimum a helpee-helper-helpee interaction.

THE RATING SCALES

Having selected the excerpts, however, the process becomes more complex. With the introduction of the rating scales the criteria of meaning and rigor dictate not only differing philosophies but also differing operations in the disposition of the excerpts. Rating scales first raise the issue of whether or not the processes of counseling and therapy—indeed, of human relations in general—are totally explicable.

Proposition II.   The development of the rating scales employed depend in large part upon the stage of evolution of the dimensions being assessed, their predictive validity, and increasing refinements and in large part upon whether the scales are viewed from the criterion of meaning or rigor, all of which reflect the stage of development of the science/art of counseling.

The Criterion of Meaning

The creative development of theoretical constructs and the operationalization of these constructs is, in a very real sense, a by-product of the commitment of the creative clinician to the welfare of his clients. By and large, then, the helping dimensions and scales reflect the dispositions of their creators. Indeed, in their eager efforts to develop more consistently effective ways of helping people the promulgators may view the dimensions discerned as "artificial dissections of more natural, effective human processes, which are known to us now only intermittently in our experience" (Carkhuff, 1968b). In addition, while grounded in human experience, the constructs are not merely exhaustive enough to account for the totality of human experience. While other variables are potential contributors, most truly facilitative processes may remain unknown to us; only the creative clinician can venture into the remaining unknown without hurting others or himself to discover benefits for others and himself.

The proponents of meaning assume a more global stance, accepting the fact that the scale discriminations are not finite and the levels of the scales by no means equidistant. Thus, the employment of the resultant product yields in many instances very gross discriminations. To be sure, it must be acknowledged that a small percentage of very high- and very low-functioning counselors may account for the significant helpee differences found in studies splitting helpers at the median. Indeed, certain helpers have a large repertoire of helping behaviors and their helpees do likewise, exhibiting pronounced tendencies over time to get high ratings on the degree to which they explore and experience themselves and, most important, on change or gain outcome criteria, including in particular behaviors related to the behaviors exhibited by the helpers (Pagell, Carkhuff, & Berenson, 1967; Pierce, Carkhuff, & Berenson, 1967). Similarly, certain other helpers who exhibit a very restrictive range of behaviors (functioning in a manner analagous to neuropsychiatric patients cast in the helping role [Pagell *et al.*, 1967], they become specialists in one or the other mode of functioning) tend, along with their helpees, to get low ratings on most criteria with which we may assess them. It may be further contended that an increased repertoire of behaviors that only the high-level–functioning helper (who has a repertoire sufficient to allow himself to be shaped by what is effective for his helpee and to shape his helpee) can offer and elicit is an implicit, if not explicit, goal of helping. It follows from this position that we must invest maximum effort in broad studies of the high-level–functioning helper. At a minimum, the proponents of meaning would argue, we must insure that we are tapping the full range of helper (or helpee) behavior in our research, so that a restrictive assessment of any one dimension will not preclude the discovery and development of other significant dimensions.

In the final analysis the proponents of meaning rely in large part upon the demonstrated empirical relationship of their ratings to a wide variety of outcome indexes. The validity data become even more imposing when we consider that similar measures of similar constructs have found support in research, suggesting that perhaps some shared, core dimensions account for the empirical evidence. The clinician-researcher must welcome attempts following on his own to articulate and clarify these core dimensions. Further, while it is likely that the improvement of the helpees of high-functioning helpers and the deterioration of the helpees of low-functioning helpers account in large part for the differences found in studies of helpee change, the proponents of meaning recognize the great number of helpers (and their helpees) who function in between these extremes. They acknowledge that the scales must be refined to a degree that will enable us in given instances, depending upon the variables involved, to generate both meaningful and valid predictions concerning the potential helpee benefits for which they were conceived. *The proponents of meaning do not, however, concede that many aspects of complex interpersonal processes can be dissected in a molecular manner and still remain effective.*

The Criterion of Rigor

The proponents of the criterion of rigor, in turn, address themselves to the highly complex and difficult task of isolating significant and independent aspects of the complex and difficult communication process of helping. From this stance it is imperative that the constructs involved not be a composite of a number of dimensions that are potentially orthogonally related. The independence of each construct must be ascertained, with most of this work presently accomplished by factor analytic work such as that by Zimmer and his colleagues (Zimmer & Anderson, 1968; Zimmer & Parks, 1967). That is, the rating scales should refer to a single type of counselor behavior or to the results of a single type of counselee behavior to avoid stimulus errors in raters' judgments. Zimmer and his colleagues argue that although the number of steps to be used in a rating scale for counselor effectiveness has never been empirically tested, it is related to the interest and sophistication of the raters. Generally, the problem involves reducing error variance and increasing true variance. When fewer discriminations can be made by raters over fewer scale divisions many additional random errors become important. In addition, these workers suggest that scaling steps should be constructed to account for the error of central tendency. The fact that a small percentage of helpers tend to get high ratings may, they offer, be an artifact of the scaling steps rather than of something implicit in the counseling relationship. Raters in general hesitate to give extreme judgments, and they tend to displace individuals in the direction of the mean of the total group. In essence the typical five-point scale used in counseling research would reduce variability of rating due to the error of central tendency and increase interjudge reliability due to the nature of the scale rather than as a reflection of true variability across a five-point scale. In order to spread the distribution, categories at either end should be created while also creating finer discriminations of responses. Finally, Zimmer and his associates argue, the level of measurement used in rating scales should be stipulated specifically, and only those permissible statistics should be employed. In rating counseling over various constructs, they suggest we force what is essentially a multidimensional quality onto a linear scale (at best what is worked with is an ordinal scale or a method of rank order) (Guilford, 1956; Stevens, 1946).

In summary, while the proponents of rigor must acknowledge, however reluctantly, the contributions of the proponents of meaning in making breakthroughs, they argue vehemently for the necessity of employing sophisticated research procedures to isolate and make operational all aspects of helper or helpee behavior that relate to significant behavioral change in the helpee.

The recommendations concerning the rating scales employed in assessing counseling may be summarized as follows.

Conclusion II: The rating scales employed are largely a function of the stage of development in the exploration of the dimensions involved:

1. Usually during the early phases of investigation the constructs created and developed by the clinician-researcher are clinically meaningful but often able to make only very gross discriminations.

2. Having achieved some degree of predictive validity, it is imperative that the procedures of rigorous research be employed in an attempt to further refine and make operational these constructs in order to generate more accurate discriminations and predictions.

THE RATING PROCESS

With the selection of excerpts and scales the preparatory phases of rating are concluded and the more controversial process of rating begins. There are a number of considerations that, potentially at least, sharply divide the proponents of meaning and rigor.

Proposition III. The rating process employed depends in large part upon whether the intent of the study is to develop clinical learnings or to replicate and establish the stability of earlier findings.

The Criterion of Meaning

While for purposes of the research and its replication it may be important that the raters not know from what session and from what part within the session the excerpts are taken, coding may not be necessary. In fact, coding may be undesirable when rating is done principally for clinical purposes. To develop clinically meaningful learnings it may be necessary for the rater to listen to the helper-helpee interactions in sequence so that he can be sensitively attuned to the subtle nuances in the exchange. In addition, it is often felt that experienced helpers, who have themselves demonstrated that they are functioning at high levels on the relevant dimensions, are justified in rating the excerpts simultaneously on all of the relevant scales involved. It may also be important for the raters to be present and to listen to the same material at the same time. While it is expected that in their own self-sustaining direction the helpers can maintain the autonomy of their discriminations, these approaches offer not only discussion opportunities but also opportunities for the helpers to argue their respective cases in the event of highly different ratings. In a very real sense, then, the clinicians' efforts reflect a greater concern for accuracy (or as close as possible a congruence of the discrimination with what is actually going on in the counseling interaction) than for reliability and replicability. Like counseling itself, the rating process, the clinicians recognize, is an effort of painstaking concentration punctuated by periodic listening lapses on the part of most raters.

In assessing the individual excerpts the rater is in effect making continual assessments of the counselor's level of functioning. In some way, if the rating level is not consistent, the rater must assign an over-all rating for the excerpt. Usually this rating is calculated on the basis of the modal level of helper functioning within the excerpt; that is, the level at which the helper is functioning most frequently, although sometimes the mean level and even less frequently the high point of the helper's level of functioning within the excerpt is employed. Similarly, although the ratings on the individual dimensions may be summed and averaged (and sometimes all of the dimensions are averaged for a mean over-all level of functioning), for many purposes and because of the inability of the scales to assess many aspects of the helpee-helper interaction the modal level of helper functioning may be the most appropriate statistic. Assessments of where the counselor is most often functioning may be more meaningful than the averages of possibly varying degrees of very high and very low levels of functioning. For example, there is evidence to indicate not only that helpers high on empathy, respect, and genuineness also confront their helpees more than low-level helpers but also that they offer relatively lower levels of facilitative conditions while confronting than the low-level helpers (Berenson & Mitchell, 1974; Carkhuff & Berenson, 1967).

In general, then, just as the scales constitute gross measures of clinically meaningful constructs, so is the rating process oriented toward the means that offer the clinician-researcher the best prospects of translating his efforts to helpee benefits. In this regard there are studies that have approximated the meaning approach and that have generated highly valid predictions of helpee or trainee outcome.

The Criterion of Rigor

The proponents of the criterion of rigor, in turn, must insist on an elaborate and painstaking coding procedure wherein excerpts are assigned code numbers and reproduced on separate reels in order to maintain anonymity. To further insure replicability raters must rate with single scales and rate in isolation.

In terms of the rating process proper, it is essential that the raters' cues for each characteristic be unique to that characteristic. As an illustration in the negative, scales containing such general statements as "infrequently" or "to some degree" do not provide the respondents with consistent reference points. In addition, raters should be able to rank cues at a point on a scale without overlap in quantitative meaning. For example, the withholding of congruence or empathy might at times be more facilitative than the demonstration of these dimensions in an overt manner, and therefore provisions should be made for a quantitative reflection of such in the rating process.

In evaluating the rating process the possibility of consistent error should be accounted for. Classically, three types of errors have been considered relevant to rating scales: (1) leniency; (2) the "halo" effect; and (3) contrast. In dealing with rating processes it should be mandatory to ascertain the degree of error due to these sources. In this regard there are analyses of variance procedures that make it possible to adjust ratings due to these errors and to compute interjudge reliability based upon the adjusted ratings (Guilford, 1954).

The ratings of excerpts should be based upon the present behavior of the helper being rated. The ratings should not be based upon past experiences with the helper, with the present rating seen as an exception to the helper's modal behavior. In addition, at this point in time we simply do not know enough about the manner in which the order of certain helper-helpee interactions contaminate the ratings.

Finally, the proponents of rigor are concerned with other potential contaminating factors. For example, the need to control the effects of content and the frequency of exposure of raters to either helper or helpee is imperative. In summary, the proponents of rigor underscore the necessity for controlling specifically what the raters are rating so that there is no stimulus residual.

The recommendations concerning the rating process employed in assessing counseling may be summarized as follows:

Conclusion III. The rating process followed will be largely a function of the stage of development of the dimensions involved:

1. If the concern of the study is to develop new, clinically meaningful learnings, simultaneous ratings on multiple scales by multiple persons may be warranted.

2. If the principal concern of the study is replication of earlier findings, rigorous methods of coding and rating in isolation are essential.

3. Due to the inadequacies of the present scales in assessing all aspects of helper-helpee interactions, the modal means of assessing both individual ratings and summarizing ratings appears most appropriate.

THE SELECTION AND TRAINING OF RATERS

The issues involved in selecting and training raters are probably the most complex and difficult of all issues. What has been thus far implicit becomes intensely explicit. The question of who can rate leads directly to the burning question of whether all of the relevant variables in human relations can ever be operationized.

Proposition IV. The issues involved in the selection and training of raters depend in large part upon whether the process is viewed from the criterion of meaning or rigor.

The Criterion of Meaning

The proponents of meaning can argue that the scales, like any clinical instruments, are only as good as the rater is sensitively attuned and effective in all other relevant areas of functioning. Thus, only those who are themselves functioning at effective levels interpersonally can make the necessary discriminations of high, moderate, and low levels of facilitative functioning. While the proponents of meaning tend to focus upon the employment of experienced helpers, they may concede that perhaps the naïve-experience continuum is not so critical (Shapiro, 1967) as the level of functioning on the relevant dimensions of the prospective rater. In this regard they can cite extensive evidence for the predictive validity of the scales in the hands of high-level–functioning helpers (Carkhuff & Berenson, 1967). In addition, there is tentative evidence to suggest the following: (1) the higher the level of conditions communicated by a helper, the more accurate are the helper's ratings when compared to the ratings of experienced experts who have demonstrated predictive validity, while the lower the level of conditions communicated, the more variable is the helper on rerating (Carkhuff, Kratochvil, & Friel, 1968); (2) discrimination is unrelated to communication among low-functioning communicators and highly related to communication among high-functioning communicators, thus suggesting that discrimination is a necessary but not sufficient condition of communication (Carkhuff, Kratochvil, & Friel, 1968); (3) the level of conditions that the objectively rated low-level communicator, whether helper or helpee, discriminates himself or others to be offering bears no positive relation to either the objective tape ratings or to each other (Carkhuff & Burstein, 1970); (4) objectively rated low-level communicators tend to rate themselves higher than high-level communicators in addition to being more variable in their rate-reratings of themselves (Carkhuff & Burstein, 1970). Simply stated, *people functioning below minimally facilitative levels on the relevant dimensions distort.* Thus, since only objective ratings have been related to constructive change, a high level of personal functioning as indicated by objective ratings by high-level–functioning persons who have demonstrably positive helpee outcomes appears critical. In summary, the proponents of meaning forward the proposition that only high-level–functioning persons can discriminate highly diverse levels of functioning. Literature in regard to both selection and training of high-level discriminators is presented in Volume I.

The Criterion of Rigor

The proponents of the criterion of rigor have perhaps much less that is unique to say about the selection and training of raters than the proponents of the criterion of meaning except insofar as they summarize their directions in relation to excerpting, scaling, and rating. In order to insure the probability of universal replication, and in distinct contrast with the criterion of meaning, they advocate that the training methodology must be such that almost everyone can be trained. Thus, persons must be trained to respond to cues defined so uniquely, referring to single types of client behavior, that anyone can be eligible for training.

In training proper, the raters should be trained specifically on individual, single scales to a sufficient degree of both intra-and interrater reliability. In addition, the proponents of rigor underscore the need to preclude all of the possible rater "sets" that interfere with the possibility of making uncontaminated ratings. Poor levels of reliability, they point out, may be a function of either the scales or the training procedures or both. In this regard, and again in contrast with the often gross discriminations yielded by the criterion of meaning, they seek very finite discriminations and aim, literally, for simple frequency tabulations that will make the rating process direct and explicit. For example, they might factor analyze the behavior of counselors in ongoing counseling interactions in the hope of discerning finite and operational behavior. Unfortunately, this activity raises questions concerning the appropriateness of the models whose behavior we analyze in order to emulate. *The ultimate hope of the proponents of rigor is to conduct analyses that will yield laws that will enable us to follow very precise patterns in both rater training and rating and, indeed, in counselor training and counseling.*

Perhaps at no point, then, are the proponents of rigor and meaning further apart than on the issue of selection and training. In effect the proponents of meaning are suggesting that we study and train only those individuals who can function at the highest levels while the proponents of rigor are suggesting that everyone be made eligible for rating.

The recommendations concerning selection and training are therefore not compatible.

Conclusion IV.   Who is selected and trained to rate is dependent upon whether the rating process is viewed from the criteria of meaning or rigor:

1. From the criterion of meaning only individuals who are themselves functioning at high levels can rate effectively.
    a. High-level–functioning discriminators can be selected and/or trained.
    b. A number of selection indexes have been developed to assess the ability to discriminate (as well as communicate).
    c. A number of programs to train raters to discriminate at high levels have been made operational.
2. With the criterion of rigor it is essential that we work toward the possibility that everyone or anyone can be trained.
    a. This approach places major emphasis upon the development of scales involving straightforward counting procedures.
    b. Unfortunately, this approach raises questions concerning the helper models employed for analyzing the critical dimensions of counseling.

MEANING AND RIGOR: SOME CRITICAL TESTS

At no point are the proponents of meaning and rigor further apart than on the issues of scaling and the selection and training of raters. In regard to scaling we in our own work have preferred to employ rating scales that involve assessments of levels of functioning for a variety of reasons. First, this approach was in keeping with the methods out of which some of these dimensions first evolved (Carkhuff & Berenson, 1967; Rogers *et al.*, 1967; Truax & Carkhuff, 1967). Second, and perhaps most important, it allowed us to develop constructs and models and to summarize data concerning levels of functioning without reference to the frequency tabulations on individual dimensions of specific norm groups. In other words, the scaling by levels imposed some structure that left us free to theorize: any given person or group must fall into the range of levels from 1 to 5, something that would not be so with frequency tabulations. However, it is to be noted that some of the dimensions such as confrontation evolved as a consequence of frequency tabulations (Carkhuff & Berenson, 1967). In one study, then, we sought to test the differential effects of ratings by levels and by frequency tabulations (Carkhuff, 1969b). Accordingly, we took one dimension that evolved in the rating by level tradition, empathy, and one that evolved by frequency tabulations, confrontation.

First, we took the most operational level of empathy, that is, the one involving the least judgment on the part of the rater, level 3. By definition level 3 indicates an essential interchangeability of the responses of both helper and helpee in terms of affect and meaning. The operational question at level 3 for the rater is, "Could the helper have said what the helpee said and could the helpee have said what the helper said?" It involves no judgments on the part of the rater as to whether the helper was additive or subtractive in his responses. We had the raters listen to entire helping sessions and tabulate the frequencies with which helpers made level 3 responses and compared them to independent data of ratings of these responses in terms of levels. We found that the helpers rated at low levels in terms of levels received very few frequency tabulations of interchangeable responses while those rated at high levels received significantly greater numbers of such responses. The evidence suggests that helpers rated at low levels are simply unable to make interchangeable responses. They do not listen or hear or communicate well enough to indicate this minimally effective level of functioning. On the other hand, helpers rated at high levels do receive a number of frequency tabulations indicating interchangeable responses. Even those who are rated as making additive responses and thus rated at levels 4 and 5 check back periodically with the helpee in order to get feedback on how well they are "tuned in." They do so by making interchangeable or level 3 responses.

The evidence for confrontation is similar, indicating that helpers rated as making confrontations with the greatest frequency were also rated to be confronting the helpees at the highest levels. It is to be noted that those helpers confronting at the highest levels or with the greatest frequency were also those who were rated as communicating empathic understanding at the highest levels or making interchangeable empathic responses with the greatest frequency, a finding consistent with previous work in this area. In summary, whether we employ rating scales involving levels of functioning or frequency tabulations, we get the same results: effective helpers receive high ratings and ineffective helpers receive low ratings.

In regard to the selection and training of raters, several critical studies are reviewed in Volume I. The most crucial studies are relevant here. The work of Shapiro (1968) indicates that "untrained raters are able to differentiate high and low levels of psychotherapeutic behavior in a manner which is similar to that of trained raters." However, the research does not indicate whether or not the ratings of either group of subjects are related to any validity criteria. In addition, without any indexes of the raters' levels of functioning there is no way of telling whether all raters may have been functioning at low levels and thus that the ratings of poor raters are as poor as the ratings of poor raters whether the raters are experienced or inexperienced. Finally, in suggesting that everyone can discriminate gross levels of functioning, this work leaves us without cues as to which raters can make the most accurate and valid predictions.

Research exploring the relationship of both level of functioning and experience to accuracy of discriminations was designed employing as criteria the gross rating scale and the expert ratings that are reviewed in Volume I (Cannon & Carkhuff, 1969). Accordingly, 80 subjects were selected from a pool of 251 subjects whose written responses to standard helpee stimulus expressions had been assessed by gross rating scales of facilitative interpersonal communication. The 80 subjects were divided into four groups of 20 of the basis of the following experience levels: (1) experienced counselors and psychotherapists; (2) graduate trainees in counseling and psychotherapy; (3) undergraduates with experience in the helping role; and (4) undergraduates with no experience in the helping role. In turn, each group of 20 subjects was divided into the 10 highest-rated and the 10 lowest-rated respondents at that experience level. The mean deviations in levels from the ratings of experts are given in Table 13-1. It can be seen that at each experience level the low-level group was functioning approximately one to one and a half communication levels lower than the high-level group. The analyses confirmed the observation that *both rater level of functioning and experience were significant sources of effect for discrimination scores.* Analyses controlling for the confounding of experience with level of functioning also yielded highly significant results. In addition, separate tests confirmed the following observations: (1) two groups of high-level–functioning subjects (I and III) were significantly more accurate in their ratings than every group of low-level–functioning subjects; (2) each of the remaining two groups of high-level–functioning subjects (V and VII) was significantly more accurate in its ratings than the two groups of low-level–functioning subjects at that experience level (VI and VIII) and none significantly different from the other two low-level groups (II and IV); (3) none of the groups of low-level–functioning subjects was significantly more accurate in its ratings than any of the groups of high-level–functioning subjects. Finally, it was concluded that the significant interaction effect between experience and levels of function-

Table 13-1. Means and Standard Deviations of Communication and Discrimination Scores

Groups	Subjects	Communication (Ratings on 5-point Scales)			Discrimination (Deviations from Experts)	
		N	Mean	sd	Mean	sd
I	High-level experienced	10	2.8	0.5	0.5	0.2
II	Low-level experienced	10	1.4	0.3	0.8	0.2
III	High-level graduate trainees	10	2.9	0.2	0.5	0.2
IV	Low-level graduate trainees	10	1.6	0.1	1.0	0.2
V	High-level experienced undergraduates	10	2.3	0.2	0.9	0.2
VI	Low-level experienced undergraduates	10	1.2	0.1	1.1	0.2
VII	High-level inexperienced undergraduates	10	2.1	0.1	0.9	0.2
VIII	Low-level inexperienced undergraduates	10	1.2	0.1	1.2	0.1
	All low-level subjects	40	1.3	0.2	1.0	0.2
	All high-level subjects	40	2.5	0.4	0.7	0.3
	All subjects	80	1.9	0.7	0.9	0.3

ing reflected the differential effects of experience at the two levels of functioning rather than the differential effects of level of functioning at the four levels of experience, thus indicating further support for the conclusion that level of functioning is a more critical indicator of accuracy of ratings than level of experience.

At this point in our development the findings would seem to lend support to the proponents of the criterion of meaning who suggest that the validity of rating scales is largely a function of the particular raters who employ these scales. They run counter to the results of Shapiro and others who indicate that neophytes rate as effectively as trained raters and do so employing gross rating scales that involve minimum effects of experience. They account for the findings of such studies with the possibility that both the neophytes and the experienced raters may have been functioning at the same levels, whether high, moderate, or low, although most likely the latter, as, for example, the very similar results of the low-level experienced (group VI) and the low-level experienced (group VIII) undergraduate groups analagous to those of the Shapiro study. On the other hand, the results of the study imply that in large part accuracy of discrimination is a function of level of functioning independent of whether the rater is therapist, rater, or client, whether trained or untrained, although, to be sure, we may be able to make diminishing probability statements in this regard. For example, an experienced therapist in the low group (II) may not discriminate as well as a graduate trainee (III) nor significantly better than experienced and inexperienced undergraduates (V and VII). In summary, not everyone can rate accurately; for that matter, if we extend the implications to their logical conclusions, not everyone can be trained to rate accurately. It simply makes good sense that, whatever the criteria, those who are experienced and who have demonstrated expertise in an area should demonstrate the most positive results. In this instance both level of functioning and experience were significant sources of effect for accurate discriminations, with level of functioning the more critical factor.

EXTENSIONS AND IMPLICATIONS

Some gaps can be bridged easily, other with difficulty, and some perhaps not at all. No doubt much of the difficulty lies in the early developmental stage of the entire helping processes. The fact is that much of the identity of the proponents of both meaning and rigor has come in the past in the reaction of each to the other. Few, in the interest of competency and effectiveness, have attempted to bridge the yawning void between them.

However, some of the issues may not be resolved. For example, the question of whether, even if we could articulate, operationalize and finally control all of the relevant dimensions of relevant human behavior, we would want to cannot be answered easily. The proponents of meaning, with a revulsion for control, vote no, while those of rigor vote yes, with each reflecting their own phenomenologies (Carkhuff, 1967c). In any event the issues that sharply divide the proponents of meaning and rigor in the investigation of helping dimensions are rooted in strong attitudinal stances and deep philosophical issues.

The proponents of meaning and rigor are most closely in tune on the more benign problems, that is, those concerning excerpting, and most sharply divided on the issues related to the preliminary phases of rating, that is, the scales and the selection and training of raters. Rigor in its impersonal stance indicates that the answer is in the scales: if we analyze counseling carefully enough we can discern and make operational all of the dimensions related to effectiveness and capture these dimensions in the appropriate rating scales. Meaning in its very personal stance suggests that the answer is in the person: some people live effectively, some can be trained to live effectively, and some must be given therapy (that is, brought to a high enough level of functioning) so that they can be trained to live effectively; in relation to rating everyone and anyone will never be able to make the discriminations necessary to generate valid predictions of outcome.

Ironically, there is a universality to the rigor message that is not present in the meaning message. Anyone can be trained to rate or even to emulate all of the relevant ways of functioning discerned from an analysis of helping. Unfortunately, this fact does raise the question of the models employed for our factor analyses (aside from the now traditional questions concerning the limitations of this statistical methodology); that is, factor analysis is as good as the data we put into it. The available base rate data indicate that there are only a very limited number of helpers who are effective—so significant, however, that without them untreated groups would fair better on the average than treatment groups. In many studies we are researching the efforts of unselected trainers who are functioning at relatively low levels to train unselected people who are functioning at relatively low levels to discriminate the levels of functioning of unselected and relatively low-level–functioning helpers, all of which culminates in the training of low-level–functioning helpers. The modal behavior of the modal helper is less than effective. The best we can hope to attain with this approach is the most effective behaviors of ineffectuals. With the recognition that effective rating and effective counseling may be highly related, *perhaps the proponents of both meaning and rigor should study only those helpers who do in fact make a difference, that is, those whose helpees repeatedly get better (and here we must do extensive and periodic outcome studies in order to avoid circularity). The choice is not between the dictates of rigor and meaning (which can be put to empirical test) but between dominance of the effectives or dominance of the ineffectives who prefer war between the competent proponents of meaning and rigor to exposure.* In summary, with the awareness that the criterion of rigor per se is not a creative process and the criterion of meaning not a stabilizing one, in the interest of the advancement of the science-art of helping it is essential that the proponents of meaning and the proponents of rigor recognize the contributions of each other. Advances in the helping area cannot be made without the free exploration and expression of the dedicated clinical researcher. Those advances that can be made cannot be stabilized and concretized so that they can be transmitted in training and helping without the scientific tools and techniques of the rigorous researcher: "we need to get on with the business of generating psychological hypotheses and proceed to do investigations and make inferences which bear on them" (Bakan, 1966, p. 436).

REFERENCES

For a more detailed discussion of the issues considered in this chapter see the asterisked readings and the references upon which the readings are based.

Bakan, D. The test of significance in psychological research. *Psychological Bulletin*, 1966, **66**, 423–437.

Berenson, B. G., & Mitchell, K. *Confrontation.* Amherst, Mass.: Human Resource Development Press, 1974.

Cannon, J. C., & Carkhuff, R. R. The effect of rater level of functioning and experience upon the discrimination of facilitative conditions. *Journal of Counseling Psychology*, in press, 1969.

Carkhuff, R. R. The contributions of a phenomenological approach to deterministic approaches to counseling and psychotherapy. *Journal of Counseling Psychology*, 1967, **14**, 570–572.

Carkhuff, R. R. *The counselor's contribution to facilitative processes.* Mimeographed manuscript, State University of New York at Buffalo, 1968. (a)

*Carkhuff, R. R. The investigation of counseling dimensions: The employment of rating scales to assess facilitative interpersonal functioning. In *The counselor's contribution to facilitative processes.* Mimeographed manuscript, State University of New York at Buffalo, 1968. (b)

Carkhuff, R. R. Helper communication as a function of helpee affect and content. *Journal of Counseling Psychology*, 1969, **16**, 126–131. (a)

Carkhuff, R. R. The differential effects of ratings by levels and frequency tabulations in determining empathy and confrontation. Unpublished research, American International College, Springfield, Mass., 1969. (b)

*Carkhuff, R. R., & Berenson, B. G. *Beyond counseling and psychotherapy.* New York: Holt, Rinehard and Winston, Inc., 1967.

Carkhuff, R. R., & Burstein, J. Objective self and client interrelationships of counselor-offered facilitative conditions. *Journal of Clinical Psychology,* 1970, **26,** 394–395.

Carkhuff, R. R., Kratochvil, D., & Friel, T. The effects of professional training: The communication and discrimination of facilitative conditions. *Journal of Counseling Psychology,* 1968, **15,** 68–74.

Carkhuff, R. R., Piaget, G., & Pierce, R. The development of skills in interpersonal functioning. *Counselor Education and Supervision,* 1968, **7,** 102–106.

Guilford, J. P. *Fundamental statistics in psychology and education.* New York: McGraw-Hill Book Company, Inc., 1956.

Kiesler, D. J., Klein, M. H., & Mathieu, P. Sampling from the recorded therapy interview: The problem of segment location. *Journal of Consulting Psychology,* 1965, **29,** 337–344.

Kiesler, D. J., Mathieu, P., & Klein, M. H. Sampling from the recorded therapy interview: A comparative study of different segment lengths. *Journal of Consulting Psychology,* 1964, **28,** 349–357.

Kiesler, D. J., Mathieu, P. & Klein, M. H. Measurement of conditions and process variables. In C. R. Rogers (ed.), *The therapeutic relationship and its impact.* Madison, Wisc.: University of Wisconsin Press, 1967. Pp. 135–185. (a)

Kiesler, D. J., Mathieu, P., & Klein, M. H. Patient experiencing level and interaction-chronograph variables in therapy interview segments. *Journal of Consulting Psychology,* 1967, **31,** 224. (b)

Pagell, W., Carkhuff, R. R., & Berenson, B. G. The predicted differential effects of high and low functioning counselors upon client level of interpersonal functioning. *Journal of Clinical Psychology,* 1967, **23,** 510–512.

Pierce, R., Carkhuff, R. R., & Berenson, B. G. The differential effects of high and low functioning counselors upon counselors-in-training. *Journal of Clinical Psychology,* 1967, **23,** 212–215.

*Rogers, C. R., Gendlin, E., Kiesler, D., & Truax, C. B. *The therapeutic relationship and its impact.* Madison, Wisc.: University of Wisconsin Press, 1967.

Shapiro, J. G. Agreement between channels of communication in interviews. *Journal of Consulting Psychology,* 1966, **30,** 535–538.

Shapiro, J. G. Relationships between expert and neophyte ratings of therapeutic conditions. *Journal of Consulting and Clinical Psychology,* 1968, **32,** 87–89.

Stevens, S. S. On the theory of scales of measurement. *Science,* 1946, **103,** 670–680.

Truax, C. B. Therapist empathy, warmth and genuineness and patient personality change in group psychotherapy: A comparison between interaction unit measures, time sample measures, patient perception measures. *Journal of Clinical Psychology*, 1966, 22, 225–229. (a)

Truax, C. B. Influence of patient statements on judgments of therapist statements during psychotherapy. *Journal of Clinical Psychology*, 1966, 22, 335–336. (b)

Truax, C. B., & Carkhuff, R. R. *Toward effective counseling and psychotherapy.* Chicago: Aldine Publishing Company, 1967.

Zimmer, J. M., & Anderson, S. Factor analyses of counselor respect, empathy and genuineness. *Journal of Counseling Psychology*, 1968, 15, 417–426.

Zimmer, J. M., & Parks, P. Factor analysis of counselor communications. *Journal of Counseling Psychology*, 1967, 14, 198–203.

14
APPLICATIONS IN
EFFECTIVE RESEARCH

When research is viewed as a means of making enlightened and systematic inquiries into what we are professing to do it is not nearly as difficult as some people make it. Indeed, the processes and effects we are attempting to achieve in practice are much more complex than the search and research processes will ever indicate to us. In our own work we have not been able to separate practice from research. Research, not a humanly meaningful end in and of itself, serves to shed light on the ingredients of effective processes in the following sequence of events: (1) the analysis of the effects of what is going on in a given area of practice; (2) the discernment of those dimensions that are most closely related to desired effects; (3) the conducting of pilot, experimental studies of the effects of these dimensions; (4) the application in training programs of those dimensions that demonstrate their relevance to the desired effects; (5) the analysis of the effects of the training program upon the trainees; and (6) the analysis of the differential effects of practice before and following training in order to determine the effectiveness of the modifications in the original practices.

A major problem in the past has been that we have not known what we were looking for in practice. Thus, we have thrown a variety of traditional testing indexes or our favorite tests into the hopper and have come out with highly questionable results. If, on the other hand, we know what it is we wish to accomplish, or at least some aspects of what we wish to accomplish, we can develop functional indexes of our effects. Thus, in a rehabilitation counselor training program one key outcome would involve the ability to relate to a typical rehabilitation case. If the trainee-products cannot do so, the program has not been effective. Accordingly, we may incorporate rehabilitation patients into the helpee role, presenting problems that for them are real and alive and assess the level of functioning of the helper in relation to them (Anthony & Carkhuff, 1970). The approach is similar in other areas.

Again our emphasis is upon interpersonal processes as the key ingredient in the social services. Accordingly, we might develop functional indexes in all of these areas; for example, ability to function in the husband and wife relationship in marital relations or ability to function in the parental role (and perhaps even ability of the child to function in his role) in parent-child relations. *The indexes employed to assess a given program as well as the program itself reflect what the program is attempting to accomplish.*

The indexes employed may be common sense ones. We simply want some means of assessing what we are doing. Often there is data readily available that do not fully indicate our intended purposes but that, nevertheless, reflect some aspects of what we are trying to do—for example, the clerical records of termination in a given agency. If, as is happening in many of our community mental health centers in so-called core areas, the rate of termination following the first session is 75 to 80 percent, then we are certainly not reaching the people we are trying to reach. If individual practitioners have a majority of helpees who do not return after one contact, or who, if they do return, request another helper, then these practitioners are not accomplishing their mission. If a teacher has a high truancy rate in her class, or, as we have seen, a first-grade teacher finds that seven stutterers develop each year in her class, then we know we have problems. If, as we have found, only 8 of 70 Upward Bound enrollees completed training and all 8 were enrollees of the same counselor, then we must study the levels of functioning of this counselor in relation to the remaining counselors. In these instances it is an abuse of the spirit of research to focus exclusively upon the helpee populations involved as many agencies do. All of our evidence indicates that we must look at the helper, although not to the exclusion of the helpee. If we must choose where to invest our time, let us study those designated more knowing by society. Let us study the practitioner instead of the client, the teacher instead of the stutterer.

There are, then, some very simple, informal ways of searching and researching the effectiveness of our programs. There is no excuse for not researching these effects. *A person cannot call himself a helper unless he is making enlightened inquiries into his efforts and modifying those efforts to make them more effective. A helper is a researcher or he is not a helper.*

A PARADIGM FOR RESEARCH IN HELPING

There are more formal procedures for assessing the effects of a given treatment or training program. These approaches are helpful in identifying the different sources of the results that might be obtained through the less formal means. There are three key ingredients to systematic research of this kind: (1) the employment of functionally meaningful indexes of outcome; (2) pre-, post-, and follow-up testing on these indexes; (3) treatment, treatment control, and control groups (see Figure 14-1).

Again the functionally meaningful indexes are requisite not only to assessment but also to the treatment or training program itself. If we cannot define the ends of our treatment, then we do not know what our treatment is about. Treatment programs should in some way lead to operational ends, however loosely defined. Accordingly, in marital counseling we must obtain some index of an improved relationship between husband and wife in order to term the process successful. All of the

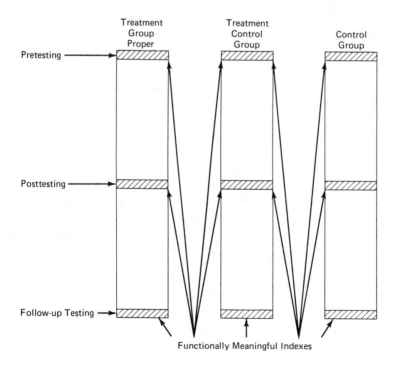

Figure 14-1. Schematic representation of research in the helping process.

Rorschach and Minnesota Multiphasic Personality Inventory (MMPI) changes in the world on the part of the helpee cannot make the process effective if the persons involved are not relating in some demonstrably improved way. However many other indexes we incorporate in our testing in order to determine how the process involved might also affect these indexes, the key ingredient remains the development of functionally meaningful indexes.

The pre- and posttreatment test administrations allow us to assess the effects of our treatment over time. We need to have an estimate of the helpee's initial level of functioning on the relevant indexes in order to determine the degree of change on these indexes. Where possible alternate forms of the indexes may be employed. Thus, for example, in parent-child counseling with parents with more than one child we have built-in alternate forms of the testing. Or we can supply different children as stand-ins. We can estimate the parents' contribution to interpersonal processes with their own children from assessing their functioning with different children. However, where the outcome is defined as precisely as in marital counseling and where there are no alternate forms available, so to speak, in our culture, this will not be the case. An additional argument must be made for the follow-up assessments, since there is reason to believe that several years later many of the effects that were once apparent have washed out due to a variety of circumstances.

Finally, different treatment and control groups allow us to distinguish the effects of treatment from the effects of many other ongoing experiences. Therefore, the treatment of preference will be incorporated in one group called the treatment proper or experimental group. A second group, termed the control group, will receive no treatment. These individuals will simply go on living as they ordinarily would with the exception of the fact of pre-, post-, and follow-up testing. A third group, and this is perhaps most important, will receive the same special attention as the treatment group for the same amount and duration of time. If possible this group will receive all of the aspects of the treatment proper except for those characteristics that are most critical to the treatment. For example, if taped excerpts are employed in a training program and evaluated in the training group proper, they would also be employed in the training control group, although they may not be employed in a way that is critical to the training proper (Berenson, Carkhuff, & Myrus, 1966). In regard to this aspect of research there must be some assurance that the individuals in the different groups are equivalent on the relevant dimensions. This may be accomplished by random assignment or matching. It is also crucial that the helpers or trainers be matched in their level of functioning on relevant dimensions. These are the basic ingredients. They are simple. They are relevant. They are meaningful. They may be employed with imagination to fit the needs of the agencies and persons involved.

We need not be overwhelmed by a need to control everything. If statistically significant effects occur only under the most controlled circumstances, then the effects are not humanly significant. They have little meaning because life, at least as we know it, does not take place under such controlled circumstances. *Only effects that are so great that they occur under conditions of only minimal methodological control have application to human functioning.*

Nor do we need to be overwhelmed by the complexities of statistics. Statistics are only tools—to be sure, very useful ones—but tools to serve our ends and not ends in themselves as so many people have made them. Significant results do not require statistics. Graphs and frequency tabulations tell the researcher much that he wants to know. In addition, simple counting tests such as Tukey's (1959) yield accurate estimates of probability statements. There are simple nonparametric techniques that have 95 percent efficiency when compared to parametric tests (Drasgow & Carkhuff, 1964). In general, the researcher would do well to remember that statistical methodologies are dictated by the design employed. Simple designs require simple statistics. However, in the event that complex statistical procedures are necessary, the inquiring practitioner may consult a statistical technician and/or hire some computer time.

Those who are sophisticated in methodology are not always equipped to ask meaningful questions. Those who have their hands and feet dirty in the soil of daily practice are best equipped to ask questions that may make a difference. We are simply not going to solve the problems in marital, labor, and, indeed, international relations by applying the generalizations of many social psychologists derived from games such as "the prisoner's dilemma." There simply is no replacement for a meaningful question and no excuse for not asking it for those who are equipped to ask it.

APPLICATIONS IN RESEARCH IN HELPING

Let us examine the methodologies developed and implemented in the areas of functional indexes, pre-posttesting, and treatment and control groups.

Functional Indexes

The principal functional index remains some form of casting the individual involved in a helping role in order to obtain some index of his optimum level of interpersonal functioning in the relevant area. Many variations of this approach have been developed, some involving human relations and others taped or written indexes. Thus, in training parents to function effectively with each other as well as with their children some index was required to estimate the initial levels of functioning of the trainee-helpers (Carkhuff & Bierman, 1970). In conjunction with learnings from other experiences (Carkhuff, 1967) it was decided to cast the parents involved in a free play situation with their problem children. In addition, the helper-trainer and his spouse were cast in the same free play situation with a child of equivalent age with the same instructions in order to determine the movement over time of the helpee-trainees toward the helper-trainer. The anticipated movement of effective helping from either active nonfacilitative or passive nonfacilitative toward the active facilitative levels at which the helper-trainer was functioning was not established.

In a study involving the training of patients in interpersonal functioning Pierce and Drasgow (1969) found that they were unable to cast severely deteriorated mental patients in the helping role prior to training. Indeed, this finding is most significant in and of itself. Accordingly, employing the helpee stimulus expressions (Carkhuff, 1969 and Volume I) as a model, they developed the following brief excerpts that were meaningful for the patients involved:

1. I feel so down. It's like everything is going against me. I get this real bad pain and can't work. I can have an operation for it but it might make me impotent. My boy is staying with my niece and her husband but they think I'm just lying and a bum, and they're giving me a real hard time. I just don't know what to do.

2. The people around here jerk me off so much. I've been sitting around on the goddamn ward for two weeks and I've seen the doctor once. I don't know what's the matter with me and nobody around here seems to want to tell me. I'm mad as hell but I'm scared to leave, too.

3. Man, I really feel great. I'm getting out of here next week, and I feel like I got a whole new start in life. For the first time since I can remember I feel relaxed. I got my old job back and my boss has been really good about the whole thing. I didn't know I could feel so great.

At the conclusion of training the researchers were able to cast the trainees in the helping role and did so with a patient at the hospital.

They also included the taped expressions again and found that on both indexes the patients (1) gained over one level in functioning and (2) demonstrated levels of functioning significantly greater than groups of control patients under different forms of treatment.

In a comprehensive study of the cumulative effects of the levels of facilitative and action-oriented dimensions upon physical, emotional, and intellectual indexes of advanced grammar school students Kratochvil, Carkhuff, & Berenson (1969) also found the need to modify the standard helpee stimulus expressions and to present them in a written form to insure full parent and teacher cooperation. Thus, the following student statements and alternative parent or teacher responses were presented to parents and teachers in order to obtain an index of both communication and discrimination:

STUDENT STATEMENTS

1. I feel so bad—I have no friends. Nobody likes me. All the other kids lunch together and play together. They always leave me out—as if they don't even care about me. Sometimes when I'm alone and all the other kids are together I feel like crying. Why doesn't anyone like me? I try to be nice, but nothing seems to work. I guess there is nothing I can do.

2. It makes me so mad! Everybody is always telling me what to do and what not to do. When I'm at home, my parents tell me what is best for me. At school it's the teacher. Even my friends bother me. Everybody pushes me around. Sometimes I feel like punching them all in the nose! They had just better leave me alone and let me do things the way I want to.

3. I'm so excited and everything is going so great! I ran for president of my class and I won; I guess the other kids really like me. And today my teacher said I was one of the best students she had ever had; she makes me feel all warm inside. And next week, during spring vacation, I'm going to have a great time with my family. I'm so happy. It's unbelievable. Some people make me feel so good.

4. I just don't know what to do. I try very hard in school, but nothing seems to sink in. I guess I'm not very smart. Nobody seems to care that I try. What really hurts is when I see my parents bragging to others about how smart my brother is; they never even mention me—they even change the subject when I'm mentioned. Oh, I wish I could do better, but I can't. The smart kids are really lucky—everybody likes them because they are smart. Sometimes I even get mad at myself because I can't do any better.

5. I get so angry in school! Everyone tells you what you have to learn, and they don't even care about what you are interested in. You are supposed

to like whatever they want to teach you. And some of the stupid things they make you do just to get a good grade! I learn more than some kids who get all A's. For me school is a waste of time. The people there make me so mad that sometimes I want to tell them that I just don't care about all their stupid subjects. But I can't, because I'd get into trouble and that would make me even more angry. I could scream and blow the school up every time I see it.

6. Each day I get up at the crack of dawn and people wonder why. I do because I have a longing to learn about myself and the things around me. It's so exciting! Each moment I see or learn something new—caterpillars become butterflies, the sun is actually bigger than the earth, or my body is made of many tiny cells. I feel like I'm bubbling over with excitement. I want to learn and discover things all day long!

7. Whenever we divide up to choose sides to play I'm always the last one picked. I'm so awkward and I don't seem to play the way the others want me to. No one ever wants me on their side. It really makes me feel bad to be the last one left. When everybody is playing I just lean against the nearest wall—sometimes I could cry; when I do I simply feel worse than ever—and all the other kids laugh at me then. I hate my body; why couldn't I have gotten a different one?

8. People get me so mad! Sometimes I feel like really letting them have it. That would at least make them stop making fun of the way I look. Just because I'm bigger than most kids my age, they call me names. The other kids call me "lardy" or "fatso." Sometimes my teacher says I'm a big bully. Even my dad and mom don't like the way I look; they kid me by saying, "You'll grow out of it, we hope." Well, they just better watch out because I'll show them I can really be a bully if I want to. I'm not going to let them make fun of me and get away with it.

9. I could just run and run and run. I feel so strong! In gym today I beat everybody on the physical fitness test. At home I get my work done faster than anyone else. I'm so full of energy and I have so many ways to use it. I'm so happy and so strong I could work and play and never stop.

HELPER RESPONSES

1. a. Maybe you just have to accept things as they are.
   b. What you should do is this. Pick out someone who might be a friend. Go up to him and eat lunch with him. And then ask him to play with you. Don't cry, don't give up.
   c. You have tried making friends but nothing works. And now you feel so alone.
   d. No matter what you do, nothing works. You even expect that it will be the same here with me.

2. a. You get so angry when people don't let you do things the way you want to. You just aren't going to let them push you around any more. And I'd better watch my step too!

    b. Everybody pushes you around so much you feel like letting them have it.

    c. Don't get so mad. I think there is a time to take orders and a time to give orders. This is what I think you should learn.

    d. Everybody gets pushed around sometime during their life.

3. a. Did you say everything is going great? What do you mean—people make you feel so good? Make sure you work hard so it might stay this way.

    b. You are getting along so well with everybody you can't believe it.

    c. You feel so good inside when there are people you can be close to— you know there is something good in you and in them. I can feel it now with you.

    d. This probably won't last long.

4. a. You have tried so hard, nothing seems to work, and nobody seems to care.

    b. You feel so sad because your efforts haven't paid off and because people close to you are ashamed of you. And now you think there is something ugly about you, and I might come to feel that way too.

    c. Have you done anything to make your parents proud of you? I'm all for letting people suffer when they deserve it.

    d. You probably need to work a little harder. Give your parents a reason to think you aren't dumb.

5. a. There are good and bad things about school. Make sure you know which is which. Try doing what your teachers want and maybe you'll get more chances to do what you want.

    b. Some people get into trouble more than others.

    c. You are mad! You're caught between expressing what you feel and being bored in school.

    d. It's like shouting in an empty room. No one can hear you.

6. a. You are full of excitement and you want to learn everything there is to learn.

    b. What about other things in your life? Are they as exciting? Are you also this excited when you are in school?

    c. Is that so? Are you on vacation now? What about the times when you didn't feel this way?

    d. Hey, you make me feel good inside! You are full of life and you want to see and feel it everywhere you go.

7. a. Are there times when you aren't the last one chosen? If so, what are these times like? You probably try a little harder then, don't you?

b. You hate how you look and everybody else does too. At times you feel so hopeless you could cry—you see nothing to do.
c. There are other kids who feel just as you do.
d. You are left out of all the fun and it's because of a body you wished you didn't have. If you were only just not you.

8. a. Have you picked on kids smaller than you? Maybe you deserve being called names.
    b. Don't show them, don't be a bully. That will simply make more trouble. You are bigger, so try being nice so you don't scare the other kids.
    c. They had better watch out, because you are big enough to let them have it and you will if they push you too far.
    d. You are big and strong, no one recognizes this, and even people close to you poke fun at you. You won't let them, or me either, make fun of you. Right?

9. a. Keep working, eat well, sleep well, and listen to what your parents tell you.
    b. It's not nice to brag so much.
    c. Using all of your energy all day long makes you happy and strong.
    d. At the same time you feel peaceful and excited inside; when you want energy it is there to use. You can face everything knowing you will be even stronger and more alive tomorrow.

While the data yielded some immediate effects such as the highest-level teacher's ability to effect significantly greater student changes on achievement indexes such as reading, a finding consistent with that of Aspy (1969) and Aspy and Hadlock (1968), they indicated that these effects "washed out," so that in the long term there were no cumulative effects, a very distressing finding.

Pre-Post Measures

This cross-sectional project provides a transition into a consideration of pre- and posttesting because it studies cumulative effects based upon a single index of present level of functioning, an approach that is not as satisfactory as long-term, longitudinal studies. The longitudinal form of research would give us indications of changes that have taken place in parent or teacher level of functioning over time. Thus, it is very conceivable that a parent who is now low was once fairly high, or a teacher who is now fairly high was once relatively low. However, longitudinal research is not always possible, and cross-sectional research may accomplish many of its aims, especially when year-to-year records are available, as in this study of cumulative effects.

The pre-, post-, and follow-up approach to assessment, then, is the approach that will insure us most of the effects under study. In our own work we remedied the faults of our earlier studies of training where we incorporated only posttesting assessments of functioning in a patient relationship (Carkhuff & Truax, 1965a). While the posttesting levels of functioning of both lay personnel and graduate students were commensurate with those of experienced and prominent professionals, and while the trainees did in fact elicit changes in the patients whom they saw (Carkhuff & Truax, 1965b), there was no way of estimating at what levels they began training. Accordingly, pre-posttesting indexes involving casting the trainee in the helping role were incorporated. Not only were objective ratings of trainee functioning obtained but also assessments by the trainee himself, the helpee whom he saw, and significant others such as roommates or spouses (Berenson *et al.*, 1966; Carkhuff, 1969; Kratochvil, 1969; Martin & Carkhuff, 1967; Pierce, Carkhuff, & Berenson, 1967). The same kinds of indexes in conjunction with therapist and expert psychiatric evaluations were employed in assessments of treatment.

In addition to these indexes other assessments such as those objective items on the Minnesota Multiphasic Personality Test on which persons can change over the course of training (Martin & Carkhuff, 1967) and treatment (Carkhuff & Bierman, 1970; Donofrio, 1968) or the Kuder neuropsychiatric items (Drasgow & Carkhuff, 1964) were incorporated. In regard to the latter treatment studies the most recent among those studying the direct effects upon parents and the indirect effects upon children of both traditional parent therapy groups and training in interpersonal functioning as a preferred mode of treatment (see Chapter 11) a variety of additional indexes, including many traditional children's tests, were included. In general, the training groups were significantly more effective than the treatment groups in effecting changes in the parents' functioning. However, where individual traditional indexes did not reflect the distinct changes obtained with the functional indexes we felt strongly that there was more basis for questioning the validity of the traditional tests than the effects on the functional indexes. In a very real sense, then, these tests become superfluous if they cannot accurately discriminate significant changes in a given individual's functioning.

Finally, the necessity for long-term follow-up studies cannot be overemphasized. The lessons learned from the Aspy and Kratochvil studies are important. While immediate effects may be demonstrated, these effects may wash out over the long run. Thus, students who have achieved a great deal under a very effective teacher may, following associations with several ineffective teachers, demonstrate very little retention of the early learning. The analogy in other helping areas suggests that if we achieved results with a given helpee and then passed the helpee on to several other ineffective helpers or significant authority figures in the helpee's environment, the effects might not hold up. There is cause for arguing not only for attempting to achieve desired ends in helping but also for preparing the helpee for associations and experiences that will not be helpful. Helping must involve preparation for handling retarding experiences as well as facilitating ones.

Training and Control Groups

While the pre-post testings provide a longitudinal control in studies of effectiveness, training control and control groups provide us with horizontal controls. They allow us to separate out the effects of our treatment from similar experiences. Again, whereas we began with only an *ad hoc* control group of professionals with which to compare our training effects (Carkhuff & Truax, 1965a), we went on to incorporate a number of different controls: pre- and posttested control groups with no intervening training (Berenson *et al.*, 1966) or treatment (Donofrio, 1968) or uncontrolled treatment experiences (Pierce & Drasgow, 1969); training control groups meeting for the same time for essentially the same purposes (except for certain critical aspects) and with the same high-level–functioning trainers (Berenson *et al.*, 1966); teaching control groups meeting for related purposes (Martin & Carkhuff, 1968); a variety of different treatment controls such as drugs and individual and group therapy groups (Pierce & Drasgow, 1969); and sequential variations in training groups (Carkhuff, Friel, & Kratochvil, 1969).

In addition, in a very real sense helpers or trainers functioning at differing or similar levels, depending upon the purposes of the study, constitute treatment controls. Thus, careful matches of trainer level of functioning and experience (Berenson *et al.*, 1966; Carkhuff, *et al.*, 1969) may serve to discern the effects of differing programs or different levels calculated to elicit different effects (Donofrio, 1968; Pagel, Carkhuff, & Berenson, 1967; Pierce & Schauble, 1970; Pierce *et al.*, 1967) may serve to study the effects of helpers offering essentially the same programs. The study of the effects of traditional psychotherapeutic treatment with parents upon both the parents and their children (Donofrio, 1968) is worth illustrating further. Professional therapists functioning at three different levels, at approximately level 3, around level 2, and around level 1.5 were assigned parents randomly. While the traditional groups effected no demonstrable changes with the exception of the self-exploration elicited by the highest-level-functioning helper, they did demonstrate more variability than a time control group. However, the point is not the results of this project as much as the programs of research it initiated. Whereas these different treatment groups were compared with each other and with the time control group, by incorporating many of the same testing indexes in further studies these groups constituted control groups for other studies. Thus, the human relations training group in both parent-child (Carkhuff & Bierman, 1970) and racial relations (Carkhuff & Banks, 1970) established significantly more positive results on comparable indexes. Other studies will follow.

A SUMMARY STATEMENT ON RESEARCH PROGRAMS

A few statements may be warranted in summary. Large-scale programs of research in the helping areas cannot be calculated in detail beforehand. If we learn from the results of our last study, we have a base for our direction in the next study. In this regard we might just briefly note the observation that many of our "professional," academic researchers do not learn from the results of their formulations and proceed accordingly. It is almost as if they do not believe their results— or, more basically, in the possibility of change. However, even given the fact that we cannot readily anticipate the next direction, we can still build research programs by incorporating overlapping dimensions and indexes that provide us with the basis for comparison.

Finally, and perhaps this is the heart of the matter, we cannot conduct research programs in helping unless we have all of the data on all of the relevant aspects of the helping process. We must know whether it is the program or the helper that is making the difference. In this regard no studies should be reported in the literature that do not enumerate the helper's and the helpee's level of functioning on the relevant dimensions—not only the level of facilitative and action-oriented dimensions at which the individual is functioning, but also an estimate of the effectiveness with which the individual implements the particular programs involved. Effective helpers may be able to effect some changes in some specifiable instances while conducting poor programs. Good programs may effect some changes in specifiable instances even under the guidance of poor helpers. Together poor helpers and poor programs can effect only negative changes. We must be able to differentiate our helpers and our programs in the interest of developing effective helpers and good programs that effect only positive changes.

REFERENCES

For a more detailed discussion of the issues considered in this chapter see the asterisked readings and the references upon which the readings are based.

*Anthony, W., & Carkhuff, R. R. The effects of rehabilitation counselor training upon discrimination, communication and helping attitudes. *Rehabilitation Counseling Bulletin*, 1970, **13**, 333–342.

Aspy, D. The effect of teacher-offered conditions of empathy, positive regard and congruence upon student achievement. *Florida Journal of Research*, 1969, **11**, 39–48.

Aspy, D., & Hadlock, W. The effects of high and low functioning teachers upon student performance. Unpublished research, University of Florida, 1968.

Berenson, B. G., Carkhuff, R. R., & Myrus, P. The interpersonal functioning and training of college students. *Journal of Counseling Psychology*, 1966, **13**, 441–446.

Carkhuff, R. R. Toward a comprehensive model of facilitative interpersonal processes. *Journal of Counseling Psychology*, 1967, **14**, 67–72.

Carkhuff, R. R. The prediction of the effects of teacher-counselor training: The development of communication and discrimination selection indexes. *Counselor Education and Supervision*, 1969, **8**, 265–272.

Carkhuff, R. R., & Banks, G. Training as a preferred mode of facilitating relations between races and generations. *Journal of Counseling Psychology*, 1970, **17**, 413–418.

Carkhuff, R. R., & Bierman, R. Training as a preferred mode of treatment of parents of emotionally disturbed children. *Journal of Counseling Psychology*, 1970, **17**, 157–161.

Carkhuff, R. R., Friel, T., & Kratochvil, D. The prediction of counselor functioning in the helping role from a variety of selection indexes. *Counselor Education and Supervision*, 1969.

Carkhuff, R. R., & Truax, C. B. Training in counseling and psychotherapy: An evaluation of an integrated didactic and experiential approach. *Journal of Consulting Psychology*, 1965, **29**, 333–336. (a)

Carkhuff, R. R., & Truax, C. B. Lay mental health counseling: The effectiveness of lay group counseling. *Journal of Consulting Psychology*, 1965, **29**, 426–431. (b)

Donofrio, D. The effects of therapist-offered conditions upon parents in group therapy and their children. Doctoral dissertation, State University of New York at Buffalo, 1968.

Drasgow, J., & Carkhuff, R. R. Kuder neuropsychiatric keys before and after psychotherapy. *Journal of Counseling Psychology*, 1964, **11**, 67–71.

Kratochvil, D. Changes in values and interpersonal functioning of nurses in training. *Counselor Education and Supervision*, 1969, **8**, 104–107.

Kratochvil, D., Carkhuff, R. R., & Berenson, B. G. Cumulative effects of parent and teacher offered levels of facilitative conditions upon indices of student physical, emotional and intellectual functioning. *Journal of Educational Research,* 1969, **63,** 161–164.

Martin, J., & Carkhuff, R. R. The effects of training upon changes in trainee personality and behavior. *Journal of Clinical Psychology,* 1968, **24,** 109–110.

Pagell, W., Carkhuff, R. R., & Berenson, B. G. The predicted differential effects of the level of counselor functioning upon the level of functioning of outpatients. *Journal of Clinical Psychology,* 1967, **23,** 510–512.

Pierce, R., & Schauble, P. Graduate training of facilitative counselors: The effects of individual supervision. *Journal of Counseling Psychology,* 1970, **17,** 210–215.

Pierce, R., Carkhuff, R. R., & Berenson, B. G. The differential effects of high and low functioning counselors upon counselors-in-training. *Journal of Clinical Psychology,* 1967, **23,** 212–215,

*Pierce, R., & Drasgow, J. Teaching facilitative interpersonal functioning to psychiatric in-patients. *Journal of Counseling Psychology,* 1969, **16,** 295–299.

Tukey, J. W. A quick, compact, two sample test. *Technometrics,* 1959, **1,** 31–48.

PART FOUR

Summary and Overview

THE HELPING PROCESS is not complete until we have translated its learnings to large-scale social action programs. Human relations institutes may serve as centers for analysis, development, and consultation on positive sources of effect in human relations problem areas (Chapter 15). Finally, any program is as good as the person who conducts it, and this person must be versed in all systems yet free of all of them (Chapter 16).

15
SOCIAL ACTION AND
THE FUTURE OF HELPING

In a very real sense both of these volumes devoted to the development of better and more complete helping services, including lay as well as professional helping, constitute contributions to large-scale social action programs. Social action programs as such are not the answer, however. The answer—if there is anything close to an answer—lies in the people who conduct these programs. We have seen program after program initiated at the federal, state, and local levels. Some few succeed but most fail, becoming bogged down in the follow-through and delivery stages. These programs flounder because no functionally meaningful criteria of effectiveness are required. They fail because frequently the best people are not in the key positions. As frequently as not those in key positions do not even have the administrative sense to facilitate the efforts of the more effective individuals among them. Indeed, often they do not have tolerance for those who can deliver, for they themselves become exposed by the contrast in style and outcome.

Until the effective helper makes translations to social action projects his contributions are limited. However, it is not enough to move into the community at large with large-scale projects. For example, most community mental health programs are largely dressed-down rather than dressed-up versions of the same old thing, with the same people always in positions of responsibility. There appears to be an implicit belief that an old storefront and a poorly clad clinician who slurs his words and uses bad grammar will get better results. Until the effective helper moves into the community at large with high-level–functioning persons, whether professional or nonprofessional, in positions of responsibility there will be no positive results on a large scale.

263

We need a whole new concept of social action. We do not need the same old people who have failed us before and will do so again. We need revolutionary social reforms based upon individuals who can achieve results. We need a reorganization of our social service systems with those functioning at high levels in the most responsible positions. We need to institute ongoing, inservice programs for those who can make a difference but who do not. We need to eliminate from our programs persons who cannot make a difference. Recurring crises bring us closer to effecting this new approach.

When we write of social service and social action programs we do not suggest "give-away" programs. When conducted by high-level–functioning, responsible adults, high levels of responsible action will be demanded from the people served by these programs. Again the promulgators and helpers conducting the programs, when they are truly effective, will constitute models for the effective living of the recipients.

There are no programs without people, and systems that have not been based upon criteria of productivity cannot facilitate productivity in the people they are supposed to serve. Systems based upon criteria of competency can.

PROPOSITIONS IN SEARCH OF A PROGRAM

What are we equipped to do? We are ready to function in several critical areas in which we have not functioned before.

Proposition I.   We are equipped to analyze the human sources of effect in human systems.

As indicated throughout these volumes, the operation of most systems is rooted in human relations. We know how to analyze the human sources of positive and negative effects in terms of the achievement of desired goals and the avoidance of undesirable consequences. We can analyze these sources by developing functional criteria of what a given agency is attempting to accomplish. For the helping areas the goals of the constructive change or gain of the helpees are quite clear. Even without the body of theoretical and empirical knowledge covered in these volumes, we are equipped to identify the individuals whose helpees flourish and those whose helpees deteriorate. We can develop criteria of competency according to whether a given individual is achieving the particular goals set for him. These criteria can be developed in very simple and fundamental ways, very often from the records of the agency secretary or clerk.

Proposition II. We are equipped to analyze the physical sources of effect in human systems.

As we found in Chapter 5 of Volume I, human systems are also in part based upon physical factors. Just as we can analyze the human sources of effect, then, we can also analyze the physical, environmental sources of positive and negative effects. Again we do so in terms of the achievement of desired goals and the avoidance of undesired goals. That is, we can discern the physical factors that make a constructive difference as well as those that do not.

Proposition III. We are equipped to introduce, reorganize, and coordinate human and environmental systems in order to maximize human conditions and outcomes.

Those human and environmental factors that foster constructive gains can be introduced. The systems into which they are integrated may be reorganized accordingly, with less emphasis given to some aspects and more to others. Again, in conjunction with facilitative physical factors, in human factors particular attention may be given to those who best meet the criteria of the setting or the program by placing such individuals in key positions.

Proposition IV. We are equipped to provide training in human relations and environmental utilization in order to maximize optimum conditions and productivity.

We can introduce training programs like or similar to those reviewed in Volume I in order to elevate the existing levels of human relations and to intensify the differences between those who are functioning effectively and those who are not. That is, we can train our highest-level–functioning persons to be trainers of others as well as to place them in other key positions. In turn, they can elevate the levels of functioning of those within the agency who can benefit from training.

Proposition V. We are equipped to provide guidance, orientation, or reorientation and consultation services.

We can provide the necessary guidance and reorientation involved in the introduction of new programs. We can give ongoing consultation services in order to provide the necessary follow-through after the initiation of the new programs. For example, with regard to proposition V, we can provide ongoing consultation to the trainers, who, in turn, will transmit the relevant learnings to those who can benefit from them. At every stage, then, we are making the most effective utilization of existing man power and providing the support necessary to make the delivery of constructive outcomes.

Proposition VI. We are equipped to provide the follow-up assessment and modification of a coordinated program.

We can follow up and study the results of our program, compare its results with those of programs existing before ours was implemented, and reorganize our program accordingly. Again, no program will unfold exactly as anticipated. *Perhaps the major proposition is this readiness to repeat the cycle and modify the program again and again in order to achieve the results intended.*

HUMAN RELATIONS INSTITUTES: A PROPOSAL

With the ability to analyze and reorganize sources of human and environmental effects and to provide human relations training and guidance as well as consultation and research services, we are ready to spell out a proposal for human relations programs. We are suggesting that strategically placed human relations institutes both in this country and throughout the world be developed. These units can be interrelated with one another through an exchange of staff and programs built around the operations of an international center. These institutes can provide broad programs of analysis, training, and consultation. They can offer community, education, industrial, institutional, and vocational services. In this context they can be funded in return for their valuable services as, for example, by industry, and thus decrease the tax dollar burden and increase the delivery to the average citizen. These institutes would constitute the core around which other service organizations could function. Perhaps most important, these institutes would make use of the effective manpower available.

Again by effective manpower we mean those individuals within a given setting who can produce on the relevant criteria. This implies a reorganization of existing manpower in terms of a criterion of competency rather than a criterion of seniority or professionalization. It also implies making use of existing manpower that is not presently being employed.

Many potential community assets are presently considered burdens by the community. For example, geriatric and hospitalized populations, welfare populations, and delinquent and criminal populations can be utilized in new and constructive ways. For example, it has been my experience that many institutionalized delinquent girls (and, for that matter, boys) assume a nourishing stance toward younger children. In my own work I feel that I can ascribe many of the therapeutically beneficial effects to the frequent contacts between my children and the delinquent girls whom I was "treating." Programs of delinquent institutions and orphanages or child-care centers could be set up side by side, with each, in effect, servicing the other. The child centers could be staffed by those delinquents who have earned the privilege and who can assume mature responsibility for others. Is that not the prime goal of rehabilitation in these institutions? These candidates could be further selected according to level of functioning and could be trained to function at even higher levels with the children, just as parents can be trained to work with their own children (see Chapter 10). They could be assigned key responsibilities according to their levels of development and functioning. To be sure, their efforts must be supervised, and this again can be accomplished by employing already existing personnel.

Jointly conceived and interlocking programs could be similarly brought about in the area of geriatric, welfare, criminal, and other populations. In addition, many other current problems could be dealt with in the same manner. The areas of marital relations, labor relations, and others could be serviced by such programs. The area of racial relations could be handled in a manner not unlike that involved in the white teacher–Negro parents communication program (see Volume I, Chapter 14). Similar programs could be implemented where the problems in human relations persist—in police relations, housing, and education—complemented by those informational, socioeconomic, and environmental programs that make success possible.

Indeed, if we are bold enough to conceive and implement an international center for human relations and community affairs, we may attend to international relations, which is perhaps in practice the lowest form of communication practiced. There is no more one-sided communication than that between nations. There are no conversations more meaningless than those that take place in United Nations and international "peace" talks. There are, apparently, no persons more ill prepared to listen, to hear, and to respond effectively than our diplomatic corps. The same principles that hold in any setting hold in this area, for here more than anywhere else we must employ our healthiest, most effective, and most experienced persons. The threat of nuclear war is the most urgent human relations problem of our time or any time, for it threatens to destroy quickly what is now only slowly decaying, man and his civilization.

The core program of the institutes, then, would involve physical and human resource planning; that is, the institutions involved must be inter-related in terms of physical and human resources. The core program would be implemented in three key stages: (1) analysis of sources of positive and negative effect in areas of human relations; (2) training of constructive agents; (3) follow-through and follow-up evaluation. Having analyzed the sources of effect, key personnel would be selected from the institutions involved to be trained. They would be trained not only to provide training experience but also to assess the effects of these training experiences. The critical aspects of these and other recommendations can and have been formulated. For example, the following brief statement of principles and purposes of the Center for Human Relations and Community Affairs of American International College in Springfield, Massachusetts, represents an early stage of one such center, which is devoting its initial efforts to the resolution and constructive management of problems in the racial relations area:

CENTER FOR HUMAN RELATIONS AND COMMUNITY AFFAIRS, AMERICAN INTERNATIONAL COLLEGE

A Brief Statement of Functions and Principles

The major problems of our times are human problems. The Center for Human Relations and Community Affairs is dedicated to the development and implementation of effective human relations programs. Its personnel is committed not only to the selection and training of human relations specialists but also to the search and research of more effective ways of helping people. Its resources are available not only to meet existing crises but also for the work of presenting the emergence of crises.

The purposes of the Center are broad in scope. While it will serve to meet community educational, child developmental, institutional, industrial, vocational and professional functions, the Center will concentrate initially upon our most pressing community problems, those involved in the area of racial relations, in the following manner:

1. the development and implementation of lay counselor and lay helper certification programs to meet ever-growing social service needs;

2. the development and implementation of in-service training programs within various educational and social service agencies;

3. the development and implementation of teacher training programs in human relations and interpersonal skills;

4. the development and implementation of community service programs staffed primarily by lay personnel;

5. the development of educational programs in human relations, degree-granting graduate programs as well as others;

6. the development and implementation of consultation programs in all areas having to do with human relations and community affairs.

The principles which will guide the Center's activities in selection and training, practice and research, are as follows:

1. the programs will involve a systematic extension of those learnings from psychology and education, counseling and psychotherapy, which translate to tangible human benefits in large-scale social action programs;
2. the programs will be directly involved in community activities—they will not be abstract academic programs;
3. the people involved in the programs must be involved in their own destinies;
4. the people involved will be trained to conduct their own in-service training programs;
5. ongoing, viable organizations must be serviced first in terms of their most pressing human relations needs;
6. there will be movement into those educational and social areas where current systems are not effective;
7. we must treat the total man in the total environment;
8. the belief that the increased employment of carefully selected and effectively trained personnel is the only way of meeting the increasingly educational and social service needs;
9. we must be dominated in our work by criteria of competency and functional utility;
10. we must be dominated in our work by the finding that by and large people learn what they are systematically taught.

Built around these kinds of centers we can not only service the already active helping programs but also develop programs in areas in which the system has not been effective, for example in the area of racial relations. In doing so we must conduct careful selection processes to select the natural black or Spanish leaders that the system has bypassed and equip them with the necessary expertise for various critical service roles so that they may cope with the difficulties that the system cannot cope with. Thus, we can develop human relations specialists to meet the crises in school integration. We can develop specialists to provide the necessary treatment and training in community clinics. We can set up preventative and rehabilitation centers in which some of the very basic physical, educational, and vocational needs, all built around an interpersonal core in which members of families can learn to live effectively with each other, can be discerned and met. We can develop specialists to provide consultation services for industry and law enforcement agencies. At all points the principle is one of training ourselves out of jobs; that is, of training trainers to conduct their own in-service training and consultation. We must equip these individuals to do for themselves what the system has not done for them. This is the only principle of contact that many of the militants of this and the next generation will accept. However, we must again keep in mind the functional criteria involving those whom we serve. We set up these programs because the system has failed. It is not enough to say that since the whites have failed, we should give the blacks a chance to fail. We can demonstrate a level of effectiveness beyond that which the system's representatives have been able to demonstrate. We must keep in mind those for whom we serve. Too many lives have been wasted already.

THE DEMONSTRATION PROGRAM: AN ILLUSTRATION

Human relations problems are not, however, exclusively racial relations problems, although, to be sure, for nonwhites in America there is no greater issue today. Indeed, the racial relations area impinges upon most other areas of concern. For example, the racial crisis compounds difficulties in industrial relations, community relations, and child development and educational programs. Nevertheless, there are many other important projects that cut across the racial relations area and, indeed, service those who are denied service in very direct ways. The following outline describes one kind of project that captures some of the central themes of these volumes. Beyond servicing the community at large, the human relations institutes could conduct those kinds of projects as part of their ongoing demonstration work. In addition, *these projects could be researched and, if proved effective, implemented on a large scale.*

LAY COUNSELOR TRAINING AND TREATMENT: A PROGRAM OF RESEARCH AND DEMONSTRATION PROJECT PLAN AND SUPPORTING DATA [1]

1. *Project Plan*
    A. *Purpose*
        The purpose of this project is to demonstrate and research the effects of a program directed toward the development of lay counselor training and treatment programs. There is extensive evidence to indicate that the levels of helper-offered facilitative and action-oriented conditions (empathy, respect, concreteness, genuineness and self-

[1] Preliminary proposal submitted to the Office of Social and Rehabilitation Services, Office of Health, Education and Welfare, Washington, D.C., 1968.

disclosure, confrontation, immediacy interpretations, etc.) are related to criteria of constructive helpee process movement (self-exploration, self-experiencing, extensiveness of problem expression, etc.) and outcome criteria (self-reports, expert reports, helper reports, reports of significant others, assessments of ward behavior, objective and projective testing, indexes of interpersonal functioning, intrapersonal functioning, degree of psychological disturbance, rate of recidivism). These findings may be extended in research and demonstration programs employing these indexes of helper- offered conditions in systematic programs.

By the term lay counselor, we mean to signify those helping persons who are not products of traditional, professional graduate programs. Lay counselor training and treatment programs have at least four functional subdivisions: (1) institutional; (2) community; (3) child-development; (4) professional. The institutional area includes the training of hospital personnel, lay as well as professional, in addition to training patients as helpers of other patients. The community area includes indigenous personnel in target areas, volunteers as well as selected personnel, with particular emphasis upon the deprived and lower classes, particularly lower class Negroes. The child-development area incorporates training parents to work with distressed children as well as developing programs integrating healthy with disturbed children and privileged with deprived children. The professional area includes training trainers to conduct programs in other geographical areas as well as ongoing training for professionals in other related areas such as teacher-counselors, lawyers, ministers and professionally trained helpers.

The design will include both experimental and control groups to assess the effects of training and treatment. Assessments will be made of the effectiveness of ongoing training and treatment programs. The results of the lay counselor training and treatment programs will be compared with these base rate data in order to determine the differential effectiveness of the programs. Briefly, the major theses, derived from earlier pilot demonstration projects in each of the four areas, are twofold:

(1) The lay counselor training programs will have a significantly constructive impact upon trainee level of functioning on dimensions related to helpee change.

(2) The lay counselor treatment programs will have a significantly constructive impact upon indices of helpee functioning.

B. *Type of Project*
  (1) Programmatic research.
  (2) Demonstration.
  (3) Research.

C. *Justification of Project*

No program of lay training and treatment has been effectively demonstrated and researched on a large scale. The employment of already available resources in lay personnel, some of which are presently considered burdens, such as patients, offers the major hope of closing the progressively widening gap between rehabilitation and social service needs and services. The possible social and economic implications are profound, including in particular the increased manpower and consequently increased treatment benefits available to helpee populations. Specifically, the selection of prospective helpers based upon validated selection indices, the training programs based upon validated training procedures and the treatment programs based upon demonstrated treatment effects, offers the promise of operational, replicable and economical programs for the employment of lay personnel. The project also establishes a training model for the development of such professional practitioners as mental health consultants who train, supervise and research the lay personnel. Finally, the impact of such a program may be to set up a "helper community" within a community. A successful program may find helpers multiplying in numbers. A large number of helping-oriented persons can attend to the ever-growing problems of education, civil disturbances and other social problems. As the project is extended an attempt will be made to secure employment within institutions and community mental health centers for high level functioning personnel as has been done in the pilot projects.

D. *Methodology*

(1) *General design:* The project involves two phases: (1) training and (2) treatment. During the initial phase, a minimum of 160 trainees will be involved, 40 in each functional area. Thus, 4 groups of a minimum of 10 trainees each will be conducted in each of the 4 functional areas. Allowing for the possibility of 20 per cent attrition, approximately 200 trainees may be involved initially. The initial concentration within each area will be as follows: *institutional*—concentration on selection and training of "helper-patients," particularly as relates to the rehabilitation of Physical Medicine and Rehabilitation and Neuropsychiatric cases; *community*—concentration on selection and training of community leaders and volunteers, particularly as relates to deprived target areas; *child-developmental*—concentration on selection and training of parents to work with own children as well as those of others; *professional*—concentration on selection and training of trainers and other professionals oriented toward social action. Results of training will be compared with those of the extensive and matched control and "training-control" group data available from pilot studies. Dur-

ing the second phase, following training, the helper-trainees will each be assigned two or more helpees for regular counseling contacts. Thus, a minimum of 320 helpees will be involved and the effects of their treatment assessed. During later phases of the project the direction and needs within each functional area will be systematically explored. Supervision will be provided throughout the second phase of the project and vocational counseling and placement opportunities made available in conjunction with the Department of Vocational Rehabilitation, the Veterans Administration, the local Employment Office and various other federal programs such as Job Corps and SEEK to those helpees whose behavior indicates a need and readiness for such.

Thus, after establishment of base rate data on training and treatment effects, trainees will be pre- and post-tested by being cast in the helping role with standard clients. Assessments of the trainees' level of functioning on helper-offered facilitative and action-oriented process dimensions (empathy, respect, concreteness, genuineness, self-disclosure, confrontation, immediacy interpretations, etc.) and helper process dimensions (self-exploration, self-experiencing, problem expression, etc.) will be obtained from ratings of trained raters employing rating scales of demonstrated reliability and validity. Trainees demonstrating minimal levels of facilitative functioning will be assigned two helpees (clients, patients, students, delinquents, etc.). Pre- and post-measures of helpee behavior and level of functioning (self-reports, expert reports, helper reports, reports of significant others, assessments of ward behavior where appropriate, objective testing such as the constructive personality change index of the Minnesota Multiphasic Personality Inventory, indexes of interpersonal and intrapersonal functioning, degree of psychological disturbance and rate of recidivism where appropriate) will be made and analyzed in order to determine the effectiveness of the treatment process.

(2) *Trainee selection indices:* The development of real-life indices of selection involving assessments of the prospective helper's communication and discrimination have received extensive construct and predictive validity support in large N studies of training outcome. Trainees who are rated above a given cut-off level gain significantly over the course of training with a high level functioning trainer while those who are rated below the cut-off level demonstrate very little positive change or gain. The communication index involves a one-half hour tape of 16 client stimulus expressions (approximately two minutes each) to which the prospective helper is asked to formulate a verbal or written response. The stimulus expressions involve 3 different

affects (depression-distress, anger-hostility, elation-excitement) crossed with 5 different content areas (social-interpersonal, education-vocational, child-rearing, sexual-marital and confrontations of the helper) plus a silence for the 16th excerpt. Communication scores are obtained from the ratings of trained raters on the facilitative and action-oriented dimensions involved. The discrimination index involves 64 counselor responses, 4 to each client stimulus expression, with calculated variations in the counselor's level of facilitative conditions and action-orientation. Thus, in a random order the following sequence of counselor responses appear: high facilitative–high active; high facilitative–low active; low facilitative–high active; low facilitative–low active. Discrimination scores are obtained by absolute deviations from the ratings of experts who have demonstrated the validity of their ratings in previous studies. Relationships between prospective helper communication and discrimination levels and indices of (1) immediate training outcome and (2) ultimate treatment outcome will be assessed.

(3)   *Training proper:* Historically, training programs have focused exclusively on either a didactive (psychoanalytic, behavioristic, trait-and-factor vocational and educational counseling) or experiential (client-centered, existential) approach. In their focus upon one or the other orientation they have all too often tended to exclude the contributions of the other approaches. The present training program focuses upon the core of conditions shared by all interview-oriented one-to-one or one-to-group helping approaches. That is, there is extensive evidence to indicate that all counseling and psychotherapeutic approaches share a common core of conditions conducive to facilitative helpee experiences. Again, the evidence in support of empathy, respect, concreteness, genuineness, self-disclosure, confrontation and immediacy is substantial although by no means unqualified. Thus, the program focuses upon a core of primary facilitative and action-oriented dimensions complemented by the unique contributions of a variety of potential preferred modes of treatment. That is, in regard to the potential preferred modes of treatment, an attempt has been made to discern the interaction of relevant variables within which the psychoanalytic, client-centered, trait-and-factor, behavioristic and existential approaches make a unique contribution to the helpee's welfare over and above the contribution accounted for by the core conditions.

In focusing upon the core conditions complemented by preferred modes of treatment the didactic and experiential approaches to training are integrated. With the aid of validated research scales on empathy, respect, concreteness, genuineness, self-disclosure, confrontation and immediacy, an attempt will be made to didactically teach the trainees to discriminate and communicate at high levels of these dimensions. For example, following the "shaping" of accurate discriminations of the dimensions involved, the trainees will listen to tapes of counseling in order to rate the process conditions of both helper and helpee and compare their ratings with their colleagues and the leader-expert. In sequence the trainees will then formulate their responses to client expressions and receive the rating feedback from all of those involved; role-play helper and helpee both in class and out of class on homework assignments with fellow trainees; have live initial contacts with distressed persons. Finally, when functioning at high enough levels, they will be assigned helpees. Throughout training the emphasis is upon immediate and concrete rating and information feedback which is made available by the trainers and other trainees in responding to tapes, role-playing and finally clinical interviews. It is imperative that discrimination and communication training take place in the context of a relationship involving high levels of conditions. Obviously, individual discriminations and communications may indicate a need for therapeutic intervention. That is, for example, an individual trainee may find that he is rating his communication response at very high levels while all others rated his response at very low levels. A need for discordance reduction is critical. In this context, quasi-group therapeutic experiences will be introduced near the mid-point of training, thus affording the trainees an opportunity to cope specifically with difficulties involved in implementing the helping role and to integrate what has been meaningful for them in the training experience. In addition, throughout training, the effects of modeling are operative and thus the trainer must be representative in all respects of the kind of effective helper we wish the trainees to become.

In the past training programs of this nature ranging from 2 years to 20 hours have been successfully implemented, with the latter appearing to be the minimal time necessary to achieve significant trainee changes. However, in view of a potential relationship between the duration of training and the retention of learning, an attempt, depending upon the prevailing conditions in each setting, will be made to allot approximately 30 hours to initial formal training time focusing upon the core conditions. In addition, this time will be complemented by an introduction to potential preferred modes of treatment and social service agencies available within the community providing these and other services (a minimum of 10 hours), supplementing the trainee's learning with knowledge that will be essential for, at a minimum, making referrals. Finally, ongoing weekly supervision will be provided the trainee-helpers when they are assigned helpees so that from 10 hours to an indeterminate number of hours may be offered in supervisory time. Thus, each trainee will receive a minimum of 50 hours of training and supervision.

(4) *Trainers:* A key to this and any other training program is the level of training of the trainer. Initially, all trainers will be experienced professionals with backgrounds in clinical or counseling psychology, psychiatry or social work. Ultimately, nonprofessionals may also be employed in some training capacity. While the differential effects of variations in trainer levels of functioning will be studied, every attempt will be made to secure only the most highly competent (based upon previously researched training and treatment) trainers for all phases of the project.

(5) *Helpee selection criteria:* Only those helpees will be included who are (1) not currently being seen in counseling or psychotherapy; (2) not diagnosed for organicity or mental retardation; (3) where appropriate, not likely to be released or unavailable over a period of a minimum of four months.

(6) *Helpee process variables and rating scales:* The following research scales will be employed for both training and rating purposes: empathy; respect or positive regard; concreteness or specificity of expression; genuineness and self-disclosure; confrontation; interpretation of immediacy (all attached). The facilitative dimensions are fully treated in texts (Carkhuff, 1969; Carkhuff & Berenson, 1967) and derived in part from earlier work (Rogers *et. al.,* 1967; Truax & Carkhuff, 1967). The action-oriented dimensions are fully treated in other texts (Berenson & Mitchell, 1974; Bierman, 1968; Carkhuff & Berenson, 1967). Both the facilitative and action-oriented dimensions are comprehensively treated and integrated in a text by Carkhuff (1969). In turn, these helper-offered dimensions have been related extensively to helper process indices such as client self-exploration (attached) and a variety of outcome indices. Most significant, in studies of lay counselor training programs, high levels of counselor-offered conditions have translated directly to significant positive behavior change in helpees (best summarized in Carkhuff, 1969; Carkhuff & Berenson, 1967; Truax & Carkhuff, 1967).

(7) *Assessment of outcome:* The problems of outcome are numerous. Briefly, however, the tasks here are twofold: (1) to assess the effects of training; (2) to assess the effects of treatment by the trainee-products. Process measures applied to standard and clinical interviews will constitute the training criteria. That is, the goals of training involve effective functioning in the helping

role. Following completion of training, this will be assessed by raters trained in the employment of the rating scales involved, in particular those related to the level of conditions offered by the helpers and the depth to which the helpees involved explore themselves. The goals of treatment, in turn, involve tangible benefits of the helpees involved. At the beginning and the end of treatment and three and six months thereafter the helpees will be assessed by the following persons: the helpees themselves; the helpee's work supervisor (where relevant); the ward nurse or attendant with whom the helpee has most contact (where relevant); an outside expert clinician; their helpers; significant "others," including spouse, relative, friend or neighbor. The helpees will be assessed on the following indices: (1) functional vocational or educational adjustment and satisfaction; (2) the degree of psychological disturbance; (3) social behavior, participation and responsibility; (4) self-care, habits and appearance. In addition, objective tests such as the constructive personality change index (CPCI) of the MMPI will be employed.

(8) *Follow-up:* In addition to the assessments at three months, six months and one year following the initiation of training, a number of variations off the theme will arise as we become more deeply involved in the project. For example, where hospitalized patients are involved, one direction might be to look toward half-way houses to be run by patients who are successfully trained and therapeutically effective.

In summary, it is within our grasp to tap the assets of resources that have been considered deficits. It is within our grasp to learn, to grow from understanding and from being understood by those the system has bypassed. It is within our grasp not simply to service the needy but to expand our humanity to incorporate a misery and a beauty we have not before known. It is not just possible. It is imperative. Too many lives have been wasted—theirs and ours!

THE FUTURE OF HELPING

Helping as we have known it cannot survive. For most intents and purposes traditional helping programs constitute the most fraudulent misrepresentation of our or any times. Even the few persons who have broken free of these orientations and who can achieve positive results cannot reach enough people in need of help to make a significant difference. The remainder must face the myths of their roles and learn what it is that can make a difference in the lives of others. Above all, however, *the would-be helpers must commit themselves to making a difference in their own lives first.* Those who cannot do so must be eliminated from critical positions in areas of human relations.

We are calling for social action. We are calling for revolution in the social services. We are calling for change from within or from without the group of those claiming to be committed to making a constructive difference in the world. And if they cannot commit themselves to actualizing these changes, then others more resourceful, more moral, and more competent must do so.

Several themes have recurred in these volumes. Some of the most critical of these are worth reiterating briefly, for they indicate the direction that human relations programs must take in the future. If we do not follow these directions, we are lost, for they constitute the way out of a huge and fearsome forest. Crises preclude the luxury of practices that have not proved themselves effective. Crises bring us to common sense considerations about what works.

Conclusion I. We must put the whole person back together.

Only the person who has the strength of his sensitivities—physical, emotional, and intellectual—and the sensitivities of his strength—physical, emotional, and intellectual—can enable others to become fully functioning participants in a fully functioning world.

Conclusion II. We must systematically select persons who can function most effectively in the helping role.

We must select individuals with the strength and sensitivities to make a constructive difference in the lives of others and recognize that not everyone can be effective in human relations.

Conclusion III. We must systematically train those persons who can function effectively in the helping role.

We must intensify the already viable resources of our most effective helper prospects in brief, systematic, efficient, and effective helping programs built around what works.

Conclusion IV. We must systematically treat those persons who are not functioning effectively in critical roles in their lives.

Again we must decide what it is we are attempting to accomplish and develop those steps necessary for accomplishing these ends most economically and effectively.

Conclusion V. We must systematically focus upon those conditions that constitute the core of effective helping processes.

Those core facilitative and action-oriented dimensions that cut across the various approaches to all human relations must be focused upon systematically in helping.

Conclusion VI. We must systematically develop the concepts and techniques of preferred modes of treatment.

The conditions under which a given set of techniques may contribute to human welfare over and above the contributions of the core conditions must be specified and the techniques refined.

Conclusion VII. We must systematically move into the environment of persons in need of help.

We cannot consider the person in need of help independent of the environment, both human and physical, from which he comes and/or to which he goes.

Conclusion VIII. We must systematically develop and interrelate those human and physical resources that have not been developed.

We must develop and interrelate, each in the cause of the other, human (in particular, nonprofessionals) and physical resources that have gone untapped or have been considered deficits in our systems.

Conclusion IX. We must systematically elevate the role of the professional.

The effective professional is the social engineer who plans, coordinates, trains, supervises, consults, and researches the effects of the programs he is promulgating, with the full recognition that he is as good as his programs and his programs are as good as he is.

Conclusion X. We must systematically inquire into what it is we are attempting to accomplish.

Continuing enlightened and systematic inquiries into our human relations efforts are the key to the continuing modification necessary for the evolution of the most effective procedures at a given point in time.

The answer, then—if there is an answer—lies in large-scale social action programs conducted by the persons best equipped to do so. It does not imply larger spending. We are simply not getting the value from our programs because by and large the programs are conceived and implemented by those who cannot achieve results. It does imply greater productivity in terms of developing and meeting criteria of competency. Private industries have long maintained passing—though not high—grades for their workers, say grades of 70. Public utility companies and the like have perhaps not set as high a standard, but they have asked for something, say grades of 60. *There have been no passing grades in civil service agencies or in the area of education, particularly those large-scale federal projects allegedly calculated to make a difference in the lives of the poor.*

A CALL TO WORK

The essence of any human relations program is the ability of the individuals who conduct it to function effectively in the helping role. Like the helping process itself, human relations begins with one person putting himself in another's position—crawling into another's skin, so to speak—seeing the world through another's eyes. The termination—if there is ever termination in effective human relations—comes with the development of an effective course of action. It is not enough to see the problem. We must both see the problem and do something about it. Understanding is where the human relations process begins, and action is where it ends.

Accordingly, in the implementation of human relations programs we have come to question not only what we have to offer but the way in which we offer it. We know that if constructive change is to take place it will take place through the efforts of those who share in their own destinies. We can facilitate these efforts *only* through transmitting all the skills that we have found to be useful and effective. In the process of transmitting these skills we have discovered that some are unnecessary and that some must be modified for the trainees who will one day be trainers themselves. In addition, we have found that we must modify our presentation of the helping process in such a way as to enable the trainee to grasp the essence of the concepts in his terms and to make operational the constructs in the most effective manner.

Human relations programs, then, if they are to be effective, require the reorganization of operations and personnel from top to bottom, *independent of the credentials of particular individuals.* Indeed, it has been the absence of criteria of competence that has influenced the choice of many persons to become helpers. Those who have been attracted by the lack of criteria of competence are not going to help to develop such criteria. Such individuals support a cause only to defeat it. They can only simulate support and pull back to neutralize the programs, because, in the end, they are not and never have been concerned with anyone but themselves. (It takes a large person to incorporate the world beyond his ego boundaries.) There will be an agreement among the supposedly divergent leaders to contain the development of meaningful programs because they all belong to the same "club."

This is not a call to arms for a new group of intellectual ineffectuals. Rather, it is a call for mature and responsible adults who have been living in the world—not protected by it—who can make a difference in the lives of others or who can with training make a difference, who can spend their lives extending their own boundaries and actualizing their own resources and who can, accordingly, do so with and for others.

We are talking about building institutions that serve the people they were built to serve—but not so big that they cannot be readily dismantled to meet immediate needs. We are talking about making use of resources we have not before known, many of which, indeed, we have traditionally considered to be liabilities rather than assets. We are talking about follow-through and delivery, a process by which we are guided to the next program by the results of the last program we conducted and the questions we asked about it.

We are talking about raising standards. We are talking about reaching for the sky, for only in this way can both earth and sky survive and grow. We are talking about a dominance of the strong rather than a tyranny of the weak in which little men are shaped to kill great men and the latter are shaped to expect it. Without these ingredients there is no future for helping or the world.

REFERENCES

For a more detailed discussion of the issues considered in this chapter see the asterisked readings and the references upon which the readings are based.

Berenson, B. G., & Mitchell, K. *Confrontation.* Amherst, Mass: Human Resource Development Press, 1974.

Bierman, R. *Counseling and child-rearing.* Mimeographed manuscript, University of Waterloo, Canada, 1968.

Carkhuff, R. R. *The Counselor's contributions to facilitative processes.* Mimeographed manuscript, State University of New York at Buffalo, 1968.

*Carkhuff, R. R. *Helping and human relations,* Vol. I. New York: Holt, Rinehart and Winston, Inc., 1969.

*Carkhuff, R. R., & Berenson, B. G. *Beyond counseling and therapy.* New York: Holt, Rinehart and Winston, Inc., 1967.

Rogers, C. R., Gendlin, E., Kiesler, D., & Truax, C. B. *The therapeutic relationship and its impact.* Madison, Wisc.: University of Wisconsin Press, 1967.

*Truax, C. B., & Carkhuff, R. R. *Toward effective counseling and psychotherapy.* Chicago: Aldine Publishing Company, 1967.

16
POTENCY IN HELPING AND LIFE

Effective facilitative and rehabilitative processes cannot be captured simply by making operational the constructs of this or any other book. Their implementation, rather, is merely another stage in the highly interactional process of developing and applying meaningful constructs. It constitutes a jumping off point in our attempts to articulate what is knowable concerning man in interaction with himself and others. With full recognition, then, of the highly tentative nature of these formulations of ignorance, these operationalizations are attempts to develop criteria of competency in helping relationships.

Unfortunately, for many practitioners the lack of criteria of competency in the helping professions has been one of the attractions of the vocation. Investigate any professional helping claim and you get "negative results." A profession bogged down in nonfunctional rituals and irrelevant outcomes requires systematic inquiries into sources of differential effectiveness in treatment programs (Volume I, Chapter 1), inquiries that, to be sure, expose those whose sole motivation has been to avoid exposure of the fact that they are more in need of help than capable of offering such.

The goals of all helping processes involve (1) understanding the physical, emotional, and intellectual world and (2) being able to act upon and develop this world (Chapter 2). The explication of the emergence of health or the evolution of dysfunctioning or psychopathology, in turn, is contingent upon the development of a comprehensive model that takes into consideration first person (Chapter 3), second person (Chapter 4), and contextual or environmental variables (Chapter 5), alone and in their various interactions.

Attempts to attain the goals of helping processes have spurred efforts to develop selection procedures based upon indexes of communication of demonstrated validity. In the hope of selecting persons who can benefit most from training and/or who can offer the most effective treatment, explorations based upon a basic principle of selection have been made operational: the best index of a future criterion is a previous index of that criterion (Chapter 6). In particular, indexes of communication (Chapter 7) and of discrimination (Chapter 8) have been made operational, with the evidence and applications (Chapter 9) suggesting that these procedures offer a promising means of differential selection.

The effects of training programs, in turn, have been found to be in large part a function of the level of functioning of the trainers, although they also depend somewhat on the level of functioning of the trainees: the trainees of trainers who are functioning (1) above minimally facilitative levels and (2) at least a level above the trainees gain the most (Chapter 10). The most effective training programs appear to be those that integrate the didactic, experiential, and modeling sources of learning and that employ the previously validated research scales in operationalizing discrimination (Chapter 11) and communication (Chapter 12) training and those that make applications in training in the core conditions (Chapter 14), particularly those that utilize role-playing techniques as an introduction to initial helping interactions (Chapter 13). In addition, training in the development of effective courses of action (15) and preferred modes of treatment (16) are also emphasized. In summary, human relations training focuses upon the core facilitative and action-oriented dimensions complemented by anything that works.

The resultant treatment procedures are closely related to the training programs. From the initial assumption that all interpersonal learning or relearning processes may have constructive or destructive consequences flow some very basic propositions (Chapter 1). Effective treatment procedures involve both the more traditionally feminine dimensions such as sensitivity and warmth as well as the more masculine dimensions such as genuineness and confrontation complemented by reality-oriented problem-solving–type activities (Chapter 2). The goals of the exploratory phase of helping involve helpee self-exploration in the relevant problem areas or areas of dysfunctioning (Chapter 3). As a function of the learnings from this exploration the helping process comes to emphasize the complex construction or reconstruction of the communication process (Chapter 4). Finally, the focus upon the translation of this self-understanding to constructive action constitutes the phase of emergent directionality in helping (Chapter 5). The crises that make up the essence of helping occur throughout the entire process, both within and outside the helping process (Chapter 6). In turn, the individual dimensions that make possible constructive directionality out of the crises can be made operational in stages (Chapter 7). The variations in applications of core conditions in effective helping (Chapter 8) and those involving specialized approaches such as behavior modification (Chapter 9) are described, with special attention given to group communication training as a preferred mode of treatment (Chapter 10).

Finally, no interpersonal processes, whether they involve training or treatment, can be effectively implemented with honesty and confidence without continuing, enlightened, and systematic inquiries. Theory and practice are seen in a highly interactional process, with each serving to extend and modify the other (Chapter 11). The problems of process and outcome in helping are put into the perspective of life and, accordingly, handled by the focus upon interpersonal functioning as the core of helping (Chapter 12). The criteria of meaning and rigor in the investigation of training and treatment modalities are addressed directly, with a principal conclusion being that there is nothing further for us to learn from the naturalistic studies of randomly selected helpers: among low-level–functioning helpers, it appears, no indexes relate to any other indexes (Chapter 13). The solution lies in studying only those helpers who have a large repertoire of responses and thus can offer differential treatment. Thus, research applications are outlined as a necessary stage of all helping programs (Chapter 14).

The attempt to extend our efforts to large-scale social action programs (Chapter 15) readily leads to an obvious conclusion: *Helping is not enough!*

PROPOSITIONS IN SEARCH OF A PERSON

Man does not help by a set of procedures alone, however fundamental they may be. In fact, these and any conclusions may be rendered sterile in ritualistic replications both within and without helping. With the thought in mind of counteracting potentially restrictive and retarding influences, we will summarize some further guiding principles—those not easily made operational—of effective helping and, indeed, of effective living. Again these are propositions to be tested and modified in daily experience.

Proposition I.   All effective human relations begin with an effective person.

The unavoidable beginning point of all effective human relations, whether in the area of child-rearing, teaching, or counseling, is with the person designated more knowing by the social system in which the parties function. This person's own life, and thus his relationships with significant others, is in the process of either deepening or deteriorating. Although open and searching, such an individual is defined and directionful, holding forcefully his integrated learnings until confronted with the new learnings discriminated by his fine sensitivities. He is as he lives —an hypothesis to be tested and modified in daily experience. The persons he influences can enjoy the same intense rewards of full emergence and life.

Proposition II.   The effective person knows that man's individual phenomenology is more basic than any system.

The systems that man chooses to adhere to reflect and describe his ways of perceiving himself and others in his world. Some people see themselves and their worlds as being "determined" and seek to populate the world with "determined" people. Others see themselves and their worlds as being "free" and seek to populate the world with "free" people. The effective practitioner in the science-art of human relations makes systematic and enlightened inquiries into his efforts in order to (1) know what is knowable by deterministic means and (2) to prepare himself for what is and will remain unknowable.

Proposition III.   The effective person knows that he is free to choose from any system in developing his own personal system.

The effective person develops his own personal cosmology. He is guided yet not dominated by it. His system is as effective as it is able to incorporate and integrate continuing experiences. It is as effective as it is able to generate meaningful and valid expectations and conclusions. It is as effective as it is open to the contributions of any and all systems as they become, at a given point in time, necessary to effect translations to tangible human benefits.

Proposition IV.   The effective person knows that no system enables man to avoid the responsibility for making individual discriminations and acting upon them.

No system, personal and integrated at the highest level or otherwise, allows man to avoid making individual discriminations. Indeed, man seeks systems, procedures and techniques in order to avoid the responsibility for making fine decisions in the individual case; he would put the system "on the line" rather than himself. Whatever it has in common with past experience, each new experience has its unique aspects, which, if left unattended, diminish the potential effectiveness of the relationship and yield no new learnings to either party to the relationship. There is no discrimination without action. Fine and sensitive discriminations demand action, whether implicitly or explicitly. To discriminate yet not to act is to reduce the validity of the next discrimination. Actions may be channeled through systems, but they are not, in the individual instance, bound to be channeled through these systems. Feelings for others that are not acted upon are simply not feelings for others. Again, as with discrimination, the individual has responsibility for his action and not the system.

Proposition V. The effective person knows that he is both the means and the ends in effective human relations.

The effective person presents both a structural model for the effects of a sustained relationship as well as an integrated means for attaining such effects. In his disposition and demeanor he is confident yet open, directionful yet flexible, integrated yet changing; he offers high levels of what he teaches. He is about what he is about, and all of his activities reflect this. He is who he is, yet is not bound by who he is. These dimensions constitute both the means and the ends of effective human relations.

Proposition VI. The effective person knows that he will involve himself only on his terms.

Knowing who he is and where he is, the effective person makes extremely fine discriminations concerning the levels at which others are functioning—in large part knowing others in their reactions to his actions. To be sure, if motivated to help another, he takes the other's experience into the fullest possible consideration. However he knows too well that dysfunctioning is largely a function of life on the terms of the unhealthy and the weak. Placing the highest premium on his own health and competence, he does not subject his energies to the waste and abuse of others. His capability for deferring, on his terms, to persons functioning at still higher levels is simply a function of his recognition that *helping must be on the terms of the healthier person.*

Proposition VII.   The effective person knows that he is capable of hurting as well as helping.

The effective helper is fully cognizant that to help some people is to destroy others. The emergence of life, both within and between persons, involves the destruction of death. The effective person is also aware that some persons, impotent and destructive, can employ his understanding and energies only to become potent and destructive, and in this respect destroy the life around them that they now in their impotence tolerate. The effective person may choose a variety of courses, including those leading directly to the destruction of these destructive forces. Finally, the effective person may engage, based upon fine discriminations unavailable to others, in activities that may for the moment, or for all time, appear "apparently" destructive to others. He does so with full responsibility for his actions, whether or not they are a function of a motivation to help.

Proposition VIII.   The effective person knows that he must implement a potent course of action based upon his own fine discriminations.

Having integrated the dimensions of the healthy male and female (life), the effective person remains unmoved by the agitated mutual reactions of either the distorted male or female (death). Neither the distorted female who sues for peace at any price nor the distorted male who commits only holocaust have a pull upon him as he proceeds in his own direction, often as seen by the others as an "extreme" or strong middle position. He is capable of accomplishing both the confrontation that leads to love and the love that leads to confrontation. He is guided by the discriminations yielded by his integrated whole male and female condition and is fully aware that the deepest level of understanding often involves filling in what is missing rather than reflecting, however deeply, what is present.

Proposition IX.   The effective person knows that he must employ all of his vast resources in all of his significant experiences.

Both to himself and to others who so motivate him, the effective person is committed to bringing to bear all of his physical, emotional, and intellectual resources in order to achieve higher and higher levels of self-actualization. He lives fully and honestly in the present, discharging all of his energies in developing further competencies in the work of his choosing, believing that a constructive future is possible only with work in the present. He lives in this moment as if it were his last, doing only those things that he would do if this moment were his last. His life has meaning because his life is meaning. The lives of others have meaning only because they come to share similar commitments.

Proposition X. The effective person knows that the only worthwhile society is a helper society.

With full recognition that a man who is looking forward is not looking back, the free man recognizes that the only meaningful society is one that serves his fellow-men. Yet he knows that in a very real sense only those who break free of such a society can return to contribute to it, and, accordingly, he reserves a special freedom for those who are not necessarily best served by any society.

A FINAL WORD

The book ends where it began—with a consideration of the effective person in all of his ramifications. The fault, it appears, lies not so much in the system or the organization or the discipline or the profession as it does in people. Some individuals can deliver and some cannot. Those who cannot deliver must be trained; those who cannot be trained must be treated; those who can be neither trained nor treated must not hold positions of responsibility in the area of human relations. Those who can deliver must be pushed to the limits of the fourth R of helping— the full realization of their full resources—and raised to positions of responsibility.

These volumes, then, challenge those who are willing and able to work and build, who can channel their energies and design their modes to meet the needs of our world in our time.

Appendix A
THE FUTURE OF HELPING

The issues of outcome, raised originally by Eysenck (1952) and extended by others (Eysenck, 1965; Levitt, 1963; Lewis, 1965; Truax and Carkhuff, 1967), have been updated by the work of Anthony and associates (1972, 1979) and Erickson (1975). Anthony's study of the long-term effects of 50 traditional psychotherapeutic treatment programs revealed a client recidivism rate of between 65% and 75% over a period of three to five years after treatment. Erickson has supported these data with his report of a ten-year recidivism rate of 77%. Put together with the earlier base rate data suggesting a two-thirds success rate, we have perhaps a good estimate of our current level of success with traditional psychotherapeutic treatment. In other words, of the two-thirds of the clients who initially improve, approximately two-thirds will deteriorate. These data suggest a lasting success rate somewhere in the range of 20% to 25% for traditional psychotherapeutic interventions on the recidivism outcome measures. Of course, traditional psychotherapeutic interventions were never set up specifically to reduce recidivism. This fact raises the question of understanding therapeutic interventions in a historic and developmental perspective.

The historic ingredients of treatment or helping interventions are, by now, well known (see Figure 1). What is perhaps not so well recognized is the principle of convergence which operates at each developmental stage; each stage of development in history and science represents the reconciliation of the seemingly disparate or divergent viewpoints of the previous stage (Berenson, 1980).

As can be seen in Phase 1, for a long time, people in need of help wandered around in a veritable desert of human nourishment, aimlessly seeking and randomly finding the most meager levels of survival help. There was no place or person to turn to. There were no programmatic forms of help available. Thus, many of the people became chronically mentally ill (C.M.I.) without hope for programmatic improvement (Frank, 1961).

Then Freud introduced a Human Revolution (Freud, 1924). In doing so, he reintegrated the body, mind, and soul of the humans affected by both the productivity

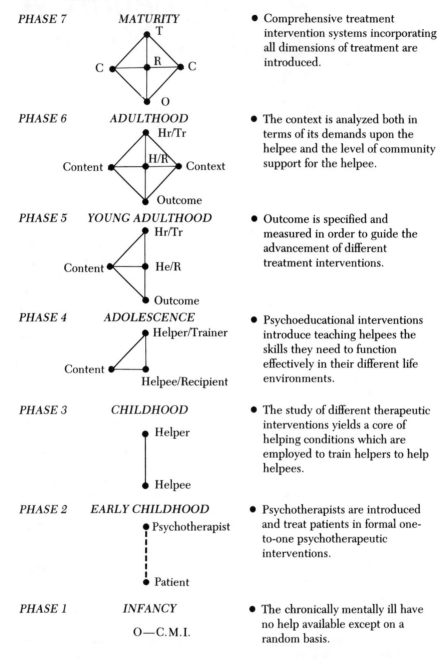

PHASE 7   MATURITY
• Comprehensive treatment intervention systems incorporating all dimensions of treatment are introduced.

PHASE 6   ADULTHOOD
• The context is analyzed both in terms of its demands upon the helpee and the level of community support for the helpee.

PHASE 5   YOUNG ADULTHOOD
• Outcome is specified and measured in order to guide the advancement of different treatment interventions.

PHASE 4   ADOLESCENCE
• Psychoeducational interventions introduce teaching helpees the skills they need to function effectively in their different life environments.

PHASE 3   CHILDHOOD
• The study of different therapeutic interventions yields a core of helping conditions which are employed to train helpers to help helpees.

PHASE 2   EARLY CHILDHOOD
• Psychotherapists are introduced and treat patients in formal one-to-one psychotherapeutic interventions.

PHASE 1   INFANCY
• The chronically mentally ill have no help available except on a random basis.

Figure 1.   A Developmental View of the Advances
in Psychotherapeutic Treatment

and waste of the Industrial Revolution. Therapists were formally appointed to intervene in the lives of the patients in order to prevent further deterioration and perhaps to affect rehabilitation (Phase 2). While the efficacy of the descendants of these psychotherapeutic interventions has been questioned severely, they did provide formal resources for people in need of help.

In the third phase of development of therapeutic interventions, all seemingly divergent therapeutic interventions were studied in order to discern a core of helping skills which were offered by effective counselors and therapists. Whatever the orientation, the effective counselors and therapists sought to organize their client's experiences and give them meaning by setting goals and developing action programs for or with the clients. These helping skills were operationalized and counselors and therapists were trained as helpers to offer high levels of helping skills to their helpees. Significant improvements in helping success rates were demonstrated in studies using traditional treatment control groups (Berenson and Carkhuff, 1966; Carkhuff, 1980; Carkhuff and Berenson, 1967, 1977; Rogers, et al., 1963; Truax and Carkhuff, 1967). In addition, these effects were generalized to other treatment modalities such as behavior modification: behavior modifiers with high levels of helping skills were significantly more effective in modifying behavior than behavior modifiers with low levels of helping skills (Mickelson and Stevic, 1971; Vitalo, 1970).

In the fourth phase of development, these seemingly divergent helping and learning approaches were integrated: the helper became a teacher and the helpee, a learner, when content was introduced as the third variable in the therapeutic equation. "Teaching as treatment" was operationalized in content that enabled the helpees to do for themselves what the helpers had previously done for them. Thus, the helpees were taught the skills that they needed to organize and give meaning to their experiences. In general, the results of outcome studies conducted at different levels suggested that skills training was more effective than other forms of helping in producing desired results: you get what you train for (Carkhuff, 1969, 1971; Carkhuff and Berenson, 1976; Vitalo, 1980).

In the fifth phase of development, the helping professionals began to address tangible outcomes in their treatment interventions. Once again, they found themselves confronted with seemingly divergent views of outcome. However, all agreed that therapeutic goals must be operationalized in observable and measurable terms. This operationalization of outcome promised to provide the basis for further refining the content and the helping delivery, thus enabling the helpees to achieve their goals more efficiently and effectively (Anthony, 1979; Carkhuff and Berenson, 1976; Paul and Lentz, 1977).

Finally, in Phase 6 of development, the real-life contexts of the helpees are being introduced as the fifth variable in the therapeutic equation so that we may fully comprehend outcome. The contexts may be analyzed to determine the helpees' needs and the contexts' requirements for effective helpee functioning. Such a contextual analysis will facilitate the specification and measurement of outcome which, in turn, will contribute to further refinement of the content and delivery process (Bachrach, 1976; Gilbert, 1978).

Together, these variables constitute the necessary ingredients in any equations for treatment effectiveness: the helpees or recipients; the helpers or trainers; the

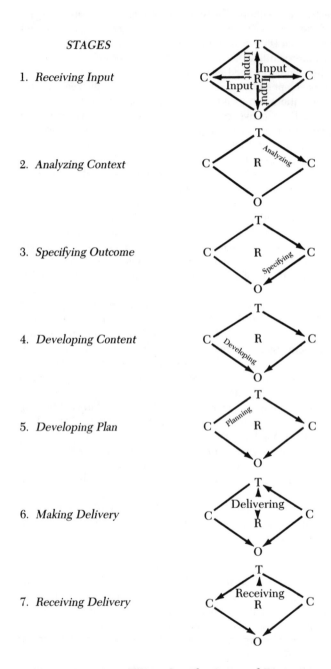

STAGES

1. *Receiving Input*

2. *Analyzing Context*

3. *Specifying Outcome*

4. *Developing Content*

5. *Developing Plan*

6. *Making Delivery*

7. *Receiving Delivery*

Figure 2. The Stages of Designing a Comprehensive Treatment System

for treatment effectiveness: the helpees or recipients; the helpers or trainers; the treatment content; the treatment outcome; and the real-life context. All must be considered, alone and sequenced in their various interactions, in order to optimize the convergence and integration of treatment interventions. All must be related in a systematic fashion in order to insure different levels of helpee outcome. Let us now look at all of these ingredients in attempting to develop a comprehensive treatment system.

TOWARD SYSTEMATIC TREATMENT

A comprehensive treatment system, then, includes all of the effective ingredients of treatment effectiveness: helpees, helpers, content, outcome, context. As can be seen in Figure 2, those designing the treatment interventions must consider every ingredient as a factor to be analyzed and operationalized.

Receiving Input

In the first stage of design, the input from the recipients of the intervention system is elicited. Thus, the helpee populations provide input regarding their needs for treatment intervention. Input may be at metabolic, conditioning, or verbal-awareness levels. The helpees provide input in regard to the following: the real-life contexts to which they may choose to return or move; the tasks or outcomes they will have to perform; the content that will help them perform; and the plan for delivering the content.

Thus, the helpees may provide input regarding their experiences of the living, learning, or working environments to which they choose to go; the things that they are going to have to do, know, and feel in those environments; and the things that they are going to have to be told, shown, or have the opportunity to do in order to learn the things they need to know.

In addition, the helpees provide input on the treatment delivery itself and their own role in receiving the delivery. Thus, the helpees provide input regarding the content which they need to learn and the delivery they need to experience in order to explore where they are, understand where they want or need to be, and act to get to their goals.

The input from the helpees initiates the systematic treatment design. The helpees do not only designate where and how they wish to function—they also provide input on their experiences of the preparation and delivery of their needed resources. The input from the helpee populations is elicited initially because all learning or helping begins with the recipients' frames of reference (Carkhuff, 1981a; Carkhuff and Berenson, 1976).

Analyzing the Real-Life Context

Having obtained the input from the helpees' frames of reference, then, the treatment designers proceed to analyze the requirements of the ingredients in the treatment system. In the second stage of a comprehensive system design, the designers analyze the requirements of the real-life context to which the helpees will go. This contextual analysis will include an analysis of the discrepancy between the helpees' current levels of functioning and the necessary or desired levels of functioning determined by the demands of the various environments to which they have chosen to go.

Thus, the task requirements of the prospective living, learning, and working environments will be analyzed in terms of their physical, emotional, and intellectual dimensions. The helpees' current levels of functioning on these required tasks will then be diagnosed. For example, interpersonal or social skills may be required at a level where the helpees can at least respond to the experience of another person. The helpees' current levels of functioning may indicate an inability to attend effectively to another person.

Finally, the context or community will be analyzed in terms of the information, resources, or incentives that it provides to support the helpees. (Where the level of support is less than facilitative, it may be necessary to treat the community as a helpee and design a comprehensive treatment system for its critical members.) The tasks required to bridge the gap between the helpees' levels of functioning and the desired or required levels of functioning in the real-life context, constitute the objectives of the treatment intervention (Carkhuff and Friel, 1981; Gilbert, 1978).

Specifying the Treatment Outcome

With the analysis of the context in hand, the designers can proceed to specify the outcome (Stage 3). The outcomes are derived from the tasks that constitute the desired results of the treatment intervention. Given the limitations of time and resources, critical tasks and subtasks must be selected to bridge the performance gap. Then these critical tasks must be defined in observable and measurable terms for the treatment intervention.

Thus, the contextual task requirements become the task objectives. These task requirements are analyzed in terms of the tasks, sub-tasks, and skills that the helpees will need to meet the task requirements. Then these critical tasks are measured. For example, with interpersonal or social skills contextual requirements, responding to the experience of another person might be a critical task. Responding could then be measured in terms of the interchangeability of the feeling and the meaning of the expression of the respondent and the respondee. These critical tasks then become the task objectives which constitute the outcome of the treatment intervention (Carkhuff and Friel, 1981; Gilbert, 1978).

Developing the Treatment Content

With the task objectives defining the outcome, it remains for the designers to specify the content of the treatment intervention (Stage 4). In developing the content, the sub-tasks are analyzed to determine the content to be delivered to the recipient population.

Thus, the sub-tasks are analyzed to include the skills, skill steps, and supportive knowledge necessary to perform the skills. The skill steps are further broken down into steps the helpee will have to do, and steps the helpee will have to think about before, during, and after doing each skill step. The supportive knowledge is broken down in terms of the facts, concepts, and principles we need to perform each step. For example, responding interpersonal skills may include the following skill steps and supportive knowledge: attending physically, observing, listening, responding to content, responding to feeling, and responding to feeling and meaning. Together, the skills, skill steps, and knowledge constitute the content of the treatment intervention (Berenson, Berenson and Carkhuff, 1978b; Carkhuff, 1981a).

Developing the Treatment Plan

With the content defined, the treatment designers proceed to plan the delivery of the content (Stage 5). The delivery plan includes the ways in which the skills content is organized to facilitate helpee reception.

Thus, the treatment plan organizes the content as follows: reviewing the content, overviewing the content, presenting the content, exercising the content, and summarizing the content. The treatment plan also includes the teaching methods to be employed to deliver the content: the didactic (telling), the modeling (showing), and the experiential (doing) methods. For example, in an effective attending skills delivery plan, the following methods will be employed: the helpees will tell, show, and do during the review in order to demonstrate their pre-treatment level of attending; both trainers and helpees will tell and show during the overview in order to compare images of the content; the trainers will tell and show and the helpees will do, during the presentation; the helpees will tell, show, do, repeat, and apply during the exercises; and the helpees will tell, show, and do during the summary to demonstrate their post-treatment level of attending. Together, the content organization, teaching methods, and application exercises constitute the treatment plan or lesson plan for delivery of the treatment content (Berenson, Berenson and Carkhuff, 1978a; Carkhuff, 1981b).

Making the Treatment Delivery

After having received recipient input, analyzed the context, specified the outcome, and developed the content and the treatment plan, the designers are now ready to make the delivery to the helpee/recipients (Stage 6). In other words, all of these tasks analyses were done in preparation for the treatment process. They occur before the recipients become involved in learning the content (see Figure 3).

As can be seen, the delivery process, itself, involves two sets of skills on the part of the helper/trainer. The first set of skills involves teaching delivery skills (TDS) which facilitate the recipients' learning from the external frame of reference of the content. The second set of skills involves interpersonal skills (IPS) which facilitate the recipients' learning from their internal frames of reference. Together, the teaching delivery and interpersonal skills constitute the delivery process (Berenson, Berenson and Carkhuff, 1979; Carkhuff, 1981a; Carkhuff, Berenson and Pierce, 1977).

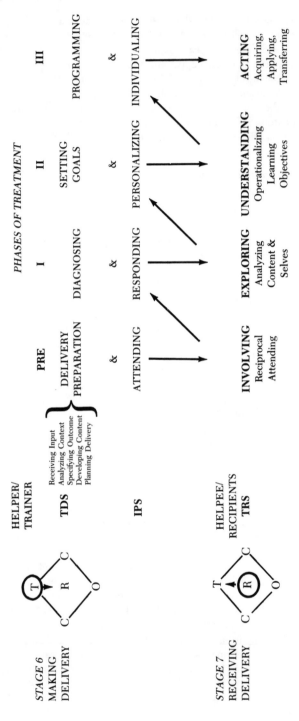

Figure 3. The Operationalization of the Treatment Process
For Recipient Populations in a Comprehensive
Treatment Intervention System

Receiving the Treatment Delivery

Although it would appear that we have discharged our responsibilities when we have made our content delivery to the recipients, that is not the case. It remains for the recipients to learn the content (Stage 7). Just as the helper/trainers have a responsibility to deliver the content, so do the recipients have a responsibility to receive the content. Clearly, the helper/trainers must help to manage the recipients' reception of the treatment delivery by teaching the recipients the skills they need to learn.

As can be seen in Figure 3, these treatment reception skills (TRS) involve the recipients in exploring where they are in relation to the learning experience by analyzing the content and themselves in relation to it; understanding where they want or need to be by operationalizing their learning goals; and acting to get from where they are to where they want to be by acquiring, applying, and transferring the content. Together, these exploring, understanding, and acting skills constitute the skills of receiving the treatment delivery (Berenson, Berenson and Carkhuff, 1981; Carkhuff and Berenson, 1981).

In summary, these are the necessary stages for designing a comprehensive treatment system: 1) receiving helpee input; 2) analyzing the context; 3) specifying the outcome; 4) developing the content; 5) developing the delivery plan; 6) making the treatment delivery; and 7) receiving the treatment delivery. These stages are sequenced in a comprehensive systems design. They are based upon historical models that are developmental and cumulative. These stages allow us to know where we are going and how to get there.

LEVELS OF OUTCOME

The treatment outcomes we have described occur within a comprehensive treatment intervention system. They define and measure the critical tasks which enable us to achieve our results, bridging the gap between the recipients' current and required levels of functioning in their chosen real-life contexts. The treatment outcomes are designed to facilitate the development of the skills content which will be delivered to the recipients. Thus, they are pivotal to the development of a comprehensive treatment system.

There are, however, other kinds of outcomes that occur both within the comprehensive treatment system and between the treatment system and society. We may consider these to be different levels of outcomes. Let us take a further look at these outcomes (see Figure 4).

Societal Outcome

Before the helper/trainer interacts with the recipients; indeed, even before the designer of a comprehensive system develops the design, society is concerned with certain outcome measures. They may be concerned in terms of costs and benefit measures. The costs involve labor, material, and administration expenditures. The

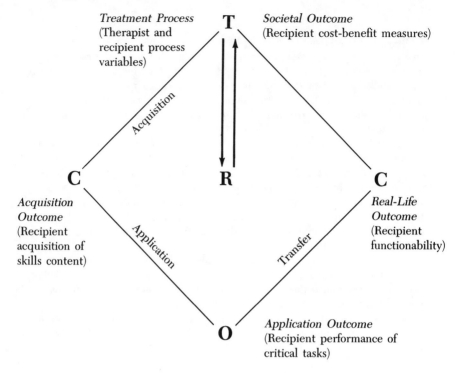

Figure 4. The Levels of Outcome
In a Comprehensive Treatment System

benefits involve the quantity and quality of the products that society receives for its expenditures.

Thus, the social outcome indices that dominate here include the following sample of measures of living, learning, and working effectiveness:

Societal Measures of Living Effectiveness
   Recidivism decreased
   Symptoms and crisis care reduced
   Length of time in residency reduced
   Economic support from state decreased
   Economic support from others decreased

Societal Measures of Learning Effectiveness
   Learning attendance and punctuality improved
   Learner adjustment improved
   Disciplinary measures decreased
   Educational performance improved
   Level of educational achievement increased

Societal Measures of Working Effectiveness
Employment placement and retention increased
Employee attendance and punctuality increased
Employee relations improved
Employment productivity increased
Employment earnings increased

All of these outcomes are of benefit to society. All of these outcomes reduce the burden of society for supporting the helpees. These societal outcome measures answer the question: What does society get out of treatment?

Real-Life Outcome

The outcomes for which we have designed our comprehensive treatment system answer the question: What does the helpee get out of treatment? These are real-life indices of outcome seen in terms of helpee benefits. They reflect what the helpee/ recipients need in order to function effectively in the living, learning, and working contexts which they have chosen. Usually, real-life outcome indices are reflected in the increase in quantity and elevation in quality of the recipients' response repertoire. These responses meet the living, learning, and working task requirements which are most effectively viewed in terms of their physical, emotional, and intellectual dimensions:

RESOURCE DIMENSIONS

Contextual Task Requirements	Physical	Emotional	Intellectual
LIVING	personal hygiene	human relations	goal setting
	physical fitness	self-control	program development
	using transportation	reducing stigma	program implementation
	shopping	problem-solving	money management
	recreating	conversing	using resources
LEARNING	sensing	listening	reading
	posturing	question-asking	writing
	paying attention	teacher relations	arithmetic
	observing	following directions	study skills
	manipulating	decision-making	hobbies
WORKING	punctuality	job interviewing	job qualifying
	using tools	job decision-making	job placement
	job strengths	employee relations	job promotion
	job endurance	job retention	work productivity
	specific job tasks	specific job tasks	specific job tasks

The issues of real-life outcome indices always revolve around the frame of reference of the individual we are evaluating. Thus, we may obtain indices of performance from the recipients themselves or any number of significant others. Again, the critical question is: What does the helpee get out of treatment? We must focus upon the most direct indices that we can to determine whether the helpees used the responses they were taught to use in the context that they chose to go to.

Application Outcome

In our design of a comprehensive treatment system, we have focused upon what we may now call application outcome. The central question here is: Can the helpees apply the critical tasks they have learned? In other words, the emphasis of the treatment programs is upon developing the helpees' abilities to apply the critical tasks that comprise the real-life transfers that the helpees want to make.

Thus, as in our illustration, interpersonal skills may be defined as the skills, knowledge, and attitudes (S,K,A) needed to attend and respond to the experiences of others. In a similar manner, career decision-making may be defined as the skills, knowledge, and attitudes needed to develop values and choose a preferred course of action. Also, specific job tasks may be defined in terms of the skills, knowledge, and attitudes needed to perform the critical tasks or sub-tasks that define the specific job tasks performance. Finally, each of these sample critical tasks may be measured as follows:

Application Outcome

LIVING
: *Interpersonal Skills*
  1. Attending by posturing and observing (S,K,A)
  2. Responding interchangeably to another's experience (S,K,A)

LEARNING
: *Career Decision-Making*
  1. Developing values and requirements (S,K,A)
  2. Developing alternative courses of action (S,K,A)
  3. Using values and requirements to choose preferred courses of action (S,K,A)

WORKING
: *Specific Job Tasks*
  1. Sub-Task #1 (S,K,A)
  2. Sub-Task #2 (S,K,A)
  3. Sub-Task #3 (S,K,A)
  .
  .
  .
  N. Sub-Task #N (S,K,A)

Other samples of application outcome might include the ability to set and define goals (planning); or to develop steps to achieve goals (program development); or to analyze tasks (learning skills and intellectual achievement); or to increase placement, promotability, and productivity skills (task performance and work productivity). The issues of application outcome revolve around the simple outcome question: Can the recipients apply the critical tasks which they have been trained to do?

Acquisition Outcome

There is another level of outcome that is often referred to in the literature. This level revolves around the acquisition question: Did the helpees acquire the skills they were taught? In other words, once the treatment content is developed and delivered, can the helpees do the skills involved?

Thus, the acquisition outcome issues are simply whether the helpees have all the skill steps and supportive knowledge they need to perform the skills and whether, indeed, they can perform the skills. In one of our illustrations, the skills content involved responding. The content of responding skills might break down as follows:

Acquisition Outcome

Skill:	Responding Skills
Skill Steps:	1. Attending physically
	2. Observing
	3. Listening
	4. Responding to content
	5. Responding to feeling
	6. Responding to meaning
Principle:	*If* the helpees can attend and respond to *another* person, *then* the others will attempt to reciprocate interpersonally *so that* there will be the basis of trust and understanding for constructive human relationships.
Concepts:	Attending, observing, listening, responding, content, feeling, meaning.
Facts:	Two or more humans in presence of each other.

In order to test the acquisition outcome, we need only to do the following: 1) determine whether the helpees can do the skills; 2) determine whether the helpees have all the skill steps they need to do the skills; and 3) determine whether the helpees have all the supportive knowledge they need to do the skill steps. The acquisition outcome issues are similar to the post-test of a teaching or training program. They reduce simply to whether or not the helpees can perform the skills.

Treatment Process Variables

Until now we have focused upon the helpee/recipient performance as the dependent variable at the different levels of outcome. At a final level of outcome, we may consider both helper/trainer and helpee/recipient variables in interaction with each other. Together, they answer the question: What did the treatment do to involve the helpees in a process leading toward improved performance?

The helper variables include those personal and social characteristics of the helper/trainers that relate to helpee involvement and performance (Paul and Lentz, 1977; Truax and Carkhuff, 1967). Generally, these characteristics manifest themselves in helping and teaching skills as we have illustrated (see Figure 3). They also are translated in a variety of therapeutic techniques which may be considered potential preferred modes of treatment.

The helpee variables include those personal and social characteristics of the helpees that relate to their involvement in the helping process. Generally, these characteristics manifest themselves in the learning skills we have illustrated (see Figure 3). In addition, they are modified by the helpee's deficit or excess of problem behaviors and competencies in the physical, emotional, and intellectual realms (Paul and Lentz, 1977; Truax and Carkhuff, 1967).

In summary, we can see the many different levels of outcome which may be considered to assess helpee progress in terms of a comprehensive treatment systems design: social outcomes, real-life outcomes, application outcomes, acquisition outcomes, and treatment process variables. If we implement a comprehensive treatment system, we are operationalizing the most basic principle of outcome: you get what you programmatically train for—no more, no less! If we can design our treatment systems comprehensively to accomplish client functionality in a real-life context, then we can refine that system so that it becomes efficient and effective for the helpee/recipient's benefit and, ultimately, perhaps even cost-beneficial for society's outcome purposes.

TOWARD DESIGNING COMPREHENSIVE FOLLOW-UP SYSTEMS

Of course, the treatment intervention is not complete with the treatment delivery. A comprehensive treatment system also involves an extensive follow-up. A treatment follow-up includes all those things which we do to insure the recipients' effective use of the skills content: 1) collecting recipient feedback; 2) monitoring the applications and transfers to the real-life context; 3) evaluating the treatment outcome; 4) modifying the content; 5) modifying the delivery plans; 6) modifying the treatment delivery process; and 7) modifying the treatment reception process (Carkhuff and Friel, 1981) (see Figure 5).

Collecting Feedback

Just as they collected the recipients' input before designing the comprehensive treatment intervention system, so must the designers now begin their follow-up by getting feedback from the recipients (Stage 1). How effective are their skills applications and transfers? What problems are they having making them? How would they modify the treatment preparation and process?

Monitoring Transfers to the Real-Life Context

The second stage in the treatment follow-up is to monitor the recipients' applications and transfers in the real-life context. The key ingredients to this step are

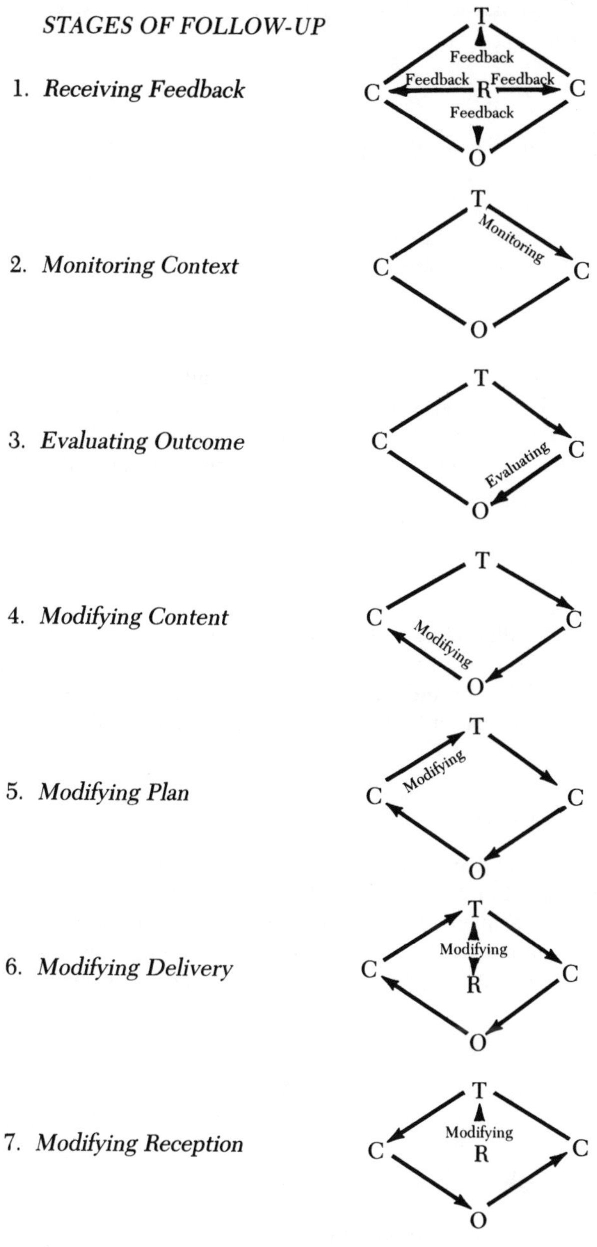

Figure 5. The Stages of Designing a
Comprehensive Follow-Up Treatment System

identifying the critical tasks to be monitored (because all tasks cannot be monitored); deciding who will monitor and what method will be used; and developing and implementing a monitoring plan.

Evaluating the Outcomes

Depending upon the results of monitoring the context, the treatment outcome may be modified to meet the needs of both the individual and the context (Stage 3). Again, the designers must provide for evaluating the recipients on selected critical tasks. Remember, these tasks define the expected performance in terms of activities and products that are measurable.

Modifying the Content

Depending upon the results of monitoring the context and evaluating the outcomes, the treatment content may also be modified to more effectively meet the outcomes and context needs (Stage 4). Thus, the skills content may be modified to incorporate new content to meet new needs and to eliminate or change old content that does not meet the current needs. The new skills content may be shared with the recipients to improve their repertoire of responses.

Modifying the Delivery Plans

Following from the modification of the content is the modification of the delivery plan (Stage 5). The delivery plan will be modified to emphasize exercises that more closely approximate the applications and transfers that the recipients are currently making. The exercises may be shared with the recipients to improve their performance.

Modifying the Treatment Delivery

Finally, along with everything else, the treatment delivery must be modified (Stage 6). Thus, more efficient and effective treatment delivery and interpersonal skills may be offered to the recipients by the helper/trainers in order to insure the reception and learning of the new content. Again, the culmination of the treatment delivery is an individualized learning program for learning the new skills.

Modifying the Treatment Reception

Along with the treatment delivery, the treatment reception must also be modified (Stage 7). Thus, the treatment reception skills of exploration, understanding, and action must be made more efficient and effective so that the recipients can more effectively acquire, apply, and transfer the skills.

In summary, the comprehensive treatment intervention system design is incomplete without the follow-up monitoring and modification: collecting feedback,

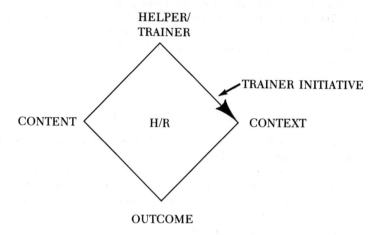

INITIAL PHASE: Trainer initiative is the initial phase of a comprehensive treatment intervention systems design.

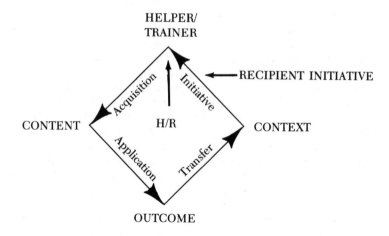

FINAL PHASE: Recipient initiative is the culminating phase of a comprehensive treatment intervention systems design.

Figure 6. The Initial and Final Phases of a Comprehensive Treatment Intervention System Design

monitoring the context, evaluating outcome, modifying the content, modifying delivery plans, modifying the treatment delivery, and modifying the treatment reception. Together, this follow-up program completes the comprehensive treatment design. In another sense, the design is never completed because the follow-up programs constitute a constant feedback system that serves to stimulate life-long learning and change.

TOWARD HUMAN INITIATIVE

The questions of outcome are the questions of human initiative: are we going to continue to attack or defend therapeutic and testing procedures designed at an earlier developmental level, or are we going to design comprehensive treatment systems which programmatically produce the results they are designed to get through systematically sequenced and integrated treatment preparation and delivery? The ultimate question of treatment outcome is the question of whether or not we are going to become truly humanistic engineers.

In summary, designing a comprehensive training system begins with designer/trainer initiative (see Figure 6). The helper/trainer takes the initiative to conduct a needs assessment in order to find what is useful for the helpee/recipients and what will make the helpee/recipients useful in the real-life contexts to which they return or go following the treatment intervention. This helper/trainer initiative stimulates treatment preparation that concludes in a treatment process making a treatment delivery to the helpee/recipients.

In a similar manner, we can see in Figure 6 that a comprehensive treatment intervention system concludes in helpee/recipient initiative. After having received the delivery, and acquired, applied, and transferred the skills, the helpee/recipients may seek to be able to initiate for themselves and others as the helper/trainers have done for them. Therefore, the helper/trainer must not only design the treatment system and implement the delivery, the helper/trainer must ultimately design training programs to give the helpee/recipients the skills that will enable them to design and implement their own treatment deliveries. A comprehensive treatment intervention system transforms helpee/recipients into helper/trainers. A comprehensive treatment intervention system culminates in human initiative.

Human initiative is the highest goal of humanity (Carkhuff, 1981b). It is what make children into adults, learners into teachers, and helpees into helpers. Human initiative enables us to design ideal systems based upon a high level of skill development and community support. It is what enables us to recognize the deficits of the real-life systems: the contexts which demand but do not support; the absence of tangible outcome to provide feedback and shape our treatment interventions; the content that emphasizes facts and concepts that are unrelated to helpee needs; the lesson plans that emphasize lecturing and directiveness rather than the kinesthetic learning necessary for the helpees to file permanent images of the skills in their brains; the delivery processes that are dominated by the preparatory task analyses rather than individualized learning programs; the reception processes that emphasize either exploration or understanding or action, each to the exclusion of the other.

Human initiative is what makes us continually strive to increase our human achievement and to expand the boundaries of our humanity. We strive to sharpen the use of an intellect which distinguishes us from all other forms of life and offers us the opportunity to describe, predict, and influence (if not control) our destinies—as individuals, as peoples, indeed, as members of a human family on this fragile spacecraft called Earth. Human initiative is what makes us truly human beings. We are asking for initiative from our helpees. Can we do less?

REFERENCES

Anthony, W. A. *The Principles of Psychiatric Rehabilitation.* Baltimore, Md.: University Park Press, 1979.

Anthony, W. A., Buell, G. J., Sharratt, S. and Altoff, M. E. The Efficiency of Psychiatric Rehabilitation. *Psychological Bulletin,* 1972, **78,** 437–456.

Bachrach, L. L. A Note on Some Recent Studies of Released Mental Hospital Patients in the Community. *American Journal of Psychiatry,* 1976, **133,** 73–75.

Berenson, B. G. *A Client Outcome Planning Model for Assessing Psychiatric Rehabilitation Interventions: A Response.* Presentation, N.I.M.H. Conference, Assessing Treatment Efficacy and Outcome. Wentworth, N.H., N.I.M.H., October 8–10, 1980.

Berenson, B. G. and Carkhuff, R. R. *The Sources of Gain in Counseling and Psychotherapy.* New York: Holt, Rinehart and Winston, 1966.

Berenson, D. H., Berenson, S. R. and Carkhuff, R. R. *The Skills of Teaching— Content Development Skills.* Amherst, Mass.: Human Resource Development Press, 1978(a).

Berenson, D. H., Berenson, S. R. and Carkhuff, R. R. *The Skills of Teaching— Lesson Planning Skills.* Amherst, Mass.: Human Resource Development Press, 1978(b).

Berenson, S. R., Berenson, D. H. and Carkhuff, R. R. *The Skills of Teaching— Teaching Delivery Skills.* Amherst, Mass.: Human Resource Development Press, 1979.

Berenson, S. R., Berenson, D. H. and Carkhuff, R. R. *The Skills of Teaching— Learning Management Skills.* Amherst, Mass.: Human Resource Development Press, 1981.

Carkhuff, R. R. *Helping and Human Relations.* Volumes I and II. New York: Holt, Rinehart and Winston, 1969.

Carkhuff, R. R. *The Development of Human Resources.* New York: Holt, Rinehart and Winston, 1971.

Carkhuff, R. R. *The Art of Helping IV.* Amherst, Mass.: Human Resource Development Press, 1980.

Carkhuff, R. R. *The Skilled Teacher.* Amherst, Mass.: Human Resource Development Press, 1981(a).

Carkhuff, R. R. *Toward Actualizing Human Potential.* Amherst, Mass.: Human Resource Development Press, 1981(b).

Carkhuff, R. R. and Berenson, B. G. *Beyond Counseling and Therapy.* New York: Holt, Rinehart and Winston, 1967; 1977.

Carkhuff, R. R. and Berenson, B. G. *Teaching as Treatment.* Amherst, Mass.: Human Resource Development Press, 1976.

Carkhuff, R. R. and Berenson, D. H. *The Skills of Learning.* Amherst, Mass.: Carkhuff Institute of Human Technology, in press, 1981.

Carkhuff, R. R., Berenson, D. H. and Pierce, R. M. *The Skills of Teaching—Interpersonal Skills.* Amherst, Mass.: Human Resource Development Press, 1977.

Erickson, R. Outcome Studies in Mental Hospitals. *Psychological Bulletin,* 1975, **82,** 519–540.

Eysenck, H. J. The Effects of Psychotherapy: An Evaluation. *Journal of Consulting Psychology,* 1952, **16,** 319–324.

Eysenck, H. J. The Effects of Psychotherapy. *International Journal of Psychiatry,* 1965, **1,** 99–178.

Frank, J. *Persuasion and Healing.* Baltimore, Md.: Johns Hopkins, 1961.

Freud, S. *Collected Papers.* London: Hogarth, 1924.

Gilbert, T. F. *Human Competence.* New York: McGraw-Hill, 1978.

Levitt, E. E. Psychotherapy with Children: A Further Education. *Behavior Research and Therapy,* 1963, **1,** 45–51.

Lewis, W. W. Continuity and Intervention in Emotional Disturbance: A Review. *Exceptional Children,* 1965, **31,** 465–475.

Mickelson, D. J. and Stevic, R. R. Differential Effects of Facilitative and Non-facilitative Behavioral Counselors. *Journal of Counseling Psychology,* 1971, **18,** 314–317.

Paul, G. L. and Lentz, R. R. *Psychosocial Treatment of Chronically Mentally Ill Patients.* Cambridge: Harvard University Press, 1977.

Rogers, C. R., Gendlin, E. T., Kiesler, D. and Truax, C. B. *The Therapeutic Relationships and Its Impact.* Madison, Wis.: University of Wisconsin, 1963.

Truax, C. B. and Carkhuff, R. R. *Toward Effective Counseling and Psychotherapy.* Chicago: Aldine, 1967.

Vitalo, R. The Effects of Facilitative Interpersonal Functioning in a Conditioning Paradigm. *Journal of Counseling Psychology,* 1970, **17,** 141–144.

Vitalo, R. *Human Resource Development.* Presentation, N.I.M.H. Conference, Assessing Treatment Efficacy and Outcome. Portsmouth, N.H., N.I.M.H., October 8–10, 1980.

Appendix B

SCALES FOR ASSESSMENT OF INTERPERSONAL FUNCTIONING

SCALE 1
EMPATHIC UNDERSTANDING IN INTERPERSONAL PROCESSES:
A SCALE FOR MEASUREMENT [1]

Level 1

The verbal and behavioral expressions of the first person either *do not attend to* or *detract significantly* from the verbal and behavioral expressions of the second person(s) in that they communicate significantly less of the second person's feelings than the second person has communicated himself.

EXAMPLES: The first person communicates no awareness of even the most obvious, expressed surface feelings of the second person. The first person may be bored or uninterested or simply operating from a preconceived frame of reference which totally excludes that of the other person(s).

[1] This scale is derived in part from "A Scale for the Measurement of Accurate Empathy," which has been validated in extensive process and outcome research on counseling and psychotherapy (summarized in Truax & Carkhuff, 1967), and in part from an earlier version that had been validated in extensive process and outcome research on counseling and psychotherapy (summarized in Carkhuff, 1968; Carkhuff & Berenson, 1967). In addition, similar measures of similar constructs have received extensive support in the literature of counseling and therapy and education. The present scale was written to apply to all interpersonal processes and represents a systematic attempt to reduce ambiguity and increase reliability. In the process many important delineations and additions have been made, including, in particular, the change to a systematic focus upon the additive, subtractive, or interchangeable aspects of the levels of communication of understanding. For comparative purposes, level 1 of the present scale is approximately equal to stage 1 of the Truax scale. The remaining levels are approximately correspondent: level 2 and stage 2 and 3 of the earlier version; level 3 and stages 4 and 5; level 4 and stages 6 and 7; level 5 and stages 8 and 9. The levels of the present scale are approximately equal to the levels of the earlier version of this scale.

In summary, the first person does everything but express that he is listening, understanding, or being sensitive to even the feelings of the other person in such a way as to detract significantly from the communications of the second person.

Level 2

While the first person responds to the expressed feelings of the second person(s), he does so in such a way that he *subtracts noticeable affect from the communications* of the second person.

EXAMPLES: The first person may communicate some awareness of obvious surface feelings of the second person, but his communications drain off a level of the affect and distort the level of meaning. The first person may communicate his own ideas of what may be going on, but these are not congruent with the expressions of the second person.

In summary, the first person tends to respond to other than what the second person is expressing or indicating.

Level 3

The expressions of the first person in response to the expressed feelings of the second person(s) are essentially *interchangeable* with those of the second person in that they express essentially the same affect and meaning.

EXAMPLE: The first person responds with accurate understanding of the surface feelings of the second person but may not respond to or may misinterpret the deeper feelings.

In summary, the first person is responding so as to neither subtract from nor add to the expressions of the second person; but he does not respond accurately to how that person really feels beneath the surface feelings. Level 3 constitutes the minimal level of facilitative interpersonal functioning.

Level 4

The responses of the first person add noticeably to the expressions of the second person(s) in such a way as to express feelings a level deeper than the second person was able to express himself.

EXAMPLE: The facilitator communicates his understanding of the expressions of the second person at a level deeper than they were expressed, and thus enables the second person to experience and/or express feelings he was unable to express previously.

In summary, the facilitator's responses add deeper feeling and meaning to the expressions of the second person.

Level 5

The first person's responses add significantly to the feeling and meaning of the expressions of the second person(s) in such a way as to (1) accurately express feelings levels below what the person himself was able to express or (2) in the event of on going deep self-exploration on the second person's part, to be fully with him in his deepest moments.

EXAMPLES: The facilitator responds with accuracy to all of the person's deeper as well as surface feelings. He is "together" with the second person or "tuned in" on his wave length. The facilitator and the other person might proceed together to explore previously unexplored areas of human existence.

In summary, the facilitator is responding with a full awareness of who the other person is and a comprehensive and accurate empathic understanding of his deepest feelings.

SCALE 2
*THE COMMUNICATION OF RESPECT IN INTERPERSONAL
PROCESSES:
A SCALE FOR MEASUREMENT* [2]

Level 1

The verbal and behavioral expressions of the first person communicate a clear lack of respect (or negative regard) for the second person(s).

EXAMPLE: The first person communicates to the second person that the second person's feelings and experiences are not worthy of consideration or that the second person is not capable of acting constructively. The first person may become the sole focus of evaluation.

---

[2] This scale is derived in part from "A Tentative Scale for the Measurement of Unconditional Positive Regard," which has been validated in extensive process and outcome research on counseling and psychotherapy (summarized in Truax & Carkhuff, 1967), and in part from an earlier version that has been validated in extensive process and outcome research on counseling and psychotherapy (summarized in Carkhuff, 1968; Carkhuff & Berenson, 1967). In addition, similar measures of similar constructs have received extensive support in the literature on counseling and psychotherapy and education. The present scale was written to apply to all interpersonal processes and represents a systematic attempt to reduce ambiguity and increase reliability. In the process many important delineations and additions have been made. For comparative purposes, the levels of the present scale are approximately equal to the stages of both the earlier scales, although the systematic emphasis upon the positive regard rather than upon unconditionality represents a pronounced divergence of emphasis and the systematic deemphasis of concern for advice-giving and directionality, both of which may or may not communicate high levels as well as low levels of respect.

In summary, in many ways the first person communicates a total lack of respect for the feelings, experiences, and potentials of the second person.

Level 2

The first person responds to the second person in such a way as to communicate little respect for the feelings, experiences, and potentials of the second person.

EXAMPLE: The first person may respond mechanically or passively or ignore many of the feelings of the second person.

In summary, in many ways the first person displays a lack of respect or concern for the second person's feelings, experiences, and potentials.

Level 3

The first person communicates a positive respect and concern for the second person's feelings, experiences, and potentials.

EXAMPLE: The first person communicates respect and concern for the second person's ability to express himself and to deal constructively with his life situation.

In summary, in many ways the first person communicates that who the second person is and what he does matter to the first person. Level 3 constitutes the minimal level of facilitative interpersonal functioning.

Level 4

The facilitator clearly communicates a very deep respect and concern for the second person.

EXAMPLE: The facilitator's responses enables the second person to feel free to be himself and to experience being valued as an individual.

In summary, the facilitator communicates a very deep caring for the feelings, experiences, and potentials of the second person.

Level 5

The facilitator communicates the very deepest respect for the second person's worth as a person and his potentials as a free individual.

EXAMPLE: The facilitator cares very deeply for the human potentials of the second person.

In summary, the facilitator is committed to the value of the other person as a human being.

SCALE 3
FACILITATIVE GENUINENESS IN INTERPERSONAL PROCESSES:
A SCALE FOR MEASUREMENT [3]

Level 1

The first person's verbalizations are clearly unrelated to what he is feeling at the moment, or his only genuine responses are negative in regard to the second person(s) and appear to have a totally destructive effect upon the second person.

EXAMPLE: The first person may be defensive in his interaction with the second person(s) and this defensiveness may be demonstrated in the content of his words or his voice quality. Where he is defensive he does not employ his reaction as a basis for potentially valuable inquiry into the relationship.

In summary, there is evidence of a considerable discrepancy between the inner experiencing of the first person(s) and his current verbalizations. Where there is no discrepancy, the first person's reactions are employed solely in a destructive fashion.

Level 2

The first person's verbalizations are slightly unrelated to what he is feeling at the moment, or when his responses are genuine they are negative in regard to the second person; the first person does not appear to know how to employ his negative reactions constructively as a basis for inquiry into the relationship.

EXAMPLE: The first person may respond to the second person(s) in a "professional" manner that has a rehearsed quality or a quality concerning the way a helper "should" respond in that situation.

In summary, the first person is usually responding according to his prescribed role rather than expressing what he personally feels or means. When he is genuine his responses are negative and he is unable to employ them as a basis for further inquiry.

[3] This scale is derived in part from "A Tentative Scale for the Measurement of Therapist Genuineness or Self-congruence," which has been validated in extensive process and outcome research on counseling and psychotherapy (summarized in Truax & Carkhuff, 1967) and in part from an earlier version that has been similarly validated (summarized in Carkhuff, 1968; Carkhuff & Berenson, 1967). In addition, similar measures of similar constructs have received support in the literature of counseling and psychotherapy and education. The present scale was written to apply to all interpersonal processes and represents a systematic attempt to reduce ambiguity and increase reliability. In the process, many important delineations and additions have been made. For comparative purposes, the levels of the present scale are approximately equal to the stages of the earlier scale, although the systematic emphasis upon the constructive employment of negative reactions represents a pronounced divergence of emphasis.

Level 3

The first person provides no "negative" cues between what he says and what he feels, but he provides no positive cues to indicate a really genuine response to the second person(s).

EXAMPLE: The first person.may listen and follow the second person(s) but commits nothing more of himself.

In summary, the first person appears to make appropriate responses that do not seem insincere but that do not reflect any real involvement either. Level 3 constitutes the minimal level of facilitative interpersonal functioning.

Level 4

The facilitator presents some positive cues indicating a genuine response (whether positive or negative) in a nondestructive manner to the second person(s).

EXAMPLE: The facilitator's expressions are congruent with his feelings, although he may be somewhat hesitant about expressing them fully.

In summary, the facilitator responds with many of his own feelings, and there is no doubt as to whether he really means what he says. He is able to employ his responses, whatever their emotional content, as a basis for further inquiry into the relationship.

Level 5

The facilitator is freely and deeply himself in a nonexploitative relationship with the second person(s).

EXAMPLE: The facilitator is completely spontaneous in his interaction and open to experiences of all types, both pleasant and hurtful. In the event of hurtful responses the facilitator's comments are employed constructively to open a further area of inquiry for both the facilitator and the second person.

In summary, the facilitator is clearly being himself and yet employing his own genuine responses constructively.

SCALE 4
FACILITATIVE SELF-DISCLOSURE IN INTERPERSONAL PROCESSES: SCALE FOR MEASUREMENT [4]

Level 1

The first person actively attempts to remain detached from the second person(s) and discloses nothing about his own feelings or personality to the second person(s), or if he does disclose himself, he does so in a way that is not tuned to the second person's general progress.

EXAMPLE: The first person may attempt, whether awkwardly or skillfully, to divert the second person's attention from focusing upon personal questions concerning the first person, or his self-disclosures may be ego shattering for the second person(s) and may ultimately cause him to lose faith in the first person.

In summary, the first person actively attempts to remain ambiguous and an unknown quantity to the second person(s), or if he is self-disclosing, he does so solely out of his own needs and is oblivious to the needs of the second person(s).

Level 2

The first person, while not always appearing actively to avoid self-disclosures, never volunteers personal information about himself.

EXAMPLE: The first person may respond briefly to direct questions from the client about himself; however, he does so hesitantly and never provides more information about himself than the second person(s) specifically requests.

In summary, the second person(s) either does not ask about the personality of the first person, or, if he does, the barest minimum of brief, vague, and superficial responses are offered by the first person.

---

[4] This scale is derived in part from "A Tentative Scale for the Measurement of Therapist Self-disclosure" (Dickenson, 1965; Truax & Carkhuff, 1967), which has been validated in process and outcome research in counseling and psychotherapy (summarized in Carkhuff, 1968; Truax & Carkhuff, 1967). In addition, similar measures of similar constructs have received support in the literature of counseling and therapy. The present scale was written to apply to all interpersonal processes and represents a systematic attempt to reduce ambiguity and increase reliability. In the process many important delineations and additions have been made. For comparative purposes, a particular point of difference in the scales is the consideration given to nonfacilitative self-disclosure in the present scale. Level 1 of the present scale is approximately equal to stages 1 and 2 of the earlier scale; level 2 to stages 3 and 4; level 3 to stages 5 and 6; level 4 to stages 7 and 8; and level 5 to stage 9.

Level 3

The first person volunteers personal information about himself which may be in keeping with the second person's interests, but this information is often vague and indicates little about the unique character of the first person.

EXAMPLE: While the first person volunteers personal information and never gives the impression that he does not wish to disclose more about himself, nevertheless, the content of his verbalizations is generally centered upon his reactions to the second person(s) and his ideas concerning their interaction.

In summary, the first person may introduce more abstract, personal ideas in accord with the second person's interests, but these ideas do not stamp him as a unique person. Level 3 constitutes the minimum level of facilitative interpersonal functioning.

Level 4

The facilitator freely volunteers information about his personal ideas, attitudes, and experiences in accord with the second person's interests and concerns.

EXAMPLE: The facilitator may discuss personal ideas in both depth and detail, and his expressions reveal him to be a unique individual.

In summary, the facilitator is free and spontaneous in volunteering personal information about himself, and in so doing may reveal in a constructive fashion quite intimate material about his own feelings, and beliefs.

Level 5

The facilitator volunteers very intimate and often detailed material about his own personality, and in keeping with the second person's needs may express information that might be extremely embarrassing under different circumstances or if revealed by the second person to an outsider.

EXAMPLE: The facilitator gives the impression of holding nothing back and of disclosing his feelings and ideas fully and completely to the second person(s). If some of his feelings are negative concerning the second person(s), the facilitator employs them constructively as a basis for an open-ended inquiry.

In summary, the facilitator is operating in a constructive fashion at the most intimate levels of self-disclosure.

SCALE 5
PERSONALLY RELEVANT CONCRETENESS OR SPECIFICITY OF EXPRESSION IN INTERPERSONAL PROCESSES: A SCALE FOR MEASUREMENT [5]

Level 1

The first person leads or allows all discussion with the second person(s) to deal only with vague and anonymous generalities.

EXAMPLE: The first person and the second person discuss everything on strictly an abstract and highly intellectual level.

In summary, the first person makes no attempt to lead the discussion into the realm of personally relevant specific situations and feelings.

Level 2

The first person frequently leads or allows even discussions of material personally relevant to the second person(s) to be dealt with on a vague and abstract level.

EXAMPLE: The first person and the second person may discuss the "real" feelings but they do so at an abstract, intellectualized level.

In summary, the first person does not elicit discussion of most personally revelant feelings and experiences in specific and concrete terms.

Level 3

The first person at times enables the second person(s) to discuss personally relevant material in specific and concrete terminology.

EXAMPLE: The first person will make it possible for the discussion with the second person(s) to center directly around most things that are personally important to the second person(s), although there will continue to be areas not dealt with concretely and areas in which the second person does not develop fully in specificity.

In summary, the first person sometimes guides the discussions into consideration of personally relevant specific and concrete instances, but these are not always fully developed. Level 3 constitutes the minimal level of facilitative functioning.

[5] This scale is derived from earlier work (summarized in Truax & Carkhuff, 1967). Similar measures of similar constructs have been researched only minimally. The present scale has received support in research on training and counseling (summarized in Carkhuff, 1968; Carkhuff & Berenson, 1967). The systematic emphasis upon the personally meaningful relevance of concrete and specific expressions represents a pronounced divergence of emphasis.

Level 4

The facilitator is frequently helpful in enabling the second person(s) to fully develop in concrete and specific terms almost all instances of concern.

EXAMPLE: The facilitator is able on many occasions to guide the discussion to specific feelings and experiences of personally meaningful material.

In summary, the facilitator is very helpful in enabling the discussion to center around specific and concrete instances of most important and personally relevant feelings and experiences.

Level 5

The facilitator is always helpful in guiding the discussion, so that the second person(s) may discuss fluently, directly, and completely specific feelings and experiences.

EXAMPLE: The first person involves the second person in discussion of specific feelings, situations, and events, regardless of their emotional content.

In summary, the facilitator facilitates a direct expression of all personally relevant feelings and experiences in concrete and specific terms.

SCALE 6
CONFRONTATION IN INTERPERSONAL PROCESSES: A SCALE FOR MEASUREMENT [6]

Level 1

The verbal and behavioral expressions of the helper disregard the discrepancies in the helpee's behavior (ideal versus real self, insight versus action, helper versus helpee's experiences).

EXAMPLE: The helper may simply ignore all helpee discrepancies by passively accepting them.

In summary, the helper simply disregards all of those discrepancies in the helpee's behavior that might be fruitful areas for consideration.

Level 2

The verbal and behavioral expressions of the helper disregard the discrepancies in the helpee's behavior.

[6] This scale is a revision of earlier versions of the confrontation scales (Anderson, Douds, & Carkhuff, 1967; Berenson & Mitchell, 1968; Carkhuff & Berenson, 1967) which have been validated in process and outcome research on counseling and psychotherapy (Berenson & Mitchell, 1969; Carkhuff & Berenson, 1967). The present scale constitutes a major revision from frequency tabulations to levels of functioning.

EXAMPLE: The helper, although not explicitly accepting these discrepancies, may simply remain silent concerning most of them.

In summary, the helper disregards the discrepancies in the helpee's behavior, and, thus, potentially important areas of inquiry.

Level 3

The verbal and behavioral expressions of the helper, while open to discrepancies in the helpee's behavior, do not relate directly and specifically to these discrepancies.

EXAMPLE: The helper may simply raise questions without pointing up the diverging directions of the possible answers.

In summary, while the helper does not disregard discrepancies in the helpee's behavior, he does not point up the directions of these discrepancies. Level 3 constitutes the minimum level of facilitative interpersonal functioning.

Level 4

The verbal and behavioral expressions of the helper attend directly and specifically to the discrepancies in the helpee's behavior.

EXAMPLE: The helper confronts the helpee directly and explicitly with discrepancies in the helpee's behavior.

In summary, the helper specifically addresses himself to discrepancies in the helpee's behavior.

Level 5

The verbal and behavioral expressions of the helper are keenly and continually attuned to the discrepancies in the helpee's behavior.

EXAMPLE: The helper confronts the helpee with helpee discrepancies in a sensitive and perceptive manner whenever they appear.

In summary, the helper does not neglect any potentially fruitful inquiry into the discrepancies in the helpee's behavior.

SCALE 7
IMMEDIACY OF RELATIONSHIP IN INTERPERSONAL PROCESSES: A SCALE FOR MEASUREMENT [7]

Level 1

The verbal and behavioral expressions of the helper disregard the content and affect of the helpee's expressions that have the potential for relating to the helper.

EXAMPLE: The helper may simply ignore all helpee communications, whether direct or indirect, that deal with the helper-helpee relationship.

In summary, the helper simply disregards all of those helpee messages that are related to the helper.

Level 2

The verbal and behavioral expressions of the helper disregard most of the helpee expressions that have the potential for relating to the helper.

EXAMPLE: Even if the helpee is talking about helping personnel in general, the helper may, in general, remain silent or just not relate the content to himself.

In summary, the helper appears to choose to disregard most of those helpee messages that are related to the helper.

Level 3

The verbal and behavior expressions of the helper, while open to interpretations of immediacy, do not relate what the helpee is saying to what is going on between the helper and the helpee in the immediate moment.

EXAMPLE: The helper may make literal responses to or reflections on the helpee's expressions or otherwise open-minded responses that refer to no one specifically but that might refer to the helper.

In summary, while the helper does not extend the helpee's expressions to immediacy, he is not closed to such interpretations. Level 3 constitutes the minimum level of facilitative interpersonal functioning.

Level 4

The verbal and behavioral expressions of the helper appear cautiously to relate the helpee's expressions directly to the helper-helpee relationship.

---

[7] This scale is a revision of earlier versions of immediacy relationship scales (Mitchell & Mitchell, 1966; Leitner & Berenson, 1967) which have been validated in process and outcome research on counseling and psychotherapy (Berenson & Mitchell, 1969; Mitchell, 1967). In addition, similar measures of similar constructs have received support in the literature of counseling and psychotherapy (Kell, 1966).

EXAMPLE: The helper attempts to relate the helpee's responses to himself, but he does so in a tentative manner.

In summary, the helper relates the helpee's responses to himself in an open, cautious manner.

Level 5

The verbal and behavioral expressions of the helper relate the helpee's expressions directly to the helper-helpee relationship.

EXAMPLE: The helper in a direct and explicit manner relates the helpee's expressions to himself.

In summary, the helper is not hesitant in making explicit interpretations of the helper-helpee relationship.

SCALE 8
HELPEE SELF-EXPLORATION IN INTERPERSONAL PROCESSES: A SCALE FOR MEASUREMENT [8]

Level 1

The second person does not discuss personally relevant material, either because he has had no opportunity to do such or because he is actively evading the discussion even when it is introduced by the first person.

EXAMPLE: The second person avoids any self-descriptions or self-exploration or direct expression of feelings that would lead him to reveal himself to the first person.

In summary, for a variety of possible reasons the second person does not give any evidence of self-exploration.

Level 2

The second person responds with discussion to the introduction of personally relevant material by the first person but does so in a mechanical manner and without the demonstration of emotional feelings.

[8] This scale is derived in part from "The Measurement of Depth of Intrapersonal Exploration (Truax & Carkhuff, 1967), which has been validated in extensive process and outcome research on counseling and psychotherapy (Carkhuff, 1968; Carkhuff & Berenson, 1967; Truax & Carkhuff, 1967, 1963, 1964, 1965). In addition, similar measures of similar constructs have received extensive support in the literature of counseling and therapy. The present scale represents a systematic attempt to reduce ambiguity and increase reliability. In the process, many important delineations and additions have been made. For comparative purposes, level 1 of the present scale is approximately equal to stage 1 of the earlier scale. The remaining levels are approximately correspondent: level 2 and stages 2 and 3; level 3 and stages 4 and 5; level 4 and stage 6; level 5 and stages 7, 8, and 9.

EXAMPLE: The second person simply discusses the material without exploring the significance or the meaning of the material or attempting further exploration of that feeling in an effort to uncover related feelings or material.

In summary, the second person responds mechanically and remotely to the introduction of personally relevant material by the first person.

Level 3

The second person voluntarily introduces discussions of personally relevant material but does so in a mechanical manner and without the demonstration of emotional feeling.

EXAMPLE: The emotional remoteness and mechanical manner of the discussion give the discussion a quality of being rehearsed.

In summary, the second person introduces personally relevant material but does so without spontaneity or emotional proximity and without an inward probing to discover new feelings and experiences.

Level 4

The second person voluntarily introduces discussions of personally relevant material with both spontaneity and emotional proximity.

EXAMPLE: The voice quality and other characteristics of the second person are very much "with" the feelings and other personal materials that are being verbalized.

In summary, the second person introduces personally relevant discussions with spontaneity and emotional proximity but without a distinct tendency toward inward probing to discover new feelings and experiences.

Level 5

The second person actively and spontaneously engages in an inward probing to discover new feelings and experiences about himself and his world.

EXAMPLE: The second person is searching to discover new feelings concerning himself and his world even though at the moment he may perhaps be doing so fearfully and tentatively.

In summary, the second person is fully and actively focusing upon himself and exploring himself and his world.

REFERENCES

Anderson, S., Douds J., & Carkhuff, R. R. The effects of confrontation by high and low confronting therapists. In *Beyond counseling and therapy*. New York: Holt, Rinehart & Winston, Inc., 1967.

Berenson, B. G., & Mitchell, K. *Confrontation in counseling and life.* Mimeographed manuscript, American International College, Springfield, Mass., 1969.

Carkhuff, R. R. *The counselor's contribution to facilitative processes.* Mimeographed manuscript, State University of New York at Buffalo, 1968.

Carkhuff, R. R., & Berenson, B. G. *Beyond counseling and therapy.* New York: Holt, Rinehart & Winston, Inc., 1967.

Dickenson, W. A. Therapist self-disclosure as a variable in psychotherapeutic process and outcome. Unpublished doctoral dissertation, University of Kentucky, 1965.

Kell, B., & Mueller, W. J. *Impact and change: A study of counseling relationships.* New York: Appleton-Century-Crofts, 1966.

Leitner, L., & Berenson, B. G. Immediate relationship scale: A revision. Unpublished research scale, State University of New York at Buffalo, 1967.

Mitchell, K. M. Therapist conditions beyond the core facilitative conditions: Immediacy and references to significant others. Paper presented at the American Psychological Association meeting, Washington, D.C., 1967.

Mitchell, R., & Mitchell, K. M. The therapist immediate relationship scale. Unpublished research scale, Michigan State University, 1966.

Truax, C. B., & Carkhuff, R. R. *Toward effective counseling and psychotherapy.* Chicago: Aldine Publishing Company, 1967.

AUTHOR INDEX

Lightface numbers refer to pages in Volume I; **boldface** numbers to pages in Volume II.

SUBJECT INDEX

Lightface numbers refer to pages in Volume I; **boldface** numbers to pages in Volume II.

Action-oriented conditions, 21, 22, 24, 26, 29, 33, 43–45, 46, 216, 217, 221, 225–228, 237, 240, 244, 259, 260 **47, 48, 50, 51, 58, 59–60, 63–64, 65 f., 72, 75, 76, 78, 79, 82, 85–86, 94, 99, 101, 105–106, 116, 117, 118, 125, 127, 182, 194, 212 ff., 251, 257, 273, 274, 276, 279, 284, 303**

Active initiative, 40

Active therapy, 51

American Journal of Psychiatry, **17**

American Journal of Psychology, 207

American Personnel and Guidance Association, 3

American Psychological Association, 3n., 4

American Psychologist, **15**

Anger-hostility, 99

Annual Review of Psychology, **184, 207**

Anxiety hierarchies, 245–246

Assessment, **276–277**

Authenticity, **90, 193**

Behavior Research and Therapy, **17**

Behavioral Science, **15**

Behavioristic approach, 237, 244–245 **62**

Behavioristic conditioning schools, **13**

Beyond Counseling and Therapy, 22n., 31n. **16, 45, 57, 69, 80, 102, 127, 221, 243, 282, 291 n.**

Brain, **207**

Careers, *see* Occupations *and* Vocations

CAUSE, **3**

Center for Human Relations and Community Affairs, **268–270**

Child-developmental concentration, **272**

Child-rearing functions, 28, 29, 99, 100 **37, 42–43, 53, 54, 226**

Childhood Education, **17**

333